Pro VS 2005 Reporting Using SQL Server and Crystal Reports

Kevin S. Goff and Rod Paddock

Apress®

Pro VS 2005 Reporting Using SQL Server and Crystal Reports

Copyright © 2006 by Kevin S. Goff and Rod Paddock

ISBN-13 (pbk): 978-1-59059-688-3

ISBN-10 (pbk): 1-59059-688-9

Printed and bound in the United States of America 9 8 7 6 5 4 3 2 1

Trademarked names may appear in this book. Rather than use a trademark symbol with every occurrence of a trademarked name, we use the names only in an editorial fashion and to the benefit of the trademark owner, with no intention of infringement of the trademark.

Lead Editor: Matt Moodie

Technical Reviewer: Jason Lefebvre

Editorial Board: Steve Anglin, Ewan Buckingham, Gary Cornell, Jason Gilmore, Jonathan Gennick, Jonathan Hassell, James Huddleston, Chris Mills, Matthew Moodie, Dominic Shakeshaft, Jim Sumser, Keir Thomas, Matt Wade

Project Manager: Sofia Marchant

Copy Edit Manager: Nicole Flores

Copy Editor: Ami Knox

Assistant Production Director: Kari Brooks-Copony

Production Editor: Katie Stence

Compositor: Molly Sharp

Proofreader: Nancy Riddiough

Indexer: Broccoli Information Management

Artist: April Milne

Cover Designer: Kurt Krames

Manufacturing Director: Tom Debolski

Distributed to the book trade worldwide by Springer-Verlag New York, Inc., 233 Spring Street, 6th Floor, New York, NY 10013. Phone 1-800-SPRINGER, fax 201-348-4505, e-mail orders-ny@springer-sbm.com, or visit http://www.springeronline.com.

For information on translations, please contact Apress directly at 2560 Ninth Street, Suite 219, Berkeley, CA 94710. Phone 510-549-5930, fax 510-549-5939, e-mail info@apress.com, or visit http://www.apress.com.

The information in this book is distributed on an "as is" basis, without warranty. Although every precaution has been taken in the preparation of this work, neither the author(s) nor Apress shall have any liability to any person or entity with respect to any loss or damage caused or alleged to be caused directly or indirectly by the information contained in this work.

The source code for this book is available to readers at http://www.apress.com in the Source Code/Download section.

This book is dedicated to my "inner circle":
my wife Gwen, her mother Diane, and my brother Steve.
I love all of you.

—Kevin Goff

Contents at a Glance

PART 1 ■■■ The Requirements: Begin with the End in Mind

PART 2 ■■■ Building the Database with SQL Server 2005

PART 3 ■■■ Defining and Building the Architecture

PART 4 ■■■ Report Writers

PART 5 ▪▪▪ Building the Client Piece

PART 6 ▪▪▪ Appendixes

Contents

PART 1 ■■■ The Requirements: Begin with the End in Mind

PART 2 ■■■ Building the Database with SQL Server 2005

PART 3 ■ ■ ■ Defining and Building the Architecture

PART 4 ■ ■ ■ **Report Writers**

PART 5 ■■■ Building the Client Piece

PART 6 ■■■ Appendixes

About the Authors

KEVIN S. GOFF is the principal consultant and founder of Common Ground Solutions, a consulting practice with 20 years of experience in building custom software solutions. He has received several awards and citations from organizations in both the public and private sector, including multiple recognitions for solutions that yielded six-figure returns on investment.

Kevin is currently a Microsoft .NET MVP for C #, and is the author of *CoDe Magazine*'s *The Baker's Dozen* series, where he selects a development topic each issue and writes 13 productivity tips. In early 2006, Microsoft featured Kevin on their internal newsletter, Microsite.

In late 2004, he wrote an article on productivity tips for Crystal Reports in .NET, a subject close to his heart. The article discussed reporting for line-of-business applications, and focused on producing efficient, effective results. The article caught the attention of many people and organizations, including Apress, and he's been talking to people and building up the ideas for this book ever since.

Kevin speaks at various conferences, .NET User Group presentations, and MSDN CodeCamp events. His company web site is www.commongroundsolutions.net, and his blog is www.TheBakersDozen.net.

ROD PADDOCK is president and founder of Dash Point Software, Inc. DPSI is an award-winning software company based in Seattle, WA. DPSI specializes in application architecture, development, and software training. Clients include Six Flags, First Premier Bank, Microsoft, the US Coast Guard and the US Navy.

DPSI specializes in Visual Studio .NET (C# and VB .NET), Visual Basic, Visual FoxPro, and SQL Server development. Rod has been a very popular speaker at a wide variety of developer conferences in North America and Europe since 1995. His most recent speaking appearance was at the DevTeach 2005 conference in Montreal, Canada. Rod was an MSDN Canada speaker in 2004 and is currently a Microsoft VB .NET MVP.

Rod is also editor-in-chief for *CoDe Magazine* (www.code-magazine.com) and has written numerous articles and books on software development.

Rod can be contacted via his web site, www.dashpoint.com, or his blog, http://blog.dashpoint.com.

About the Technical Reviewer

JASON LEFEBVRE is vice president and founding partner of Intensity Software, Inc. (www.intensitysoftware.com), which specializes in providing custom Microsoft .NET applications, legacy system migration, and boxed software products. Jason has been using Microsoft .NET since its Alpha stages in early 2000 and uses Visual Studio and the Microsoft .NET Framework daily while creating solutions for Intensity Software's clients. Jason has been a participating author for a number of books and has written numerous articles about Microsoft .NET–related topics. Jason has been building software professionally for over 10 years.

Acknowledgments

I love books. For years I wanted to be a novelist, but I traded in my storylines and plots for a computer. But as it turns out, truth can be more interesting than fiction.

The sequence of events and professional support I've received remind me of the famous "six degrees of separation." So going back in time, *mille mercis* to the following:

- The Apress team of Sofia Marchant, Matthew Moodie, Jason Lefebrve, Katie Stence, and Ami Knox for their work and incredible patience.

- Ewan Buckingham for his efforts and encouragement on the initial chapters.

- Dominick Shakeshaft for reading my articles in *CoDe Magazine* and offering me the great opportunity of writing for Apress.

- Rod Paddock and Markus Egger for taking a chance on me as a new columnist for *CoDe Magazine* in the summer of 2004.

- The great books that changed my life and inspired me to become a writer—such how-to books as Yair Alan Griver's *The Visual FoxPro Codebook* and Allen Holub's *Compiler Design in C* inspired me to write.

- Folks in the .NET community like Bonnie Berent and Cathi Gero, who helped me ascend the .NET learning curve; and Mike Antonovich, my first boss in early 1988, who gave me terrific guidance to last an entire career.

- A special thanks to Matthew Moodie at Apress. A first-time author couldn't ask for a better development editor than Matt.

Mass quantities of Red Bull, Hot Tamales candy, and Starbucks Caramel Macchiato were consumed while I wrote this book. I listened to Charlie Parker, Cannonball Adderley, ELP, and Rush until my ears bled. And two Persian cats constantly vied for my attention.

I've saved the best for last. My "inner circle" is my wife Gwen, her mother Diane, and my brother Steve, and I love you all.

Et toujours notre bon vielle ami . . . Mike A.

Kevin Goff

First and foremost, I want to thank my wife Jessica, daughter Krysta, and son Isaiah. Without the support of family, none of this would be possible.

Second, I want to thank my coauthor Kevin Goff. Kevin is 100% responsible for the successful completion of this book. This book started with a column Kevin wrote in *CoDe Magazine* that prompted editors at Apress to contact Kevin. Thanks for having me on board.

Next, I would like to thank the crew we worked with at Apress. Thanks Sofia, Matt, Katie, Ewan, and Ami. Props go out to our tech editor Jason Lefebvre. Working with Apress has been a great experience.

I also want to thank a bunch of people who contributed to this book in many untold ways. John Petersen, the Zerfas family (Dan, Terry, and PJ), Erik Ruthruff, Markus Egger, Ellen Whitney, Art Sanchez, the Wolff family (Mark, Dana, Allie, and Adam), Jim Duffy, Miguel Castro, and too many others to mention. Friendship is one of the most important aspects of life. Thanks for being there . . .

Finally, this book was written with the help of Starbucks, Korn, Stone Sour, Godsmack, Van Halen, AC/DC, *Stargate SG1*, *Battlestar Gallactica*, *Family Guy*, and lots of *South Park* (go Kenny, Kyle, Eric, and Stan) . . .

Rod Paddock

Introduction

This book is about building a distributed reporting solution using Visual Studio .NET 2005, Crystal Reports .NET, and SQL Server 2005. The book demonstrates some proven methodologies for building data-driven .NET business reporting applications. The book also utilizes my Common Ground Framework for Visual Studio 2005, a collection of reusable classes to increase your productivity in building such applications.

The book will walk you through a complete reporting application for a fictitious construction company. The application contains several reports, both detailed and summarized, along with different types of business charts. The reports reflect many of the common types of report content that users ask for.

The application will run in a distributed environment, with separate layers for data access, business classes, web services/remoting, and the reporting and client layers. Along the way, you'll see a large supply of code and techniques for the following:

- Writing T-SQL 2005 stored procedures

- Building an architecture for web services and .NET remoting

- Building a reusable data access library using .NET Generics

- ADO.NET data handling and strongly-typed DataSets

- Subclassing Windows Forms controls and building reusable user-interface modules for reporting

- Using the Crystal Reports .NET designer to construct complex report layouts

- Automating common Crystal Reports tasks

- Generating PowerPoint slides from a .NET application.

As a regular columnist for *CoDe Magazine*, each edition in my *The Baker's Dozen* series presents 13 productivity tips on a different technology, to help developers to become more productive and efficient. To borrow a cliché, this book is like a *Baker's Dozen* on steroids.

I set out to build the type of book and demo application that I could have used when I began the .NET learning curve. While no one can learn any technology overnight, my goal was to write a book of technical steps/walkthroughs to help folks become more comfortable and proficient in building .NET applications with these types of requirements; and also to present a set of reusable classes that you can leverage for your .NET applications.

Why a Book on Reporting?

In 1988 I developed my first application report. It was a text-based report for an old FoxBase for DOS application, based on notes and phone conversations with a client. Little did I know that almost 20 years later I would build hundreds of reports and graphs, and then write a book about constructing reporting solutions.

By the time I completed my first report, my level of consciousness of the entire application—the data and what users wanted out of it—grew by leaps and bounds. Suddenly all the lightbulbs came on about the application and the data. So I've always gravitated towards the reporting functionality of an application—it gives me a clear picture of the entire application. Like so many developers in today's world of agile development, you never know when you may be asked to switch from module A to module X, so understanding what users will ultimately want out of the application will increase your ability to be flexible.

If the eyes are indeed the windows to the soul, reports are a view into an application. They reflect the data of the application (even if in a synthesized form). They are used as a tool for business analysis. For some managers, the reports are the reason for the application!

And somewhat tongue-in-cheek: Richard Campbell (of DotNetRocks! fame) said to me last year that people reviewing the reports are usually the ones signing the paychecks!

Reports play a critical role in business applications. Project stakeholders expect reports to summarize and efficiently present data to business users and decision markers to help evaluate and analyze business performance. This book will arm .NET developers with the necessary skills and tools to address reporting requirements and produce sophisticated output using Crystal Reports.

Fast-forward to the present: in late 2004, I wrote an article in *CoDe Magazine* on tips for using Crystal Reports—the article focused on reporting for line-of-business applications. The article caught the attention of many people and organizations—including Dominic Shakeshaft, the editorial director for Apress. Mr. Shakeshaft sent me an e-mail and asked me whether I was interested in writing a book on reporting. So here we are.

Many people ask me what report writer I use. I respond with two answers. First, I use Crystal Reports. Other tools may have specific features, but Crystal Reports remains the best general-purpose reporting tool for Windows-based development. Second, I tell people that the **report writer constitutes a small portion of building reporting solutions**. That is the segue into the structure and general content of this book.

What's Covered in This Book?

This book isn't "just" about Crystal Reports. It's a book that covers the reporting process from beginning to end. Sure, it's important to develop fancy reports and cool-looking graphs. Eye candy sells. But there's so much more to building reports than the final output. In most cases, the process involves the following:

- Establishing the report requirements and defining the report content and output.

- Defining the report input parameters and report data result sets.

- Developing a set of strongly-typed DataSets that represent the result sets.

- Building the back-end database stored procedures to query the databases and produce the result sets.

- When necessary, writing any additional application code using ADO.NET to synthesize the database result sets into the final result sets that the report itself will utilize. (This is needed if the back-end database doesn't contain all the functionality to produce the final result set—so it may need to be a two-step process.)

- Building the necessary infrastructure to support a distributed environment. Users may be running the reports internally on an intranet, or remotely. A solution may require code so that components can communicate across application boundaries (e.g., web service or remoting solutions).

- Constructing a set of classes to deal with database and stored procedure access.

- Developing the reports themselves using a report writer. (See? The report writer didn't appear until the seventh bullet point.) The reports will utilize the strongly-typed DataSets as the design-time data source.

- Building client interface forms for users to make report selections (date range, other report options).

- Generating the report, displaying the report output, and allowing the user to export the report to different formats, such as PDF.

- Generating PowerPoint presentation slides directly from a .NET application.

- Archiving output, so that users can retrieve the image of a report at the time it was generated.

To increase the coverage of report writers, my editor at *CoDe Magazine* and good friend Rod Paddock wrote two outstanding chapters on ActiveReports.NET and SQL Server Reporting Services 2005. Rod also inspired the chapter on middleware data summarization, for those using databases that don't have a rich programming language like T-SQL. So if you're using one of those two report writers, you can still walk away with material to leverage in your applications.

Focus on the Distributed Model

As stated at the beginning, this book focuses on a distributed model and techniques you can employ in each layer. It means many things, both obvious and not so obvious. For the former, it means the client piece can't directly access the database, since the database is likely sitting behind a server and a firewall, and therefore the client piece has no direct access. For the latter, it means that reports can't directly access the database either. In both cases, the book demonstrates different methods, from strongly-typed interfaces to XML schema definitions.

The Philosophy of the Book

For years now, I've delivered presentations at different conferences and user groups on this very topic. I took a database application I wrote for a construction company and modified it to become a "training application" on how to build distributed reporting solutions. In all my years as a reader, the best books were those that provided meaningful exercises. So this is very much a "how-to" book with real-world examples. It covers stored procedures, data access layers, remoting interfaces, web services, Winforms development—and tons of code. As an added attraction, the book presents techniques for generating Office/PowerPoint output. I hope you find this book meaningful.

There are two general themes I've tried to maintain throughout this book. One is a theme that an old college professor advocated when writing papers: "idea-packing." He stressed the practice of value in each and every sentence and paragraph, making each one count. From that day, I made that one of my mantras: to pack as much meaningful information into each paragraph as possible.

The second theme borrows from the Steven Covey premise of "Begin with the End in Mind." In this-e book, we'll build each layer by first presenting the end vision, and then working backward to identify the necessary steps. We build each piece in enough detail that each set of chapters could stand as a book on its own.

So as this book is divided into parts for database code, middleware, report interfaces, etc., the goal is to make the content in each part rival the content of entire books on the subject.

The Source Code for This Book

You can download the code for this book by visiting my web site (www.commongroundsolutions.net) as well as the Apress web site (www.apress.com). There is a link on the main page specifically for the book and the download project. My site also contains a link for contact information, should you have any questions about the book or the code.

The download project is a single ZIP file called ProVS2005Reporting.zip. It contains three files inside:

- The SQL 2005 database (ConstructionDB.zip).

- The entire Visual Studio 2005 demo solution (ConstructionApp.zip). This contains both the Construction Demo project and my Common Ground Framework for Visual Studio 2005.

- A Microsoft Word document named INSTALL.DOC that contains complete installation instructions and latest release notes.

I use this application and the reporting framework as a training application for professional conferences, .NET User Group presentations, and MSDN CodeCamp events. The demo application itself is an ongoing effort, so you can expect it to grow with more functionality and more report examples. Feel free to visit my blog at www.TheBakersDozen.net for followup discussions on the book.

What You'll Need to Run the Demo Application

You'll need the professional version of Visual Studio 2005, which includes Crystal Reports .NET. You do not need to purchase the standalone version of Crystal Reports, as all of the reports were built using the version of Crystal that's integrated with VS 2005. You will also need SQL Server 2005. And, as we all need these days, plenty of memory and disk space . . .

Have You Considered "This"? Why Doesn't It Do "That"?

For all the features and functionality in this application, I'm sure that folks will read this and say, "Why aren't you using Crystal crosstabs?" or "Why didn't you try web services another way?" or "Why didn't you show how to use Crystal Reports in web forms?" and so on. As a reader, I've done it for years (and still do it!). It's impossible to cover everything, as I soon discovered when writing this book!

However, your feedback is very important. As I mentioned earlier, I use this application as part of my training efforts, and I'm periodically enhancing it. So if you have any thoughts or suggestions, feel free to contact me. An author once told me that the truly good books are ones that not only present meaningful material, but also inspire others to come up with new ideas. So I hope this book achieves both objectives for you.

Miscellaneous Notes

There are reports that appear in the application, though we don't fully cover them in the book. For instance, we cover the stored procedure for the construction job summary/profit report in Chapter 3, but we don't fully cover the Crystal report itself. Conversely, we covered specific reports in Crystal in Chapter 9, but we don't talk about the stored procedures.

This isn't an omission: our goal is to cover as many different capabilities, without duplicating effort. We certainly could step through the Crystal Report for the construction job summary/profit report, but the process wouldn't cover any Crystal techniques that we don't cover in other reports.

To Sum It All Up

At the risk of repetition, the goal is to show reusable code/classes and reusable techniques/methodologies. In many instances, we'll start a section by showing the end result and then work backward to identify the necessary key steps. I was 22 years old when I started my career, and I thought that building software and talking/writing about it was the best job anyone can ever have. Sure, the waywardness of business can affect the most passionate of all of us, but I'm about to turn 42, and I still love this as much as I did 20 years ago. It is just so much fun!

Thank you for purchasing the book! We hope you appreciate the work and find it useful.

Kevin S. Goff
Lead Author

■ ■ ■

PART 1

The Requirements: Begin with the End in Mind

The opening chapter sets the stage for the entire text. We present a real-world situation: a manager and business analyst define a set of general reporting requirements for an application. You work to solidify the requirements. Then you work with other developers to build the architecture and components for the system.

CHAPTER 1

Defining the Requirements

As we stated in the introduction to this part, this chapter presents the scenario on which the entire text is based. Here it is:

You arrive at work on Monday morning. Your manager sees you and pulls you into his office. He informs you that the developer working on a .NET/SQL Server application for a client has left your organization. The application is a job-costing system for a construction company. The developer managed to finish the data entry piece of the application. Your manager goes on to say that there are ten reports that the company has promised the client for the application. Because you've built reports for the company in the past, your manager decides to pull you from your current project to build the reports.

You take a deep breath and ask your manager the following questions: "What types of reports?" "Do you have specs?" "How much time will I have?" Your manager answers that he doesn't have the details, but he's scheduled a 10 a.m. meeting with the company business analyst who has all the information on the reports. When you ask again how much time you'll have, your manager responds, "Right now, we're a week behind schedule. The reports were due to be delivered at the end of this week. I may be able to buy some time if we can demonstrate some progress—but we need to come through on this quickly." Your manager finishes by saying that the company can't invoice the client until all reports are complete.

Your instincts tell you to say something right away, but you decide to wait until after you speak with the business analyst. You return to your desk and type a detailed e-mail to the programmer who will be taking over your work. Finally, you take 30 minutes to study the database schema of the construction application (found in Appendix B), and then you go to the 10 a.m. meeting.

The First Meeting: Defining the Requirements

You arrive at the 10 a.m. meeting in the conference room, where your manager and the company analyst are waiting. The analyst asks you how much you know about the construction application. You answer that you haven't seen much of the application, but you reviewed the database just prior to the meeting, and you have an idea of what the application stores. The analyst asks you if you can provide an overview, based on what you reviewed. You pull out the notes you took earlier and answer that you know the application stores the following:

1. Workers, classified as either regular employees or subcontractors.

2. Hourly pay rates per worker, with an effective date.

3. Hourly overhead rates, such as liability insurance, work comp, health insurance, etc., with an effective date. Some rates only apply to employees.

4. A client/customer table with general customer information and customer logos.

5. A construction job table that contains each job number, the client, and job start/close date.

6. A timesheet table that contains a row for hours worked by worker, job, and date. You let them know that you found that hours are broken out by regular hours and overtime hours, and that you also realize that a worker may work on multiple jobs in one day.

7. A materials table that stores data for all materials purchased for a job. Each material purchased falls into one of a handful of categories (petty cash, fuel, stone, and standard material).

8. An invoice table that contains a reference to the job(s) associated with the invoice.

9. A receivables table that stores money received for each invoice.

The analyst accepts that you have a basic understanding of the data and gives you an abbreviated tour of the application, which consists of data entry and lookup screens. He then hands you a batch of stapled papers: some are Excel report printouts, some are Word document printouts, and a few are handwritten charts. You ask for a few minutes to read through the documents, which present the following:

1. A printout of an Excel spreadsheet that the client was using for timesheets. The spreadsheet lists each name, date worked, job description, and regular hours/overtime hours worked. At the bottom of the spreadsheet, the client has asked for the following:

   • A date prompt to print timesheets based on a date range.

   • An option to display columns for the hourly rate, overtime rate, and overhead rate that would be applied to the daily hours, as well as the total labor dollars. (Only users with rights to see rates can select this option.)

   • An option to print timesheets for specific jobs.

   • An option to select one worker, multiple workers, just employees, or just subcontractors.

   • The main sort order is division: within this, the option to sort on name, hours worked, or total labor dollars.

   • Subtotals of hours worked (and labor dollars, if applicable) by employee, division, and then grand totals.

2. An Excel printout of a report titled Construction Job Profile Report, which should show all details on a construction job. It contains four sections:

   • A header section that lists the job number, client name, job description, create and close date, and summary totals for labor costs, material costs, and profit dollars/margin

- A summary of labor: one line for each worker on the job, total number of hours, and total labor dollars

- A detail list of materials purchased for the job (material name, date purchased, and amount)

- A list of each overhead category, the total overhead dollars for the job, and the total overhead dollars for the year

- A list of invoices for the job, and invoices paid

The requested options for this report are as follows:

- Date range: job created (or closed) between two dates.

- Select specific construction jobs.

- Each page should contain a single job. The only sort order is job number.

3. An Excel printout of a report titled Construction Job Summary Report. The report displays one line per job number, with the following columns (measures):

- Job Number, Description, and Client Name

- Labor Profit $ and Total Labor $

- Material Profit $ and Total Material $

- Profit Margin $

- Total Profit $

- Total Dollars Billed, Total Dollars Received, and Balance (Amount Due)

The requested options for the report are as follows:

- The user must be able to sort on any column. A user may want to rank order jobs by Material Profit, or by Balance, etc.

- The user must be able to define a filter condition on any column (e.g., only jobs with a balance greater than $5,000, total received greater than $25,000, etc.).

- The user must be able to highlight certain pieces of information in red (e.g., profit above a certain amount).

4. A handwritten Gantt pictorial chart that shows a timeline of construction jobs for a client or time range. The hard copy shows the chart at the top and a data summary at the bottom.

5. A printout of an MS word document for the new client invoice. The invoice displays summary information at the top, and then details identical to the construction profile, as well as past due invoices and notes. The invoice should also display both the company logo as well as a client logo, if one is on file.

6. A handwritten aging receivables report that shows invoices that have not been paid. The unpaid invoice amounts should show in standard aging bracket time periods (aged 1–30 days, 31–60 days, etc.). The user must be able to run the report at a detail level (by invoice) or summarized by customer. The client has also asked that they be able to change the date range of the aging brackets. For example, they may want to run for 1–15 days, 16–45 days, etc.

7. A complex handwritten chart that shows three sections on a single page:

   - A line chart that shows total costs (materials and labor) by month. The chart should show two lines in different colors—one for this year, and one for the same time period a year ago.

   - A pie chart that shows the breakdown of labor and costs.

   - A data recap for the first graph.

   - The graph is run by location.

8. A simpler version of the preceding chart that shows monthly costs and revenue (profit).

9. A printout of PowerPoint slides—the president promised the client that the software would automatically generate a quarterly PowerPoint presentation. The client has been generating the presentation manually. The presentation contains the following:

   - A title page with the company name and logo

   - A table of contents page

   - A list (table) of the top five construction jobs based on profit, along with details

   - A list of the top five workers based on hours and the jobs they worked on

   - A slide for the following charts that compare data to a previous quarter (selected by the user):

     - A line chart comparing profit

     - A bar chart showing materials and labor (last year as a line)

Appendix A contains more information (and actual client-generated examples) of these reports.

In addition, on a separate page the client has stated that all reports (except for the PowerPoint presentation) follow specific rules and specific output guidelines. They recognize that all their existing reports and printouts are inconsistent, and they want the new reports to have a common and consistent appearance. The rules are as follows:

1. All reports must use the same font. They prefer either Arial or Verdana.

2. Every report must allow the user to enter a footnote that will appear on the bottom of every page.

3. Every report must be saved to PDF—not only so that users can e-mail PDFs to other people, but also so that there is a documented record of every report that was run. For example, someone can see what an invoice looked like at the time it was actually printed.

4. The name of the user who ran the report should appear on the report.

5. The page number and number of pages should appear on every report.

6. The software must retain user selections for reports. If the user runs a timesheet report for two workers and for a specific date range, the software should make those the default selections if the user closes/reopens the application and runs the same report.

The analyst also explains that while the data entry piece of the software is a desktop application, some of the company managers or sales force will need to access the reports remotely. These users might run the reports from within the corporate network, or they might run the software from a remote location such as a hotel room, customer location, etc.

Finally, your manager chimes in. After hearing the details about the reporting module, he realizes that much of the functionality could be applied to two upcoming client projects—neither of which use SQL Server. He asks if the reports can be written to utilize different databases. He acknowledges that the work is more than what was initially believed, but states that the time put against the reports can be leveraged on these other projects.

You tell the analyst and your manager that you're going back to your office to digest everything and to talk to some other technical developers, and that you'll get back to them in a few days.

Building the Plan of Attack

You look over the tasks at hand, you do some research, and over the course of the week you begin to map out a general architecture that addresses every requirement. Because your manager wants to use elements of this solution for other projects, you plan on developing certain areas for configuration and reuse.

- You plan to use SQL Server 2005 stored procedures to query the databases and generate the result sets. Your company database administrator (DBA) has tremendous experience in writing stored procedures. You will provide the DBA with the schema, and you will define both the input parameters and the query/result set requirements (using strongly-typed DataSets, as described later in this list) for each of the reports. Armed with this information, the DBA can build and test the stored procedures independently of any other development efforts.

- Related to the database—you will support multiple databases/database servers. You expect to utilize a test database as well as the production database, and would like to easily toggle back and forth between the two.

- You will construct a set of classes in C# for the client application to use either web services or remoting to communicate with the back-end business layer. This includes building a set of generic interfaces to work with either approach. Once again, you will document the technical requirements and parameters for these classes and see whether you can assign this work to another developer.

- You will build a generic data access layer (DAL) in C#. The DAL will manage the connection to the back-end database. The DAL will call the database stored procedures, return the results, and allow the developer to set certain properties during the stored procedure execution process (such as setting a custom timeout for specific reports).

- You will build strongly-typed DataSets to represent the result sets that SQL Server produces.

- You will design the reports and graphs using the Crystal Reports designer that ships with Visual Studio 2005. You will set each report's DataSource to the corresponding strongly-typed DataSet. The Crystal Reports designer in VS 2005 allows developers to preview reports while designing.

- You will write a set of generic classes in C# to seamlessly integrate the reports with the application so that the user can preview or print reports. The classes will also export reports to a PDF format.

- You will write a Winform client application in C# that will perform the following:

  - Prompt for a user ID and password, and then communicate with the back-end through either web services or remoting (using the **generic connection object**) to validate.

  - Prompt the user for a list of reports and present a user interface form to make the necessary selections for a report (date range, workers, jobs, etc.). The interface also prompts for a report footnote.

  - Call the back-end report logic through the generic connection object, and send the report input selection parameters. Each report will have a separate .NET interface that defines the report parameters and return result set. When the application uses web services, the web service will return report result sets as an XML string. When the application uses remoting, the back end will return the result sets as a DataSet, serialized in a binary format.

  - Receive the result sets from the back end, bind the result sets to the report object associated with the Crystal Report, and display the report. (Note: the application will invoke a client-side business object to determine whether any report measures should be blank, based on the user's access level.)

  - Automatically generate a PDF version of the report and catalog the PDF with the user name, date/time generated, and footnote.

  - Allow users to view and print previously generated reports.

  - Generate the PowerPoint presentation described in the requirements using a set of VB classes for Office 2003 automation you previously developed.

  - Store user selections as an XML file so that users do not need to retype/repick selections from the last report.

  - Automatically update itself via Visual Studio 2005 Click-Once capability.

Building a Report Draft and Report Style Guide

To establish a common appearance for reports, you draft a version of the timesheet report in Microsoft Word, and email it to the client (see Figure 1-1).

Date: 12/8/2005		**Acme Construction Company**								Page 1 of 1
Time: 3:55:01 PM		**Time Sheet Report with Rates**								

Time Period: 11/07/2005 to 11/08/2005

Division	Name	Date	Job #	Reg	OT	Total	Reg	OT	OverHead	Total Labor $
				--------Hours----------			---------- Rates $/Hr ------------			
North	Kevin Goff	11/07/05	117	8.00	1.00	9.00	20.00	30.00	25.12	416.08
			216	2.00		2.00	20.00		25.12	90.24
		11/08/05	117	8.00	1.00	9.00	20.00	30.00	25.12	416.08
		Worker Totals:		18.00	2.00	20.00				922.40
	*J. Goff	11/07/05	119	7.00		7.00	21.00		20.11	287.77
		11/08/05	119	7.25		7.25	21.00		20.11	298.05
		Worker Totals:		14.25		14.25				585.82
		North Division Totals:		32.25	2.00	34.25				1,508.22
		Company Totals:		32.25	2.00	34.25				1,508.22

Run by John Smith	User Footnote: Test of TimeSheet report, showing labor and overhead rates	Source: Construction Test
	System Footnote: An asterisk indicates subcontractors	Database

Figure 1-1. *A draft version of the timesheet report*

You also sent the client a **report rule sheet**, shown in Figure 1-2, to confirm the rules associated with the report.

Report Rule Sheet: TimeSheet Report

General Narrative:
The timesheet report displays the number of daily hours each worker recorded. If a worker recorded time for multiple jobs in one day, then each job is listed as a separate line. The report displays regular hours and overtime hours as separate columns. The report should subtotal hours for each worker, for each division, and then for the company.

A second version of the report (available only for users who have the rights to view labor rates) shows everything described above, as well as the regular and overtime pay rates for each worker. The report also shows the hourly labor overhead rate for each worker. Note that subcontractors will generally have a lower overhead rate, as some individual rates only apply to regular employees. Total labor dollars are calculated, both for the worker as well as subtotals by division and company.

Options
- Employee criteria options
  - Select for one or more employees (default is all employees)
  - Filter on base employees / subcontractors / both
  - Select for an entire Division
- Other criteria options
  - Filter on one or more Construction Jobs (default is all jobs)
- Enter a date range
- Enter a user footnote
- Output format
  - Simple Format (only shows dates and hours worked)
  - Complex Format (shows simple format, plus labor rates, overhead rates, and total labor $)
- Rank order
  - By Division/ Name
  - By Division/Total Hours Worked
  - By Division/Total Labor Dollars
- Save selections so that they can be run again
- Generate PDF automatically, so that report can be viewed again

Rules
- Only users with **ShowRates** rights can run output format #2
- The report should not page break in the middle of a worker. Make sure that a worker's time records always show on one page. (The only exception is if the date range is so long that it's impossible to show an entire worker on one page)
- Indicate that a worker is a subcontractor by placing an asterisk next to the worker's name
- Always runs in landscape

Figure 1-2. *Report rule sheet for the timesheet report*

Finally, to build on the client's concept of a **report style guide**, you incorporate common formatting you've established on other reporting projects with what the client provided. You propose the following to the client:

- All reports will use the Verdana font for report header and footer content.

- All other report content (data, column headings, section names, etc.) will use the Arial font.

- All report titles will use 14-point bold.

- All report subtitles will use 12-point bold.

- Any secondary subtitles will use 10-point type.

- Numeric columns will be right-aligned with their headings, where applicable.

- All other columns (text, date, etc.) will be left-aligned with their headings, where applicable.

- Report headings will use 9-point bold (the only exception is reports with many measures, which will use 8-point type).

- Report content will use 8- or 9-point type, depending on level of content.

- Report footers will always contain the name of the user who generated the report, the data/project source, user footnotes, and a system footnote (if necessary).

Summary

In this chapter, we've covered the requirements for the reporting application. We've presented the specific content for each report, as well as the options that each report must provide. This book will cover the capabilities of Crystal Reports and how you can build the reports to specification. We've also talked about the primary technical requirements for the application, as well as the environments in which users will run the reports: from these requirements, you can see that building a complete solution will be much more than just covering the report writer capabilities. A theme throughout this book is that building a full-blown reporting solution is much more than just the report writer. While the report writer is arguably the most visible aspect of reporting, it represents just a portion of the entire picture.

As stated in the introduction, the purpose of this book is to cover all the major aspects of reporting and present a methodology for building reporting solutions. With each chapter, we will begin by listing the technical requirements for the chapter topic—that process will lead us into the actual code to perform the necessary tasks.

As this book will cover all the major components of a distributed application, we'll be doing a great deal of "traveling" across many technical areas. What's the most valuable tool when you travel for the first time? A map—and in this instance, a roadmap. Appendix C contains a technical roadmap for our application. Just like you would with a regular roadmap, take a look at the roadmap before you begin—and don't hesitate to read it again if you feel you're not finding your way!

Much of the code in this text comes from Kevin Goff's Common Ground Framework for Visual Studio 2005, a set of productivity classes for all major tiers of a distributed application. Appendix D contains a complete reference for all the components of the framework.

PART 2

■■■

Building the Database with SQL Server 2005

In Part 2, you begin your quest toward building the reports by analyzing the data require-ments for the reports. You will write stored procedures in SQL Server 2005 to retrieve data and generate the result sets for the reports. To do so, you must define both the input param-eters and the result sets for each report. You will review those definitions with the DBA, who will write and test the stored procedures. Chapter 2 presents a methodology to build the database code for the Timesheet report. The code utilizes some of the new features in T-SQL 2005, such as PIVOT and APPLY. The chapter also covers some reusable code for sub-sequent reports. Chapter 3 discusses T-SQL code for other reports, and covers additional new language features in SQL Server 2005. (For developers using SQL Server 2000, the last section of Chapter 3 will contain equivalent T-SQL 2000 code where possible.)

CHAPTER 2

■■■

Generating Result Sets with T-SQL 2005 Stored Procedures and UDFs

As we stated in Chapter 1, you will define the input parameters and result sets for each report, and then deliver this to the DBA. This process potentially leads to more analytical depth—writing a spec for someone else will often lead you to consider things more thoroughly than writing a spec for yourself. This chapter covers the first report, which is the Timesheet report. The first report will take a little longer, partly because we'll introduce some functions that you can leverage in subsequent reports in Chapter 3.

In this chapter, you'll do the following:

- Learn about SQL result sets for reports and build the result set for the Timesheet report.

- Build an SQL stored procedure solution for handling a variable number of user selections (the user may select a number of workers, or jobs, etc.).

- Write queries to calculate labor costs by joining daily timesheet records with rates, where the database stores rates with an effective date.

- Utilize the new PIVOT keyword in SQL Server 2005 to translate rows of data (regular hours, overtime hours) into result set columns.

- Utilize the new APPLY operator to directly apply the results of table-valued user-defined functions (UDFs) to queries that call those UDFs.

This chapter assumes a basic understanding of SQL syntax. You don't need to be a wizard at building SQL statements, but you will need to understand JOIN and WHERE clauses, outer joins, and SQL Server user-defined functions.

Defining the Result Set

Take the first report, the Timesheet report, and build a specification. You can review it and see if you're comfortable passing it on. Table 2-1 lists the parameters for the report, and Table 2-2 lists the result set that you will want the back-end SQL queries to generate.

Table 2-1. *Draft of Parameters for Timesheet Report*

Input Parameter	Description
Starting Date	Starting date range
Ending Date	Ending date range
JobList	A list of jobs (or all)
WorkerList	A list of workers (or employees only, or subcontractors only, or all)
Sort Option	Division/name, division/hours worked, division/labor dollars
DetailOption	Only show hours, or show hours plus labor rates

Table 2-2. *Draft of Result Set for Timesheet Report (Three Tables)*

Table	Column	Description
Table1	**Worker List (One Row for Each Worker/Division)**	
	DivisionFK	The division the work was done in
	WorkerFK	The worker FK
	First Name	Worker's first name
	Last Name	Worker's last name
	EmployeeFlag	Whether the worker is an employee or a subcontractor
	RegularHours	Sum of regular hours for the worker/division
	OverTimeHours	Sum of overtime hours for the worker/division
	TotalHours	Sum of total hours for the worker/division
	*TotalLabor	Sum of labor dollars for the worker/division
Table2	**Unique Division List (One Row for Each Division)**	
	DivisionFK	The division
	Description	The division name
	RegularHours	Sum of regular hours for the worker/division
	OverTimeHours	Sum of overtime hours for the worker/division
	TotalHours	Sum of total hours for the worker/division
	*TotalLabor	Sum of labor dollars for the worker/division
Table3	**Table Containing Detail-Level Timesheet Data**	
	DivisionFK	The division the work was done in
	WorkerFK	The worker FK
	WorkDate	Date worked
	JobMasterFK	The job number
	RegularHours	Regular hours worked
	OverTimeHours	Overtime hours worked

Table	Column	Description
	TotalHours	Sum of regular hours and overtime hours
	*HourlyRate	Regular rate per hour
	*OverTimeRate	Overtime rate per hour
	*OverheadRate	Overhead rate per hour
	*TotalLabor	Total labor dollars for the day

Your final product will be a strongly-typed DataSet that models the result set in Table 2-2. The data in the result set will mirror the final contents of the report. The report will ultimately read the result set and display the data in the result set. Just as an input screen would not contain business calculations, the report will not create and display report content that does not appear in the result set. The report is, by nature, an extension of the UI: the only responsibility of the report is to present the prepared and complete result set.

■**Caution** Notice how we said "the only responsibility of the report"—the report should not contain calculations or logic or rules (with the exception of logic to display things in different colors or fonts, and even then it should be data driven).

This concept means that the result set should be complete. This practice leads to two important benefits:

- If you wanted to replicate the output in a different format using a different reporting tool, you could use the result set in its entirety and concentrate on the presentation, without worry of searching for calculations.

- The result set serves as documentation for the reporting process and a model for the report content. A reporting solution with a complete and comprehensive result set will be easier to maintain than a reporting solution that takes a partial result set and adds reporting data in different layers.

Finally, some notes as part of the spec:

- A worker may work on jobs for two different divisions. If so, the worker will appear twice in the list, once for each division.

- An asterisk (*) indicates the column should be populated only if the detail option is set from the input parameters. If not, these columns should be zero.

- Rate changes may take effect in the middle of a period. When querying rates for a given date, you must determine the effective date for a specific day.

Right away, you see two technical challenges. First, you must deal with the input parameters for the list of jobs and the list of workers (when they are selected). The list may contain one key value, or two, or ten, etc. The list may be empty, which indicates that all jobs/workers should be selected. This will be the case for other reports that allow a variable number of selections. So your stored procedures must be able to work with a variable list of keys representing selections.

The second challenge is to deal with rates changing. A rate change (either for a pay rate or an overhead rate) may take effect in the middle of a period. Your SQL queries will need to account for this. Many reports and queries must take this into account, so reusable database code will be valuable to calculate the labor rates for any given day.

Fortunately, the DBA knows some powerful tricks in T-SQL 2005 to meet these challenges.

Querying on a Variable Number of Selections

The requirements for the first (and many other) reports state that the system must allow the user to select one employee per job, or multiples, or all. Essentially, you want to pass a variable number of integer keys (representing the user selections) and query the database against those integer keys. The DBA knows that one way to accomplish this in SQL Server 2005 is to pass a comma-separated list of integers to a stored procedure and, inside the stored procedure, convert the list of integers to a temporary table that you can use in subsequent JOIN statements. This process is as follows:

- Pass a comma-delimited list of integer keys (representing the selections) to a stored procedure. For example, if the user selects Worker One and Worker Two, which map to WorkerPK values of 1111 and 1112, then the system would pass a parameter of 1111,1112 as a string.

- In the stored procedure, create a table-valued user-defined function called CommaListToTable (see Listing 2-1). The UDF will receive the comma-delimited list as a parameter and will return a table variable. The code in Listing 2-1 iterates through the keys in the comma-delimited list and creates a table variable that subsequent queries can use in JOIN or WHERE statements. Figure 2-1 shows a quick example of this UDF.

■**Note** We can't take credit for the idea of this UDF—we've only made minor modifications. Several versions and variations of this UDF exist on the SqlTeam.com and DotNetMonster.com web sites, as well as other .NET and SQL newsgroups.

Listing 2-1. *Code to Convert a Comma-Separated List to a Table Variable*

```
CREATE FUNCTION  [dbo].[CommaListToTable] (@cList VarChar(MAX))
RETURNS @IntKeyTable TABLE
     (IntKey INT, Counter int   PRIMARY KEY CLUSTERED ([IntKey])  ) AS
BEGIN
```

```
DECLARE @nPosition INT
DECLARE @cTempValue VARCHAR(max)
DECLARE @nIntKey int
DECLARE @nCounter int
SET @nCounter = 0

SET @cList = RTRIM(@cList) + ','
-- So right now you might have  '1111,2222,'
-- (Careful if the CSV already ended with a comma,
-- you'll wind up with an extra 0 in the key table)

-- See if comma exists in list
-- (Use PATINDEX to return pattern position within a string
WHILE PATINDEX('%,%' , @cList) <> 0
      BEGIN
            SET @nCounter = @nCounter + 1
            -- Get the position of the comma
          SELECT @nPosition =  PATINDEX('%,%' , @cList)
            -- Get the key, from beginning of string to the comma
          SELECT @cTempValue = LEFT(@cList, @nPosition - 1)

            SET @nIntKey = CAST(@cTempValue AS INT)
            -- Write out to the Keys table (convert to integer)
            INSERT INTO @IntKeyTable
                VALUES (@nIntKey, @nCounter)

            -- Wipe out the value you just inserted
             SELECT @cList = STUFF(@cList, 1, @nPosition, '')
        END
RETURN
END
```

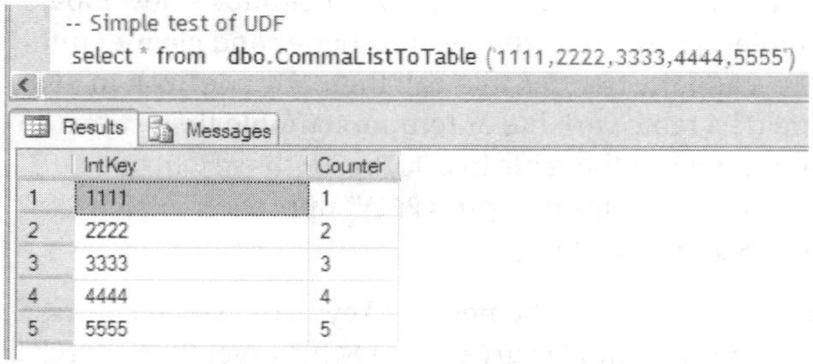

```
-- Simple test of UDF
select * from  dbo.CommaListToTable ('1111,2222,3333,4444,5555')
```

	IntKey	Counter
1	1111	1
2	2222	2
3	3333	3
4	4444	4
5	5555	5

Figure 2-1. *Quick example of using CommaListToTable, which returns a table variable*

Listing 2-2 shows another example of using `CommaListToTable`, with Figure 2-2 illustrating the output.

Listing 2-2. *Code to Utilize CommaListToTable*

```
DECLARE @cList VARCHAR(10)
SET @cList = '1,2,3'   -- Variable list of Integer keys

SELECT LKOverHead.* FROM LKOverHead
     CROSS APPLY dbo.CommaListToTable(@cList) AS TList
          WHERE LKOverHeadPK = TList.IntKey
```

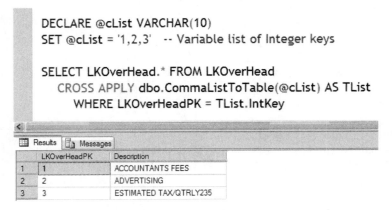

Figure 2-2. *Output example using CommaListToTable*

While developers could use this technique in SQL Server 2000, SQL Server 2005 expands the capability through two important enhancements:

- Developers can apply the results of a table-valued UDF directly in a query (note the use of the new `APPLY` keyword in Listing 2-2). As the name implies, `APPLY` allows developers to directly apply the results of a table-valued UDF: the result is better and cleaner integration between table-valued UDFs and the queries that call them. By contrast, in SQL Server 2000, developers had to create a table variable or temporary table first, store the results of the UDF in the table, and then use the table in a `JOIN`. For those who are still using SQL Server 2000, Listing 2-3 demonstrates the "pre-APPLY" approach (which works in both SQL Server 2000 and SQL Server 2005).

- The `VarChar` parameter in `CommaListToTable` uses the new `MAX` keyword, which allows developers to store up to 2 billion bytes in a single `VarChar`. (In SQL Server 2000, `VarChar` variables were limited to 8,000 bytes.)

Listing 2-3. *Your Second Example Stores Results of the UDF in a Table Variable*

```
DECLARE @cList VARCHAR(10)
SET @cList = '1,2,3'    -- Variable list of integer keys

DECLARE @tTempList TABLE (IntKey int)

INSERT INTO @tTempList (IntKey)
    SELECT IntKey FROM dbo.CommaListToTable(@cList)
```

Handling Variable Selections with XML

Developers can also use XML for managing and querying against variable selections. To apply the previous example to XML, suppose you've created an XML string with a root name of ACCOUNTS and a record tag of Account, as follows:

```
<ACCOUNTS>
    <Account  IntKey='1' />
    <Account  IntKey='2' />
    <Account  IntKey='3' />
</ACCOUNTS>
```

You can pass that XML string to a stored procedure and use it against subsequent queries by doing the following:

- Declare an integer variable to hold an XML document, and use the system stored procedure sp_xml_preparedocument.

- Create a temporary table or table variable to receive the contents of the XML document.

- Query the XML document with the system UDF OPENXML, and insert the results of that query into a table variable or temporary table.

```
DECLARE @cAccountData VARCHAR(MAX)
SET @cAccountData = '<ACCOUNTS>
  <Account  IntKey="1" />
  <Account  IntKey="2" />
  <Account  IntKey="3" /></ACCOUNTS>'
DECLARE @hdoc int
EXEC sp_xml_preparedocument @hdoc OUTPUT, @cAccountData
DECLARE @tAccounts TABLE (IntKey int)

INSERT INTO  @tAccounts (IntKey)
        SELECT IntKey FROM
            OPENXML (@hdoc, '/ACCOUNTS/Account',1) WITH (IntKey int)
SELECT * FROM @tAccounts

-- You can now use the contents of tAccounts in subsequent JOIN statements

EXEC sp_xml_removedocument @hDoc
```

SQL Server 2005 contains many new XML capabilities that we'll cover further in Chapter 3.

Table-Valued UDFs and How to APPLY Them

The requirements to determine rates and labor dollars for any given worker per workday gives you an opportunity to demonstrate different capabilities with user-defined functions. In this example, you need to determine two sets of rates:

- The hourly overhead rate (stored in OverHeadRate) for any given day

- The regular hourly work rate and overtime work rate (stored in WorkerRate) for any given day

Figures 2-3 and 2-4 show the LKOverHead and OverHeadRate tables.

	LKOverHeadPK	Description
1	1	ACCOUNTANTS FEES
2	2	ADVERTISING
3	3	ESTIMATED TAX/QTRLY235
4	4	EXTRA: FUEL
5	5	HEALTH INSURANCE
6	6	LIABILITY INSURANCE
7	7	MISC EQUIPMENT
8	8	MOBIL PHONES
9	9	OFFICE PHONES
10	10	RENT
11	11	SKID LOADER
12	12	TRUCK INSURANCE
13	13	TRUCKS
14	14	UTILITIES
15	15	W. COMP

Figure 2-3. *LKOverHead master lookup table*

	OverHeadRatePK	LKOverHeadFK	HourlyRate	EffectiveDate	EmployeeFlag
1	1	1	0.70	2006-01-01 00:00:00.000	0
2	17	1	0.85	2006-01-09 00:00:00.000	0
3	2	2	0.22	2006-01-01 00:00:00.000	0
4	3	3	1.08	2006-01-01 00:00:00.000	1
5	4	4	0.27	2006-01-01 00:00:00.000	0
6	5	5	1.62	2006-01-01 00:00:00.000	1
7	6	6	0.19	2006-01-01 00:00:00.000	0
8	7	7	0.22	2006-01-01 00:00:00.000	0
9	8	8	0.32	2006-01-01 00:00:00.000	0
10	9	9	0.11	2006-01-01 00:00:00.000	1
11	18	9	0.16	2006-01-09 00:00:00.000	1
12	10	10	0.52	2006-01-01 00:00:00.000	1
13	11	11	0.59	2006-01-01 00:00:00.000	0
14	12	12	0.22	2006-01-01 00:00:00.000	0
15	13	13	2.16	2006-01-01 00:00:00.000	0
16	14	14	0.05	2006-01-01 00:00:00.000	1
17	15	15	1.08	2006-01-01 00:00:00.000	1

Figure 2-4. *OverHeadRate table (note the rate increase for two overhead categories)*

Note two pieces of data in the OverHeadRate table. First, the EmployeeFlag indicates whether the rate applies to employees only (value of 1) or all workers (value of 0). Second, the EffectiveDate indicates the date that the specific rate goes into effect. From the tables in Figures 2-3 and 2-4, you can see that the overhead rate for accountants' fees increased from 70 cents to 85 cents on January 9. The system logic must calculate labor dollars by matching the labor date against the correct rate for that date.

Listing 2-4 introduces your second UDF, GetOverHeadRate. A developer calls GetOverHeadRate and passes two parameters: an effective date and a flag for whether the function should include employee-only overhead rates or all overhead rates. The query utilizes a subquery that reads OverHeadRate a second time to determine the maximum rate and date given the effective date. The main query matches up on this date to return the correct rate.

Listing 2-4. *UDF GetOverHeadRate to Determine Sum of Overhead Rate*

```
CREATE FUNCTION [dbo].[GetOverHeadRate]
(

    @dEffectiveDate DateTime, @lEmployeeFlag bit)
RETURNS decimal (14,2)
AS
BEGIN

    DECLARE @dHourlyRate DECIMAL(14,2)
    -- Query Overhead Rate, match each one on the maximum date given
    -- the date parameter (@dEffectiveDate)

    SET @dHourlyRate = (SELECT SUM(HourlyRate)
        FROM OverHeadRate  OHR
            JOIN (SELECT LKOverHeadFK,MAX(EffectiveDate) AS EffectiveDate
                            FROM OverHeadRate OVTemp
                            WHERE  EffectiveDate <= @dEffectiveDate
                            GROUP BY LKOverHeadFK )  OHTemp
                ON OHTemp.LKOverHeadFK = OHR.LKOverHeadFK AND
                                    OHR.EffectiveDate =
                                    OHTemp.EffectiveDate
        WHERE CASE  WHEN @lEmployeeFlag = 1 THEN 0 ELSE EmployeeFlag END = 0)
            -- Use parameter to determine whether to filter on EmployeeFlag
    RETURN @dHourlyRate
END
```

The goal of the code in Listing 2-4 is to determine the overhead labor rate per hour for a given day, either for employees or subcontractors. Let's look at the code from the inside out:

First, you must determine the "active" rates for a specific date. A rate may have changed three times in a year, and you need to know the rate for a specific point in time. So for each rate you must find the most recent effective date that is on or before the effective date parameter. If rates were changed on March 1, April 15, and July 30, a query based on an effective date of June 1 would look for the rate of April 15 (the most recent, or "maximum," date on or before June 1). Therefore, your innermost query must retrieve each rate record based on the effective date parameter. The query in the following code is an example of a derived table that you can use in the outer query:

```
SELECT LKOverHeadFK,MAX(EffectiveDate) AS EffectiveDate
     FROM OverHeadRate OVTemp
          WHERE  EffectiveDate <= @dEffectiveDate
    GROUP BY LKOverHeadFK )  OHTemp
```

Next, you can join the `OverHeadRate` table against this derived table (based on the Rate ID key column, and the actual effective date), and optionally filter on the `EmployeeFlag` to filter out any overhead rates that are not relevant to subcontractors:

```
SET @dHourlyRate =
   (SELECT SUM(HourlyRate)
      FROM OverHeadRate  OHR
         JOIN (OHTemp)   -- See code earlier for query that produces derived table
            ON OHTemp.LKOverHeadFK  = OHR.LKOverHeadFK AND
               OHTemp.EffectiveDate = OHR.EffectiveDate
       WHERE
          CASE  WHEN @lEmployeeFlag = 1 THEN 0
                       ELSE EmployeeFlag END = 0)
```

As you can see, breaking down Listing 2-4 from the inside out helps to understand what may initially appear to be a complicated query!

Moving On: UDF to Get Worker Rates

As the requirement to retrieve labor rates for a given time period will be used across multiple reports, you'll want to create reusable code to retrieve rates for any given worker and time period. Other reports may use this detail information or perhaps summarize it. Figure 2-5 shows the rates you'll need to query.

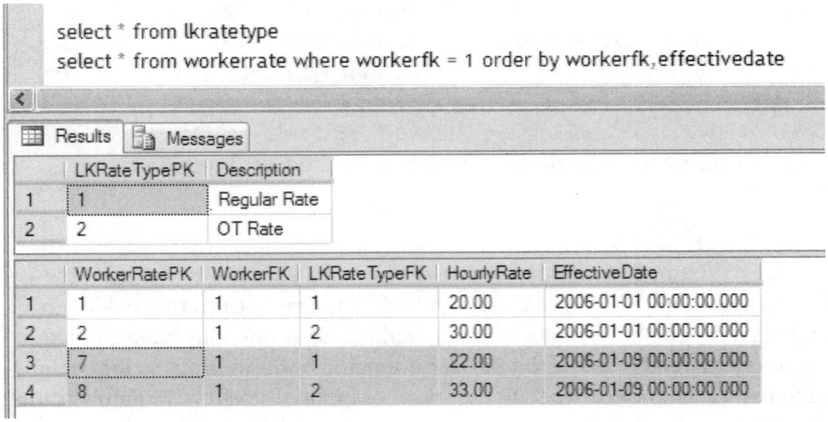

```
select * from lkratetype
select * from workerrate where workerfk = 1 order by workerfk,effectivedate
```

	LKRateTypePK	Description
1	1	Regular Rate
2	2	OT Rate

	WorkerRatePK	WorkerFK	LKRateTypeFK	HourlyRate	EffectiveDate
1	1	1	1	20.00	2006-01-01 00:00:00.000
2	2	1	2	30.00	2006-01-01 00:00:00.000
3	7	1	1	22.00	2006-01-09 00:00:00.000
4	8	1	2	33.00	2006-01-09 00:00:00.000

Figure 2-5. *Example of rates—note the worker rate inceases on 1-9-06*

Listing 2-5 contains code to return the regular pay rate, overtime rate, and overhead rate (using the UDF from Listing 2-4) for a worker for each day in a given date range.

Listing 2-5. *UDF GetWorkerRates to Get All Rates (Overhead and Labor)*

```
CREATE FUNCTION [dbo].[GetWorkerRates]
( @nWorkerFK int, @dStartDate DATETIME, @dEndDate DATETIME )
RETURNS
@tWorkerRates TABLE
(WorkerFK int, WorkDate DateTime, OverHeadRate decimal(10,2),
        RegularRate decimal(10,2), OTRate decimal(10,2))
AS
BEGIN
    DECLARE @lEmployeeFlag BIT
    SET @lEmployeeFlag = (SELECT EmployeeFlag FROM Worker
                                        WHERE WorkerPK = @nWorkerFK)

    INSERT INTO @tWorkerRates
        SELECT * FROM (SELECT TS.WorkerFK, TS.WorkDate,
            dbo.GetOverHeadRate(TS.WorkDate,@lEmployeeFlag) AS OverHeadRate,
                    WR.hourlyrate  AS HourlyRate, TS.LKRateTypeFK
        FROM (SELECT WorkerFK,WorkDate,LKRateTypeFK FROM TimeSheets
                            WHERE WorkerFK =  @nWorkerFK
                            GROUP BY WorkerFK,WorkDate,LKRateTypeFK) AS TS
          JOIN WorkerRate WR ON TS.WorkerFK = WR.WorkerFK AND
                    TS.LKRateTypeFK = WR.LKRateTypeFK
        WHERE WR.EffectiveDate =
                    (SELECT MAX(EffectiveDate) FROM WorkerRate WrTemp
                      WHERE WRTemp.LKRateTypeFK = TS.LKRateTypeFK AND
                        EffectiveDate <= WorkDate AND WrTemp.WorkerFK =
                            TS.WorkerFK)
                      AND WorkDate >= WR.EffectiveDate
                      and TS.Workerfk = @nWorkerFK
                      AND WorkDate BETWEEN @dStartDate AND @dEndDate) AS TEMP
        PIVOT (  SUM(HourlyRate) FOR LKRateTypeFK In ( [1],[2])) As X

RETURN
END
```

Here's a breakdown of the preceding code:

- Declares a table variable called tWorkerRates, which stores the overhead and labor rates for each day represented by the date range for the worker.

- Creates a derived table called TS, which retrieves all the timesheet rows for the worker and date range.

- Calls the UDF GetOverHeadRate (refer back to Listing 2-4) to determine the overhead rate for the worker and each date worked.

- Matches the data from TS against the data from WorkerRate. As the data in TS is daily data, the matching is performed based on maximum effective date on or before the date worked (similar to the matching performed in the query in Listing 2-4).

Finally, note the new PIVOT keyword at the bottom of the query. We will cover the new PIVOT capability in more detail in the next chapter—but the timesheet data is a good introduction to pivoting.

As you saw in Figure 2-5, the database will store multiple timesheet rows for each kind of time stored (regular hours and overtime hours). You need to create a flat row structure for the report to display regular labor and overtime labor on the same line. The PIVOT keyword allows you to (as the definition of pivot suggests) convert the two rows (e.g., keying in or pivoting on LKRateTypeFK) into the two columns for standard time and overtime.

Note the specific syntax for the PIVOT:

```
PIVOT (   SUM(HourlyRate) FOR LKRateTypeFK In ( [1],[2]))
```

Pivoting essentially involves three things: what you are pivoting on (the sum of the HourlyRate column), based on some column (LKRateTypeFK) being a set of values (1 or 2). Note that the list of values is essentially as static as a list of SELECT columns: you would need to use dynamic SQL if the list is variable.

■**Note** This example introduces the new PIVOT command. Chapter 3 provides a more detailed example, where you will build a result set for the aging receivables report and pivot rows of invoices into aging brackets based on date range.

Putting It All together: Stored Procedure GetTimeSheetData

While building components and UDFs is very important, it's always important (and fun) to write the final procedure that ties it all together! Listing 2-6 contains the code for GetTimeSheetData, the main stored procedure to retrieve timesheet data and rates.

Listing 2-6. *Stored Procedure GetTimeSheetData*

```
CREATE PROCEDURE [dbo].[GetTimeSheetData]
    -- Add the parameters for the stored procedure here
    @dStartDate DATETIME, @dEndDate DATETIME, @cJobList VARCHAR(MAX),
    @cWorkerList VARCHAR(MAX), @nSortOption int, @lShowDetails bit
```

```
AS
BEGIN
    SET NOCOUNT ON;

    -- Table variable to hold results
    DECLARE @tTimeSheets TABLE
        (DivisionFK int, WorkerFK int, WorkDate DateTime,
        JobMasterFK int, Hourlyrate decimal(14,2), OTRate decimal(14,2),
        OverHeadrate decimal(14,2), TotalLabor decimal(14,2),
        RegularHours decimal(14,2), OTHours decimal(14,2))


    INSERT INTO @tTimeSheets
    SELECT * FROM
        (SELECT DivisionFK,  TimeSheets.WorkerFK, TimeSheets.WorkDate,
         JobMasterFK, LKRateTypeFK, RegularRate, OTrate, OverheadRate,
         0 AS TotalLabor, HoursWorked
         FROM Timesheets
        CROSS APPLY dbo.GetWorkerRates
                (TimeSheets.WorkerFK,@dStartDate,@dEndDate) as EmpRates
        CROSS APPLY dbo.CommaListToTable(@cJobList) AS JobList
        CROSS APPLY dbo.CommaListToTable(@cWorkerList) AS WorkerList

        WHERE  Timesheets.WorkerFK= EmpRates.WorkerFK AND
                    Timesheets.WorkDate = EmpRates.WorkDate
            AND CASE
                WHEN @cJobList  = '' THEN 1
                WHEN JobList.IntKey = TimeSheets.JobMasterFK THEN 1
                ELSE 0 END = 1

            AND CASE
          WHEN @cWorkerList  = '' THEN 1
          WHEN WorkerList.IntKey = TimeSheets.WorkerFK  THEN 1
          ELSE 0 END = 1      ) as temp

        -- Result set for timesheet details
        PIVOT (  SUM(HoursWorked) FOR LKRateTypeFK In ( [1],[2])) As X

        -- Could have been done in the query, but you can "munge" it afterwards
    UPDATE @tTimeSheets
        SET RegularHours = COALESCE(RegularHours,0),
        OTHours  = COALESCE(OtHours,0),
         OTRate  = COALESCE(OtRate,0),
        TotalLabor = (RegularHours * HourlyRate) + (OTHours * OTRate) +
                        ( (RegularHours + OtHours) * OverHeadRate)
```

```
-- Result set for employee summary
SELECT TS.DivisionFK,Worker.WorkerPK,FirstName, LastName,
            Worker.EmployeeFlag, SUM(RegularHours) AS RegularHours,
            SUM(OTHours) AS OtHours, SUM(RegularHours + OTHours)
                                                        AS TotHours,
            SUM(TotalLabor) AS TotalLabor
FROM Worker
    JOIN @tTimeSheets TS ON WorkerPK = WorkerFK
GROUP BY TS.DivisionFK, Worker.WorkerPK, FirstName,
                LastName, Worker.EmployeeFlag

-- Result set for division summary
SELECT TS.DivisionFK,Division.Description,
        SUM(RegularHours) AS RegularHours,
        SUM(OTHours) AS OtHours, SUM(RegularHours + OTHours)
                                                        AS TotHours,
        SUM(TotalLabor) AS TotalLabor
FROM Division
    JOIN @tTimeSheets TS ON DivisionPK = DivisionFK
GROUP BY TS.DivisionFK, Division.Description


-- Result set for timesheet details
SELECT DivisionFK, WorkerFK , WorkDate , JobMasterFK , RegularHours,
            OTHours, ISNULL(RegularHours,0) + ISNULL(OTHours,0) AS TotHours,
            HourlyRate , OTRate , OverHeadRate, TotalLabor
FROM  @tTimeSheets

END
```

Once again, we'll break down what this code does. In this case, you

- Declare a table variable called tTimeSheets, which stores the detail line item data for the timesheets.

- Utilize the CROSS APPLY capability with the UDF CommaListToTable (refer back to Listing 2-1) for both the variable number of jobs (or none) in cJobList and cWorkerList. Note also the CASE statements, which only execute the WHERE clause if the corresponding variables contain data.

- Utilize the CROSS APPLY capability with the UDF GetWorkerRates (refer back to Listing 2-5) to match up timesheet hours with labor pay and overhead rates.

- Again, use the PIVOT capability to convert multiple rows of timesheet hours (regular and overtime) into one row for the report.

- Create summary result sets by employee and division (for the report). Figure 2-6 shows an example of running the stored procedure for a single job and a single worker, Figure 2-7 shows an example for all jobs and a single worker, and Figure 2-8 shows the result of running the stored procedure for many jobs and all workers.

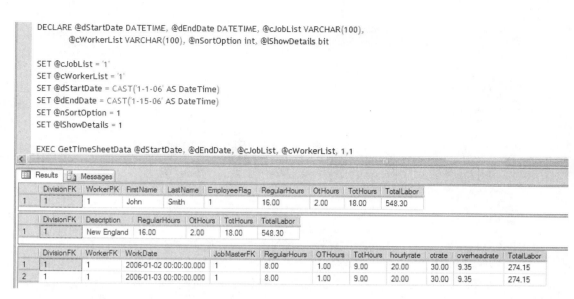

```
DECLARE @dStartDate DATETIME, @dEndDate DATETIME, @cJobList VARCHAR(100),
        @cWorkerList VARCHAR(100), @nSortOption int, @lShowDetails bit

SET @cJobList = '1'
SET @cWorkerList = '1'
SET @dStartDate = CAST('1-1-06' AS DateTime)
SET @dEndDate = CAST('1-15-06' AS DateTime)
SET @nSortOption = 1
SET @lShowDetails = 1

EXEC GetTimeSheetData @dStartDate, @dEndDate, @cJobList, @cWorkerList, 1,1
```

	DivisionFK	WorkerPK	FirstName	LastName	EmployeeFlag	RegularHours	OtHours	TotHours	TotalLabor
1	1	1	John	Smith	1	16.00	2.00	18.00	548.30

	DivisionFK	Description	RegularHours	OtHours	TotHours	TotalLabor
1	1	New England	16.00	2.00	18.00	548.30

	DivisionFK	WorkerFK	WorkDate	JobMasterFK	RegularHours	OTHours	TotHours	hourlyrate	otrate	overheadrate	TotalLabor
1	1	1	2006-01-02 00:00:00.000	1	8.00	1.00	9.00	20.00	30.00	9.35	274.15
2	1	1	2006-01-03 00:00:00.000	1	8.00	1.00	9.00	20.00	30.00	9.35	274.15

Figure 2-6. *Testing the result set with one job and one worker*

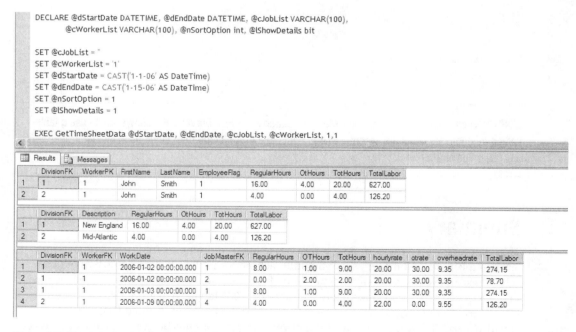

```
DECLARE @dStartDate DATETIME, @dEndDate DATETIME, @cJobList VARCHAR(100),
        @cWorkerList VARCHAR(100), @nSortOption int, @lShowDetails bit

SET @cJobList = ''
SET @cWorkerList = '1'
SET @dStartDate = CAST('1-1-06' AS DateTime)
SET @dEndDate = CAST('1-15-06' AS DateTime)
SET @nSortOption = 1
SET @lShowDetails = 1

EXEC GetTimeSheetData @dStartDate, @dEndDate, @cJobList, @cWorkerList, 1,1
```

	DivisionFK	WorkerPK	FirstName	LastName	EmployeeFlag	RegularHours	OtHours	TotHours	TotalLabor
1	1	1	John	Smith	1	16.00	4.00	20.00	627.00
2	2	1	John	Smith	1	4.00	0.00	4.00	126.20

	DivisionFK	Description	RegularHours	OtHours	TotHours	TotalLabor
1	1	New England	16.00	4.00	20.00	627.00
2	2	Mid-Atlantic	4.00	0.00	4.00	126.20

	DivisionFK	WorkerFK	WorkDate	JobMasterFK	RegularHours	OTHours	TotHours	hourlyrate	otrate	overheadrate	TotalLabor
1	1	1	2006-01-02 00:00:00.000	1	8.00	1.00	9.00	20.00	30.00	9.35	274.15
2	1	1	2006-01-02 00:00:00.000	2	0.00	2.00	2.00	20.00	30.00	9.35	78.70
3	1	1	2006-01-03 00:00:00.000	1	8.00	1.00	9.00	20.00	30.00	9.35	274.15
4	2	1	2006-01-09 00:00:00.000	4	4.00	0.00	4.00	22.00	0.00	9.55	126.20

Figure 2-7. *Testing the result set with all jobs, one worker*

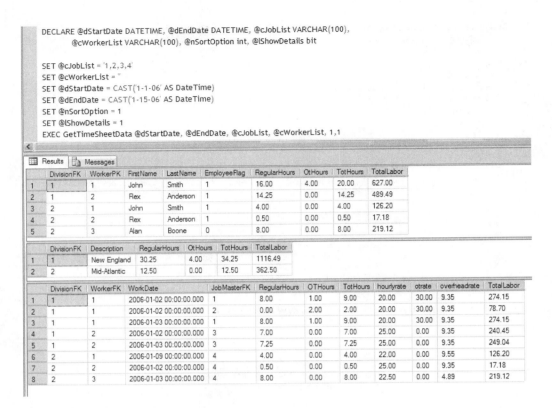

```
DECLARE @dStartDate DATETIME, @dEndDate DATETIME, @cJobList VARCHAR(100),
        @cWorkerList VARCHAR(100), @nSortOption int, @lShowDetails bit

SET @cJobList = '1,2,3,4'
SET @cWorkerList = ''
SET @dStartDate = CAST('1-1-06' AS DateTime)
SET @dEndDate = CAST('1-15-06' AS DateTime)
SET @nSortOption = 1
SET @lShowDetails = 1
EXEC GetTimeSheetData @dStartDate, @dEndDate, @cJobList, @cWorkerList, 1,1
```

Figure 2-8. *Testing the result set with many jobs, all workers*

■Note The new APPLY operator has additional capabilities. SQL Server 2005 allows you to use a table-valued function in a subquery, where the arguments to the UDF come from columns in the outer query. We will cover this in Chapter 3.

Summary

This chapter covered the complete stored procedure requirements for the first report. You learned the value of full result sets, you built techniques for handling variable lists of user selections, and you constructed a table-valued user-defined function that you can leverage in other queries. You also looked at two new T-SQL 2005 language features: PIVOT, to convert rows into columns, and APPLY, to directly apply the results of table-valued UDFs. In addition, you also learned that the maximum size of VarChar variables has been significantly enhanced in SQL Server 2005.

In the next chapter , you will build result sets for other reports, and you'll look more closely at some of the new SQL Server 2005 language features. Roll up your sleeves and get ready for some heavy T-SQL!

CHAPTER 3

■ ■ ■

More T-SQL 2005 Stored Procedures

In the previous chapter, you built the complete SQL code for the timesheet report. You also constructed several new user-defined functions (UDFs) and utilized some new SQL Server 2005 language features. In this chapter, you'll do the following:

- Build the result sets for the **construction job summary** report, which will make further use of the APPLY capability.

- Build the stored procedure for the **aging receivables** report, which will further utilize the PIVOT capability.

- Learn about a wide variety of different language features in T-SQL, and how they can be used both for your reporting requirements as well as general database tasks that developers typically face. Here is a list of what we'll cover:

  - How to query for the top N rows in a table, where N is a variable number, by using the new TOP N capability in SQL Server 2005. (In previous versions of SQL Server, the N was a literal.)

  - Building stored procedures to recursively query against hierarchical data, using the new **common table expression** capabilities in SQL Server 2005.

  - How to perform audit trail logging using Update triggers.

  - How to get immediate feedback on updates using the new OUTPUT and OUTPUT INTO keywords in SQL Server 2005.

  - How to build queries dynamically using dynamic SQL, and how to build alternative solutions by using the CASE statement and the COALESCE function.

  - Ranking result sets using the new built-in **ranking** functions in SQL Server 2005.

  - Implementing TRY...CATCH error-handling (including nested error handling) in SQL Server 2005.

  - Using the LIKE keyword to perform partial text searches.

  - Working with XML data.

- Using `Dateparts` to work with `Datetime` data

- A cleaner alternative to `IN` and `NOT IN`

- One final look at the `APPLY` operator in SQL Server 2005 for correlated subqueries

- Get a brief look at SQL Server 2000 code for functional equivalents of certain features we've covered in the last two chapters.

Building the Construction Job Summary Report

Back in Chapter 1, we identified a job summary and profit report that displays aggregate totals (labor, materials, profit, etc.) for each construction job. Figure A-2 in Appendix A shows an example of the report. The report allows an end user to sort on any aggregate column, so it is an easy way to see which jobs were the most profitable, had the least amount of labor, etc. Fortunately, you're already part of the way there: you can leverage some of the UDFs you wrote in Chapter 2.

The construction job summary report contains one line per construction job (i.e., one job in the `JobMaster` table). Table 3-1 lists the measures for the report, along with a brief description that the client has provided.

Table 3-1. *Measures for the Construction Job Summary Report*

Column	Description
Total Labor $	Sum of hours worked on the job, multiplied by labor and overhead rates
Total Material $	Sum of material purchased for the job
Labor Profit $	Sum of hours worked on the job, multiplied by an additional labor profit rate
Material Profit $	Total Material $, multiplied by a material markup percentage
Addtl Labor Profit $	Additional lump-sum labor profit dollars, passed on to the client
*Total Profit $	Sum of the three profit figures
*Total Contracted Amt	Total Labor $ + Total Material $ + Total Profit $
Total Amount Billed	Amount actually invoiced to date
Total Amount Received	Total amount received to date
*Balance	Difference between total billed and total received
*Total Profit %	Total Profit % divided by Total Contracted Amt, expressed as a %

Of course, any SQL code should derive from a specification that defines these calculations in more technical detail. The specification may also reveal opportunities for reusable functions. So let's take a second look at the report's measures (excluding the ones marked with an asterisk, which are just simple calculations of the calculated columns).

- *Total Labor $*: Must retrieve all workers who worked on the job and the hours they worked (from the `TimeSheets` table), determine their labor rates and overhead rates, and summarize this data.

- *Total Material $*: Must retrieve all material purchases for the job from `Materials`.

- *Labor Profit $*: Must sum the hours worked on the job (from `TimeSheets`) and multiply it by `JobMaster.AdditionalHourlyRate`.

- *Material Profit $*: Take the data from Total Material $ and multiply it by `JobMaster.MaterialMarkupPct`.

- *Addtl Labor Profit $*: This is simply the column `JobMaster.AdditionalLabor`.

- *Total Amount Billed*: The sum of `Invoices.InvoiceAmount` for all invoices related to that construction job.

- *Total Amount Received*: The sum of `Receipts.AmountPaid` for that construction job (must join `Receipts` to `Invoices`).

If you want to continue with the practice of using user-defined functions, you are looking at **three** new functions to retrieve data at the construction job level. The first must calculate the labor statistics (and can utilize some of the existing UDFs you built in Chapter 2), the second must calculate the material purchase costs, and the third must retrieve the invoice information.

Determining the Total Labor Data

First, let's take a look at the UDF to determine total labor data at the job level. In a nutshell, doing so requires the following steps:

- Determining the employees who worked on a job

- Determining the number of hours they worked each day on the job

- Determining the rates (`GetWorkerRates` from Listing 2-5 in Chapter 2)

- Bringing that data together, rolling up (summarizing) those figures, and applying any additional labor profit (markups) defined for the job

Listing 3-1 displays the UDF to determine the number of hours a worker works on a job. The query is fairly simple: it retrieves hours from `TimeSheets` and performs the `PIVOT` operations to convert rows for regular hours and OT hours into columns. Note the use of the `COALESCE` function: this handy function allows you to write code to handle instances where you want to query on either one job or all. If the calling procedure passes a `NULL` value for the `JobNumber` parameter, the query will simply join the `JobNumber` column to itself—essentially retrieving every job. (Later in this chapter, we'll cover `COALESCE` in a little more detail.)

Listing 3-1. *UDF GetWorkerHours*

```
CREATE FUNCTION [dbo].[GetWorkerHours]
( @nWorkerFK int, @dStartDate DATETIME, @dEndDate DATETIME, @nJobNumber int  )
RETURNS
@tWorkerHours TABLE
( WorkerFK int, WorkDate DateTime,   RegularHours decimal(10,2), OTHours
  decimal(10,2) )
```

```
AS
BEGIN
        -- You may want hours for just one job, or for all jobs,
        -- so use COALESCE

        -- Again, use PIVOT to place hours into Regular and OT

        INSERT INTO @tWorkerHours
            SELECT * FROM (
                    SELECT  WorkerFK, Workdate,  LKRateTypeFK, HoursWorked
                        FROM TimeSheets
                            WHERE  WorkerFK = @nWorkerFK
                                AND JobMasterFK = COALESCE(@nJobNumber,JobMasterFK))
                                AS Temp
            PIVOT (   SUM(HoursWorked) FOR LKRateTypeFK In ( [1],[2])) As X
        RETURN
END
```

Now that you have functions to retrieve both hours and rates, you can put it all together in yet another function, GetJobLaborTotals (see Listing 3-2). Note the CROSS APPLY references to dbo.GetWorkerHours and dbo.GetWorkerRates. Also, note the code in step 1: the UDF creates a derived table (WorkerList) to determine each worker and the minimum/maximum date worked for the job.

The UDF joins the results from WorkerList with the results of the GetWorkerHours and GetWorkerRates (WorkerHours and WorkerRates).

Listing 3-2. *GetJobLaborTotals for a Single Job*

```
CREATE FUNCTION [dbo].[GetJobLaborTotals]
(
        @nJobMasterFK int
 )
RETURNS
@tTotalJobCosts   TABLE
(
        JobMasterFK int, TotJobHours decimal(14,2), Labor decimal(14,2), LaborProfit
          decimal(14,2)
)
AS
BEGIN

        INSERT INTO @tTotalJobCosts
            SELECT JobMaster.JobMasterPK, TotJobHours,Labor,
                (TotJobHours * AdditionalHourlyRate) +
                        ISNULL(JOBMASTER.AdditionalLabor,0) AS LaborProfit
            FROM JobMaster
                JOIN
                (SELECT    JobMasterPK, SUM(ISNULL(RegularHours,0) +
```

```
                              ISNULL(OTHours,0)) AS TotJobHours ,
                                SUM(ISNULL((RegularHours * RegularRate),0) +
                                ISNULL((OTHours * OTRate),0) +
                                  (( ISNULL(RegularHours,0) + ISNULL(OTHours,0)) *
                                OverHeadRate))  AS Labor
                     FROM JobMaster

                     -- Step 1, From TimeSheets, get workers on the job,
                     -- and for each one, their minimum and maximum Work Date
                     -- (to use for calls to GetWorkerHours and GetWorkerRates)
                     -- Derived table called WorkerList
               JOIN (SELECT JobMasterFK, WorkerFK,MIN(WorkDate) AS MinWorkDate,
                            MAX(WorkDate) AS MaxWorkDate
                          FROM TimeSheets
                           GROUP BY JobmasterFK,workerfk) AS  WorkerList
                 ON WorkerList.JobMasterFK = JobMaster.JobmasterPK

                     -- Step 2,  take each WorkerFK/MinWorkDate/MaxWorkDate on the job,
                     -- get their hours worked and daily rates  (as hours and rates)
                   CROSS APPLY dbo.GetWorkerHours
                       (WorkerList.Workerfk,MinWorkDate,MaxWorkDate,JobMasterPK)
                          AS WorkerHours
                 CROSS APPLY dbo.GetWorkerRates
                        (WorkerList.Workerfk, MinWorkdate,MaxWorkdate)
                           AS  WorkerRates
              WHERE JobMasterPK = @nJobMasterFK AND
                          Workerlist.WorkerFK = WorkerRates.WorkerFK  AND
                           WorkerRates.WorkerFK = WorkerHours.WorkerFK AND
                           WorkerRates.Workdate = WorkerHours.Workdate
                    GROUP BY JobMasterPK) AS TempJob
             ON TempJob.JobMasterPK = JobMaster.JobMasterPK

       RETURN
END
```

Retrieving Material Purchases

Second, you need a simple UDF to retrieve material purchases associated with the job. Fortunately, this is much easier to create than the previous UDFs. Listing 3-3 displays the UDF for GetJobMaterials. The UDF simply queries Materials on the JobNumber to summarize the purchases, and also applies any markup percentage to determine material profit.

Listing 3-3. *GetJobMaterials*

```
CREATE FUNCTION [dbo].[GetJobMaterials]
    (@nJobNumberFK int  )
RETURNS
```

```
@tMaterials TABLE
(
     JobMasterFK int, PurchaseAmount decimal(14,2), MaterialProfit decimal(14,2)
)

AS
BEGIN
     INSERT INTO @tMaterials
          SELECT JobMasterFK,SUM(Purchaseamount) AS PurchaseAmount,
                         SUM(PurchaseAmount * MaterialMarkupPct) AS MaterialProfit
          FROM JobMaster
               LEFT JOIN Materials ON JobMasterPK = JobMasterFK
          WHERE JobMasterPK = @nJobNumberFK
          GROUP BY JobMasterFK

     RETURN
END
```

Retrieving Invoiced Amounts and Payments

Third, you need a simple UDF to retrieve any invoiced amounts and any payments associated with the job. Again, this is a simple UDF. Listing 3-4 displays the UDF for GetJobInvoiceTotals. The UDF simply queries the Invoices table on JobNumber (and the Receipts table on Invoice number) to retrieve any invoices amounts and payments.

Listing 3-4. *GetJobInvoiceTotals*

```
ALTER FUNCTION [dbo].[GetJobInvoiceTotals]
(  @nJobNumberFK int  )
RETURNS
     @tInvoices TABLE
     (JobMasterFK int, InvoiceAmount decimal(14,2), AmountPaid decimal(14,2),
      Balance decimal(14,2)  )
AS
BEGIN
     DECLARE @InvoiceAmount decimal(14,2), @AmountReceived Decimal(14,2)
     SET @InvoiceAmount = (SELECT SUM(InvoiceAmount) FROM InvoiceJob
                                        WHERE JobMasterFK = @nJobNumberFK)
     SET @AmountReceived = (SELECT SUM(AmountReceived) FROM Receipts
                                        WHERE JobMasterFK = @nJobNumberFK)

     INSERT INTO @tInvoices
        VALUES (@nJobNumberFK, @InvoiceAmount, @AmountReceived,
              @InvoiceAmount - @AmountReceived)
     RETURN
END
```

Putting It All Together

Finally you can put it all together. Listing 3-5 lists the final stored procedure (GetJobSummaries) to produce the result set for the report. Once again, the stored procedure utilizes many topics we've previously covered: use of the APPLY operator, use of the CommaListToTable function, and use of the CASE statement to either query on all jobs (if the JobList parameter is blank) or on the contents of the JobList parameter.

Listing 3-5. *GetJobSummaries, Final Stored Procedure to Produce Report Result Set*

```
CREATE PROCEDURE [dbo].[GetJobSummaries]
    -- Add the parameters for the stored procedure here
    @cJobList VARCHAR(MAX)

AS
BEGIN
    -- SET NOCOUNT ON added to prevent extra result sets from
    -- interfering with SELECT statements.
    SET NOCOUNT ON;

    SELECT   JobMasterPK, ClientName, JM.Description, TotJobHours, Labor, LaborProfit,
        PurchaseAmount, MaterialProfit , MaterialProfit + (TotJobHours *
        AdditionalHourlyRate) + JM.AdditionalLabor AS TotalProfit,
        Labor + PurchaseAmount + MaterialProfit +
     (TotJobHours * AdditionalHourlyRate) + JM.AdditionalLabor
      AS ContractedAmount,
        InvoiceAmount, AmountPaid , Balance
    FROM JobMaster JM
        -- Table-valued UDF to create table of jobs
        CROSS APPLY dbo.CommaListToTable(@cJobList )   AS JobList
        -- Table-valued UDF - returns total hours, labor, & labor profit for a job
        CROSS APPLY dbo.GetJobLaborTotals (JM.JobMasterPK) AS JobLaborTotals
        -- Table-valued UDF - returns materials purchased/profit for a job
        CROSS APPLY dbo.GetJobMaterials ( JM.JobMasterPK) AS Materials
        -- Table-valued UDF to return amounts invoiced and amounts received
        CROSS APPLY dbo.GetJobInvoiceTotals(JM.JobMasterPK) AS JobInvoices

            WHERE JobLaborTotals.JobMasterFK = JM.JobMasterPK
                AND JobInvoices.JobmasterFK = JM.JobMasterPK
                AND Materials.JobMasterfK = JM.JobMasterPK
                -- Either join on the list of jobs selected, or run for ALL
                AND CASE
                    WHEN @cJobList  = '' THEN 1
                    WHEN JobList.IntKey = JobMasterPK THEN 1
                    ELSE 0 END = 1
END
```

Figure 3-1 shows an example of running GetJobSummaries.

```
EXEC GetJobSummaries '1,2'
```

	JobMasterPK	ClientName	Description	TotJobHours	Labor	LaborProfit	PurchaseAmount	MaterialProfit	TotalProfit	ContractedAmount
1	1	KINGSTON CONSTRUCTION	Job #1	18.00	548.30	36.00	1000.00	70.00	106.0000	1654.3000
2	2	GOLDGATE CONTRACTING	Job #2	2.00	78.70	0.00	2000.00	100.00	100.0000	2178.7000

Figure 3-1. *Example result set for construction job summary report*

Building the Result Sets for an Aging Receivables Report

Before we cover the queries for the aging receivables report, you need to define a new database table. The requirements for the aging receivables report call for configurable aging brackets. While aging brackets normally run in 30-day increments (1–30 days, 31–60 days, etc.), the client may want to run for custom ranges. Table 3-2 lists the structure for the table AgingBrackets.

Table 3-2. *Table for Data-Driven Aging Brackets (AgingBrackets)*

Column Name	Type	Description
StartDay	int	First day of the bracket range (e.g., day 31)
EndDay	int	End day of the bracket range (e.g., day 60)
BracketNumber	int	Bracket number for the aging columns (e.g., 2)
BracketLabel	char(50)	"31-60 Days"

Figure 3-2 displays the default entries.

```
SELECT * FROM AgingBrackets
```

	StartDay	EndDay	BracketNumber	BracketLabel
1	1	30	1	< 30 Days
2	31	60	2	31-60 Days
3	61	90	3	61-90 Days
4	91	120	4	91-120 Days
5	121	999999	5	> 120 Days

Figure 3-2. *Default values for table AgingBrackets*

Listing 3-6 presents the stored procedure GetAgingReceivables. The code produces the result sets for the aging receivables report. Of interest are the following:

- The code uses the CommaListToTable UDF for a variable number of customers.

- The code joins the Invoices table against the AgingBrackets table and calculates the number of days each invoice is aged (with respect to the aging date) by using dateparts (the parameter in the DateDiff function).

- The code determines the corresponding aging bracket for the number of days aged and PIVOTs on that bracket to produce the aging bracket columns.

- In additional to the detailed result sets, the stored procedure also produces summary result sets for the aging bracket and the list of customers. These will also be used on the final report output.

Listing 3-6. *Complete Stored Procedure for Retrieving Aging Invoices*

```
CREATE PROCEDURE [dbo].[GetAgingReceivables]
    @cCustomerList VARCHAR(MAX), @dAgingDate DateTime, @lShowDetails bit
AS
BEGIN
    SET NOCOUNT ON;

    -- Table variable to hold results
    DECLARE @tAgingDetails TABLE
        (ClientFK int, InvoiceNumber char(20), InvoiceDate DateTime,
TotalAged decimal(14,2),  Bracket1 decimal(14,2), Bracket2 decimal(14,2),
Bracket3 decimal(14,2), Bracket4 decimal(14,2), Bracket5 decimal(14,2) )

    INSERT INTO @tAgingDetails
        SELECT * FROM
            -- Grab open invoices, determine balance owed
            (SELECT  ClientFK, InvoiceNumber, InvoiceDate, 0 AS TotalAged,
                            InvoiceAmount-SUM(ISNULL(AmountReceived,0)) AS AmountOwed,
              ABR.BracketNumber
            FROM Invoices Inv
                -- Determine days aged, find the corresponding bracket
              JOIN AgingBrackets ABR ON DateDiff(dd,InvoiceDate,@dAgingDate)
                                BETWEEN ABR.StartDay and ABR.EndDay
              LEFT JOIN Receipts RCT ON InvoicePK = INvoiceFK
            -- If run for selected customers
            CROSS APPLY dbo.CommaListToTable(@cCustomerList) AS CustomerList
            WHERE InvoiceClosed = 0
            -- Check if customers selected....if not, run for all
            AND CASE
                WHEN @cCustomerList  = '' THEN 1
                WHEN CustomerList.IntKey = Inv.ClientFK  THEN 1
```

```
            ELSE 0 END = 1

        GROUP BY
            ClientFK, InvoiceNumber,InvoiceDate,InvoiceAmount,ABR.BracketNumber)
     AS Temp
     -- Pivot amount owed into the correct bracket
     PIVOT (  SUM(AmountOwed)  FOR BracketNumber In ( [1],[2],[3],[4],[5]))
     As Brackets



    -- Post query munging, set the total aged column
    -- (helpful in summarizing)
    UPDATE @tAgingDetails SET TotalAged = ISNULL(Bracket1,0) +
                                          ISNULL(Bracket2,0) +
                                          ISNULL(Bracket3,0) +
                                          ISNULL(Bracket4,0) +
                                          ISNULL(Bracket5,0)


-- Four result sets

    -- 1) Return detail aging data...if detail option was not selected, just bring back
empty structure
     IF @lShowDetails = 1
        SELECT * FROM @tAgingDetails
      ELSE
         SELECT * FROM @tAgingDetails WHERE 1=0


    -- 2) Summary aging data
        SELECT ClientFK,SUM(Bracket1) AS Bracket1,
                        SUM(Bracket2) AS Bracket2,
                        SUM(Bracket3) AS Bracket3,
                        SUM(Bracket4) AS Bracket4,
                        SUM(Bracket5) AS Bracket5,
                        SUM( TotalAged ) AS TotalAged
        FROM @tAgingDetails GROUP BY      ClientFK

    -- 3) The aging brackets (to display descriptions on the report)
    SELECT * FROM AgingBrackets

    -- 4) Client names for clients in the report
    SELECT ClientPK, ClientName FROM Client
        JOIN @tAgingDetails ON ClientPK = ClientFk
        GROUP BY ClientPK,ClientName
END
```

Figures 3-3 and 3-4 show two different examples of running the aging receivables report: one for a single customer, and one for all customers.

```
DECLARE @dAgingDate DateTime, @cCustomerList varchar(100), @lShowdetails bit

SET @dAgingDate =GETDATE()
SET @cCustomerList = '2'
SET @lShowDetails = 1

EXEC GetAgingReceivables @cCustomerList, @dAgingDate, @lShowDetails
```

	ClientFK	InvoiceNumber	InvoiceDate	TotalAged	Bracket1	Bracket2	Bracket3	Bracket4	Bracket5
1	2	2005-1954	2005-05-01...	12000.00	0.00	0.00	0.00	0.00	12000.00

	ClientFK	TotalAged	Bracket1	Bracket2	Bracket3	Bracket4	Bracket5
1	2	12000.00	0.00	0.00	0.00	0.00	12000.00

	StartDay	Endday	BracketNumber	BracketLabel
1	1	30	1	< 30 Days
2	31	60	2	31-60 Days
3	61	90	3	61-90 Days
4	91	120	4	91-120 Days
5	121	999999	5	> 120 Days

	ClientPK	ClientName
1	2	GOLDGATE CONTRACTING

Figure 3-3. *Running the aging receivables report for one customer, as of today*

```
DECLARE @dAgingDate DateTime, @cCustomerList varchar(100), @lShowdetails bit
SET @dAgingDate = CAST('1-1-06' AS DateTime)
SET @cCustomerList = ''
SET @lShowDetails = 1
EXEC GetAgingReceivables @cCustomerList, @dAgingDate, @lShowDetails
```

	ClientFK	InvoiceNumber	InvoiceDate	TotalAged	Bracket1	Bracket2	Bracket3	Bracket4	Bracket5
1	1	2005-0662	2005-09-01...	0.00	0.00	0.00	0.00	0.00	0.00
2	1	2005-0778	2005-10-01...	2000.00	0.00	0.00	0.00	2000.00	0.00
3	1	2005-1209	2005-12-18...	3500.00	3500.00	0.00	0.00	0.00	0.00
4	1	2005-2182	2005-12-01...	3000.00	0.00	3000.00	0.00	0.00	0.00
5	2	2005-1954	2005-05-01...	12000.00	0.00	0.00	0.00	0.00	12000.00
6	3	2005-0944	2005-08-01...	13000.00	0.00	0.00	0.00	0.00	13000.00
7	3	2005-1001	2005-10-18...	17500.00	0.00	0.00	17500.00	0.00	0.00

	ClientFK	TotalAged	Bracket1	Bracket2	Bracket3	Bracket4	Bracket5
1	1	8500.00	3500.00	3000.00	0.00	2000.00	0.00
2	2	12000.00	0.00	0.00	0.00	0.00	12000.00
3	3	30500.00	0.00	0.00	17500.00	0.00	13000.00

	StartDay	Endday	BracketNumber	BracketLabel
1	1	30	1	< 30 Days
	31	60	2	31-60 Days

	ClientPK	ClientName
1	1	KINGSTON CONSTRUCTION
2	2	GOLDGATE CONTRACTING
3	3	L& L EXCAVATING INC.

Figure 3-4. *Running the aging receivables report for all customers, as of January 1*

■Note Chapters 2 and 3 have made heavy use of T-SQL User-Defined functions. Our goal is to demonstrate reusability. However, this is just one application. In your applications, you may choose to take some of the UDFs and incorporate them directly into the higher-level queries. There are always trade-offs between reusability and performance: use the knowledge of your specific situations to judge which approach is best.

General SQL Server Programming Tasks

You can think of this next section as a miscellaneous section, albeit a large one. In different online forums, user groups, or client interactions, we've seen the same or similar questions asked over and over. So let's take some time and cover different database programming tasks that developers face: some might have relevance to reporting applications, though perhaps not directly related to the application in this book. Other tasks may be outside the scope of reporting applications, but are still important areas that SQL developers will want to examine. For that reason, we'll simply use the Northwind database that comes with SQL Server 2000 for this next section.

TOP N Reporting

Let's take a look at the new TOP N capability in T-SQL 2005. As a basic explanation, TOP N instructs SQL Server to only return the first N number of rows in the result set, based on whatever sort order you specify. In SQL Server 2000, the N had to be a literal: to execute TOP N queries in SQL Server (where N was variable), the developer had to construct a SQL string and then execute it dynamically. While this worked, it resulted in code that is arguably a bit more difficult to maintain—not to mention that it probably discouraged less-experienced developers who wanted to avoid dynamic SQL altogether. Alternatively, the developer could set the ROWCOUNT system variable to limit the result set: this had limitations in more complex SQL statements and also required you to restore it afterwards.

Fortunately, SQL Server 2005 allows developers to specify a variable. This should encourage developers to place code for TOP N reporting in the database layer, as opposed to implementing a portion of it outside the database. Listing 3-7 demonstrates a simple but meaningful example of retrieving the TOP N jobs based on labor profit—by using one of the UDFs you previously built.

Listing 3-7. *Code to Demonstrate TOP N*

```
DECLARE @nTop int
SET @nTop = 5
SELECT TOP(@nTop) JobMasterPK, LaborProfit
    FROM JobMaster
        CROSS APPLY dbo.GetJobLaborTotals(JobMaster.JobMasterPK) JobLabor
    WHERE JobLabor.JobMasterFK = JobMaster.JobMasterPK
    ORDER BY LaborProfit DESC
```

By default, using TOP N will return the number of rows specified by N. If you want to return the top N% rows, you can use the PERCENT keyword:

```
SELECT TOP(@nTop) PERCENT...
```

The TOP variable can even be the result of a UDF or any expression that returns an integer, such as the following query from the Northwind Orders database:

```
SELECT TOP( SELECT COUNT(*) FROM SHIPPERS ) * FROM ORDERS
```

In SQL Server 2005, you can also use the TOP N capability with INSERT, UPDATE, and DELETE statements, to limit the scope of the command.

```
-- Create a table variable with three rows, but only update the first two
DECLARE @tTest1 TABLE ( Amount decimal(10,2))
INSERT INTO @ttest1 VALUES ( 100)
INSERT INTO @ttest1 VALUES ( 200)
INSERT INTO @ttest1 VALUES ( 300)
UPDATE TOP(@nTop)      @tTest1 SET Amount = Amount * 10

-- Now create a second table variable,
-- and insert the first two rows from the first one
DECLARE @tTest2 TABLE ( Amount decimal(10,2))
INSERT TOP(2) @tTest2      SELECT * FROM @tTest1 order by amount
```

Common Table Expressions/Recursive Queries

Prior to SQL Server 2005, performing a recursive query (i.e., a query that calls another query) meant creating temporary tables and writing multiple SQL statements. A common example is querying hierarchical data. While not specifically part of the examples, you want to take a minute to look at a powerful new way to query hierarchical data in SQL Server 2005.

SQL Server 2005 allows developers to perform true recursive queries through common table expressions (CTEs). CTEs are similar to derived tables, and they allow you to write recursive queries in a single SQL statement.

As a basic example, take a look at the music hierarchy presented in Table 3-3.

Table 3-3. *Music Hierarchy Stored in MusicData*

Data	Primary Key	Parent Key
Musicians	1	NULL
Jazz	2	1
Rock	3	1
Classical	4	1
Saxophone	5	2
Trumpet	6	2
Guitar	7	3
Piano	8	4
Charlie Parker	9	5
John Coltrane	10	5
Miles Davis	11	6
Eddie Van Halen	12	7
Franz Liszt	13	8

For any given search name (might be an instrument, a musician, etc.), you want to determine that name's parent row, and then its parent, and so on, all the way up to the top of the hierarchy. While this may seem a meaningless example, imagine if this were a sales hierarchy, or even a product bill-of-material structure.

Listing 3-8 contains a query to retrieve a specific row and all parent rows. There are three elements to this query. First, you declare a CTE (MusicTree) with column names. You can think of this as similar to a derived table. Second, the inside query (or anchor query) retrieves the row based on the search criteria (in this case, Charlie Parker). Finally, the recursive query performs a join between the results in MusicTree and each parent, until the search is exhausted (i.e., reaches the top level).

Listing 3-8. *Example of Recursive Queries and CTEs*

```
DECLARE @cSearch char(50)
SET @cSearch = 'Charlie Parker'
;
WITH MusicTree (ResultName, PKValue)
    AS (SELECT   Name, ParentPK
        FROM MusicData
        WHERE Name = @cSearch
    UNION   ALL
        SELECT   Name, parentPK
            FROM MusicData
                INNER JOIN MusicTree ON PKValue = MainPK   )
SELECT  * FROM   MusicTree
```

The results are displayed in Table 3-4.

Table 3-4. *Results of Recursive Query*

Result Name	PKValue
Charlie Parker	5
Saxophone	2
Jazz	1
Musicians	NULL

By default, SQL Server 2005 supports 100 recursion levels. For more information and examples on this powerful new feature, check for either CTEs or Recursive CTEs in the SQL Server 2005 help system.

While this example may seem a bit simple, there are many serious applications for common table expressions. For example, you may be building an e-commerce solution with a standard set of database tables. However, one client may have three levels of product/item hierarchy, another client may have four, etc. You can store the hierarchies in a fixed database schema and use recursive queries to deal with many different parent-child relationships. Another example might be the storage of menu options in a database: at any one time, you may need to retrieve and display available menu options, based on the current menu selection.

Implementing Audit Trail Functionality

Storing database changes is a common requirement in database systems. For certain key pieces of data in an application, a client will want to know every time the data was changed: who changed it and when, the value of the data before the change, and the value of the data after the change. A frequent question on technical forums is how to implement audit trail functionality. Sometimes the person asking the question will know part of the answer but is missing some piece of the puzzle. Perhaps the person knows that Update triggers are part of the answer but isn't quite sure of the syntax. Other times, that person believes (erroneously) that the UPDATED function can be used to determine whether columns have changed.

Update triggers are indeed the area where audit trail processing occurs. An Update trigger is a specific type of stored procedure that fires every time an UPDATE statement executes against the table. Update triggers provide access to two critical system tables that contain the state of the row before it was updated (Deleted) and after it was updated (Inserted). Before we take you into full-blown audit trail functionality, we'll first show you a simpler use of the Inserted system table to get a taste of what you can do with it.

For example, suppose you have a column in a Client table called LastUpdated: you want to always store the server date and time on any updated row(s). Even if someone manually changes a row in the Client table outside the application (in Query Analyzer, SQL Management Studio, etc.), you always want LastUpdated to reflect the date and time the changes occurred. You can implement the following code in an Update trigger:

```
CREATE TRIGGER Upd_Client ON dbo.Client
FOR UPDATE
AS
     UPDATE Client
          SET LastUpdated = GETDATE()
     FROM Client C
          JOIN Inserted I
          ON I.PrimaryKey = C.PrimaryKey
```

Again, the Inserted system table contains one row for every row that was updated. So if someone manually executes an Update system that affects five rows, the trigger will fire once, and the Inserted table will contain the five rows. You can join against the Inserted table on the table's primary key column to update the LastUpdated column.

■**Note** In SQL Server, an Update trigger fires once per UPDATE statement. Never try to assign the value of a column from the Inserted or Deleted system tables to a variable under the assumption that the Inserted/Deleted tables will only contain one row. This is a common beginner's mistake that usually leads to a runtime error.

Now that you see how you can use the Inserted system table, let's take a look at detecting database changes and then logging them. Table 3-5 shows the structure for an audit trail log that will serve as your history for every database change: you want to insert into this table every time a change occurs.

Table 3-5. *Structure for an Audit Trail History (AuditTrail)*

ColumnName	Type	Description
TableName	char	The name of the table where the change occurred
PrimaryKey	int	The primary key value of the row that was changed
LastUpdated	datetime	The date/time of the change
ColName	char	The name of the column that was changed
OldValue	varchar	The value of the column before the change
NewValue	varchar	The value of the column after the change

Listing 3-9 shows the code for an Update trigger on the Product Master table to track changes, by querying the Inserted and Deleted tables. For this example, you'll check the PRICE and DESCRIPTION columns for changes, and write the values from Inserted and Deleted into your AuditTrail log. Take notice that when you write out the old/new value of Price to the audit log, you must convert the price column from a decimal column to a character column.

Listing 3-9. *Update Trigger to Detect and Log Price Changes*

```
CREATE TRIGGER Upd_Price ON dbo.Price
FOR  UPDATE
AS
     DECLARE @dLastUpdate DATETIME
     SET @dLastUpdate = GETDATE()
     -- Set the last Update for rows updated
     UPDATE Price
         SET LastUpdate = @dLastUpdate
     FROM Price P
         JOIN Inserted I
         ON I.PrimaryKey = P.PrimaryKey

  -- Write out to the audit Log, for rows where price changed

     INSERT INTO AuditTrail (TableName, PrimaryKey, LastUpdate, ColName,
         OldValue, NewValue, UserKey)
         SELECT 'PRICE' AS TableName, I.PrimaryKey, @dLastUpdate AS LastUpdate,
             'Price' AS ColName,  CONVERT(CHAR(20),D.Price) AS OldValue,
             CONVERT(CHAR(20),I.Price) AS NewValue,
             I.UserKey
         FROM Inserted I
         JOIN Deleted D ON D.PrimaryKey = I.PrimaryKey
         WHERE I.Price <> D.Price
```

■**Note** Another common "beginner's mistake" is to use the UPDATED function (or COLUMNS_UPDATED) to detect which column(s) have changed. These functions return a value of true for columns that were referenced in an UPDATE statement. Because an UPDATE statement may do nothing more than update a column value with the same value before the update, you would be logging a change that didn't occur. Audit trail logging needs to join the Inserted and Deleted tables to examine before/after values.

Getting Immediate Feedback with OUTPUT and OUTPUT INTO in SQL Server 2005

In your audit trail solution in the previous section, you must query against the AuditTrail log to view the list of changes. In most instances, that will be fine, but there may be cases where you want immediate feedback on what has been changed. SQL Server 2005 allows you to specify an OUTPUT clause on an UPDATE statement so that you can immediately output the before/after changes.

In SQL Server 2000, the Inserted and Deleted system tables (that we mentioned in the previous section) were only available inside an Update trigger. SQL Server 2005 expands the visibility of Inserted/Deleted by allowing you to specify them in an OUTPUT clause of an UPDATE statement. The following code snippet creates a table variable with three rows and updates the amount column of the first two. In your UPDATE statement, you can OUTPUT rows from Inserted/Deleted to immediately see what was changed.

```
DECLARE @tTest1 TABLE ( RowNum int, Amount decimal(10,2))
INSERT INTO @ttest1 VALUES (1, 100)
INSERT INTO @ttest1 VALUES (2, 200)
INSERT INTO @ttest1 VALUES (3, 300)
UPDATE      TOP(2)  @tTest1      SET Amount = Amount * 10
     OUTPUT Inserted.RowNum,Deleted.Amount,Inserted.Amount

     -- You can also OUTPUT into a temporary table for later use in the procedure
```

■**Note** While the OUTPUT and OUTPUT INTO statements provide considerable convenience, do not use them in place of audit trail functionality in Update triggers. Update triggers give you the protection of firing for **any** update, even ones beyond the control of your application. Think of OUTPUT and OUTPUT INTO as shortcuts if you need immediate feedback on what was changed, without having to make another callback to the server to call the AuditTrail log.

Using Dynamic SQL (and Finding Alternatives)

A common (and sometimes controversial) subject is using dynamic SQL to programmatically construct SQL syntax on the fly, and then executing it using the SQL Server system stored procedure sp_executesql. Dynamic SQL is most often used when some key piece of information on a SQL query (such as a table name, column name, or result set structure) is not known until runtime. While some purists may argue that dynamic SQL is a symptom of a faulty overall design, the reality is that some developers will face situations where some significant aspect of a query is not known until runtime.

Dynamic SQL syntax can be a bit daunting, so Listing 3-10 shows two examples of dynamic SQL.

Listing 3-10. *Examples of Dynamic SQL*

```
USE northwind
-- Will return orders where EmployeeID = 5
DECLARE @cSQLSyntax nvarchar(2000)
DECLARE @cTableName varchar(20)
SET @cTableName = 'Orders'
SET @cSQLSyntax = N'SELECT * FROM ' + @cTableName  + ' WHERE EmployeeID = 5'
EXEC sp_executesql @cSQLSyntax


-- Return a column into an output variable.
-- Query must only contain one row, else an error will occur
-- (query could also be a SUM that returns a scalar value).


DECLARE @cValue nVarChar(30)
DECLARE @cColumnName varchar(20)
SET @cColumnName = 'OrderID'
SET @cSQLSyntax = N' SELECT @cValue = ' + @cColumnName + '   FROM'
SET @cSQLSyntax = @cSqlSyntax + ' Orders  where employeeid = 1'
EXECUTE SP_EXECUTESQL @cSQLSyntax, N'@cValue nVarChar(30) OUTPUT', @cValue OUTPUT
SELECT @cValue
```

However, there are instances where other approaches offer benefits over dynamic SQL. Suppose you have a form (or web page) that allows users to retrieve customers based on several input criteria (first and last name, address, city, zip, etc.) The user may enter one field, two fields, or many fields. You need to write a stored procedure to examine all possible parameters, but only query on those that the user entered.

You could write a stored procedure that examines each parameter, constructs a SQL SELECT string based on parameters the user filled out, and executes the string using dynamic SQL. Many SQL developers opt for this approach.

Alternatively, you can use the SQL Server COALESCE function (see Listing 3-11). COALESCE, available both in SQL Server 2000 and SQL Server 2005, provides you with an alternative approach that arguably leads to cleaner T-SQL code. For each search condition, you pass COALESCE two values: the search variable, and a value to use if the search variable is NULL. So for any search values that the user did not specify, the search defaults to the column being equal to itself. This approach is still very fast, even when querying against millions of rows.

Listing 3-11. *Using COALESCE to Deal with Many Parameters, Where Some Could Be NULL*

```
DECLARE @city varchar(50), @state varchar(50), @zip varchar(50),
        @FirstName varchar(50), @LastName varchar(50),
        @Address varchar(50)

SET @FirstName = 'Kevin'
SET @State = 'NY'

SELECT * FROM CUSTOMERS WHERE
             FirstName = COALESCE(@FirstName,FirstName) AND
             LastName = COALESCE(@LastName,LastName) AND
             Address = COALESCE(@Address,Address) AND
             City = COALESCE(@City,City) AND
             State = COALESCE(@State,State) AND
             Zip = COALESCE(@Zip,Zip)
```

Another instance where dynamic SQL is often used is when an SQL statement may have a conditional ORDER BY or GROUP BY clause. As a somewhat contrived and simple (but meaningful) example, suppose you want to sum the freight in the Northwind Orders database, and group it either by EmployeeID or ShipVia method. Some developers might either use dynamic SQL to construct the query (including the group by) at runtime or duplicate the code and change the GROUP BY. You can utilize a CASE statement to build a simpler solution:

```
DECLARE @nGroupOpt int
SET @nGroupOpt = 1    -- 1 for employee, 2 for ship method

SELECT CASE @nGroupOpt WHEN 1 THEN EmployeeID ELSE ShipVia END AS GroupColumn,
    SUM(Freight) AS TotFreight
    FROM ORDERS
    GROUP BY  CASE @nGroupOpt WHEN 1 THEN EmployeeID ELSE ShipVia END
    ORDER BY TotFreight DESC
```

New Functions in SQL Server 2005 to Assign Ranking Values

Suppose you want to rank the top orders by customer, in descending sequence (for orders greater than $500). You may want to use the ranking order number as a display column on a report. As part of the result set, you want to return a ranking number, as demonstrated here:

Customer	Rank	Description
Customer A	1	Highest order
Customer A	2	Second highest order
Customer A	3	Third highest order
Customer B	1	Highest order

And so on.

The following query reads the Northwind Orders database for orders greater than $500. It uses the new ROW_NUMBER OVER function to assign row numbers based on a particular order and the new PARTITION keyword to group the ranking.

```
use northwind

SELECT  CustomerID, OH.OrderID, OrderDate,
(UnitPrice  * Quantity) as Orderamount,
    ROW_NUMBER() OVER (PARTITION BY CUSTOMERID
  ORDER BY  (UnitPrice  * Quantity) DESC)
  AS OrderRank
  FROM Orders OH
     JOIN [dbo].[Order Details] OD
          ON OH.OrderID = OD.OrderID
  WHERE  (UnitPrice * Quantity) > 500
       ORDER BY CUSTOMERID, OrderAmount  DESC
```

Implementing Better Error Handling with TRY...CATCH

SQL Server 2005 implements TRY...CATCH functionality to trap runtime errors. You can use syntax similar to the syntax that .NET developers have been able to use for years. This allows you to gracefully check for (and manage) runtime errors and exceptions.

Consider the following code:

```
DELETE  from Orders where orderid = 10336
```

This will generate a runtime error because of the constraint between the Order header and Order detail tables in the Northwind database. However, you can wrap this in a basic TRY...CATCH block as follows:

```
BEGIN TRY
    DELETE  from Orders where orderid = 10336
END TRY
BEGIN CATCH
    SELECT  ERROR_NUMBER() AS ErrNum, ERROR_SEVERITY() AS ErrSev,
      ERROR_STATE() as ErrState,  ERROR_MESSAGE() as ErrMsg;
END CATCH
```

This code will return the error information in a result set, and will continue on. You can even build nested TRY...CATCH blocks for more complicated stored procedure requirements!

■**Note** If you plan to return error conditions as a result set, the data access layer that reads the result set must be prepared to handle a result set that contains this structure.

Using LIKE to Perform Text Searches

The T-SQL LIKE command allows developers to search for patterns within strings. A common use would be searching for the phrase "XP" within a text/character column that contains "skills include Windows XP, FrontPage, etc.". Developers can use the LIKE command and the wildcard percentage character (%) to perform pattern matching.

You can use LIKE in multiple ways, depending on the type of search you want to perform. Most searches need to check for a pattern that exists anywhere within a column. However, some searches only need to return rows where a column begins with a search pattern. Additionally, some searches may be interested in rows where a column ends with a search pattern. Here are some examples:

```
Search anywhere in the column
SELECT * FROM Applicants WHERE Skills LIKE '%XP%'

-- Search where skills begins with XP
SELECT * FROM Applicants WHERE Skills LIKE 'XP%'

-- Search where skills ends with XP
SELECT * FROM Applicants WHERE Skills LIKE '%XP'
```

Additionally, developers can use the single wildcard underscore character (Name LIKE '_EVIN'),

Working with XML Data

SQL Server 2000 provided many great capabilities for working with XML data, and SQL Server 2005 adds even more new functions through the new XML data type and XML querying capabilities. Let's look at two different examples for getting XML data into tables (and also querying out of XML-stored data).

Listing 3-12 shows two different examples of reading XML-supplied data into a simple address table. The first uses attribute-centric mapping. The second uses element-centric mapping and also demonstrates nested columns.

Listing 3-12. *Reading XML Data into Database Columns*

```
-- First example
DECLARE @cXMLDoc XML
declare @hdoc int
SET @cXMLDoc = '<AddressType  >
    <AddressRecord
        AccountID = "1"
        Street="31 Main Dr" City="Philly" State="PA" Zip="12345"/>
    <AddressRecord
        AccountID = "2"
        Street="1 Wilson Dr" City="Newark" State="NJ" Zip="22222"/>
</AddressType>'
```

```
EXEC sp_xml_preparedocument @hdoc OUTPUT, @cXMLDoc

SELECT * FROM OPENXML (@hdoc, '/AddressType/AddressRecord',1)
   WITH (AccountID int,Street varchar(100), City varchar(100),
         State varchar(10), Zip varchar(13))

GO
-- Second example, uses an Address tag to specify nested columns

DECLARE @cXMLDoc XML
declare @hdoc int
SET @cxmldoc =
'<customer>
     <Customernum>48456</Customernum>
     <Firstname>Kevin</Firstname>
     <Lastname>Goff</Lastname>
     <Address>
        <city>Allentown</city>
        <state>PA</state>
     </Address>
</customer>'

EXEC sp_xml_preparedocument @hdoc OUTPUT, @cxmldoc
DECLARE @tTemp TABLE (Customernum int, Firstname char(50),
     Lastname char(50), City char(50), State Char(10))

insert into @ttemp
     SELECT *  FROM OPENXML (@hdoc, '/customer',2)
              WITH (Customernum int,Firstname varchar(50),Lastname varchar(50),
         city varchar(50) './Address/city',
         state varchar(50) './Address/state')
```

To reverse the examples, let's assume you're storing address information in the new XML column DataType and need to query based on one of the XML columns. To make things even more interesting, let's suppose you need to query on a subset of a column. Listing 3-13 provides an example of this.

Listing 3-13. *Querying from XML Data*

```
declare @tTest table (address xml)
insert into @ttest values ('<Address >
   <AddrRecord
       AccountID = "1"
       Street="31 Main Dr" City="Newark" State="NJ" Zip="11111" />
   </Address>' )
```

```
insert into @ttest values ('<Address >
  <AddrRecord
      AccountID = "2"
      Street="1 Wilson Rd" City="Philly" State="PA" Zip="22222"/>
  </Address>' )
```

```
SELECT * FROM @ttest

  WHERE Address.exist('/Address/AddrRecord [contains(@City,"hil")]') = 1
```

Using Date Parts

Suppose you need to retrieve daily order information and summarize it by a week-ending date (Saturday). You want to write a UDF that converts any date during the week to a Saturday date for that week. You can use SQL Server's DATEPART functions to solve this requirement. As the name implies, DATEPART returns a specific part of a date: day of week, month, year, quarter, etc. (Check SQL Server Books Online for all possible DATEPART options.)

In the following example, you call the DATEPART function and ask it to return the value of the weekday for the date in question , subtract that value from 7, and then add that result to the initial date. That will give you the Saturday date for the week!

```
CREATE FUNCTION dbo.GetEndOfWeek
    (@dDate DateTime)
    -- Converts date to the Saturday date for the week
RETURNS DateTime AS
BEGIN
    DECLARE @dRetDate DateTime
    SET @dRetDate = @dDate + ( 7-DATEPART(weekday,@dDate))

RETURN @dRetDate
END
```

You can then use this UDF as part of a query against orders, to summarize the data by the week-ending Saturday date.

```
SELECT dbo.GetEndOfWeek(OrderDate) AS WeekEnding,
   SUM(Amount) AS WeekAmount
   FROM OrderHdr
   GROUP BY dbo.GetEndOfWeek(OrderDate)
```

■**Note** By default, SQL Server's setting for the first day of the week is Sunday. To set the first day of the week to a different day (e.g., summarize sales from Monday to Sunday instead of Sunday to Saturday), use the SET DATEFIRST <NumberVar> command: check the help system for details on the DATEFIRST option.

A Cleaner Alternative to IN: INTERSECT and EXCEPT

Most SQL developers have written queries that filtered result sets based on values simply existing (or not existing) in other tables. In SQL 2000, developers used the IN keyword. For example, if you wanted to query against construction jobs that, among other things, had invoices (or didn't have invoices), you'd write the following code:

```
SELECT JobMasterPK
    FROM JobMaster
        WHERE JobMasterPK IN
            (SELECT JobMasterFK FROM Invoices)

SELECT JobMasterPK
    FROM JobMaster
        WHERE JobMasterPK NOT IN
            (SELECT ISNULL(JobMasterFK,0) FROM Invoices)
```

SQL Server 2005 implements the INTERSECT and EXCEPT operators, which are part of the SQL-99 standard. You can write these same two queries as follows:

```
SELECT JobMasterPK
    FROM JobMaster
        INTERSECT SELECT JobMasterFK FROM Invoices

SELECT JobMasterPK
    FROM JobMaster
        EXCEPT  SELECT JobMasterFK FROM Invoices
```

Note that in the first set of examples, you must check for NULL values when searching for jobs that do not have invoices: in the second set of examples, EXCEPT (and INTERSECT) are able to handle NULL values for you.

APPLY Revisited: Using UDFs with Correlated Subqueries

Suppose, in the Northwind database, you want to know which customers have had at least two orders for more than $5,000 (or five orders for more than $1,000 dollars, etc.) variable.

Your first step is to build a table-valued UDF called GetCustOrders. The UDF contains two parameters (customer ID and dollar threshold), and returns a table variable of orders for that customer that exceed the threshold.

```
CREATE FUNCTION [dbo].[GetCustOrders]
   (@CustomerID AS varchar(10), @nThreshold AS decimal(14,2))
RETURNS @tOrders TABLE (OrderID int, CustomerID varchar(10),
                                OrderDate datetime, OrderAmount decimal(14,2))


AS
BEGIN
```

```
        INSERT INTO @tOrders
          SELECT  OH.OrderID, CustomerID, OrderDate, (UnitPrice  * Quantity)
          AS Orderamount
     FROM Orders OH
      JOIN [dbo].[Order Details] OD
          ON OH.OrderID = OD.OrderID
         WHERE CustomerID =  @CustomerID AND
           (UnitPrice  * Quantity)  > @nThreshold
   ORDER BY OrderAmount  DESC
RETURN
END
Go
```

Your next step is to run that UDF against every customer in the database and determine which customers have at least two orders from the UDF. Ideally, you'd like to construct a subquery to pass each customer as a parameter to the UDF. Here's where the power of T-SQL Server 2005 comes in.

In SQL Server 2000, table-valued functions within a correlated subquery could not reference columns from the outer query. Fortunately, T-SQL 2005 removes this restriction and allows you to use a table-valued function in a subquery, where the arguments to the UDF come from columns in the outer query. You can now build a subquery that calls your UDF and passes columns from the outer query as arguments to the UDF:

```
DECLARE @nNumOrders int, @nMinAmt decimal(14,2)
SET @nNumOrders = 2
SET @nMinAmt = 5000.00
SELECT CustomerID FROM Customers
    WHERE  (SELECT COUNT(*) FROM
    DBO.GetCustOrders_GT_X(CustomerID,@nMinAmt)) >=@nNumOrders
```

Using SQL Server 2000

You've used three new functions in SQL2005: TOP N, APPLY, and PIVOT. Implementing similar or comparable capabilities in SQL Server 2000 is as follows:

- To achieve TOP N capability in SQL Server 2000, you must use dynamic SQL to construct and execute a SQL statement where the N value is unknown until runtime. Listing 3-14 shows a brief example. Note the use of the system stored procedure sq_executesql.

- To APPLY the results of a table-valued UDF in SQL Server 2000 to every row in the inner expression, you'll need to create a temporary table (or table variable, or derived table) and then perform a JOIN. Listing 2-3 back in Chapter 2 demonstrates a simple example of this.

- To convert source table rows into destination columns, you must hand-code a conversion process by using CASE statements. Listing 3-15 contains an equivalent code snippet for the aging receivables report that utilized a PIVOT back in Listing 3-6.

Listing 3-14. *Equivalent Code in SQL Server 2000 to Demonstrate TOP N*

```
DECLARE @nRows int
SET @nRows = 5
DECLARE @cSQL nvarchar(2000)

SET @cSQL = N'SELECT TOP ' + CAST(@nRows AS VARCHAR(5)) + ' * FROM Customer'
EXEC sp_executesql @cSQL
```

Listing 3-15. *Equivalent Code in SQL Server 2000 to Demonstrate PIVOT*

```
SUM(CASE WHEN DDate BETWEEN @dAgeDate-30 AND @dAgeDate
    THEN DBalance ELSE 0 END) AS Age30 ,

SUM(CASE WHEN DDate BETWEEN @dAgeDate-60 AND @dAgeDate-31
    THEN DBalance ELSE 0 END) AS Age60 ,

SUM(CASE WHEN DDate BETWEEN @dAgeDate-90 AND @dAgeDate-61
    THEN DBalance ELSE 0 END) AS  Age90 ,

SUM(CASE WHEN DDate BETWEEN @dAgeDate-120 AND @dAgeDate-91
    THEN DBalance ELSE 0 END) AS  Age120 ,

SUM(CASE WHEN DDate < @dAgeDate - 120
    THEN DBalance ELSE 0 END) AS  AgeGT120,

SUM(CASE WHEN DDate > @dAgeDate
    THEN DBalance ELSE 0 END) AS NotAged,
     SUM(DBalance) AS TotBalance
```

Summary

In this chapter, you spent some more time looking at the new APPLY and PIVOT capabilities. You also looked at other new language features, such as variable TOP N, recursive queries with common table expressions, OUTPUT, and new XML features. You also took a look at other tasks, such as audit trail logging, and how you can build solutions to address them. Hopefully these last two chapters have provided valuable insight into how you can use T-SQL to generate result sets and solve many other database problems.

Recommended Reading

Bob Beauchemin and Dan Sullivan. *A Developer's Guide to SQL Server 2005*. Boston, MA: Addison-Wesley, 2006.

Itzik Ben-Gan et al. *Inside Microsoft SQL Server 2005: T-SQL Querying*. Redmond, WA: Microsoft Press, 2006.

Shawn Wildermuth. "Making Sense of the XML DataType in SQL Server 2005." CoDe Magazine, May/June 2006.

PART 3

■ ■ ■

Defining and Building the Architecture

Now that you've completed the database requirements, we will shift the focus to the application layer (middle-tier) components of your solution. The general theme to this part is developing components that execute on the server—not on the client side. There are four chapters to this part. Chapter 4 defines the back-end interfaces that the client will utilize. This chapter will also cover the general architecture for accessing the back end (using either web services or remoting). The content segues into Chapter 5, which presents the complete business object and data-access layer. Chapter 6 integrates typed DataSets into the equation. Chapter 7 demonstrates the use of typed DataSets and ADO.NET in environments that require additional data summarization outside of the database. Installations that cannot make full use of stored procedure code must perform postquery data-munging—Chapter 7 presents several examples that demonstrate the power of ADO.NET and typed DataSets.

CHAPTER 4

■ ■ ■

Building Remoting/Web Service Solutions with Interfaces

The initial requirements stated that users must be able to use the client software components to view the reports either internally or while traveling. In this chapter, we will show you how to build a step-by-step solution for this requirement that includes web services, remoting, and interfaces. Many developers who are new to .NET and/or distributed computing in general often ask questions regarding how components in a web-based/distributed environment "talk" to each other. Unlike thick-client applications where most or all of the code and classes reside on one computer or one server, the components of a distributed application will reside on different domains. This chapter covers the following:

- Using the philosophy of "begin with the end in mind," we'll present some technical diagrams that depict the end result that you're going to build.

- We'll talk about web services and remoting: how they work, the differences between the two, the coding requirements, and the benefits/advantages and downsides to each of them.

- We will discuss interfaces and how valuable they are in a distributed environment. We'll also show you how to build interfaces using .NET Generics so that classes implementing your interfaces can return more than one type of data.

- You will build a remoting solution, first focusing on the server-side components and then the client-side components.

- You will build a web service: again, we will cover the server side first, and then show how to access it on the client side.

- In perhaps the most important part of this chapter, you will build a general factory class that allows you to abstract out all the intricacies and complexities of web services and remoting into a class that you can reuse in other applications.

- Finally, you will explore a number of specific remoting features of Visual Studio 2005, such as the new security enhancements for TCP remoting, the new IPC client channel for remoting on a single physical computer, and how .NET Generics in Visual Studio 2005 can streamline your use of remoting interfaces.

■Note Several parts of this chapter have appeared in one form or another from Kevin Goff's *Baker's Dozen Productivity Series* in *CoDe Magazine*. See the introduction to this book for the actual issues.

Begin with the End in Mind

When building a solution that contains multiple moving parts, a diagram of the end result can help you see the big picture. In this section, you'll look at diagrams for your remoting solution, your web services solution, and how you'll integrate them into one system. This section will cover some material and technical terms that may be new to you: don't worry, we will be discussing them in more detail throughout this chapter. We're showing these diagrams now to help you visualize the final solution and how all the pieces work together.

.NET Remoting

.NET remoting is the process whereby one .NET class/application (class A) in a specific domain calls the method of another .NET class (class B) in a different domain. The .NET code for class B executes on the domain where class B resides. Class B communicates with class A through internal .NET messaging.

The application to which class A resides does not have the code for class B, nor does it even have a reference to the DLL for class B. However, you can use the combination of .NET remoting and .NET interfaces for class A to call class B in a strongly-typed manner.

■Note You can use .NET remoting when all directly related components are .NET components. You cannot use non-.NET code as part of a remoting architecture.

Figure 4-1 shows a diagram of the .NET remoting process for the aging receivables report.

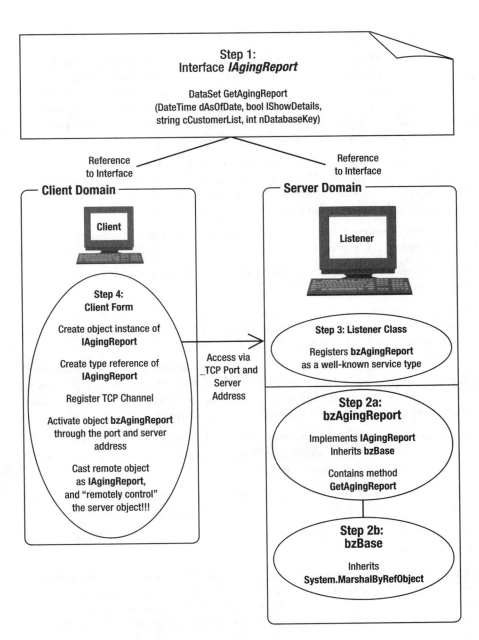

Figure 4-1. *Overview of remoting*

You can build a remoting solution in four general steps:

1. First, you define a .NET interface, IAgingReport. Interfaces by themselves do nothing: they provide value in conjunction with classes/objects that implement them. The IAgingReport interface contains a reference to the method GetAgingReport, which receives parameters and returns a DataSet with the results. Both the client and server domains will have a reference to this interface. The interface allows the client piece to access the remote server class in a strongly-typed manner.

2. Second, you must build your server-side class (bzAgingReport) to perform the actual processing for the aging receivables report. (In reality, this class will use a data access method that we'll cover in the next chapter.) The class bzAgingReport is the "target" of the remoting call. You have three requirements for bzAgingReport:

   - It must **implement** the IAgingReport interface (the client will be activating this class by means of the interface).

   - It must **inherit from** your base business class (which has some base support properties and methods).

   - It must **inherit from** the .NET system class System.MarshalByRefObject. This is the base class for objects that communicate across application domain boundaries by exchanging messages using a proxy.

     This presents a challenge for you, as .NET does not support multiple inheritance. However, while a single .NET class cannot inherit from multiple classes, you can still achieve the end result by inheriting from MarshalByRefObject in the base class. We'll cover this in Listings 4-2 and 4-3 later in this chapter.

3. Third, you need to build a server "listener" that registers bzAgingReport on one of the server domain's TCP port numbers. You will register it as a WellKnownServiceType so that the client piece can communicate with it.

4. For your fourth and final step, you can build your client code to remote with bzAgingReport. The code will essentially perform the following:

   - Open a new TCP channel (eventually referencing the same port number that the server listener specified).

   - Activate bzAgingReport using the port number, server address, and a type reference to IAgingReport. (The type reference must match the object type that you registered as a well-known service back in step 3.) When you activate an object that inherits from MarshalByRefObject, .NET will automatically download a proxy object for bzAgingReport to the client domain.

   - Take the result of the activation (a .NET proxy object) and cast it to IAgingReport so that you can utilize bzAgingReport in a strongly-typed manner. You can then call the method GetAgingReport in bzAgingReport. Each time you use properties and methods in bzAgingReport, .NET automatically sends messages back and forth between the local proxy and the actual server-side object so that the actual code executes on the domain where you registered bzAgingReport.

■**Note** When you want to call/activate a class remotely, that class **must** inherit from
`System.MarshalByRefObject`. This is the base class for objects that communicate across application
domain boundaries by exchanging messages using a proxy.

.NET Web Services

By contrast, .NET web services require fewer steps. Figure 4-2 depicts the process of running
the aging receivables report through a web service, which requires three general steps.

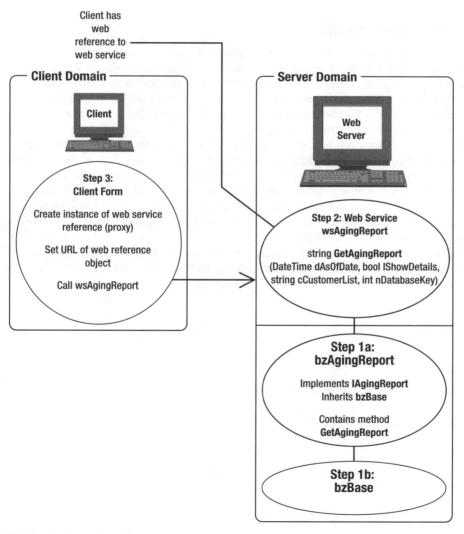

Figure 4-2. *Overview of web services*

1. First, you construct your server-side class (bzAgingReport) in the same way you constructed it in the remoting scenario.

2. Second, you build an ASP.NET 2.0 web service called wAgingReport. The web service will receive the four parameters for the aging receivables report (as of date, the option for details, the list of customers, and the database key). Unlike the remoting scenario, which returned a DataSet to the calling procedure, the web service returns a string in an XML format. This allows non-.NET clients to access/consume the web service.

3. Finally, in the client piece, you add a web reference to the web service and code against an object reference to this web reference. The web reference serves as a proxy for messaging with the actual web service, via XML.

Your Development Goals

This chapter will present code in C# to address the requirements of the web service and remoting scenarios. You'll build the interfaces first, since by definition they serve as the contract that any classes implementing them will contain specific properties and methods. You'll look at each part of the code in isolation, and then at the end you'll build some reusable factory classes that you can use in other applications. As you'll see, your factory classes will hide the complexities of remoting and even web services.

One of the goals of this text is to frequently show the end result, so that you can visualize the big picture while you're building individual pieces. As you go through each piece of code (interfaces, remoting code, etc.), it helps to understand where you're going with all this.

First, take a look at the general solution/project structure that you're going to build. Figure 4-3 shows a subset of your final development solution. In this chapter (and the next few chapters), you'll be writing code for several of the files in these projects to address the requirements depicted back in Figures 4-1 and 4-2.

Note in Figure 4-3 that you have two primary solution folders: Common Ground Framework and Construction Demo. The former contains some reusable functionality for remoting and data access techniques, while the latter contains projects for your business solution.

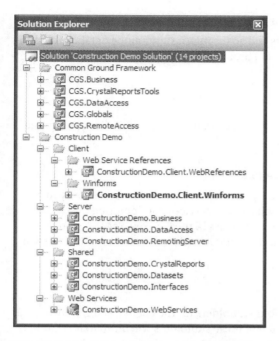

Figure 4-3. *Partial development solution for the construction demo*

Primary Folder #1: The Common Ground Framework

As stated back in Chapter 1, much of this book uses code from Kevin Goff's **Common Ground Framework for Visual Studio 2005**, a set of reusable classes for multitier .NET development. In this chapter and the next few chapters, we'll be covering code for the following projects:

The Base Business Class (CGS.Business)

In our overview of remoting, we stated as a requirement that all business objects must implement an interface, must inherit from a base object, and must also inherit from System.MarshalByRefObject (to meet remoting requirements). Since .NET does not support multiple inheritance, your business objects will derive from a base business object in this project (CGS.Business), which in turn will derive from System.MarshalByRefObject. You will see this base class (cgsBaseBusinessObject.cs) in Listing 4-2 later in this chapter.

The Crystal Reports Tools Class (CGS.CrystalReportsTools)

You will use Crystal Reports .NET to build your report files, using the version of Crystal Reports that comes with Visual Studio 2005. You will need to write code to integrate these reports with your application, and you will also need functionality to preview, print, and export reports. We will cover this project in detail in Chapter 12.

The Base Data Access Class (CGS.DataAccess)

As part of your architecture, all database access will go through a stand-alone database compo-nent. This component will interact with the stored procedures you wrote in Chapters 2 and 3. We will cover this component in Chapter 5.

The System Globals Class (CGS.Globals)

The system architecture will utilize some global properties, primarily in the client part of the application. We will cover these in Chapter 13.

The Communication Factory Class (CGS.RemoteAccess)

In the beginning of this chapter, we mentioned a general factory class that will allow you to abstract out all the intricacies and complexities of web services and remoting into a class that you can reuse in other applications. This factory class in the CGS.RemoteAccess project (cgsRemoteAccess.cs) contains the code for this functionality, which we'll cover in Listings 4-8 and 4-9 later in this chapter.

Primary Folder #2: the Construction Demo

The Construction Demo folder is divided into four subfolders for the client, server, web service, and shared components of the application. Each of these subfolders will ultimately contain several projects: but for simplicity, you'll start by covering the necessary projects for the aging receivables report.

The Client Section

The Client folder contains projects for the client-side aspects of the application, such as the Windows Forms and web server references.

The Client Web References Class (ConstructionDemo.Client.WebReferences)

The client application will need .NET web references to the construction web services. Because you want your web services to implement the same reporting interfaces that your .NET business objects implement, you will subclass these .NET web references to implement your reporting interfaces. You will subclass the aging receivables report for the web service (wAgingReport.asmx) as wAgingReportRef.cs. You will see this in Listing 4-7 later in the chapter.

This project requires a reference to the DLL ConstructionDemo.Interfaces, as well as a web reference to the server web service wAgingReport.asmx.

This project also requires a reference to the .NET System DLL System.Web.Services.

The Client Winforms Classes (ConstructionDemo.Client.Winforms)

This project will eventually contain the Windows Forms for your application. The test code in this chapter to activate/consume remoting/web service objects (Listings 4-7 through 4-9) will reside in this project.

This project requires the following .NET DLL references from the ConstructionDemo namespace: Client.WebServices, DataSets, and Interfaces.

The Server Section

The server folder contains projects for the server-side aspects of the application, such as the client-specific business objects and data access objects, as well as a remoting server to honor client remoting requests. You'll see in many instances that these classes derive from your base classes in the Common Ground Framework.

The Server Business Classes (ConstructionDemo.Business)

You will store all of your server-side business objects in this project. Listing 4-3 later in this chapter shows an example of the bzAgingReport object for the aging receivables report: the class inherits from your base business object (cgsBaseBusinessObject) and implements your IAgingReport interface. Remember that cgsBaseBusinessObject inherits from System.MarshalByRefObject, so that you can use your business objects with .NET remoting. Ultimately your business classes will integrate with your data access component (in Chapter 5) to return data.

■**Note** The naming convention you will use here requires you to preface all business objects with bz. You will preface any web services that call their corresponding business objects with w (for example, bzAgingReport and wAgingReport).

This project requires the following .NET DLL references from the ConstructionDemo namespace: DataAccess, DataSets, and Interfaces. The project also inherits from the Common Ground Framework classes CGS.Business and CGS.DataAccess.

The Server Data Access Classes (ConstructionDemo.DataAccess)

You will define a data access class for each report and store the classes in this project. These classes will inherit from your base data access class (cgsDataAccess) and will interact with your database stored procedures. The business objects will call these data access classes. We will cover this section in detail in Chapter 5.

This project requires a reference to the DLL ConstructionDemo.Interfaces, as well as the Common Ground Framework class CGS.DataAccess.

The Server Remoting Server (ConstructionDemo.RemotingServer)

You'll need to build a remoting "listener" application that registers all of the server-side business objects as well-known service types, so that client-side code can activate them through remoting. We'll cover this later in Listing 4-4.

This project requires the following .NET DLL references from the `ConstructionDemo` namespace: `Business` and `Interfaces`. The project also requires a reference to the Common Ground framework class `CGS.Business`.

The Construction Demo Shared Section

Some applications (including ours) may use components on both the client and server side. Both the client piece and the server tier of the `Construction Demo` will refer to the `interfaces` that you build. Your application will also utilize typed DataSets that represent the structure.

The Shared Interface Classes (ConstructionDemo.Interfaces)

This project contains all of the interfaces for your reports. Listing 4-1 will show an example of a report interface for your aging receivables report (`IAgingReport`). You will utilize .NET Generics to build a generic interface so that classes implementing these interfaces can return a DataSet, or a custom collection, or even an XML string.

The Shared Typed DataSet Classes (ConstructionDemo.DataSets)

The project contains all of the typed DataSets for your application. Chapter 6 will cover typed DataSets in detail. The typed DataSet objects are not dependent on any other application component; however, they are used as references in both the client and server tiers.

The Crystal Reports Classes (ConstructionDemo.CrystalReports)

The project contains all of the Crystal Report files for your application. Chapters 8 and 9 will cover these in detail. The reason they are in a shared folder, and not the client folder, is to support the idea that reports might be run in batch mode on the server.

This project requires the following .NET DLL references from the `ConstructionDemo` namespace: `DataSets`.

The Client Web Service Section

As your application will support XML web services, you must build a project with web services for your reports. While the web services are a server-side element, they may reside on a different location; you will separate them into their own folder.

The Client Web Service Classes (ConstructionDemo.WebServices)

This project contains all of the web service definitions for each of the reports. The client piece will directly consume these services when the user runs a report over a web service connection. We will cover the web service for the aging receivables report (`wAgingReport.asmx`) later in Listing 4-6.

This project requires the following .NET DLL references from the `ConstructionDemo` namespace: `Business`, `DataSets`, and `Interfaces`.

■Note The preceding discussion of the development solution is just an overview. For more details on the development solution, check the Technical Roadmap in Appendix C.

Remoting and Web Services

Your general architecture will support two methods to access the back end: web services and TCP remoting. You will build an ASP.NET project as a web service, which contains C# code that will call the necessary business objects. Users accessing the application outside of corporate headquarters will in turn connect to the application via this web service. Visual Studio 2005 greatly simplifies the process of building .NET web services because, when you build a web service, Visual Studio creates a proxy web reference that the client component will utilize. (However, you'll subclass that proxy to fully integrate with the interfaces in Listing 4-1. More on that later in this chapter.)

Now for remoting. You will also build a remoting server to accommodate internal users. While web services can be used for this kind of user, remoting will generally outperform web services, and doesn't require IIS (when using TCP remoting). It is also true that some people view remoting as more complex than web services. While it does require a little more work, you can build some reusable code and techniques to take the sting out of it. Let's start with a few concepts.

Suppose you have two components, A (a client-side DLL) and B (a server-side DLL). B may have ten different methods to perform different actions on the server side. The definitions for these methods would be stored in an interface similar to that in Listing 4-1 (which you'll see later). Remoting is a technique where A activates a reference to B and uses the interface to instruct B to execute one of B's methods on the domain where B resides.

OK, so how does the activation take place? Well, the activation takes place through a port—either a TCP port or an HTTP port.

■Note This book only covers TCP remoting.

In this context, the port represents a connection for the client program to access back-end functions. It is a two-step process: the server side registers each back-end object as a well-known type and associates it with a port channel, and then the client side activates the desired back-end object through that same port. Last, but perhaps most critically, any back-end class that executes via a remoting call **must** inherit from System.MarshalByRefObject. This is absolutely essential: MarshalByRefObject allows objects to communicate across application boundaries via a proxy. You'll get a runtime error if you omit it.

Finally, Visual Studio 2005 offers two new capabilities for TCP remoting that further accentuate its capabilities. First, Microsoft has implemented new security features for remoting. Second, developers can now pass DataSets across application domains in a true binary format, which reduces the size by a factor of six.

General Usage Notes for .NET Remoting

Keep these points in mind about .NET remoting:

- First and foremost, .NET remoting will only work with .NET components.

- Use .NET interfaces when you implement remoting.

- In Visual Studio 2005, you can pass/return a DataSet across an application boundary in a true binary format.

General Usage Notes for .NET Web Services

And now, a few general things you'll want to remember about .NET web services:

- Use ASP.NET web services (and the Web Services Enhancements, or WSE) when your requirements include SOAP or service-oriented architectures. Also use web services if non-.NET clients will need to access the application (platform independence).

- If your web service returns a result set from a DataSet, first convert the DataSet to an XML string by using the `DataSet.GetXml()` function, and then return the XML string.

Defining the Interface

A common definition/description of an interface is a contract that guarantees how a class will behave, and what properties and methods the class will contain. When you create an instance of a class that implements the interface, you can be assured that the class will contain every property and method that the interface defined. Think of the interface as the bullet point list of what will be in the class.

This assurance is critical in a distributed environment. The code for the back-end logic to build the reporting data will reside on a different domain than the client Winform component. So ultimately you will need to call methods in business objects that don't exist on the client domain. You can do this by creating strongly-typed interfaces that both the client-side and server-side code will share. The interfaces define each method call, the parameters, and the return value types.

The value of interfaces increases even further in multideveloper environments. One or more developers might build the back-end pieces, while a UI developer works on the client piece. The interfaces serve as their common language. Later in this chapter we'll show you how to activate the code associated with these interfaces.

In Chapter 1, we listed all of the reports and their general requirements. The client component for running the reports will utilize an interface for executing the actual back-end code

to retrieve the reporting data. Listing 4-1 contains the interface definitions for the construction reporting module, which you'll store in the project ConstructionDemo.Interfaces.

Listing 4-1. *Report Interfaces (ReportInterfaces.cs)*

```
using System;
using System.Collections.Generic;
using System.Text;

namespace ConstructionDemo.Interfaces
{
    // Utilizes .NET Generics - parameter declaration for a DataSet,
  //  or custom list,
   // or even an XML string
   public interface IAgingReport <T>
   {
      T GetAgingReport(DateTime dAsOfDate, bool lDetails, string cClientList,
                               int nDBKey);
   }

   public interface ITimeSheetReport <T>
   {
       T GetTimeSheetReport(DateTime dStartDate, DateTime dEndDate,
               bool lShowDetails, string cJobList, string cEmployeeList,
               int nDBKey);
   }
   // etc., etc.

}
```

The code in Listing 4-1 provides your first glimpse of .NET Generics. You may be wondering . . . what is the <T>? That is the placeholder for a data type. You can specify a placeholder
for the interface and fill it in during the implementation. The classes that implement this
interface can fill it in with a DataSet, or a typed DataSet, or a custom collection—or even
(as you'll see when you get to web services) an XML string representing a DataSet. This will
ultimately allow your client code to access either a web service object (which will return an
XML string) or a remoting object (which will return a typed DataSet) using the same interface.

There is nothing significant about the actual letter *T*: it is just a type parameter declaration inside the placeholder, for classes that implement the interface. You can call it anything
you want (except for a .NET keyword).

Building a Remoting Application

The next two sections cover the "meat and potatoes" of writing code for remoting and web
services. In each section, we'll focus on the server-side aspects first, and then we'll talk about
the necessary code and processes on the client side.

Writing the Server-Side Code

There are four steps to building the server-side components for remoting in your reporting solution:

1. You need to create strongly-typed interfaces that contain definitions for your back-end objects. Fortunately, you've already performed that step, in Listing 4-1. At the risk of repetition, these interfaces are the cornerstone to any distributed solution. They provide the language by which both sides communicate. As you'll see in the next section, the client-side component will utilize this interface to access the actual back-end functionality.

■**Note** The interface contains no actual code for any of the methods. Its only significance is that any class that implements this interface must have methods with the same name and parameters. As you'll see later, that's all the client side needs.

---

2. You need to build external business objects that implement the interfaces from Listing 4-1. Chapter 7 will cover the contents of the business objects in detail. This section merely creates a stub. However, as you're about to see, even setting up the structure and inheritance is important. There are three requirements for your external business objects:

   a. They all must implement the corresponding report interface in `ReportInterfaces` (`IAgingReport`, for instance).

   b. They must inherit from the .NET system class `MarshalByRefObject`. As stated back in the section "Begin with the End in Mind," the back-end remoting objects must inherit from this class, which enables remote code to execute the class on the domain of the external method.

   c. Your business objects must inherit from a base business object (as you may want to store base business behavior in a base object).

   Right away, you face a challenge. While a single .NET class can inherit from one class and one interface, it **cannot** inherit from multiple classes. You can resolve this by defining a base business object (`BaseBzObject`, which is shown in Listing 4-2 in the upcoming section) that inherits from `MarshalByRefObject`. Then you can define the actual business object (`bzAgingReport`) to inherit from `BaseBzObject` and implement `IAgingReport`. This way, `bzAgingReport` still picks up the critical inheritance of `MarshalByRefObject` from the `BaseBzObject`.

3. Having addressed the inheritance issue in step 2, you can construct your first actual business object. Listing 4-3 (in the upcoming section) contains a stub function for `bzAgingReport`. Note the reference to the base class `BaseBzObject` and the implementation of `IAgingReport`.

4. Build a listener, which is a remoting server that registers `bzAgingReport` on a specific TCP channel. The client class can access and activate registered classes through the TCP port and server address. Listing 4-4 later in this chapter shows an example of this.

Building the Remoting Object with MarshalByRefObject

Listings 4-2 and 4-3 demonstrate what we described previously: a base business class (cgsBaseBusinessObject.cs, in Listing 4-2) that inherits from System.MarshalByRefObject, and then your aging report class (bzAgingReport.cs, in Listing 4-3) that implements the IAgingReport interface and inherits from the base business class. The cgsBaseBusinessObject class will reside in your base CGS.Business project, while the bzAgingReport class will reside in your ConstructionDemo.Business class (with a .NET reference to CGS.Business).

Listing 4-2. *The Base Business Object cgsBaseBusinessObject.cs*

```
using System;
using System.Collections.Generic;
using System.Text;

namespace CGS.Business
{
    public class cgsBaseBusinessObject : System.MarshalByRefObject
    {
        // Base business object methods go here
        public cgsBaseBusinessObject()
        {
            // TODO: Add constructor logic here
        }
    }
}
```

Once again, the most important thing to note here is the inheritance of MarshalByRefObject: the aging report class must inherit from this class in order for remoting to work.

Listing 4-3. *Stub Method for the Aging Report Object*

```
using System;
using System.Collections.Generic;
using System.Text;
using System.Data;
using ConstructionDemo.Interfaces;
using CGS.Business;
using ConstructionDemo.Datasets;
using ConstructionDemo.DataAccess;



namespace ConstructionDemo.Business
{
    public class bzAgingReport : cgsBaseBusinessObject, IAgingReport<DataSet>
    {
        public DataSet GetAgingReport(DateTime dAsOfDate, bool lDetails,
                                      string cClientList, int nDBKey)
```

```
        {
            // Return new daAgingReport().GetAgingReport(
            //                      dAsOfDate, lDetails, cClientList, nDBKey);
            // You haven't yet defined your data access class, so for now
            // you'll comment it out and return an empty DataSet
            return new DataSet();
        }
    }
}
```

A few key points on the code in Listing 4-3:

- The class implements your IAgingReport interface and fills in the type parameter as a standard DataSet. In Chapter 6, you will replace this with a typed DataSet for the aging receivables report.

- The class calls the data access class, which you will build in the next chapter.

Building a Server Listener for Remoting Objects

After you construct your back-end remoting objects, you need to set up a listener on the server (or domain where the remoting objects reside). The listener will register a channel on a specific TCP port and then will register each object as a well-known service type. Once registered, your client-code can activate these server-side objects using the same TCP port, the name of the object, and a type reference to the corresponding interface.

■**Note** A remoting listener must be running on the server domain. If the client piece tries to activate back-end objects that have not been registered as well-known service types by the listener, the client piece will receive a runtime system error.

The development solution back in Figure 4-3 contains a Windows Forms project called ConstructionDemo.RemotingServer, which performs the tasks just listed. Listing 4-4 contains the code for a basic listener that you can include in a Windows console application on the server end.

Listing 4-4. *A Basic Remoting Server/Listener*

```
using System.Runtime.Remoting;
using System.Runtime.Remoting.Channels;
using System.Runtime.Remoting.Channels.Tcp;
using System.Runtime;

// You can place this code in the Load event of the form, or in a command button
// to launch the listener
```

```
TcpServerChannel Tcps;
int nTCPPort = 8228;    // For demo purposes, would normally come from a config file

Tcps = new TcpServerChannel(nTCPPort);
ChannelServices.RegisterChannel(Tcps);    // Register the channel

// Create a listener - client code can activate object with the same type, using the
// port number and server address
RemotingConfiguration.RegisterWellKnownServiceType (
    typeof(bzAgingReport.bzAgingReport),
    "bzAgingReport",   WellKnownObjectMode.Singleton);
```

■**Note** You must manually add a .NET reference to `System.Runtime.Remoting` when you build the remoting listener.

Building the Client-Side of a Remoting Piece

Now that you've established an interface and a server-side business object, you need to write code to access this back-end object using remoting. The steps are as follows:

1. Add a reference to the `System.Runtime.Remoting` namespace (by right-clicking in Solution Explorer and choosing Add Reference).

2. Define an object reference to the `IAgingReport` interface (call it `oAgingReport`). You'll eventually use the object reference to access the back-end method `GetAgingReport()`, as if you had direct access to it.

3. Define a type reference to `IAgingReport` (the server-side needs this to match up on object types).

4. Open a TCP channel (for purposes of demonstration, you're hard-coding port 8228 and the TCP address)

5. Activate the remote object and cast the return value to `IAgingReport`. At this point, `oAgingReport` can access any properties and methods defined in `IAgingReport`.

   Listing 4-5 demonstrates a complete example of using remoting.

Listing 4-5. *Client Code to Access the Back End via Remoting*

```
using System.Runtime.Remoting;
using System.Runtime.Remoting.Channels;
using System.Runtime.Remoting.Channels.Tcp;
using ConstructionDemo.Interfaces;
using System.Data;
```

```
IAgingReport oAgingReport;
Type tReport = typeof(IAgingReport)
ChannelServices.RegisterChannel( new
      TcpClientChannel());

oAgingReport =
   (IAgingReport)Activator.GetObject(  tReport,
      "tcp://localhost:8228/bzAgingReport");

DataSet dsResults = oAgingReport.GetAgingReport(dAsOfDate, true, cClientList, 1);
```

■**Note** Just like with the server-side remoting listener, you must manually add a .NET reference to
System.Runtime.Remoting when you build the client piece.

Building a Web Service

We'll now cover the necessary steps for building and consuming a web service. Just like we did with the remoting scenario, we'll cover the steps on the server-side as you build your first web service. Next, you'll learn how to test out the web service using nothing more than Internet Explorer. Then you'll see how to integrate the web service into your application.

■**Note** This section uses **Web Application Projects** for **Visual Studio 2005**. Microsoft offers web application projects as an alternative to the Website project model that comes with Visual Studio 2005. Some
developers who used the Visual Studio .NET 2003 Web project model were not satisfied with the new Website
project model in Visual Studio 2005. In response to developer feedback, Microsoft built the Web Application
Projects add-in: this add-in provides a Visual Studio 2005 Web project model option that works like the Visual
Studio .NET 2003 Web project model. Developers can now use Web Application Projects as an alternative to
the Website project model already available in Visual Studio 2005. The "Recommended Reading" section at
the end of this chapter provides the URL for this add-in.

Building a Web Service

Next, you'll create a web service project (ConstructionDemo.WebServices) and build the web service for your aging receivables report.

Creating the Web Service Project

Create a new project in Visual Studio 2005, and select ASP.NET Web Service Application as the project template (Figure 4-4). You can store your web services in wherever location is best for your setup, either on your local host (C:\INETPUB\WWWROOT) or in another folder.

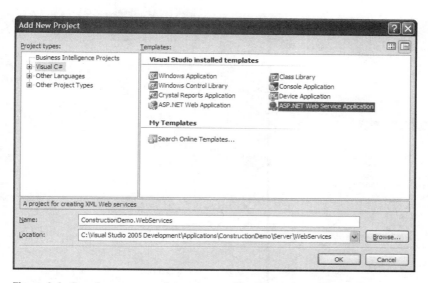

Figure 4-4. *Creating a new web service application using Web Application Projects for VS 2005*

By default, Visual Studio 2005 creates a default web service called `Service1.asmx`. While you can rename this to whatever name you desire, we prefer to erase the default web service and create a new one with the name we want (in this case, `wAgingReport`). To do so yourself, right-click and select Add New Item in Solution Explorer and add a new web service for the project (see Figure 4-5).

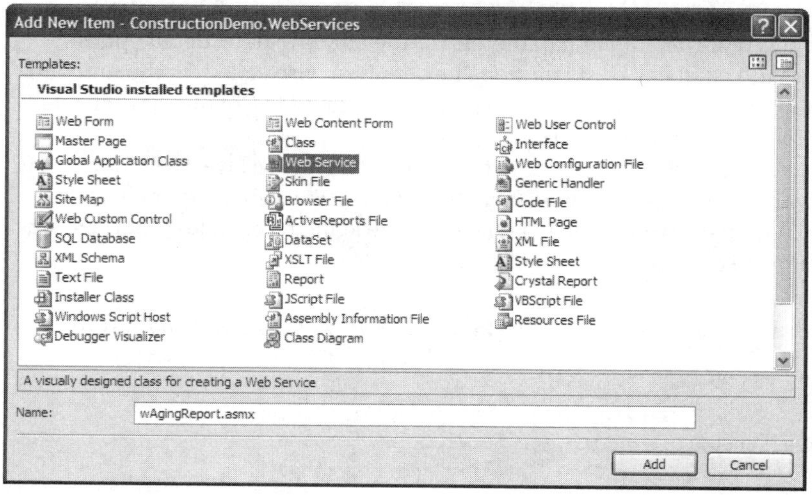

Figure 4-5. *Adding a new web service to the project*

After adding the new web service, Solution Explorer now displays the new web service, along with the associated C# class file, as shown in Figure 4-6.

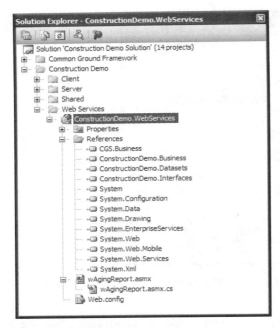

Figure 4-6. *Web application project, with a web service for the aging receivables report*

Next, you need to add a method to the web service to start execution of the aging receivables report. This will be a public method that the web service will expose to outside clients that wish to run the aging receivables report as a web service. Remember that the definition for the aging receivables report included parameters for the effective date, detail option, optional list of clients, and database key identifier. The definition also called for the function to return an XML string representing the result sets that you defined in Chapter 3 when you covered the stored procedure for the aging receivables report.

Unfortunately, you don't (yet) have anything that calls the database layer: we'll cover that in the next chapter when we discuss building data access layers. For right now, you'll simply build a stub function within the web service that receives the aging receivables report parameters and returns a dummy string, as shown in Listing 4-6.

Listing 4-6. *Example of a Web Service for the Aging Receivables Report (wAgingReport.asmx)*

```
namespace ConstructionDemo.WebServices
{
    public class wAgingReport : System.Web.Services.WebService,
                                        IAgingReport<string>
    {
        [WebMethod]
        public string GetAgingReport(DateTime dAsOfDate, bool lShowDetails,
                            string cCustomerList, int nDBKey)
        {
            return
```

```
            "This will eventually be the XML result set for the aging report";
        }
}
}
```

After you build the additional components in the next chapter, we'll come back to this and "fill in the blanks."

Defining the Web Service Location As a Shareable Web Folder

Your next step is to test the web service, which you can do through Internet Explorer. However, there is one step you need to take before you can test, and that is to set up the web service folder as shareable. If you navigate to the folder in Windows Explorer, right-click and choose Properties, and go to the Web Sharing tab of the Properties sheet (see Figure 4-7), you can define the folder as a shareable folder on the default web site.

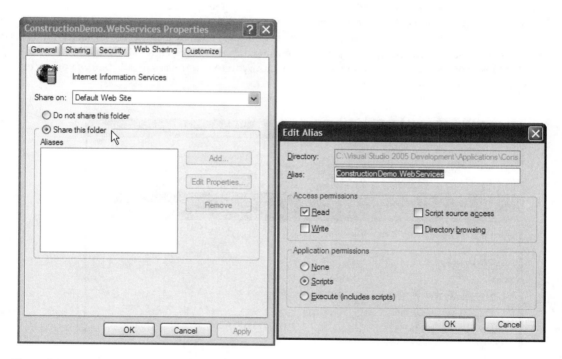

Figure 4-7. *Setting a folder for local web sharing*

Testing the Web Service

Even before you integrate the web service project into your client application, you can test the basic mechanics of the web service by using Internet Explorer. As demonstrated in Figure 4-8, you launch the browser and enter **http://localhost/ConstructionDemo.WebServices/ wAgingReport.asmx** in the address bar. If you type the address correctly, the local web server will execute the web service you specified and list all available methods in the web service.

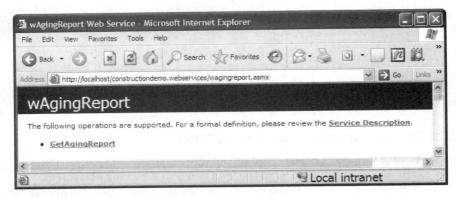

Figure 4-8. *Testing the web service using Internet Explorer*

You only have one method in your web service, so you select GetAgingReport, which contains four parameters. When you execute the web service programmatically, you will pass the appropriate parameters; however, since you have not yet specified any, the web server passes a message back to the browser to prompt for the parameters (see Figure 4-9). Again, when you "hook this up" to a data access layer, this will allow you to test the result sets before you write any client-side code.

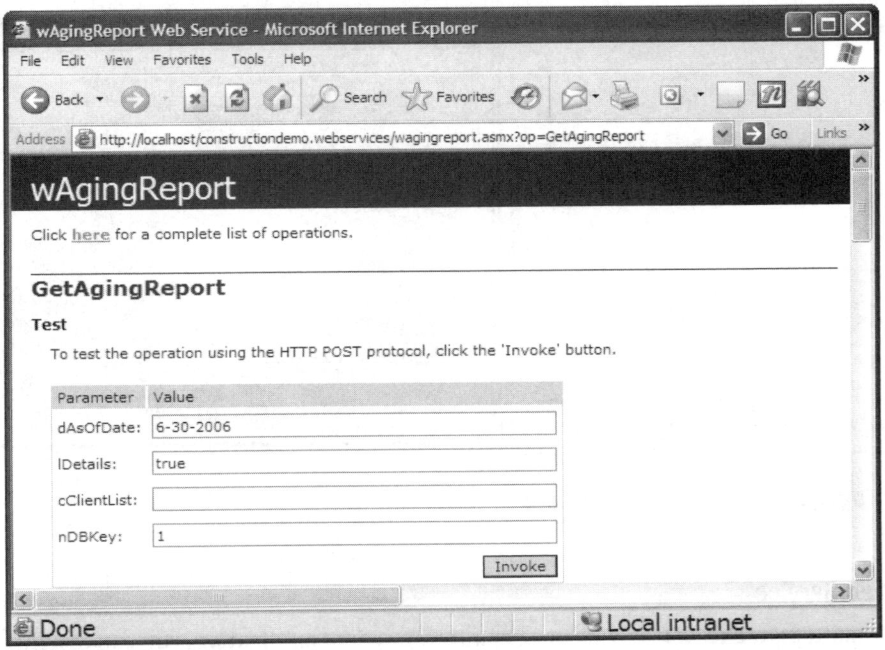

Figure 4-9. *Web service parameters*

After you enter the parameters and click Invoke, the web service will execute whatever method code exists in the web service for that specific function. Since you merely inserted a dummy string into the web service, all you will see is that string as the result (see Figure 4-10).

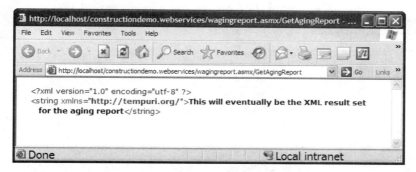

Figure 4-10. *Testing the web service using Internet Explorer*

■**Tip** Internet Explorer is an excellent way to perform basic testing of web service functions.

Using the Web Service from a Client Application

Once you're comfortable with your web service wAgingReport, your next step is to add a reference (actually, a web reference) to wAgingReport in your client application.

Creating a Web Reference Project

The development solution back in Figure 4-3 included a project called ConstructionDemo. Client.WebReferences. We stated that this particular project would reference all of the web services in ConstructionDemo.WebServices. When you add web service references to another .NET project, Visual Studio does not bring forward any interface implementations you defined in the web service. Because your client-side code will activate back-end web services (and business objects) through your interfaces, you will subclass the web service references and implement the interface in the subclass. That way, even when .NET regenerates your web references any time you update/refresh a web service, your technique of subclassing the web reference will retain the interface implementation.

You begin by adding the new project (ConstructionDemo.Client.WebReferences) as a class library project to your development solution, Immediately, you can right-click the new project to add the web references (see Figure 4-11).

Adding References to Your Web Services

Next, you need to add a specific web reference to the web service. In a sense, you will be using the web reference in the same manner that the remoting client uses the remoting interface—to "discover" what properties and methods are exposed by the web service. So you right-click the project name and select Add Web Reference. Visual Studio 2005 then displays a dialog, shown in Figure 4-12, so that you can begin adding the web reference.

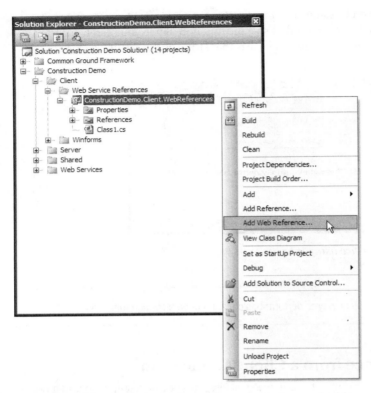

Figure 4-11. *Add web service project to current solution and adding a web reference*

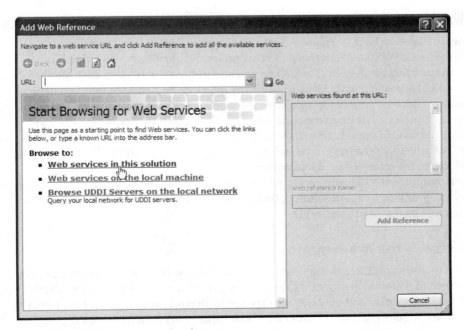

Figure 4-12. *Adding a new web reference*

This dialog provides you with different options for locating the web service that you want. Since you added the web service project to your solution, you can take the first option to quickly retrieve the web service. Had you not added the web service project to your solution, you could still retrieve the web service by selecting the second option to browse from the web services on the local machine. You can also retrieve the desired web service by typing the URL in the address bar at the top of the screen.

However, you selected the option to browse for web services in the current solution: since you opened the web service project wAgingReport in the current solution, Visual Studio 2005 displays it for you to confirm and select (see Figure 4-13).

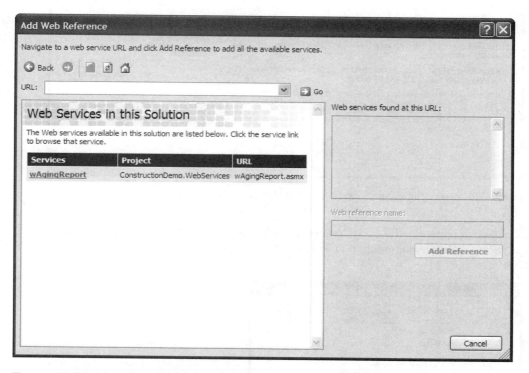

Figure 4-13. *Selecting the web service wAgingReport as a reference*

After you select the web service, Visual Studio 2005 adds a web reference to the service in your current project. By default, VS 2005 adds the reference with the name of "localhost"; however, you can rename it to the desired name (usually the original name of the service), as shown in Figure 4-14.

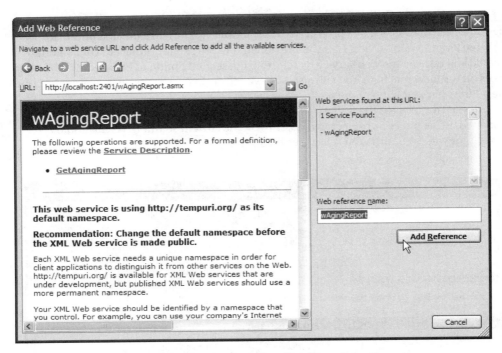

Figure 4-14. *Renaming the web reference from "localhost" to wAgingReport*

After you rename the web reference and add the reference, Visual Studio will update your project with the web reference that you added (see Figure 4-15).

Figure 4-15. *The web reference now renamed as wAgingReport*

Subclassing Your Web Reference to Implement Your Interfaces

Also note in Figure 4-15 that you've renamed the default class in your new
`ConstructionDemo.Client.WebReferences` from `Class1.cs` to `wAgingReportRef.cs`. Your
next step is to subclass the web reference to implement `IAgingReport`. You need to do this
because Visual Studio does not carry forward `IAgingReport` from the server-side web service
`wAgingReport` to the web reference. Listing 4-7 shows the code for `wAgingReportRef`.

Listing 4-7. *Subclassing the Web Reference to Implement the Interface*

```
// wAgingReportRef.cs
// Subclasses the web service reference to implement IAgingReport

using System;
using System.Collections.Generic;
using System.Text;
using ConstructionDemo.Interfaces;


namespace ConstructionDemo.Client.WebReferences
{
    public class wAgingReportRef : wAgingReport.wAgingReport, IAgingReport<string>
    {

    }
}
```

That's it! You've filled the basic requirements on the client side for your web services.
To utilize your web services on the client side, all you have to do is add a reference to
`ConstructionDemo.Client.WebReferences` and write code against the web references that you
subclassed (`wAgingReportRef`).

As an example, Figure 4-16 shows the web service reference being instantiated, with
IntelliSense used for statement completion of the web service method `GetAgingReport`. Should
you need to specify a different URL than the default URL when you created the web service,
you can change the URL property of the web reference object.

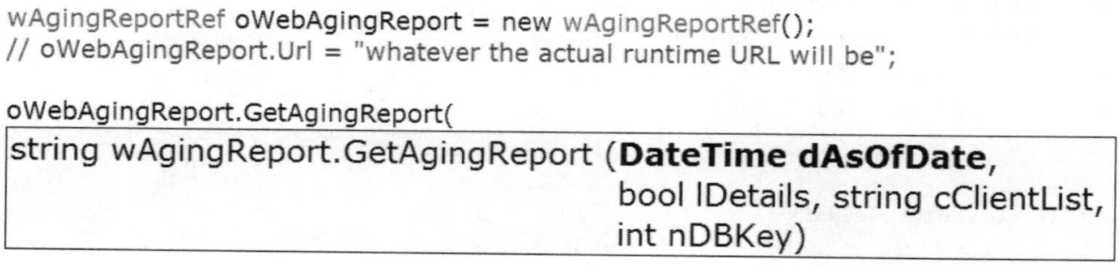

```
wAgingReportRef oWebAgingReport = new wAgingReportRef();
// oWebAgingReport.Url = "whatever the actual runtime URL will be";

oWebAgingReport.GetAgingReport(
```

string wAgingReport.GetAgingReport (**DateTime dAsOfDate**,
bool lDetails, string cClientList,
int nDBKey)

Figure 4-16. *Using IntelliSense to discover the method(s) in the web service*

Tip A common beginner's question on web services is how to specify the actual location (URL) of the web service at runtime, if the location differs from the design-time URL. Just as Grant is buried in Grant's tomb, the web service object has a URL property for you to specify the runtime URL!

Creating a Factory to Simplify the Process

In the previous section, we separately covered access using two code bases, one for web services and the other for remoting. However, in the end you're striving for a common code base that handles both situations seamlessly and that also hides as much of the complexity of remoting and web services as possible from the rest of the application.

Listing 4-8 presents `cgsRemoteAccess.cs`, a generic factory class for returning a remote object that you can cast to either a remoting interface or a web service object. This class will reside in the `CGS.RemoteAccess` project. Listing 4-9 demonstrates the use of the class. Note that in Listing 4-9, you do not need to specify any specific remoting logic—just merely whether you are using remoting or web services, as well as the type interface references to the back-end objects. The factory class returns an object that you can cast to the desired interface and utilize in a strongly-typed manner.

Note Listing 4-9 is a very basic example of using the remote access factory class to consume a web service. Listing 6-3 in Chapter 6 will provide a more complete example.

In Chapter 13,which covers client access in detail, we'll cover the specific properties of this generic factory class, and how you can utilize them for maximum flexibility and power.

Listing 4-8. *A Factory-Based Approach to Generic Remote Objects*

```
using System;
using System.Data;
using System.Runtime;
using System.Runtime.Remoting;
using System.Runtime.Remoting.Channels;
using System.Runtime.Remoting.Channels.Tcp;
using System.Web.Services.Protocols;


namespace CGS.RemoteAccess
{
public class ClientRemoteAccess
{

  // Supported enumerations
public enum ConnectionTypeOptions {WebServices=1, TcpRemoting };
```

```csharp
// Set at startup when user logs in and
// selects the connection profile

private static DataSet _DsAvailableConnections;
public DataSet DsAvailableConnections
{   get {return _DsAvailableConnections  ;}
    set {_DsAvailableConnections  = value;}  }

private static string _cDescription;
public string cDescription
{   get {return _cDescription  ;}
    set {_cDescription  = value;} }

// Set at startup when user logs in and selects the
// connection profile


private static ConnectionTypeOptions _nConnectionType;
public ConnectionTypeOptions nConnectionType
{   get {return _nConnectionType  ;}
    set {_nConnectionType  = value;}  }

// Set at startup when user logs in, comes from
//connection profile, default is 8228

private static int _nTCPPort;
public int nTCPPort
{   get {return _nTCPPort  ;}
    set {_nTCPPort  = value;} }

private static string _cTcpServer;
public string cTcpServer
{   get {return _cTcpServer  ;}      // this is concatenated with the port
    set {_cTcpServer  = value;}  }

private static string _cWebServiceURL;
public string cWebServiceURL
{   get {return _cWebServiceURL  ;}
    set {_cWebServiceURL  = value;}  }


private Type _tInterface;
public Type tInterface
{   get {return _tInterface  ;}
    set {_tInterface  = value;} }
```

```
private string _cServiceName;
public string cServiceName
{   get {return _cServiceName ;}
    set {_cServiceName  = value;} }

private SoapHttpClientProtocol _wService;
public SoapHttpClientProtocol wService
{    get {return _wService ;}
     set {_wService  = value;}    }


public ClientRemoteAccess()
{
    this.nTCPPort = 8228;
}

public bool UsingWebServices()
{
    if(this.nConnectionType == ConnectionTypeOptions.WebServices)
        return true;
    else
        return false;

}

// Required naming convention is for all web service objects to begin with 'w',
// and all business objects to begin with 'bz'

// Service name will be referenced with a 'base' name (AgingReport, for instance)
private string cWSPrefix = "w";
private string cBzPrefix = "bz";


public object GetAccessObject()
{
    // Type reference to back-end interface
    Type oInterface = this.tInterface;
    string cServiceName = this.cServiceName;

    // Object reference to web service (if used)
    SoapHttpClientProtocol ows = this.wService;

    // Generic back-end object (will be cast to interface)
    object oAccessObject = new object();

    switch(this.nConnectionType)
    {
```

```
            case ConnectionTypeOptions.TcpRemoting:
                // TCP remoting....must create new TCP channel
                IChannel[] myIChannelArray = ChannelServices.RegisteredChannels;
                if(myIChannelArray.Length ==0)
                    ChannelServices.RegisterChannel( new TcpClientChannel());
                // Activate back-end object
                oAccessObject = Activator.GetObject( oInterface,
                        this.cTcpServer.ToString().Trim() + ":" +
                        this.nTCPPort.ToString().Trim()  + "/" + cServiceName  ) ;
                break;
            case ConnectionTypeOptions.WebServices:
                // Set URL of instantiated web service object
                ows.Url = this.cWebServiceURL.ToString() + "/" + cWSPrefix +
                                    cServiceName + ".asmx";
                oAccessObject = ows;
                break;
        }

    return oAccessObject;
}
}
}
```

■**Note** The project for the code in Listing 4-8 (cgsRemoteAccess) requires .NET references to
System.Web.Services and System.Runtime.Remoting.

Listing 4-9. *Example of Using the Factory Class*

```
// To get a result set from the back end,
// you need to instantiate the remote access class,
// and provide it with some information

// A type-reference to the server-side Interface     (IAgingReport)
// The name of the service
// (the back-end object name, or the name of the web service)
// If web services are being used, an object reference to a web service

// Then you call GetAccessObject,
// which returns a generic object that you can cast to your interface

IAgingReport<string>  oAgingReport;

// Create instance of remote access class
```

```
oRemoteAccess = new CGS.RemoteAccess.ClientRemoteAccess();
// Type reference to the remote interface, plus the name of the web service
oRemoteAccess.tInterface = typeof(IAgingReport<string>);
oRemoteAccess.cServiceName = "AgingReport";

// Need to specify whether you're using web services or remoting.
// In this example of using the factory, you'll try web services.
// You'll handle remoting with the typed DataSet in Chapter 6.

oRemoteAccess.nConnectionType =
 ClientRemoteAccess.ConnectionTypeOptions.WebServices

// Create instance of web service, if web services were selected at startup
if(oRemoteAccess.UsingWebServices())
     oRemoteAccess.wService = new wAgingReportRef();

// Get an object reference to the remote object    (which you can cast)
oAgingReport = (IAgingReport<string>)oRemoteAccess.GetAccessObject();

// Begin/End parameters
DateTime dStartDate = DateTime.Today;

// Remote object contains a function to get the result set

string cXMLResults = oAgingReport.GetAgingReport(dStartDate,true,"",1);

// Now that you've received the results from the web service as XML, you
// can convert it to a DataSet, and do whatever you need with it.
```

New Features for Remoting in Visual Studio 2005

After the release of Visual Studio 2003, many individuals in this industry stated that .NET remoting was essentially "going away." News of Windows Communication Foundation (formerly known as Indigo) further reinforced this belief. However, a large number of developers continued to use remoting and requested enhancements for the next version of .NET. Microsoft responded with new remoting functionality (primarily in the area of security) in Visual Studio 2005 that we'll cover in this section.

Secure TCP Remoting and TCP Channel Timeouts

In Visual Studio 2003, the only way to implement secure remoting was to use HTTP remoting (as opposed to TCP remoting) and host the remoting objects in IIS. TCP remoting in Visual Studio 2005 supports encryption and authentication using Security Support Provider Interface (SSPI).

You can implement secure TCP remoting by specifying remoting configuration parameters in a dictionary object, both on the server and client side. On the **server-side**, you can implement the following when you establish a new TcpServerChannel:

```
IDictionary oDict = new System.Collections.Hashtable();
oDict.Add("port", 8228);
oDict.Add("secure", true);
oDict.Add("impersonate", true);
oDict.Add("protectionlevel", "EncryptAndSign");

TcpServerChannel serverChannel = new TcpServerChannel(oDict, null);
ChannelServices.RegisterChannel(serverChannel);
```

The corresponding client-side code is as follows (note that you can also use the new connection timeout parameter):

```
IDictionary oDict = new System.Collections.Hashtable();
oDict.Add("secure", "true");
oDict.Add("tokenImpersonationLevel", "Impersonation");
oDict.Add("protectionlevel", "EncryptAndSign");
oDict.Add("connectionTimeOut", 1000);
TcpClientChannel oChannel = new TcpClientChannel(oDict, null);
ChannelServices.RegisterChannel(oChannel);
```

The New IPC Client Channel

While not specifically part of this book's development project, in some instances, both the client and server components of a remoting architecture may run on the same physical computer. One example might be development testing, where you might want to mimic a distributed environment on a stand-alone system. While you could still utilize TCP remoting, port 8228, and the localhost address, Visual Studio 2005 allows access to the IPC channel for maximum performance. The IPC channel defines a communication channel for remoting using the Windows IPC system and bypasses any network communication across application domains: as a result, the IPC channel is significantly faster than the TCP channels.

Of course, you can only use the IPC channel between domains on the same physical computer. However, it offers the advantage of additional performance for testing (or any instances where two or more applications/objects need to access each other).

To utilize the IPC client channel, all you need to do is take the client code from the previous section and replace TcpClientChannel with IpcClientChannel as follows:

```
IpcClientChannel oClientChannel = new IpcClientChannel(oDict, null);
ChannelServices.RegisterChannel(oClientChannel);
```

Serializing DataSets in a Binary Format

As we stated earlier in this chapter, Visual Studio 2005 allows you to serialize DataSets across remoting application boundaries in a true binary format. Many data-centric applications pass and receive data that either began (or will end) in ADO.NET DataSets. In Visual Studio .NET 2003, developers often serialized this data as XML strings, because of the overhead of DataSets. Fortunately, Visual Studio 2005 has improved this situation by allowing developers to serialize DataSets as a true binary format (when using TCP remoting). The actual syntax is

```
MyDataSet.RemotingFormat = SerializationFormat.Binary
```

This will reduce the size of the transferred data by at least a factor of 6.

Using .NET Generics to Simplify Remoting Interfaces

In a database application, you might have a dozen modules, each containing a method to retrieve data for a primary key. That might mean GetProduct, GetAccount, GetCostCenter, etc. And then you might have other categories of functions for the various modules. Does that mean you are potentially facing a proliferation of interfaces?

This is one of the areas where .NET Generics in Visual Studio 2005 can help you out. Generics can help simplify situations where you have multiple classes that differ only by an internal type. In this instance, you can define a generic interface that receives a single primary key integer (it could be an account key, a product key, or a cost center key) and returns a DataSet (it could be account results, product results, or cost center results).

The first step is to define the interface and specify a placeholder for the parameter (in case you might have specific business objects that return custom collections instead of a DataSet). Note that the <T> placeholder indicates a generic. When we refer to the actual type, we will represent it in the same way. The following code demonstrates a reference to an object that implements this generic interface:

```
public interface IRemoteGenericResultSet<T>
{
T GetResults(int nID);
}
```

The second step is to define the business objects that implement IRemoteGenericResultSet:

```
namespace ProductBzObject
{
    public class ProductBzObject: System.MarshalByRefObject,
                                   IRemoteGenericResultSet<DataSet>
{
public DataSet GetResults(int nID)
{
// Do something, return a result set for the product file
}
}

namespace CostCenterBzObject
{
    public class CostCenterBzObject: System.MarshalByRefObject,
                                     IRemoteGenericResultSet<DataSet>
```

```
{
public DataSet GetResults(int nID)
{
// Do something, return a result set for the cost center file
}
}
```

Finally, on the client side, you can execute each back-end object using nothing more than a string for each specific class and the generic interface. Note that the following client code doesn't contain any type references to a specific module. We've build a simple method called RemoteGeneric to illustrate this:

```
DataSet ds1 = this.RemoteGeneric("ProductBzObject",100);   // PK Value
DataSet ds2 = this.RemoteGeneric("CostCenterBzObject",300);  // PK Value


private DataSet RemoteGeneric(string cRemoteClass, int nPK)
{
string cServer = "tcp://localhost:8228";
object oRemoteObject =
Activator.GetObject(
typeof(IRemoteGenericResultSet<DataSet>),
cServer + "/" + cRemoteClass);

IRemoteGenericResultSet<DataSet> oRemoteBzObject =
oRemoteObject as
                    IRemoteGenericResultSet<DataSet>;
return oRemoteBzObject.GetResults(nPK);
}
```

Summary

We've covered a great deal in this chapter. Even though you need to develop additional components before you can actually run anything meaningful, you've tackled a significant milestone in building your general infrastructure.

We presented two diagrams that covered the general architecture using either web services or remoting, and we stressed the value of interfaces as part of our model of distributed computing. We performed a walk-through with code for both web services and remoting, and presented a reusable factory class for distributed computing: this factory class allows application developers to focus on the business aspect of their tasks without needing to worry about technical terms/namespaces/functions directly associated with web services and remoting. Finally, we covered some new functions in Visual Studio 2005 that add value to remoting functionality, such as secure TCP remoting, serializing DataSets in binary format, and the use of .NET Generics to add both simplicity and flexibility to remoting interfaces.

In the next chapter, you'll learn how to build a data access layer and explore business objects in more detail. At that point, you'll be able to perform some integration testing. You'll also be able to interactively test your back-end processes by calling some of the stored procedures through your data access layer and manually generate some of the report result sets.

Recommended Reading

Ingo Rammer and Mario Szpuszta. *Advanced .NET Remoting, Second Edition*. Berkeley, CA: Apress, 2005.

Ingo Rammer and Christian Weyer. .NET Remoting FAQ. www.ThinkTecture.com/Resources/RemotingFAQ/default.html.

Microsoft Corporation. "Introduction to Web Application Projects." http://msdn.microsoft.com/vstudio/default.aspx?pull=/library/en-us/dnvs05/html/WAP.asp. April 2006.

■ ■ ■

CHAPTER 5

Building a Data Access Layer

In this chapter, we'll show you how to construct a data access layer (DAL) for the example application. The DAL will communicate with a back-end database server to retrieve (and save) data. You'll start by defining the requirements for a DAL that you can use for many applications—your reporting application as well as many different types of applications. Then you'll see the C# code to address these requirements. Finally, you'll learn some techniques to expand the functionality of the DAL.

So in this chapter, we'll cover the following:

- The requirements, and features that you want in a data access layer, and a diagram depicting how data access fits within your architecture

- How most developers initially construct a data retrieval procedure

- How you can build a data retrieval process to implement your desired functionality

- How to use .NET Generics to write an abstract retrieval process that can automatically populate any DataSet (including a typed DataSet) from a stored procedure

- The complete code that you'll use for the data access class, which we present when we "track back" over the project in the section "Looking at Where You Are" (You'll also update some of the code presented for your business object and web service from Chapter 4.)

- Some of the new ADO.NET capabilities in the SQL Server Provider for Visual Studio 2005 that you can use to extend your data access component, such as multiple active result sets, provider factories to easily support multiple database products, and asynchronous command execution to run multiple back-end database processes

Overview: What Is a Data Access Layer?

A DAL is an application component that communicates with the back-end database. Its primary function is to execute commands against the database, through a provider component. The DAL manages database connections, retrieves data from the database server, and sends data to the database server. Other application components (such as business objects) retrieve and save data by using the DAL—so you can think of the DAL as the funnel for all database requests in your application.

Requirements for a DAL

Before you construct your DAL, take a look at the requirements. Many of your requirements will reflect an interest in reusing your DAL for many different applications, with no modifications:

- The DAL should contain functionality to open a database connection, execute a stored procedure, close the connection, and return the results to the calling function.

- The DAL should handle connection strings.

- The DAL should handle a variable number of input parameters.

- The DAL should be able to work against different databases and even different database servers. The calling application may need to retrieve data from server A/database B one minute, and then server C/database D the next minute.

- A developer should be able to set a custom database timeout for a specific database operation.

- The DAL should be built as a class from which custom classes can inherit, to gain access to the public properties and methods of the DAL.

- The DAL should be the only. . . repeat, **only** . . . component that communicates with the back-end database. No other pieces of the software should access the database.

Figure 5-1 illustrates how this data access layer will fit into your application.

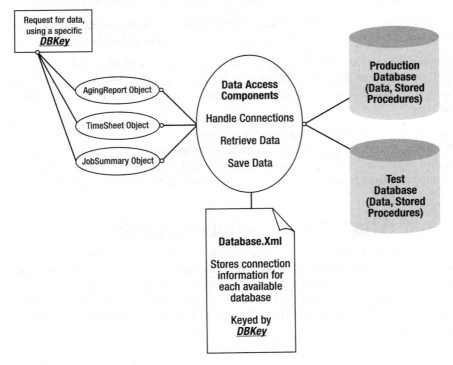

Figure 5-1. *Diagram of data access layer*

Building a Data Access Class

Some developers may start a DAL with a function similar to that shown in Listing 5-1.

Listing 5-1. *Simple Method to Retrieve Data from a Stored Procedure*

```
using System;
using System.Data;
using System.Data.SqlClient;
using System.ComponentModel;
using System.Collections;
using System.Collections.Generic;

public DataSet SPRetrieveData(string cProcName)
{
  SqlConnection oSqlConn = new SqlConnection("user id=sa;password=;
    initial catalog=MyDatabase; data source=MyServer");

  DataSet DsReturn = new DataSet();

  SqlDataAdapter oSqlAdapter = new SqlDataAdapter(cProcName, oSqlConn);
  oSqlAdapter.SelectCommand.CommandType = CommandType.StoredProcedure;

  oSqlAdapter.Fill( DsReturn,"MyData");
  oSqlConn.Close();

  return DsReturn;
}
```

While this will work in specific situations, you need to expand it to cover all of your requirements.

■**Note** Throughout this chapter, any code listings assume that namespace `using` statements appear at the top of the code listing, particularly for the `System.Data`, `System.Data.SqlClient`, and `System.Collections.Generic` namespaces.

Handling Multiple Databases with a DBKey Identifier

Let's start with the requirement to handle connections and support multiple databases. Your application will need to access different database servers (test server, production server, etc.). Since you want to use the DAL in many different applications, you don't want to hard-code any application-specific entities into the base DAL.

At startup, the application will prompt the user for which database to use. The application must inform the DAL which database should be used, and you will use an `integer` key identifier for each specific database. You will define your database connection information in a configuration file called database.xml, which will reside on the server side, in the same area where the DAL runs. Listing 5-2 shows an example of this file.

Listing 5-2. *database.xml*

```
<DataBase>
  <ConnectionInfo>
    <DBKey>1</DBKey>
    <UserID>sa</UserID>
    <password>sa2000</password>
    <DataSource>KCI890TEST</DataSource>
    <InitialCatalog>ConstructionDemo</InitialCatalog>
    <MultipleActiveResultSets>false</MultipleActiveResultSets>
    <AsynchronousProcessing>false</AsynchronousProcessing>
    <Connectiontimeout>30</Connectiontimeout>
  </ConnectionInfo>
  <ConnectionInfo>
    <DBKey>2</DBKey>
    <UserID>sa</UserID>
    <password></password>
    <DataSource>KCI890PROD</DataSource>
    <InitialCatalog>ConstructionProdt</InitialCatalog>
    <MultipleActiveResultSets>false</MultipleActiveResultSets>
    <AsynchronousProcessing>false</AsynchronousProcessing>
    <Connectiontimeout>230</Connectiontimeout>
  </ConnectionInfo>
</DataBase>
```

Note the element DBKey in each row. Your database.xml file will contain a unique DBKey for each possible database. Your client-side solution (which we'll cover in Chapter 13) will prompt the user for the database to be used ("use test database," "use production database," etc.). The client-side configuration file will contain these same DBKey values. All calls from the client side to the back end will pass this DBKey, which the DAL will use when opening database.xml to retrieve the specific database information. The DAL can then create a database connection using this information.

Listing 5-3 shows two methods that meet the requirements for managing connections and supporting different database servers. The two methods work to open the database.xml file, retrieve the database definition based on the requested database key, and return a SQL connection object.

■**Note** Chapter 13 will demonstrate the client-side functionality for determining which database to use.

Listing 5-3. *GetConnection and BuildDBConnectionString*

```
public SqlConnection GetConnection(int nDatabaseKey)
{
  return new SqlConnection(this.BuildDBConnectionString(nDatabaseKey));
}

private string BuildDBConnectionString (int nDatabaseKey)
{
  string cDBConnectionString="";
  DataSet DsDBInfo = new DataSet();

  // Retrieve the XML file in the current domain/folder
  // (Don't use GetCurrentDirectory, it isn't always reliable!)
  AppDomain currentDomain = AppDomain.CurrentDomain;
  string cFileXml=currentDomain.BaseDirectory+"database.xml";


  // Open the XML file, create a primary key on the DBKey,
  // so that you can perform a quick FIND

  // (You could also use a RowFilter or SELECT)
  DsDBInfo.ReadXml(cFileXml);
  DsDBInfo.Tables[0].PrimaryKey =
    new DataColumn[] {DsDBInfo.Tables[0].Columns["DbKey"]};
  DataRow Dr = DsDBInfo.Tables[0].Rows.Find(nDatabaseKey);

  cDBConnectionString = "user id="  + Dr["UserID"].ToString().Trim() + ";" +
                "password=" + Dr["Password"].ToString().Trim() + ";" +
                "initial catalog=" + Dr["InitialCatalog"].ToString().Trim() + ";" +
                "data source=" + Dr["DataSource"].ToString().Trim() + ";" +
                "Connect Timeout=" + Dr["ConnectiontimeOut"].ToString().Trim()   ;

  return cDBConnectionString;
}
```

■**Note** In Listing 5-3, the BaseDirectory property of the current application domain object determines
the current directory. This is more reliable than the commonly used GetCurrentDirectory function, which
isn't fully reliable if the application changes the active directory.

In addition to the code in Listing 5-3, you can also take advantage of the new SqlConnectionStringBuilder object, which exposes the connection string elements as strongly-typed properties. Listing 5-4 demonstrates an alternative to the BuildDBConnectionString from the preceding listing.

Listing 5-4. *VS 2005 Code to Utilize the New Connection String Builder Object*

```
public string BuildDatabaseConnectionString(int nDatabaseKey)
{
  DataSet DsDBInfo = new DataSet();
  AppDomain currentDomain = AppDomain.CurrentDomain;

  string cFileXml=currentDomain.BaseDirectory+"database.xml";

  DsDBInfo.ReadXml(cFileXml);
  DsDBInfo.Tables[0].PrimaryKey =
    new DataColumn[] {DsDBInfo.Tables[0].Columns["DbKey"]};
  DataRow Dr = DsDBInfo.Tables[0].Rows.Find(nDatabaseKey);

  SqlConnectionStringBuilder oStringBuilder = new SqlConnectionStringBuilder();
  oStringBuilder.UserID = Convert.ToString(Dr["UserID"]);
  oStringBuilder.Password = Convert.ToString(Dr["PassWord"]);
  oStringBuilder.InitialCatalog = Convert.ToString(Dr["InitialCatalog"]);
  oStringBuilder.DataSource = Convert.ToString(Dr["DataSource"]);
  oStringBuilder.ConnectTimeout = Convert.ToInt32(Dr["ConnectiontimeOut"]);
  oStringBuilder.MultipleActiveResultSets =
        Convert.ToBoolean(Dr["MultipleActiveResultSets"]);
  oStringBuilder.AsynchronousProcessing =
        Convert.ToBoolean(Dr["AsynchronousProcessing"]);


  return oStringBuilder.ConnectionString;
}
```

■**Note** In Listing 5-4, you reference two new connection string settings for multiple active result sets and asynchronous processing. These are new settings for the ADO.NET System.Data.SqlClient namespace in Visual Studio 2005, and we'll cover them later in this chapter in the sections "Multiple Active Result Sets" and "Asynchronous Processing Made Simple."

Handling Stored Procedure Parameters

Next, let's take a look at input parameters. Your DAL must support stored procedures, which will have a variable number of parameters. Some stored procedures may have no parameters, while others may have a small handful, and some might have many. Your solution must allow developers to pass a variable number of parameters to the DAL.

Your DAL solution will populate an ArrayList of parameters, and pass the ArrayList to the DAL. The DAL will iterate through the ArrayList and pass the necessary parameters to the stored procedure. Listings 5-5 and 5-6 demonstrate an example of calling the DAL with an ArrayList of SQL parameters, as well as the DAL code for reading the ArrayList.

Listing 5-5. *Custom DAL Code to Call the Base Method SPRetrieveData*

```
public DataSet ValidateUserID(string cUserID, string cPassword, int nDBKey)
{
  // Build array list of parameters for the stored procedure
  ArrayList aSqlParms = new ArrayList();
  aSqlParms.Add(new SqlParameter("@cUserID",cUserID));
  aSqlParms.Add(new SqlParameter("@cPassword",cPassword));

  // Call SPRetrieveData, passing the name of the stored proc,
  // the DB key to be used, and the array list of parameters
  DataSet DsReturn = this.SPRetrieveData("SPValidateUserID",nDBKey,aSqlParms);

  return DsReturn;
}
```

Listing 5-6. *SPRetrieveData*

```
protected virtual DataSet SPRetrieveData(string cProcName,
                                  int nDBKey, ArrayList aParameters)
{
  // Get the connection object
  SqlConnection oSqlConn = this.GetConnection(nDBKey);

   DataSet DsReturn = new DataSet();

  // Open a data adapter, set the command type
  SqlDataAdapter oSqlAdapter = new SqlDataAdapter(cProcName, oSqlConn);
  oSqlAdapter.SelectCommand.CommandType = CommandType.StoredProcedure;

  // Look through the array list of SQL parameters
  foreach(SqlParameter oParms in aParameters) {
    oSqlAdapter.SelectCommand.Parameters.Add(oParms);
  }

  oSqlAdapter.Fill( DsReturn,"MyData");
  oSqlConn.Close();

  return DsReturn;
}
```

Implementing a Custom Timeout

You're getting closer to meeting your final requirements. Another requirement is the option of specifying a custom timeout for individual queries/stored procedures. While your database.xml file contains a setting for a timeout, you may have a special stored procedure that takes longer to execute. You can create an overload for SPRetrieveData, to optionally supply an additional parameter for a custom timeout. Listing 5-7 contains the complete listing for your data access class to demonstrate this.

Listing 5-7. *SPRetrieveData, with an Overload for a Custom Timeout*

```
using System;
using System.Data;
using System.Data.SqlClient;
using System.ComponentModel;
using System.Collections;
using System.Collections.Generic;

namespace CGS.DataAccess
{
  public class cgsDataAccess
  {

    protected string TableName;

    private SqlConnection GetConnection(int nDatabaseKey)
    {
      return  new SqlConnection(this.BuildDatabaseConnectionString(nDatabaseKey));
}

    public string BuildDatabaseConnectionString(int nDatabaseKey)
    {
      DataSet DsDBInfo = new DataSet();
      AppDomain currentDomain = AppDomain.CurrentDomain;

      string cFileXml=currentDomain.BaseDirectory+"database.xml";

      DsDBInfo.ReadXml(cFileXml);
      DsDBInfo.Tables[0].PrimaryKey =
        new DataColumn[] {DsDBInfo.Tables[0].Columns["DbKey"]};
      DataRow Dr = DsDBInfo.Tables[0].Rows.Find(nDatabaseKey);

      SqlConnectionStringBuilder oStringBuilder = new SqlConnectionStringBuilder();
      oStringBuilder.UserID = Convert.ToString(Dr["UserID"]);
      oStringBuilder.Password = Convert.ToString(Dr["PassWord"]);
      oStringBuilder.InitialCatalog = Convert.ToString(Dr["InitialCatalog"]);
      oStringBuilder.DataSource = Convert.ToString(Dr["DataSource"]);
      oStringBuilder.ConnectTimeout = Convert.ToInt32(Dr["ConnectiontimeOut"]);
      oStringBuilder.MultipleActiveResultSets =
```

```
          Convert.ToBoolean(Dr["MultipleActiveResultSets"]);
     oStringBuilder.AsynchronousProcessing =
          Convert.ToBoolean(Dr["AsynchronousProcessing"]);

   return oStringBuilder.ConnectionString;
}


// Overload for a stored procedure, DB key, but no parameters or custom timeout
protected virtual DataSet SPRetrieveData(string cProcName, int nDBKey)
{
   return this.SPRetrieveData(cProcName, nDBKey, new ArrayList(), 0);     }


// Overload for a stored procedure, DB key, parameters, no custom timeout
protected virtual DataSet SPRetrieveData(string cProcName, int nDBKey,
                                         ArrayList aParameters)
{
   return this.SPRetrieveData(cProcName, nDBKey, aParameters, 0);     }


// Overload for all parameters:
// stored procedure, DB key, parameters, custom timeout
protected virtual DataSet SPRetrieveData(string cProcName, int nDBKey,
                  ArrayList aParameters,  int nCommandTimeOut)
{
   // Get the connection object
   SqlConnection oSqlConn = this.GetConnection(nDBKey);

   DataSet DsReturn = new DataSet();

   // Open a data adapter, set the command type
   SqlDataAdapter oSqlAdapter = new SqlDataAdapter(cProcName, oSqlConn);
   oSqlAdapter.SelectCommand.CommandType = CommandType.StoredProcedure;

   // If someone specified a timeout, use it
   if(nCommandTimeOut > 0) {
     oSqlAdapter.SelectCommand.CommandTimeout=nCommandTimeOut;
   }

   // Look through the arraylist of SQL parameters
   foreach(SqlParameter oParms in aParameters)  {
     oSqlAdapter.SelectCommand.Parameters.Add(oParms);
   }

   oSqlAdapter.Fill( DsReturn,"MyData");
   oSqlConn.Close();

   return DsReturn;
  }
 }
}
```

Using Your Basic Data Access Class

Finally, Listing 5-8 shows a custom data access class that inherits from your base data access class. The listing utilizes the methods in your base data access layer to return the result sets for the aging receivables report.

Listing 5-8. *Custom Data Access Class for the Aging Receivables Report*

```
using System;
using System.Data;
using System.Data.SqlClient;
using System.ComponentModel;
using System.Collections;
using CGS.DataAccess;

namespace ConstructionDemo.DataAccess
{
  public class AgingReportDataAccess : cgsDataAccess
  {
    public AgingReportDataAccess ()
    {
    }

    public DataSet GetAgingReport(DateTime dAsOfDate, bool lDetails,
                                 string cClientList, int nDBKey)
    {
      ArrayList aSqlParms = new ArrayList();

      aSqlParms.Add(new SqlParameter("@dAsOfDate",dAsOfDate));
      aSqlParms.Add(new SqlParameter("@lDetails",lDetails));
      aSqlParms.Add(new SqlParameter("@cClientList",cClientList));

      DataSet DsReturn=this.SPRetrieveData("GetAgingReceivables", nDBKey,aSqlParms);

      return DsReturn;
    }
  }
}
```

Are You Satisfied with This?

You've built a basic process to retrieve data from stored procedures. You could stop here and move on, but there's just one little hitch. As you'll see in Chapter 6, you're using typed DataSets in your application—yet the data access method you just built only populates regular untyped DataSets.

You can certainly build another process to read untyped DataSets into your typed DataSets. That would certainly work, but wouldn't it be great if you could somehow pass a reference to a typed DataSet into the data access layer, and have the data access layer populate it for you?

Now, you may be thinking, "How can I possibly do that, unless somehow I make my base data access class aware of the typed DataSet?" That would surely couple the base data access class with your application DataSets, which is something you surely don't want. Could you use .NET reflection? Perhaps, though some solutions utilizing reflection tend to be nonstandard, clumsy, and don't perform well.

Fortunately, there is painless way to do this. In the next section, we'll show how .NET Generics can help you to populate your application DataSets, while keeping your base data access class "generic."

Populating Typed DataSets Using .NET Generics

We use stored procedures and typed DataSets heavily. One of our many "holy grail" quests for years has been to populate a typed DataSet **directly** from a stored procedure, while still maintaining a level of separation between the typed DataSet and the database connection.

For a long time, we used a base method in our data access class to populate a plain vanilla DataSet from a stored procedure with parameters (essentially the same code from the previous listings in this chapter). Afterwards we would merge the DataSet into a typed DataSet. This certainly worked, but meant additional code and an additional processing step.

What we wanted to do was pass an instance of a typed DataSet into the base method, and have the base method serve as a factory—to pump out a populated typed DataSet, without needing an actual reference to the typed DataSet.

.NET Generics allow you to create such a class and then use it (as demonstrated later in this section in Listings 5-9 and 5-10). The steps are as follows:

1. Create an instance of a typed DataSet from the project (we'll use the aging receivables report as our example).

2. Create a typed list of SQL parameters for the stored procedure (instead of using `ArrayList`).

3. Call the data access class method (`ReadIntoTypedDs`), passing an instance of the typed DataSet, the name of the stored procedure, and the typed list of parameters for the stored proc.

4. Create the data access method `ReadIntoTypedDs` (see Listing 5-9), and specify a typed placeholder for the first parameter and for the return value. Note the restriction that the parameter must be a DataSet, since code inside the method will use DataSet-specific properties and methods.

```
public T ReadIntoTypedDs<T>
    (T dsTypedDs, string cStoredProc, List<SqlParameter> oParmList,
            int nDBKey, int CommandTimeOut)  where T : DataSet
```

5. Define the standard connection object, data adapter, etc.

6. Elbow grease time! SQL Server returns stored procedure result sets with actual names of Table, Table1, Table2, etc. (Please don't ask why!) When you designed your typed DataSet, you might have used more descriptive names (dtClient, dtDetails, etc.) Therefore, you need to map the names Table, Table1, etc., to the names in your typed DataSet, using the TableMappings command of the data adapter.

7. Fill the DataSet from the data adapter, and return it.

Note that the method in Listing 5-9 uses the GetConnection function covered earlier.

Listing 5-9. *A Data Access Method to Retrieve Data Directly into a Typed DataSet*

```
public T ReadIntoTypedDs<T>(T dsTypedDs, string cStoredProc,
        List<SqlParameter> oParmList, int nDBKey, int nCommandTimeOut )
                                                where T : DataSet
{

    SqlConnection oSqlConn = this.GetConnection(nDBKey);
    SqlDataAdapter oSqlAdapter = new SqlDataAdapter(cStoredProc, oSqlConn);
    oSqlAdapter.SelectCommand.CommandType = CommandType.StoredProcedure;

    if(nCommandTimeOut > 0)
        oSqlAdapter.SelectCommand.CommandTimeout = nCommandTimeOut;

    foreach (SqlParameter oParm in oParmList)
        oSqlAdapter.SelectCommand.Parameters.Add(oParm);

    int nTableCtr = 0;
    foreach (DataTable Dt in dsTypedDs.Tables)
    {
        string cSource = "";
        // Tricky part...
        // first result set from sql is Table, 2nd is Table1, 3rd, is Table2
        // So you have to check the counter and set the source string correctly
        if (nTableCtr == 0)
            cSource = "Table";
        else
            cSource = "Table" + nTableCtr.ToString().Trim();
        oSqlAdapter.TableMappings.Add(cSource, Dt.TableName.ToString());
        // Set the mapping from the original table name to the corresponding one
        // in your typed dS
          nTableCtr++;
    }

    oSqlAdapter.Fill(dsTypedDs);
    oSqlConn.Close();

    return dsTypedDs;
}
```

Listing 5-10 shows an example of directly populating a typed DataSet. You will see how to make use of this when we cover typed DataSets in the next chapter: the key point is that you are able to use .NET Generics to populate your application DataSets using a base method, simply by defining a typed parameter placeholder in the base class and then declaring the actual DataSet in the method that calls it. This demonstrates the power (and simplicity) of .NET Generics!

Listing 5-10. *Using the Method to Populate a Typed DataSet*

```
int nDBKey = 1;

cgsDataAccess oDataAccess = new cgsDataAccess();
dsAgingReport odsAgingReport = new dsAgingReport();

// Type-safe list of SQL parameters
List<SqlParameter> oParms = new List<SqlParameter>();

oParms.Add(new SqlParameter("@cCustomerList", ""));
oParms.Add(new SqlParameter("@dAgingDate", DateTime.Today));
oParms.Add(new SqlParameter("@lShowDetails", true));

// You can have a base data access class read the results of a stored procedure
// DIRECTLY into a typed DataSet....no need to do a MERGE
odsAgingReport =
      oDataAccess.ReadIntoTypedDs(
              odsAgingReport,"GetAgingReceivables",oParms,nDBKey,100);
```

Note that the first line in Listing 5-10 references the typed DataSet dsAgingReport (from the ConstructionDemo.Datasets project) that we'll cover in Chapter 6. This typed DataSet represents the structure of the data for the stored procedure result sets: your goal is to populate an instance of this object with the data from the stored procedure, and ultimately push the contents into the actual report.

■**Note** We will cover typed DataSets in detail in Chapter 6.

Looking at Where You Are

After a few iterations of building a data access class, you're ready to "nail down" some of your code and move on. In Chapter 4, your business object and web service for the aging receivables report (bzAgingReport and wAgingReport) contained "stub" code for an empty DataSet and a dummy string, until you constructed an actual data access component. Now you can go back and "fill in" some of the blanks. Though we still have to cover the typed DataSet for the aging receivables report, things are starting to crystallize. You will make use of the typed DataSet throughout this section.

Remember that the following projects contain references to other projects in the application. Refer to either the project overview that accompanies Figure 4-3 back in Chapter 4 or the Technical Roadmap in Appendix C for details.

The Aging Report Business Object (bzAgingReport)

Listing 5-11 contains the complete revised code for bzAgingReport.cs (in the ConstructionDemo.Business project). The class creates an instance of the application data access class that will use the typed DataSet (daAgingReport, covered later in Listing 5-13) and calls the method GetAgingReport() with the specified parameters. Note that your implementation of IAgingReport in the business object declares dsAgingReport (your typed DataSet, which we'll cover in the next chapter) as the type parameter.

Listing 5-11. *Revised bzAgingReport.cs in the ConstructionDemo.Business Project*

```
using System;
using System.Collections.Generic;
using System.Text;
using ConstructionDemo.Datasets;
using ConstructionDemo.DataAccess;
using CGS.Business;
using ConstructionDemo.Interfaces;

namespace ConstructionDemo.Business
{
    public class bzAgingReport : cgsBaseBusinessObject, IAgingReport<dsAgingReport>
    {
        public dsAgingReport GetAgingReport(DateTime dAsOfDate, bool lDetails,
                                string cClientList, int nDBKey)
        {
            return new daAgingReport().GetAgingReport(dAsOfDate, lDetails,
                            cClientList, nDBKey);
        }
    }
}
```

The Aging Report Web Service (wAgingReport.asmx)

Listing 5-12 contains the complete revised code for the web service wAgingReport.asmx (in the ConstructionDemo.WebServices project). Once again, this class also implements IAgingReport, but here you define a string as the type parameter for the interface, as your web service must return an XML string to accommodate non-.NET clients that may need to consume the service.

Listing 5-12. *Revised wAgingReport.asmx Web Service*

```
using System;
using System.Data;
using System.Web;
using System.Collections;
using System.Web.Services;
using System.Web.Services.Protocols;
using System.ComponentModel;
using ConstructionDemo.Interfaces;
using ConstructionDemo.Business;


namespace ConstructionDemo.WebServices
{
    /// <summary>
    /// Summary description for wAgingReport
    /// </summary>
    [WebService(Namespace = "http://tempuri.org/")]
    [WebServiceBinding(ConformsTo = WsiProfiles.BasicProfile1_1)]
    [ToolboxItem(false)]
    public class wAgingReport: System.Web.Services.WebService, IAgingReport<string>
    {

        [WebMethod]
        public string GetAgingReport(DateTime dAsOfDate, bool lDetails,
                    string cClientList, int nDBKey)
        {

            string cXML = new bzAgingReport().GetAgingReport(
              dAsOfDate, lDetails, cClientList, nDBKey).GetXml();

            return cXML;
        }
    }
}
```

The Aging Report Data Access Class (daAgingReport.cs)

Listing 5-13 contains the complete code for the aging report data access class (daAgingReport.cs in the ConstructionDemo.DataAccess project). Note that this class inherits from your base data access class, so that you can utilize the base method ReadIntoTypedDs.

Listing 5-13. *Aging Report Data Access Class*

```csharp
using System;
using System.Collections.Generic;
using System.Text;
using System.Data;
using System.Data.SqlClient;
using CGS.DataAccess;
using ConstructionDemo.Datasets;



namespace ConstructionDemo.DataAccess
{
    public class daAgingReport : cgsDataAccess
    {


        public dsAgingReport GetAgingReport(DateTime dAsOfDate, bool lDetails,
                                            string cClientList, int nDBKey)
        {

            List<SqlParameter> oParms = new List<SqlParameter>();

            oParms.Add(new SqlParameter("@cCustomerList", cClientList));
            oParms.Add(new SqlParameter("@dAgingDate", dAsOfDate));
            oParms.Add(new SqlParameter("@lShowDetails", true));

            // You can have a base data access class read
            // the results of a stored procedure
            // DIRECTLY into a typed DataSet....no need to do a MERGE
            dsAgingReport odsAgingReport = new dsAgingReport();
            odsAgingReport = this.ReadIntoTypedDs(odsAgingReport,
                        "[dbo].[GetAgingReceivables]", oParms, nDBKey, 0);

            return odsAgingReport;


        }
    }


}
```

Your Final Data Access Class (cgsDataAccess.cs)

Listing 5-14 contains the complete code for the data access class that you'll use in the application. This class resides in the CGS.DataAccess project.

Listing 5-14. *Data Access Class for the Application* (cgsDataAccess.cs)

```csharp
using System;
using System.Data;
using System.Data.SqlClient;
using System.ComponentModel;
using System.Collections;
using System.Collections.Generic;

namespace CGS.DataAccess
{
    public class cgsDataAccess
    {


        private SqlConnection GetConnection(int nDatabaseKey)
        {
            return  new SqlConnection(this.BuildDatabaseConnectionString
                    (nDatabaseKey));
        }

        public T ReadIntoTypedDs<T>(T dsTypedDs, string cStoredProc,
                    List<SqlParameter> oParmList, int nDBKey) where T : DataSet
        {
            return this.ReadIntoTypedDs(dsTypedDs, cStoredProc,
                                        oParmList, nDBKey, 0);
         }




        public T ReadIntoTypedDs<T>(T dsTypedDs, string cStoredProc,
            List<SqlParameter> oParmList, int nDBKey, int nCommandTimeOut )
                where T : DataSet
        {

            SqlConnection oSqlConn = this.GetConnection(nDBKey);
            SqlDataAdapter oSqlAdapter = new SqlDataAdapter(cStoredProc, oSqlConn);
            oSqlAdapter.SelectCommand.CommandType = CommandType.StoredProcedure;

            if(nCommandTimeOut > 0)
                oSqlAdapter.SelectCommand.CommandTimeout = nCommandTimeOut;


            foreach (SqlParameter oParm in oParmList)
                oSqlAdapter.SelectCommand.Parameters.Add(oParm);
```

```
    int nTableCtr = 0;
    foreach (DataTable Dt in dsTypedDs.Tables)
    {
        string cSource = "";
        // Tricky part...first result set from sql is Table, 2nd is Table1,
        //   3rd is Table2
        // So you must check the counter and set the source string correctly
        if (nTableCtr == 0)
            cSource = "Table";
        else
            cSource = "Table" + nTableCtr.ToString().Trim();
        oSqlAdapter.TableMappings.Add(cSource, Dt.TableName.ToString());
        // Set the mapping from the original table name
        // to the corresponding one in your typed dS

        nTableCtr++;
    }

    oSqlAdapter.Fill(dsTypedDs);
    oSqlConn.Close();

    return dsTypedDs;
}


public string BuildDatabaseConnectionString(int nDatabaseKey)
{

    DataSet DsDatabaseInfo = new DataSet();
    AppDomain currentDomain = AppDomain.CurrentDomain;

    string cFileXml=currentDomain.BaseDirectory+"database.xml";
    DsDatabaseInfo.ReadXml(cFileXml);
    DsDatabaseInfo.Tables[0].PrimaryKey =
        new DataColumn[] {DsDatabaseInfo.Tables[0].Columns["DbKey"]};
    DataRow Dr = DsDatabaseInfo.Tables[0].Rows.Find(nDatabaseKey);

    SqlConnectionStringBuilder oStringBuilder =
                    new SqlConnectionStringBuilder();
    oStringBuilder.UserID = Convert.ToString(Dr["UserID"]);
    oStringBuilder.Password = Convert.ToString(Dr["PassWord"]);
    oStringBuilder.InitialCatalog =
                Convert.ToString(Dr["InitialCatalog"]);
    oStringBuilder.DataSource = Convert.ToString(Dr["DataSource"]);
```

```
            oStringBuilder.ConnectTimeout =
                    Convert.ToInt32(Dr["ConnectionTimeOut"]);
            oStringBuilder.MultipleActiveResultSets =
                    Convert.ToBoolean(Dr["MultipleActiveResultSets"]);
            oStringBuilder.AsynchronousProcessing =
                    Convert.ToBoolean(Dr["AsynchronousProcessing"]);

            return oStringBuilder.ConnectionString;

        }


    public cgsDataAccess()
    {
        // TODO: Add constructor logic here
    }
    }
}
```

Once again, we'll cover the typed DataSet in the next chapter, which will help to complete the picture.

Extending a Data Access Class

You now know the basic requirements of your data access class. Next, you'll learn about extending your data access class. Some of the following capabilities will utilize new capabilities in Visual Studio 2005:

- Multiple active result sets

- Loading DataSets without using data adapters

- Supporting multiple database products

- Asynchronous processing

While you won't actually incorporate any of these functions into your data access class, they are still important enhancements that are worth being aware of.

Multiple Active Result Sets

First, let's look at multiple active result sets, which many refer to as MARS. Some developers prefer the ADO.NET DataReader; but Visual Studio .NET 2003 contained a limitation where a single connection object only supported one DataReader. Situations calling for multiple concurrent readers needed to use multiple SQL connections. Visual Studio 2005 supports multiple active readers on a single connection—according to Microsoft, this was one of the most highly requested enhancements. Listing 5-15 demonstrates an example of MARS.

Listing 5-15. *Example of Multiple Active Result Sets*

```
SqlConnection oSqlConn = this.GetConnection(nDatabaseKey);
SqlCommand cmd1 = new SqlCommand("SELECT * FROM Table1",oSqlConn);
SqlCommand cmd2 = new SqlCommand("SELECT * FROM Table2",oSqlConn);
SqlDataReader rReader1 = cmd1.ExecuteReader();
SqlDataReader rReader2 = cmd2.ExecuteReader();
```

■**Note** You must set `MultipleActiveResultSets=true` in the connection string to enable this functionality on a connection object.

Loading a DataSet from a DataReader

Second, Visual Studio 2005 now allows developers to easily load DataReader content into a
DataTable or DataSet, thus reducing the need for the `DataAdapter` class. Listing 5-16 demonstrates a brief example of this.

Listing 5-16. *Loading a DataTable Without a Data Adapter*

```
SqlConnection oSqlConn = this.GetConnection(nDatabaseKey);
SqlCommand cmd1 = new SqlCommand("SELECT * FROM Table1",oSqlConn);
SqlDataReader rReader1 = cmd1.ExecuteReader();
DataTable DtTable = new DataTable();
// Note the second parameter, for overwriting or preserving changes
DtTable.Load(rReader1,LoadOption.OverwriteChanges);
```

Using Provider Factories to Support Multiple Database Products

Third, some database applications must support multiple database products (e.g., an application must support both SQL Server and Oracle). In Visual Studio .NET 2003, developers needed
to code against interfaces for IDbConnection, IDbAdapter, etc., and then write case statements
to determine the connection object to use. Visual Studio 2005 introduces new provider factory
classes to simplify the process.

   You must do two things to use provider factories. First, you must specify a provider string
in MACHINE.CONFIG for each data provider you intend to support. Listing 5-17 shows an example.

Listing 5-17. *Machine.CONFIG Entry for a Provider String*

```
// Each data provider to be used must have a provider string in the machine.config
// <DbProviderFactories>
//    <add name="SqlClient Provider"
//        invariant="System.Data.SqlClient"
//        description=".Net Framework Data Provider for SqlServer"
//        type="System.Data.SqlClient.SqlClientFactory", System.Data,
//        Version=2.0.0.0, Culture=neutral, PublicKeyToken="SomeString"/ >
// </DbProviderFactories>
```

Note the invariant attribute (essentially, the name of the database provider): the second step is to supply this name to the ADO.NET provider factory classes. Listing 5-18 shows an example of using the factory classes to perform database queries.

Listing 5-18. *Using the Provider Factory Classes*

```
DbProviderFactory oFactory =
  new DbProviderFactories.GetFactory("System.Data.SqlClient");
DbConnection oConn = oFactory.CreateConnection();
DbCommand oCommand = oFactory.CreateCommand();
oCommand.CommandText = "SELECT * FROM <sometable> WHERE <cond>";
DbParameter oParm = oCommand.CreateParameter();
oParm.ParameterName = "@MyParameter";
oParm.Value = 12345;
oCommand.Parameters.Add(oParm);
oConn.Open();
IdataReader oReader = oCommand.ExecuteReader();

// Execute your code against the reader, then close
oReader.Close();
oConn.Close();
```

Asynchronous Processing Made Simple

Fourth, Visual Studio 2005 now allows developers to easily process database tasks asynchronously. In Visual Studio .NET 2003, developers needed to use asynchronous delegates to simulate asynchronous processing, a task that many developers chose not to implement. Fortunately, the SQL Server data provider in Visual Studio 2005 now supports asynchronous database interactions, thanks to two new features: new member functions in SqlCommand and a new IAsyncResult interface that represents the status of an asynchronous operation.

The SqlCommand object contains the following new member functions that you can use for asynchronous processing:

- BeginExecuteReader() and EndExecuteReader()

- BeginExecuteNonQuery() and EndExecuteNonQuery()

- BeginExecuteXmlReader() and EndExecuteXmlReader()

Visual Studio 2005 provides three methods for working with asynchronous commands:

- *Polling method*: This requires using the new IsCompleted property.

- *The callback model*: The developer specifies a function to be executed when the asynchronous command completes. The BeginXXX() methods contain an overload for a delegate parameter.

- *Synchronization objects (the wait model)*: The IAsyncResult object listed previously contains a WaitHandle property.

Note the `Begin` and `End` prefixes on each of these methods. These all implement the new `IAsyncResult` interface in Visual Studio 2005. Any time you begin an asynchronous process using one of the methods just listed, the method returns an `IAsyncResult` object that represents the status of the asynchronous process. Table 5-1 lists the main properties of `IAsyncResult`.

Table 5-1. *Main Properties for IAsyncResult*

Property	Description
`AsyncState`	Object that contains information about the asynchronous process. For example, you can cast this object to the `SqlCommand` associated with the process (particularly valuable in the callback model).
`AsyncWaitHandle`	`WaitHandle` object that you can use (in conjunction with the wait model).
`CompletedSynchronously`	Property that indicates whether the asynchronous operation completed synchronously.
`IsCompleted`	Property that indicates whether the asynchronous operation has completed (used in the polling model).

■**Note** You must set `Async=true` in the connection string for asynchronous processing to work.

Asynchronous Processing Using the Polling Model

Listing 5-19 demonstrates the polling model, which is the simplest form of asynchronous processing. As the name implies, you can poll the new Boolean property `IsCompleted`, which indicates whether the asynchronous operation is finished. You can issue the `BeginExecuteReader()` method, perform other tasks, and then check to see whether `IsCompleted` is true.

Listing 5-19. *Basic Asynchronous Processing Using the Polling Method*

```
SqlConnection oSqlConn = this.GetConnection(nDatabaseKey);
oSqlConn.Open();
SqlCommand oCmd = new SqlCommand("SELECT * FROM Orders", oSqlConn);
IAsyncResult oAR = oCmd.BeginExecuteReader();

while (oAR.IsCompleted == false) {
  // Do something while waiting
}

SqlDataReader r = oCmd.EndExecuteReader(oAR);
oMyConn.Close();
```

Asynchronous Processing Using the Callback Model

You can also define and register an event handler in conjunction with asynchronous command execution. As shown in Listing 5-20, you define an asynchronous callback delegate that should be called when the asynchronous process completes. You then pass that delegate as a parameter to one of the overloads for BeginExecuteReader. The actual event that you define (GetResult) will receive the IAsyncResult object and will cast the object's AsyncState property as the original SqlCommand object. From there, you can capture the data from the reader.

Listing 5-20. *Basic Example of the Callback Model*

```
SqlConnection oSqlConn = this.GetConnection(nDatabaseKey);
oSqlConn.Open();
SqlCommand oCmd = new SqlCommand("SELECT * FROM Orders", oSqlConn);
AsyncCallback oCallBack = new AsyncCallback(GetResult);

oCmd.BeginExecuteReader(oCallBack, oCmd,CommandBehavior.CloseConnection);

public void GetResult(IAsyncResult result)
{
    SqlCommand oCmd = (SqlCommand)result.AsyncState;
    SqlDataReader rdr =oCmd.EndExecuteReader(result);
    //  Do something with the reader
}
```

Asynchronous Processing Using the Wait Model

You can implement asynchronous processing in conjunction with utilizing multiple active result sets. This demonstrates some of the true power that ADO.NET offers in Visual Studio 2005. You may need to retrieve multiple sets of data to populate multiple data-bound controls in the user interface. You might also need to concurrently retrieve data from different data sources (which might even include multiple physical databases), and then define a specific point where no further processing should occur until all retrieval processes are complete.

You can start your retrieval processes asynchronously, and use WaitHandles to define where all subsequent execution should wait until all the retrieval processing has finished. The final example (Listing 5-21) utilizes the wait model, where you create an array of WaitHandle objects (from the System.Threading namespace)

In Listing 5-21, you set out to retrieve data from multiple tables. Once again you call BeginExecuteReader, which returns an IAsyncResult object. The IAsyncResult object exposes a property called AsyncWaitHandle, which you store in a WaitHandle array. Finally, you call WaitAll (again, from the System.Threading namespace) and pass your WaitHandle array as a parameter. You are guaranteed that no further code execution will occur until all retrievals complete.

■**Tip** Alternatively, you can use WaitAny, which also receives an array of WaitHandles. Execution will wait until any of the processes associated with those handles completes.

Listing 5-21. *Basic Example of the Wait Model*

```
SqlConnection oSqlConn = this.GetConnection(nDatabaseKey);
oSqlConn.Open();
SqlCommand oCmd1 = new SqlCommand("SELECT * FROM Orders", oMyConn);
SqlCommand oCmd2 = new SqlCommand("SELECT * FROM shippers", oMyConn);

WaitHandle[] oHandles = new WaitHandle[2];

IAsyncResult oResult1 = oCmd1.BeginExecuteReader();
IAsyncResult oResult2 = oCmd2.BeginExecuteReader();

oHandles[0] = oResult1.AsyncWaitHandle;
oHandles[1] = oResult2.AsyncWaitHandle;

WaitHandle.WaitAll(oHandles);

SqlDataReader oReader1 = oCmd1.EndExecuteReader(oResult1);
SqlDataReader oReader2 = oCmd2.EndExecuteReader(oResult2);


oMyConn.Close();
```

■ **Note** You cannot use WaitHandles in a Single Threaded Apartment Model (STAThread).

A Final Word on Asynchronous Command Execution

The new capabilities in ADO.NET to implement asynchronous processing provide great power to scale out complex back-end processing tasks. Of course, any technology that exposes this much power should be used judiciously, For instance, asynchronous processing using DataReaders can potentially lock a data buffer on the server: this may be accentuated by any additional waiting for other processes. Also, your implementation of asynchronous processing may cause a performance hit on the server. In general, it is best to use asynchronous processing on operations that you know will require some time on the server, and where you could be performing other critical tasks while waiting for those processes to complete.

Summary

In this chapter, you saw how to build a data access component that allows you to work with multiple back ends and to run different back-end database processes. You also wrote code to leverage .NET Generics, so that you can populate any DataSet (including a typed DataSet) from a stored procedure. You also looked at some of the new capabilities in the SqlClient database provider for Visual Studio 2005 that allow you to implement multiple active result sets, provider factories, and asynchronous command processing.

Now that you've constructed a data access layer, your next step is to look at the content and format of what the data layer returns. Your result sets will contain data for aging receivables reports, timesheets, and other reporting data: we'll introduce you to a technique for representing this data in a strongly-typed manner, using strongly-typed DataSets. The next chapter will demonstrate how typed DataSets can simplify any processing of the result sets. We'll also show how to utilize the strongly-typed result sets in the business layer, to execute any necessary postquery data manipulation.

■ ■ ■

CHAPTER 6

Using Strongly-Typed DataSets

In this chapter, we'll talk about strongly-typed DataSets (which we'll refer to as simply typed DataSets) and how they help in a reporting solution. We'll explain what typed DataSets are and we'll cover the different ways you can build and integrate them into your reporting process. We'll also look closely at the many benefits they provide at different stages of an application. In the next chapter, we'll look at some advanced uses of typed DataSets. Specifically in this chapter, we'll cover the following:

- What typed DataSets are and how they differ from untyped DataSets.

- How to create typed DataSets: you can either generate them from your stored procedure result set structures or create them manually.

- Specific benefits of typed DataSets in detail.

- How you can use typed DataSets not only for reporting, but also for some of the new data-binding capabilities of the `DataGridView` in Visual Studio 2005.

- Some of the shortcomings of typed DataSets, and some of the ways you can work around them.

- A look back at **the entire architecture** up to this point. We'll review what you're now able to accomplish and how you can use your back-end processes to populate an instance of a typed DataSet for your report.

Note Your application will store typed DataSets in a separate project, `ConstructionDemo.Datasets`. You will use the typed DataSets to store the result sets from your stored procedures, and you'll bind the typed DataSets into your Crystal Reports files when you generate the reports.

What Are Typed DataSets?

A typed DataSet is a strongly-typed container for collections of business entity data and inherits from the `System.Data.DataSet` class. However, unlike the standard DataSet that features late binding and weak typing, typed DataSets provide strongly-typed access to data. This means that they expose table, column, and relation objects as named properties, rather than generic collection elements. Essentially, you can write code as `MyRow.ClientName`, as opposed to `MyRow["ClientName"]`.

Typed DataSets also give you the ability to use IntelliSense for statement completion and type checking at compile time. In the context of reporting, they aid in data-driven report design and provide an excellent form of self-documentation of stored procedure result sets. Also (as you'll see in the next chapter), when you need further massaged and summarized result sets, typed DataSets add a level of efficiency and structure to the code you write. Typed DataSets also simplify data binding. Several of the visual designers in Visual Studio 2005 are capable of reading typed DataSet definitions, which simplifies the process of constructing user interfaces. And last but **certainly** not least, typed DataSets improve your productivity when building reports with Crystal Reports (which you'll see later in this book).

Building Typed DataSets for This Application

In this chapter, we'll walk you through the steps to construct typed DataSets. First, you'll build a typed DataSet from a prebuilt schema; then, you'll construct a typed DataSet manually using the Visual Studio 2005 typed DataSet editor.

Building a Utility to Generate a Typed DataSet from Your Stored Procedures

In Chapter 3, we covered the stored procedure and the result set for the aging receivables report. Because you've already established the entire result set, you can easily use it to create a typed DataSet. You'll do it by writing a simple Windows Forms developer utility that does the following:

1. The utility calls the stored procedure `GetAgingReceivables`, which you wrote back in Chapter 3. You'll call the stored procedure using your base data access class (`cgsDataAccess`).

2. This will return a standard untyped DataSet. You'll take the DataSet, set the table names the way you want them, and write out the DataSet as an XML Schema Definition (XSD) file.

3. Finally, you'll read the XSD into your `ConstructionDemo.Datasets` project as a typed DataSet.

Here are the steps you'll take to build this utility. You'll build it specifically for the aging receivables report, though you'll easily see how to expand this to cover schema generation from the other application stored procedures.

1. First, create a new stand-alone Windows forms project, and add a .NET reference to `CGS.DataAccess`, your base data access class. (Call the project `DeveloperUtilities`.)

2. Make sure to store your `Database.XML` (from Chapter 3) in the `BIN\DEBUG` folder of the project you're creating (or in the folder where the project executable will reside). Unlike all the other code in this book, which is designed for a distributed architecture, this utility assumes direct access to the database server and DataSource.

3. Change the name of the default form in the project from Form1 to FrmGenerateSchemas. In the default form for the project, add a command button called btnGenerateAgingSchema.

4. Paste the code in Listing 6-1 into the new form (FrmGenerateSchemas).

Listing 6-1. *Utility Form to Generate XML Schemas*

```csharp
using System;
using System.Collections.Generic;
using System.ComponentModel;
using System.Data;
using System.Drawing;
using System.Text;
using System.Windows.Forms;
using System.Data.SqlClient;
using CGS.DataAccess;

namespace DeveloperUtilities
{
    public partial class FrmGenerateSchemas : Form
    {

        string cLocation = "c:\\MyXmlFiles\\";
        int nDBKey = 1;


        public FrmGenerateSchemas()
        {
            InitializeComponent();
        }

        private void btnGenerateAgingSchema_Click(object sender, EventArgs e)
        {
            this.GenerateAgingSchema();
        }


        private void GenerateAgingSchema()
        {
            // Create SQL parameters using a type-safe list
            List<SqlParameter> oParms = new List<SqlParameter>();

            oParms.Add(new SqlParameter("@cCustomerList", "1"));
            oParms.Add(new SqlParameter("@dAgingDate", new DateTime(2006, 1, 1)));
            oParms.Add(new SqlParameter("@lShowDetails", true));
```

```
        // Call your form method, which calls the base CGS data access class
        DataSet dsReturn = this.GetResults("GetAgingReceivables", oParms);

        // Set the names, for both the set name and the table names

        dsReturn.DataSetName = "dsAgingReport";
        dsReturn.Tables[0].TableName = "dtAgingDetails";
        dsReturn.Tables[1].TableName = "dtAgingSummary";
        dsReturn.Tables[2].TableName = "dtAgingBrackets";
        dsReturn.Tables[3].TableName = "dtClients";

        string cXMLFile = cLocation + "dsAgingReport.xsd";
        dsReturn.WriteXmlSchema(cXMLFile);
        MessageBox.Show(cXMLFile + " successfully created!");

    }


    private DataSet GetResults(string cStoredProc, List<SqlParameter> oParms)
    {

        cgsDataAccess oBaseData = new cgsDataAccess();
        DataSet dsReturn = new DataSet();
        return oBaseData.ReadIntoTypedDs(dsReturn, cStoredProc, oParms,
                                                                nDBKey);


    }

  }
}
```

After you run the code in Listing 6-1, you can create the aging report typed DataSet from the XSD. To do so, open (or create) the project ConstructionDemo.Datasets. The project is created as a .NET class library. Once you create/open the project, load Solution Explorer, right-click, choose Add ➤ Existing Item, and then navigate to the folder that contains dsAgingReport.xsd (the file you created in Listing 6-1). Figure 6-1 shows the end result—a typed DataSet in Solution Explorer. Any project in the solution that needs to use the typed DataSet for the aging receivables report must add ConstructionDemo.DataSets as a .NET reference.

Figure 6-1. *Solution Explorer after adding the XSD*

Figure 6-2 shows the `dsAgingReport.xsd` file in the Visual Studio 2005 default DataSet Editor.

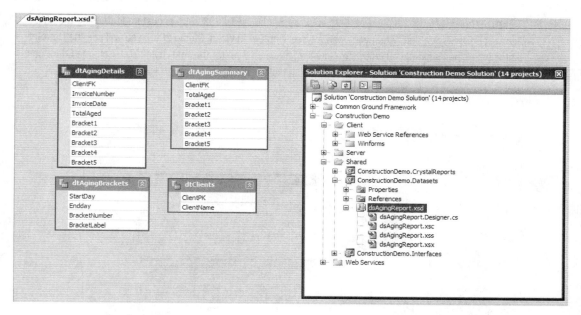

Figure 6-2. *Default DataSet Editor*

You can choose other methods for viewing/editing the typed DataSet by right-clicking the DataSet in Solution Explorer and selecting Open With to bring up the dialog shown in Figure 6-3.

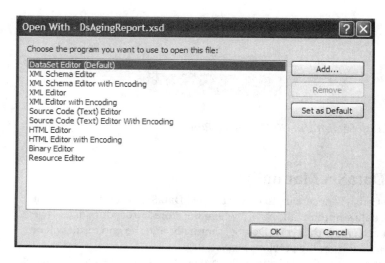

Figure 6-3. *Options for editing a typed DataSet*

Finally, Figure 6-4 shows the XML Schema Editor that many utilized in Visual Studio 2003.

> ■**Note** Those who used typed DataSets in Visual Studio .NET 2003 were accustomed to using the XML Schema Editor. By default, when you open a typed DataSet in Visual Studio 2005, you will see the DataSet Editor, which has a simplified interface. However, those who prefer the "old-style" XML Schema Editor can select the XML Schema Editor from the Open With dialog.

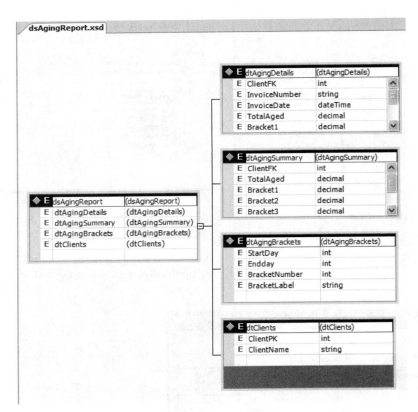

Figure 6-4. *Viewing a typed DataSet using the XML Schema Editor*

Creating a Typed DataSet Manually

There may be situations where it is necessary to create a typed DataSet (to build a report or to write some middleware data summarization), but where the stored procedure doesn't yet exist. In this instance, you can create the typed DataSet manually, and the end result will be the same as if you had created it from the previous steps.

To create a typed DataSet manually, navigate to the project that stores the typed DataSets, right-click, and choose Add ➤ New Item. Visual Studio 2005 will display a dialog box like the one in Figure 6-5, where you can select DataSet as the installed template and enter the name.

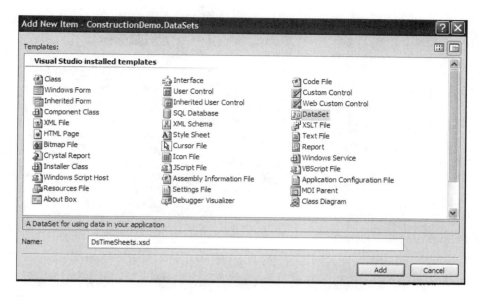

Figure 6-5. *Adding a new typed DataSet*

After clicking Add in the dialog, Visual Studio 2005 will display the DataSet Designer (see Figure 6-6).

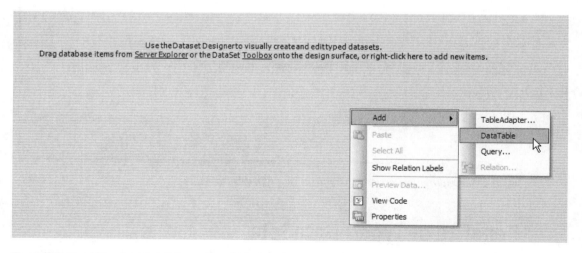

Figure 6-6. *Creating a new typed DataSet with the default DataSet Designer*

Once you begin creating DataTables within the typed DataSet, you can right-click to add columns (see Figure 6-7) or right-click to view/set the properties of an individual column (see Figure 6-8).

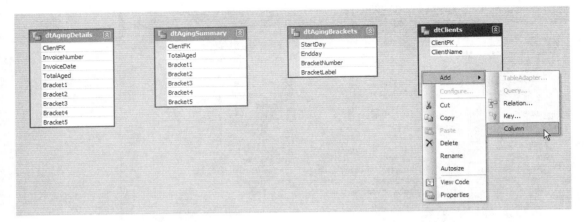

Figure 6-7. *Adding columns to a typed DataSet*

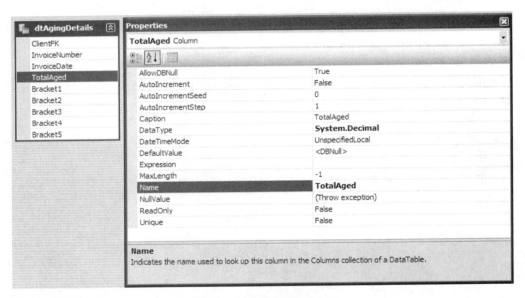

Figure 6-8. *Viewing properties of a column in a typed DataSet*

Benefits of Typed DataSets

Typed DataSets have many benefits over standard DataSets. Let's take a look at how they simplify and enhance the development process.

Strong Typing

Typed DataSets give you the ability to use IntelliSense for statement completion and type checking at compile time as shown in Figure 6-9. Compare that to an untyped example as shown in Figure 6-10. Note that in the second example, you cannot use IntelliSense, so you must type the column name correctly (or receive a runtime error), and you must cast the column object to the correct DataType.

```
Masonry.DataSets.DsMasonryTimeSheets oTimeSheets = new DsMasonryTimeSheets();

foreach(DsMasonryTimeSheets.DtMasonryTimeSheetsRow oRow in oTimeSheets.DtMasonryTimeSheets.Rows) {
    int nHoursWorked = oRow.Ho
```

Figure 6-9. *Example of statement completion with typed DataSets*

```
foreach(DataRow dr in oTimeSheets.Tables["DtTimeSheets"].Rows) {
    // no statement completion, we must make sure to type the column name correctly,
    // or we'll get a nasty run-time error

    // we also must cast the column to the necessary data type
    int nHoursWorked = Convert.ToInt32(dr["HoursWorked"]);
```

Figure 6-10. *Example of an untyped DataSet*

Typed DataSets also make it easy to define default column values when you add new DataRows (see the DefaultValue property back in Figure 6-8).

Easier Traversing of Hierarchical Data

If a typed DataSet contains table relations, the XML Schema Definition tool adds methods to the typed DataSet class for traversing hierarchical data. For example, a developer can write parent/child code for the tables DtOrderHeader and DtOrderDetail by using two methods that the .NET schema definition tool automatically generates: GetDtOrderDetailRows() and GetDtOrderHeaderRow(). A developer can use DataSet annotations to define alternate naming conventions: we'll cover this later in the chapter in the section called "Overcoming the Shortcomings."

Find Your Way Easier

Additionally, if you define a primary key for any table in a typed DataSet, the class exposes a FindXXX() method associated with the column name. A developer can perform a find against a table with a primary key of OrderID by using the pregenerated method FindByOrderID(). If the primary key is a concatenation of two columns (for example, CustomerID and OrderID), the developer would use FindByCustomerIDOrderID().

In general, there's less code to write because the typed DataSet class contains generated code for building the schema and creating the necessary table, column, row, and relation objects. The code you do have to write can be cleaner, more compact, and easier to maintain.

Null Value Handling

Working with null values is a little easier when using typed DataSets. Each typed DataRow contains a method to check whether a column value is null: `MyRow.IsAddressNull()`. The DataRow also contains a second method to set a column value to null: `MyRow.SetAddressNull()`. Again, we'll cover annotations later, which also provide flexibility in dealing with nulls.

But Wait—More Benefits!

The benefits that typed DataSets have over normal DataSets are not the only advantages you gain by using them. Let's look at some more.

Reporting

Typed DataSets are valuable in the reporting process, as we'll demonstrate in later chapters. A developer can design report content from a typed DataSet definition, even before the stored procedures are constructed. Once again, the typed DataSet becomes a form of documentation for the report DataSource. We've developed hundreds of reports using different methodologies and find typed DataSets to be the most efficient.

■**Note** There is a common misconception that utilizing or even referring to typed DataSets in the presentation tier is an example of coupling the presentation tier with the data tier, and therefore not a good practice. The methodology in this book populates the typed DataSets in the data access/business layer, which is completely outside the client piece. The same general approach would be required to populate custom business collections. The DataSet project resides outside of both tiers, and it used as a reference for tiers that either need to populate it or bind to it.

Subclassing

Since a typed DataSet is a class that inherits from `System.DataSet`, you can further subclass a typed DataSet to add validation code or any other methods. Alternatively, you can also take advantage of the new partial class capability in Visual Studio 2005 to add method code for your DataSet.

Simplify Data Binding

Typed DataSets can simplify design-time data binding—a developer can define a DataSource in the property sheet. Because your sample application stores all typed DataSets as a separate project DLL, a developer can add the DLL to the Visual Studio toolbox, and then drop an instance of the typed DataSet onto a form as a precursor to design-time data binding. Developers who define DataSources in code still gain the advantage of table/column name discovery through IntelliSense.

Using Typed DataSets with Designer Tools

You can used typed DataSets with many different designer tools. Visual Studio 2005 provides new designer tools for use with typed DataSets to potentially increase your productivity in building user-interface modules. Let's take a look at them.

Using Typed DataSets for Reports

Although we won't walk you through the creation of the actual reports using Crystal Reports and typed DataSets until Chapters 8 and 9, we'll give you a quick overview here. In a broad nutshell, to build reports, you go through two steps. First, you open the typed DataSet schema that you'll use to design the report (`dsAgingReport`, for instance) using the Crystal Reports **Database Expert** (see Figure 6-11).

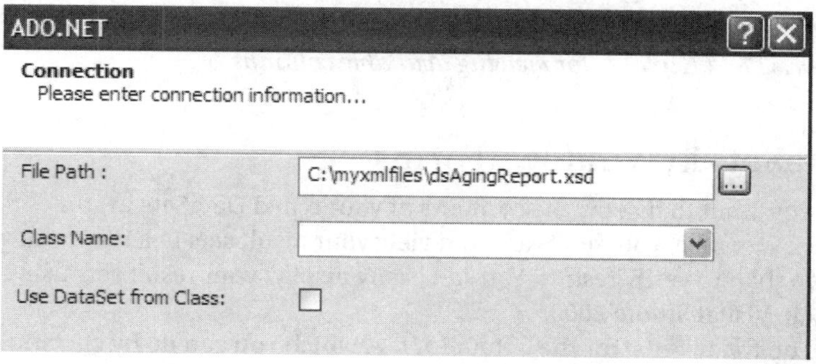

Figure 6-11. *Specifying a typed DataSet for a report using the Crystal Reports Database Expert*

Second, once you've specified the typed DataSet as the design-time DataSource, you can use the Crystal Reports **Field Explorer** (see Figure 6-12) to drag/drop data columns onto the report layout area, as needed.

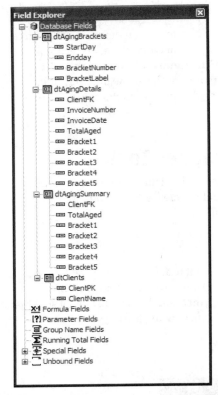

Figure 6-12. *The Crystal Reports Field Explorer, for viewing available columns*

Viewing Typed DataSets in Windows Forms

There may be times where you want to display the contents of your typed DataSets in something other than a report. For instance, you may want to review your result sets in a Windows Form—if for no other reason than to verify results. You can easily display your result sets using the improved DataGridView in Visual Studio 2005.

Your first step is to pull up the task list for the DataGridView, which you can do by clicking in the upper-right corner of the control (see Figure 6-13).

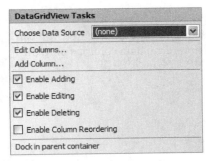

Figure 6-13. *Retrieving the DataGridView tasks to view available options*

You'll want to click Choose Data Source from Figure 6-13. Visual Studio will then display the pop-up window in Figure 6-14, where you'll select the option Add Project Data Source.

Figure 6-14. *Selecting a design-time DataSource for the DataGridView*

Next, you need to specify the type of DataSource to bind to the DataGridView. Note that at design time, any form or report that you build will not have any direct connection to a database connection or web service. All that you have (and all that you need) is the result set definitions in your database project (ConstructionDemo.DataSets). As shown in Figure 6-15, you will select Object as your DataSource Type.

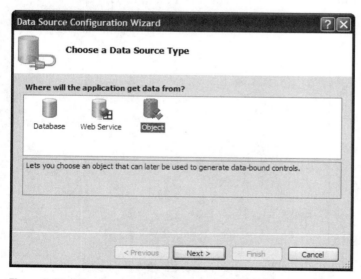

Figure 6-15. *Selecting an object as a design-time DataSource*

Once you select Object, Visual Studio 2005 will display all available objects that either reside in the current project or were defined as .NET references in the current project. Simply by adding ConstructionDemo.DataSets as a reference to your current project, you can select the desired DataSet (dsAgingReport) as shown in Figure 6-16.

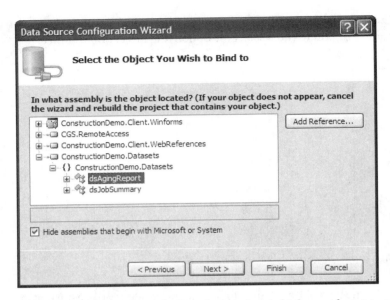

Figure 6-16. *Selecting from the DataSets project (which must be set as a reference)*

Since dsAgingReport contains four DataTables, you need to specify which table to display (which will become the value of the DataMember property of the DataGridView). In Figure 6-17, you can select the desired table from the pop-up DataSource for the DataGridView.

Figure 6-17. *Select the corresponding data member—in this case, the summary data table*

Now that you've specified the DataSource, Visual Studio 2005 automatically generates all of the column objects for the DataGridView. You can customize the column headings, alignment, and overall appearance (see Figure 6-18).

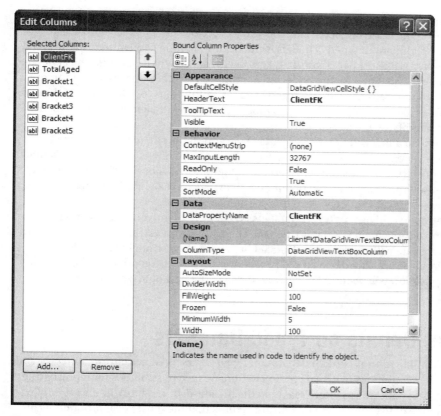

Figure 6-18. *Columns from the design-time DataSource*

At runtime, you can bind the DataGridView to an instance of a populated dsAgingReport object, as follows:

```
this.grvSummary.DataSource = dsAgingReport.dtAgingSummary
```

Note Chapter 13 will cover more details for design-time data binding and displaying result sets using Windows Forms in Visual Studio 2005.

Overcoming the Shortcomings

Typed DataSets aren't perfect, because they carry overhead. While certain specific aspects of typed DataSets are faster than untyped DataSets, instantiating a complex typed DataSet can be costly. Of course, costly is a relative term. In many instances, we are talking about half a second, which, for many applications, is meaningless. But for some, it's the low-hanging fruit.

An application that frequently creates an instance of the same typed DataSet will spend a measured percentage of time on the creation process. Uri N. has developed a proxy class for typed DataSets so that the actual creation only needs to occur once. You can find his article and source code on the Code Project at www.codeproject.com/csharp/TypedDSProxy.asp.

Another complaint about typed DataSets is the default naming conventions in the typed DataSet class for items like the DataTable/DataRow objects and methods/events. The generated names may not be consistent with the preferred naming conventions on your development projects. Fortunately, developers can use typed DataSet annotations to solve some of the common naming issues, by allowing developers to modify the names of elements in the typed DataSet without modifying the actual schema.

Annotations also allow you to specify a nullValue annotation to instruct the typed DataSet class how to react when a column is DbNull. You can optionally tell the typed DataSet to return an empty string or a default replacement value. Shawn Wildermuth demonstrates typed DataSet annotations in an excellent online article that you can find in the recommended reading section at the very end of this chapter.

Another common criticism of typed DataSets is that developers must update them any time a stored procedure changes. That is true (and in reality, if you add a column or table to a result set, the new data will appear in the DataSet: it just won't be strongly-typed). However, if new columns or tables are added to a stored procedure, chances are good that other components of the application will be modified as well to reflect the new data (screens, reports, validations, etc.).

The Great Debate on Typed DataSets

Many blogs and online forums contain debates on typed DataSets versus custom objects. While the new List class capabilities in Visual Studio 2005 create new possibilities for representing data, typed DataSets continue to offer great benefits in data-driven, report-intensive applications. Ironically, one of the things that has surprised us is that the most vocal proponents of typed DataSets have understated how valuable typed DataSets are to the reporting process.

For ubiquitous line-of-business, data-driven applications, the typed DataSet approach provides many benefits. Tasks such as two-way data binding, filtering, sorting, XML integration, setting up relationships between data objects, preserving rowstate information, merging changes, and complex reporting operations are much easier with typed DataSets.

You may have to write additional code—sometimes a substantial amount of code—in the absence of DataSets. Those eschewing typed DataSets should ask themselves—is it worthwhile? And with the performance enhancements in ADO.NET 2.0, will custom code to accomplish these tasks execute as quickly as native ADO.NET 2.0 capabilities? In our opinion, the ability to effectively finish an application more quickly using native capabilities in .NET is a fundamental argument that developers should seriously evaluate when opting for approaches that exclude DataSets.

Stop the Presses! Something Doesn't Match

Unless you're a perfect developer who has never made a mistake, you've probably discovered midway through a process that some aspect of the design needs to be changed or tweaked. (We once knew a project manager who told his developers, "Once I thought I made a mistake—but it turned out I was wrong.")

Well, as the saying goes, "Houston, we have a problem." The dtAgingBrackets table in dsAgingReport contains one row for each aging bracket: it mirrors the AgingBrackets table in the database. However, you need to display the aging bracket labels as column headings; there-fore, a flat one-row table with a column for each bracket will serve you better than a table with one row for each bracket.

You could certainly modify the stored procedure to PIVOT the rows into columns. Another approach would be to manually add a DataTable to dsAgingReport with a fixed num-ber of columns for each bracket. Call the new DataTable dtBracketColumns, with five string columns (Bracket1 through Bracket5). When you populate an instance of dsAgingReport, you can write some .NET code to scan through the rows in dtAgingBrackets and create a single dtBracketColumns. You need to modify bzAgingReport (in the ConstructionDemo.Business project) as shown in Listing 6-2 to populate the columns in your new table so that you can easily add a "nonnormalized" row to dtBracketColumns for the report.

Listing 6-2. *Modified Aging Report Business Class to Manually Add a Row*

```
using System;
using System.Collections.Generic;
using System.Text;
using ConstructionDemo.Datasets;
using ConstructionDemo.DataAccess;
using CGS.Business;
using ConstructionDemo.Interfaces;

namespace ConstructionDemo.Business
{
    public class bzAgingReport : cgsBaseBusinessObject,
                                IAgingReport<dsAgingReport>
    {
        public dsAgingReport GetAgingReport(DateTime dAsOfDate, bool lDetails,
                                string cClientList, int nDBKey)
        {
            dsAgingReport odsAgingReport = new dsAgingReport();
            odsAgingReport = new daAgingReport().GetAgingReport(
                    dAsOfDate, lDetails, cClientList, nDBKey);

            string[] Brackets = new string[5];

            for(int nRowCtr=0;nRowCtr<5;nRowCtr++)
                Brackets[nRowCtr] =
                    odsAgingReport.dtAgingBrackets[nRowCtr].BracketLabel;

            odsAgingReport.dtBracketColumns.AdddtBracketColumnsRow
                    (Brackets[0],Brackets[1],Brackets[2],Brackets[3],Brackets[4]);

            return odsAgingReport;

        }
    }
}
```

■Note The code in Listing 6-2 is a small example of the capabilities in ADO.NET. Chapter 7 shows a variety of different techniques in ADO.NET for processing data.

Breakpoint: The Architecture As It Stands

Time to take a deep breath and look at what you've accomplished! While you're not generating reports yet, you're able to retrieve data from the back end. Listing 6-3 shows code from a test form in the client piece.

Listing 6-3. *Your Client Code, Which Calls the Back End to Populate the Aging Report DataSet*

```
using System;
using System.Collections.Generic;
using System.ComponentModel;
using System.Data;
using System.Drawing;
using System.Text;
using System.Windows.Forms;
using CGS.RemoteAccess;
using ConstructionDemo.Interfaces;
using ConstructionDemo.Client.WebReferences;
using ConstructionDemo.Datasets;
using System.IO;

// Form initialization code

// Test for web services
this.TestAgingReport(ClientRemoteAccess.ConnectionTypeOptions.WebServices);

// Test for remoting (must have remoting server listener application running)
this.TestAgingReport(ClientRemoteAccess.ConnectionTypeOptions.TcpRemoting);


private void TestAgingReport(ClientRemoteAccess.ConnectionTypeOptions oConnType)
{

    // Create an instance of your Remote Access Factory class
    ClientRemoteAccess oRemoteAccess = new ClientRemoteAccess();

    // You need to set five properties for the factory

    // 1) A type reference to the interface
    oRemoteAccess.tInterface = typeof(ConstructionDemo.Interfaces.IAgingReport<>);
```

```
// 2) The base name of the back-end object
oRemoteAccess.cServiceName = "AgingReport";

// 3) Connection type (remoting or web services)
oRemoteAccess.nConnectionType = oConnType;

// 4) Back-end server address (could be a URL or TCP server address)
oRemoteAccess.cTcpServer = "tcp://localhost";
oRemoteAccess.nTCPPort = 8228;

oRemoteAccess.cWebServiceURL =
        "http://localhost/ConstructionDemo.WebServices/";

// 5) If you're using the web, create instance of local web proxy
//      (subclassed reference)
if (oRemoteAccess.UsingWebServices()==true)
    oRemoteAccess.wService = new wAgingReportRef();


// Now that you've set properties for the factory,
// get an object reference to the back-end object
object oReturnObject = oRemoteAccess.GetAccessObject();

// Create instance of typed DataSet
dsAgingReport dsAgingReport = new dsAgingReport();

// Set some parameters for the aging receivables report
DateTime dAsOfDate = new DateTime(2006,1,1);
bool lUseDetails = true;
string cClientList = "";
int nDBKey = 1;

// If you're using web services,
// create instance of Interface object (as an XML string),
// call back-end method GetAgingReport,
// and convert the XML string back to your typed DataSet

if (oRemoteAccess.UsingWebServices()==true)
{

    IAgingReport<string> oAgingReport;
    oAgingReport = (IAgingReport<string>)oReturnObject;
    string cXMLResults = oAgingReport.GetAgingReport
                    (dAsOfDate, lUseDetails,cClientList,nDBKey);

    dsAgingReport.ReadXml(new StringReader(cXMLResults),
            XmlReadMode.InferSchema);
}
```

```
    else
    {
        // If you're using remoting, create instance of Interface object
        // (as your typed DataSet),
        // call back-end method GetAgingReport, which returns result
        // directly into your typed DataSet
        IAgingReport<dsAgingReport> oAgingReport;
        oAgingReport = (IAgingReport<dsAgingReport>)oReturnObject;
        dsAgingReport = oAgingReport.GetAgingReport
                        (dAsOfDate,lUseDetails,cClientList,nDBKey);
    }

    // At this point, dsAgingReport has been populated!
    // You can use it for your report
}
```

Breaking Down the Code

The code in Listing 6-3 represents a **significant** milestone. It references a great deal of functionality that you've built along the way to retrieve data from the back end and makes use of virtually every technique we've covered so far. Let's step through the different areas of the code:

Setting the References and Namespaces

First, you'll need to set the following .NET references for Listing 6-3:

- `CGS.RemoteAccess.DLL`, which contains the factory method `GetAccessObject`.

- `ConstructionDemo.Client.WebReferences`, which contains the subclassed web references that implement the same generic interface as their remoting business object counterparts. For this example, `ConstructionDemo.Client.WebReferences` contains a web reference (`wAgingReport`) for the server-side aging report web service (`wAgingReport`) that you created back in Chapter 4.

- `ConstructionDemo.Datasets`, which contains all of your typed DataSet definitions (including `dsAgingReport`) as a separate project.

- `ConstructionDemo.Interfaces`, which defines all of the report interfaces (including `IAgingReport`) so that the client-side can communicate with the back-end server.

At the top of Listing 6-3, you'll include several using statements for your .NET references (`ConstructionDemo.Interfaces`, etc.). This allows you to reference objects from these namespaces without needing to specify the entire namespace (i.e., `IAgingReport` versus `ConstructionDemo.Interfaces.IAgingReport`).

■**Note** Appendix C contains the complete technical roadmap and technical reference guide for the application. If you're unsure about a particular reference or the functionality of a particular class, refer to Appendix C.

Using the Factory Communication Class

Second, you'll create an instance of the factory communication class (ClientRemoteAccess) that you built back in Chapter 4. You'll also set the necessary properties for ClientRemoteAccess to function (the server address, how you're connecting, etc.). Table 6-1 lists all the important properties that RemoteAccess class will need and use for handling remote communications. Once you create an instance of ClientRemoteAccess and then set the relevant properties, you can then call the method GetAccessObject, which will return a standard .NET object that you can cast to IAgingReport. At that point, you can work with the back-end object in a strongly-typed manner and discover/execute the methods that IAgingReport exposes (GetAgingReport).

Table 6-1. *RemoteAccess Properties*

Property	Description
ConnectionTypeOptions	An enumeration of available connection options
nConnectionType	The ConnectionTypeOption to be used
tInterface	Type reference to .NET interface to be used
wService	Object for web reference (if web services are being used)
cWebServiceURL	Web service URL (if web services are being used)
cTcpServer	TCP server address (if remoting is being used)
nTcpPort	TCP port number (if remoting is being used)
cServiceName	The name of the back-end object/web service

Handling the Web Reference

Third, as the test in Listing 6-3 uses web services, you need to create an instance of the web service reference (wAgingReport). wAgingReport is your .NET-generated proxy for the actual back-end web service. Here's where you need to put your ".NET thinking cap" on.

When you run a report, you want the same client-side code base to activate and access the report's web service or its business object. Your factory class (RemoteAccess) does much of that work for you. However, your interface-based approach requires that both the web service reference and the business object must implement IAgingReport.

For the business object, this is no problem: your aging report business object implements IAgingReport (and inherits from your base class object that derives from MarshalByRefObject for remoting). Additionally, you defined your web service (wAgingReport) on the server side to implement IAgingReport. So why the need for a thinking cap?

Here's why: when .NET generates the web service reference/proxy class (which you named as wAgingReport on the client side), .NET drops the reference to IAgingReport. (Interfaces aren't relevant to non-.NET clients that look to consume web services.) Therefore, you need to modify wAgingReport on the client side to implement the interface. Unfortunately, you can't simply open wAgingReport in the client project and modify it to implement IAgingReport. (Well, you "could," but .NET will overwrite your modifications any time you update/refresh the web service.)

Fortunately, the solution isn't difficult. If you'll recall back in Listing 4-7 in Chapter 4, you subclassed the client-side `wAgingReport` as `wAgingReportRef` and implemented `IAgingReport` in `wAgingReportRef`:

```
public class wAgingReportRef :
                        wAgingReport.wAgingReport , IAgingReport<string>
```

■Tip Don't try to implement an interface directly in the web reference proxy, as .NET's default behavior is to overwrite it when you update/refresh the web reference. If you need a .NET web reference proxy to implement an interface, subclass the web reference proxy and implement the interface in your subclass. That way, anything you define in the subclass will still be preserved any time you update/refresh the web reference.

Calling the Back End

You're almost there! The code in Listing 6-3 contains a block of code that handles the actual call to `GetAgingReport` in two different ways, based on whether you're using web services or remoting. In Chapter 13, you'll see how to combine these into one method for simplicity, but let's talk about them separately here.

When you call the back end via web services, you must prepare to handle the result set as an XML string. Remember that the web service might some day be consumed by a non-.NET client, so the web service must return a format that other systems can read (XML). So your type reference to `IAgingReport` must specify a `string` as a placeholder. Additionally, you need to convert the return XML string to a typed DataSet so that you can ultimately bind it with the report (or any other data-bound controls you might use). You can easily accomplish this by creating a `StringReader` from the return XML string, and then pass the resulting `StringReader` object to the DataSet's `ReadXml` method.

```
dsAgingReport.ReadXml(
        new StringReader(cXMLResults), XmlReadMode.InferSchema);
```

When you call the back end via remoting, the process is a bit more "direct," as you're executing a process that is designed for pure .NET-to-.NET communications. The back-end remoting object for the aging receivables report returns an instance of `dsAgingReport`, so all you need to do is specify as such in the placeholder for `IAgingReport`: in this instance, you have assurances that your call to `GetAgingReport` will return an instance of `dsAgingReport`.

Some Improvements for Later

The code in Listing 6-3 represents everything that your framework allows you to do, at this point. Some of the steps in the code are manual steps: we'll cover the following functionality later in the book to simplify these steps:

1. At the top of the code, you needed to set options for the server address and your communication method (web services or remoting). You shouldn't have to do that every time you need to retrieve data: you'll want to specify that once, at the beginning of the application, based on how the end user signs on to the application.

2. You manually defined the report parameters (as of date, list of clients, etc.). You'll want to present the end user with an options dialog to make these selections.

3. You built an `If...then...else` block: the block handles the return result set as an XML string if you're connecting through web services and handles the return result set as a DataSet if you're connecting through remoting. You can simplify this code further with one more class, which we'll cover in Chapter 13.

■**Note** Listing 6-3 represents a significant milestone. While you're not yet generating reports, and you still have a few tweaks to make, you are able to retrieve strongly-typed data from the back end using your existing architecture and factory class.

Summary

This chapter provided an overview of typed DataSets, as well as their benefits. We covered the different ways to build them and provided an overview of ways to use them. The end of this chapter represented a breaking point to review the overall architecture and what you can currently accomplish.

In the next chapter, we'll cover the benefits of typed DataSets in more detail with some practical examples. We'll also address one of the larger criticisms about .NET—that ADO.NET is not powerful enough to handle extensive data-summarization operations.

Recommended Reading

Brian Noyes. *Data Binding with Windows Forms 2.0: Programming Smart Client Data Applications with .NET*. Boston, MA: Addison-Wesley, 2006.

Shawn Wildermuth. "Improving Typed DataSets." `www.ondotnet.com/pub/a/dotnet/2003/03/31/typeddatasetannotations.html`. March 2003.

■ ■ ■

CHAPTER 7

Middleware Data Summarization Using Typed DataSets

Throughout this book, we've emphasized the role of stored procedures as a key component in reporting applications. This assumes that developers are using a database that supports stored procedures as well as a strong SQL implementation. In some instances, however, the back-end database may not fully support the types of data summarization and aggregation that we covered back in the chapters that discussed SQL Server stored procedures. And even if developers are using a database that supports these features, the development standards might strongly discourage (or even prohibit) the use of database-specific features. In either situation, developers may face the challenge of returning partially summarized (or even unsummarized) data from the database, and then performing the final summarization before generating the report. This chapter takes one of the report result sets (the aging receivables report) and demonstrates how you can utilize the features of ADO.NET to produce the same result as if you had used stored procedures.

Capabilities in ADO.NET

ADO.NET is not a full-blown data management module with SQL support. For that reason, ADO.NET is sometimes undervalued as a tool for working with data. However, ADO.NET contains more functionality than is commonly recognized. One of the (many) challenges in learning .NET is building an understanding of everything that ADO.NET can do.

If you ever read *Cyrano de Bergerac* (or saw one of the movies based on it, or even the movie *Roxanne*), you may recall in the beginning that Cyrano challenges himself to come up with a number of creative insults for his nose. Well, this chapter makes the promise to demonstrate ten different techniques in ADO.NET, using the aging receivables report as an example. The ten are as follows:

1. Creating an instance of a typed DataSet and adding rows using strong typing

2. Setting default data column values for new rows

3. Looping through strongly-typed row collections

4. Performing date math and other miscellaneous date functions

5. Performing lookups

6. Filtering data

7. Performing the equivalent of a SELECT DISTINCT

8. Working with data relations

9. Computing subtotals automatically

10. Computing subtotals manually

If you wish to "skip ahead" and see the end result, Listing 7-10 contains the complete source code for this example. All code listings prior to that show individual pieces that correspond to the preceding ten points.

After we cover these ten areas, we'll close out the chapter by looking at some miscellaneous tips for using ADO.NET.

The Scenario: Produce an Aging Report Result Set from a Flat List of Invoices

We'll intentionally make this a worst-case scenario: your only result set from the database is a flat list of invoices that you'll store into a typed DataSet called dsInvoices, as shown in Table 7-1.

Table 7-1. *Flat List of Invoices As a Result Set*

ColumnName
ClientPK
ClientName
InvoiceDate
InvoiceNumber
InvoiceAmount

The goal is to process this data into the typed DataSet definition for the aging receivables report (dsAgingReport), which we presented back in Chapter 6. For convenience, we'll display the structure for dsAgingReport in Table 7-2.

Table 7-2. *Structure for Result Set*

TableName	ColumnName	Data Type
dtAgingBrackets	StartDay	Int32
	Endday	Int32
	BracketNumber	Int32
	BracketLabel	String

TableName	ColumnName	Data Type
dtAgingDetails	ClientFK	Int32
	InvoiceNumber	
	InvoiceDate	
	TotalAged	
	Bracket1	
	Bracket2	
	Bracket3	
	Bracket4	
	Bracket5	
	TotalAged	
		String
		DateTime
		Decimal
		Decimal
		Decimal
		Decimal
		Decimal
		Decimal
		Decimal
		Decimal
dtAgingSummary	ClientFK	Int32
	TotalAged	Decimal
	Bracket1	Decimal
	Bracket2	Decimal
	Bracket3	Decimal
	Bracket4	Decimal
	Bracket5	Decimal
dtBracketColumns	Bracket1	String
	Bracket2	String
	Bracket3	String
	Bracket4	String
	Bracket5	String
dtClients	ClientPK	nt32
	ClientName	tring

In order to read through the invoices from the structure in Table 7-1 and populate the result set for the structure in Table 7-2, you'll need to perform the following steps (most of which use ADO.NET functionality):

1. Create an instance of both data structures.

2. Manually populate the bracket definitions (aging bracket 1 is for invoices that have aged between 1 and 30 days, bracket 2 for 31 to 60 days, etc.).

3. Establish a report "as-of" date (i.e., the effective date of the report).

4. Read through each invoice, and determine the number of days it has aged from the as-of date. If it has aged at least one day, insert a row into the aging details table (dtAgingDetails), determine the bracket to which the aging amount belongs by looking up the number of days in the bracket table, and place the amount into the corresponding bracket in dtAgingDetails.

5. Build the dtClients table by determining the unique set of clients in the source dtInvoices table.

6. Calculate subtotals on the aging bracket columns for each client.

For those who like to jump to the end to see how things turn out, Listing 7-10 at the end of the chapter contains the final listing for these tasks. The remainder of this chapter covers each of the individual steps.

Step 1: Creating an Instance and Adding Rows

Once you've created the typed DataSet definition (see Chapter 6 for details on creating it), you can create an instance object with the code in Listing 7-1. Once you've created an object instance, you need to manually add bracket definitions for each aging bracket that the final report will present.

You can add rows one of two different ways. First, you can use the method that Visual Studio 2005 creates when you define a strongly-typed DataTable. Note the AdddtAgingBracketsRow() methods in Listing 7-1: VS 2005 builds these methods automatically and establishes the parameters based on the columns in the DataTable. Figure 7-1 demonstrates how IntelliSense assists with statement completion by displaying all of the column parameters.

Listing 7-1. *Creating the Aging Report Typed DataSet and Manually Adding Rows*

```
dsAgingReport odsAgingReport = new dsAgingReport();

// Fill in the aging brackets manually (as if you'd pulled them from the database)

odsAgingReport.dtAgingBrackets.AdddtAgingBracketsRow(  1, 30, 1, "< 30 days");
odsAgingReport.dtAgingBrackets.AdddtAgingBracketsRow( 31, 60, 2, "31-60 days");
odsAgingReport.dtAgingBrackets.AdddtAgingBracketsRow( 61, 90, 3, "61-90 days");
odsAgingReport.dtAgingBrackets.AdddtAgingBracketsRow( 91, 120, 4, "91-120 days");
odsAgingReport.dtAgingBrackets.AdddtAgingBracketsRow(121, 99999, 5, "> 120 days");
```

odsAgingReport.dtAgingBrackets.AdddtAgingBracketsRow(

▪2 of 2▪	dsAgingReport.dtAgingBracketsRow
	dtAgingBracketsDataTable.AdddtAgingBracketsRow (
	int StartDay,
	int Endday,
	int BracketNumber,
	string BracketLabel)

Figure 7-1. *Statement completion*

You can also add a new row by creating an instance of a new strongly-typed row object, populating the strongly-typed properties that correspond to the columns, and then adding the row object. Listing 7-2 demonstrates this approach. Note that the developer can still use IntelliSense for each of the column properties.

Listing 7-2. *An Alternate Way of Adding Rows*

```
dsAgingReport odsAgingReport = new dsAgingReport();
dsAgingReport.dtAgingBracketsRow oNewRow =
        odsAgingReport.dtAgingBrackets.NewdtAgingBracketsRow();
oNewRow.StartDay = 1;
oNewRow.Endday = 30;
oNewRow.BracketLabel = " < 30 days ";
oNewRow.BracketNumber = 1;
odsAgingReport.dtAgingBrackets.AdddtAgingBracketsRow(oNewRow);
```

Step 2: Creating Default Column Values for New Rows

When you add new rows to a DataTable, you may want to define default values. For instance, you may want to store a value of zero in a numeric column, if you don't explicitly provide a value. This way you don't have to perform null value checking during aggregation operations.

The DataSet editor in Visual Studio 2005 allows you to easily define default values (see Figure 7-2), similar to the way SQL developers can define default column values.

You can define not only default values to avoid null situations, but also calculated columns that include summarizations from other related tables. We'll revisit this a little later.

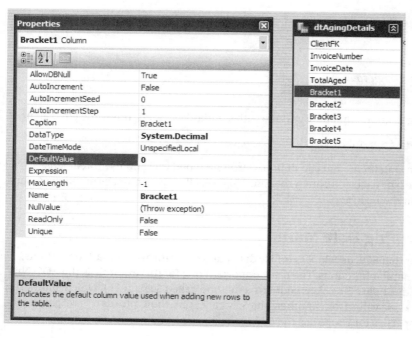

Figure 7-2. *Setting default values*

> **■Note** It's often important to set the `DefaultValue` of numeric columns to zero, especially when those columns will be summarized. ADO.NET functions that summarize numeric data do not deal with NULL values very well. So unless there is business significance to NULL values (which there isn't for this report), make sure to set `DefaultValues` to zero.

Step 3: Looping Through Strongly-Typed Rows

Once you've created an instance of both the source invoices and the final result set, you can loop through the invoice rows. Figure 7-3 provides a code snippet that demonstrates how to loop through rows.

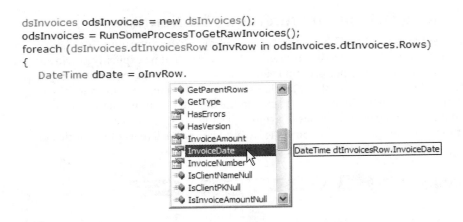

Figure 7-3. *Looping through rows*

For those trying to apply what they've done with standard DataSets, this is the equivalent of

```
foreach (DataRow dr in MyTable.Rows)
```

In your `foreach` statement, you can define a strongly-typed row and use IntelliSense to determine the values for each column in the row. This will allow you to perform the necessary date comparisons in the next step.

Step 4: Performing Date Math

In the same manner that SQL developers utilize date parts to perform date math operations, ADO.NET provides similar functions. The most important one for this example is the ADO.NET `TimeSpan` class. The .NET `DateTime` class contains a method called `Subtract()`, which allows you to subtract one `DateTime` value from another. The `Subtract()` method returns a `TimeSpan` object, which contains properties for you to see the difference in terms of days, hours, seconds, etc.

You can use the TimeSpan class as shown in Listing 7-3 to determine how many days an invoice has aged, based on the as-of date. Again, a TimeSpan object contains many properties that you're encouraged to explore.

Listing 7-3. *Looping Through Invoice Rows and Determining How Old an Invoice Is*

```
dsInvoices odsInvoices = new dsInvoices();
int nDaysAged;
TimeSpan ts;
DateTime dAsOfDate = DateTime.Today;

foreach (dsInvoices.dtInvoicesRow oInvRow in odsInvoices.dtInvoices.Rows)
{
  ts = dAsOfDate.Subtract(oInvRow.InvoiceDate);
  nDaysAged = ts.Days;
  if (nDaysAged > 0) {
    // If it's aged, process it
  }
}
```

Step 5: Performing Lookups on Primary Keys

While the example doesn't utilize this, developers often will define a primary key on a Data-Table and then perform subsequent lookups based on a primary key value. You can define a primary key by right-clicking a column in the DataSet designer and selecting the Set Primary Key option. Visual Studio 2005 will automatically create a method in the typed DataSet class (using the column name as part of the method name) to simplify any lookups (see Listing 7-4).

Listing 7-4. *Performing Lookups*

```
// If you haven't defined a PrimaryKey in the DataSet designer,
// you can define one in code, by either of the following two lines

// odsAgingReport.dtAgingDetails.PrimaryKey =
//   new DataColumn[] { odsAgingReport.dtAgingDetails.InvoiceNumberColumn };

// odsAgingReport.dtAgingDetails.PrimaryKey =
//   new DataColumn[] { odsAgingReport.dtAgingDetails.Columns["InvoiceNumber"] };

// Note that "FindByInvoiceNumber" was generated by VS 2005, because you
// established it as a primary key

dsAgingReport.dtAgingDetailsRow oLookupRow =
  odsAgingReport.dtAgingDetails.FindByInvoiceNumber("Invoice 111-AA");
decimal nAmount = oLookupRow.TotalAged;
```

Step 6: Filtering

Once you determine that an invoice has aged a certain number of days, you need to search the aging bracket table for the bracket number associated with the number of days. While ADO.NET doesn't provide a full-blown implementation of SQL syntax, it often provides enough capabilities for basic and intermediate lookups.

Listing 7-5 demonstrates a lookup into the aging bracket table to determine the bracket associated with the specific number of days an invoice has aged. Specifically, you're using the `DataTable.Select()` method and passing the filter syntax (days aged between the `StartDay` and `EndDay` for the bracket). The method returns an array of standard DataRows (as opposed to strongly-typed rows); however, you can cast any of the rows as strongly-typed rows to regain the strong-typing as you determine the resulting bracket.

Listing 7-5. *Filtering*

```
dsAgingReport odsAgingReport = new dsAgingReport();
dsInvoices odsInvoices = new dsInvoices();
DateTime dAsOfDate = DateTime.Today;
int nBracket;
int nDaysAged;
TimeSpan ts;
string cDateExpr;

foreach (dsInvoices.dtInvoicesRow oInvRow in odsInvoices.dtInvoices.Rows)
{
        ts = dAsOfDate.Subtract(oInvRow.InvoiceDate);
        nDaysAged = ts.Days;

        if (nDaysAged > 0)  {   // if it's aged, process it
            dsAgingReport.dtAgingDetailsRow oNewRow =
            odsAgingReport.dtAgingDetails.NewdtAgingDetailsRow();
        oNewRow.ClientFK = oInvRow.ClientPK;
        oNewRow.InvoiceDate = oInvRow.InvoiceDate;
        oNewRow.InvoiceNumber = oInvRow.InvoiceNumber;
        cDateExpr = "StartDay <= " + nDaysAged.ToString() +
            " AND EndDay >= " + nDaysAged.ToString();

        DataRow[] dr = odsAgingReport.dtAgingBrackets.Select(cDateExpr);
        // You should only get one row back, so look for the first row
        nBracket = ((dsAgingReport.dtAgingBracketsRow)dr[0]).BracketNumber;
        // Continue processing...
    }
}
```

While not part of this example, a developer could loop through the array of DataRows as well: as an example, the filter syntax might have been all invoices greater than $1,000. Listing 7-6 shows a variety of different filter capabilities.

Listing 7-6. *Examples of Different RowFilter Capabilities*

```
dsInvoices odsInvoices = new dsInvoices();
string cFilterExpr = "";

// Date handling
cFilterExpr = "InvoiceDate >= '01/31/2006' AND InvoiceDate <= '02/28/2006'";
cFilterExpr = "InvoiceDate >= #01/31/2006";

// Full and partial text searches
cFilterExpr = "ClientName = 'JONES CONSTRUCTION'";

// Search for "Construction" anywhere
cFilterExpr = "ClientName LIKE '%CONSTRUCTION%'";

// Search for names that start with "Construction"
cFilterExpr = "ClientName LIKE 'CONSTRUCTION%'";

// Numeric data
cFilterExpr = "InvoiceAmount > 1000";

// Combining AND/OR
cFilterExpr = "(ClientName LIKE '%BUILDING%' OR ClientName LIKE %HOMES%')
                        AND InvoiceAmount > 5000";

// Using the IN function
cFilterExpr = "InvoiceAmount IN (1000,2000,3000)";
cFilterExpr = "ClientName IN ('Jones Construction','Smith Construction')";
cFilterExpr = "ClientName NOT IN  ('Jones Construction','Smith Construction')";

// Using the ISNULL function
cFilterExpr = "ISNULL(InvoiceAmount,-9999)=-9999";

// Using the PARENT (or CHILD) function
cFilterExpr =  "Parent(RelName) = like '%NATIONAL'";

DataRow[] dr = odsInvoices.dtInvoices.Select(cFilterExpr);
```

■**Note** Visual Studio 2005 ADO.NET RowFilter syntax does not support full set-based (i.e., JOIN) operations. However, you can reference multiple DataTables in a RowFilter using the Parent and Child functions, **provided** you've established an ADO.NET relation between the DataTables.

Step 7: Performing the Equivalent of SELECT DISTINCT

In Visual Studio .NET 2003, a common complaint about ADO.NET was the lack of any native ability to perform the equivalent of a SQL SELECT DISTINCT, which would return a unique set of rows based on a list of columns. A developer may have a result set of 500 rows that represents X number of unique states, and would like to easily perform a SELECT DISTINCT to determine what states they are. The only choices in VS .NET 2003 were to either perform the query in SQL Server or write custom ADO.NET code to loop through the results and determine the unique states manually.

Fortunately, Visual Studio 2005 provides native capabilities to perform a basic SELECT DISTINCT. The DataView (or DefaultView) of a DataTable contains a new method called ToTable(),(), which contains an overload to create a new table of distinct rows based on a comma-separated string of columns. In the overload, you pass a Boolean to indicate that you want to create a list of unique results, and then your series of columns to determine the uniqueness.

You need this new functionality, because in this example all you have is a list of invoices with a ClientPK and a client name. There could be hundreds or thousands of invoices that span a dozen or so clients. Your result set requires a unique list of clients. Listing 7-7 demonstrates how to build a DataTable of unique clients. Note that the example takes the resulting DataTable and merges it right into your typed DataSet using the ADO.NET Merge function, which (in the example in Listing 7-7) allows you to merge the contents of the temporary table into the dtClients table of your typed DataSet odsAgingReport.

Listing 7-7. *Performing a SELECT DISTINCT*

```
odsAgingReport.dtClients.Merge(
    odsInvoices.dtInvoices.DefaultView.ToTable(
                true, "ClientPK", "ClientName"));
```

■**Tip** This new functionality in ADO.NET (a functional equivalent to SELECT DISTINCT) is available as an overload in the DefaultView.ToTable method. Many developers are unaware of this functionality because it exists as an overload, and therefore is not obvious to some. When you use .NET Framework methods, utilize IntelliSense as much as possible to see what other functionality exists.

Step 8: Handling Data Relations

Although your final code solution doesn't utilize data relations, it's still worth the time to explore them. You can establish ADO.NET DataRelation objects between DataTables that are related based on some key value. In Figure 7-4, you can see we've established a relation between dtClients and dtAgingDetails, and also a relation between dtAgingDetails and dtAgingSummary, simply by dragging the Client primary key from one table to another.

When you establish data relations, ADO.NET automatically creates a method for the strongly-typed row of the parent table, so that you can easily read the corresponding child table(s). By default, the name of the method will be Get<ChildTableName>Rows(), so your example will have a method called GetDtAgingDetailsRows().

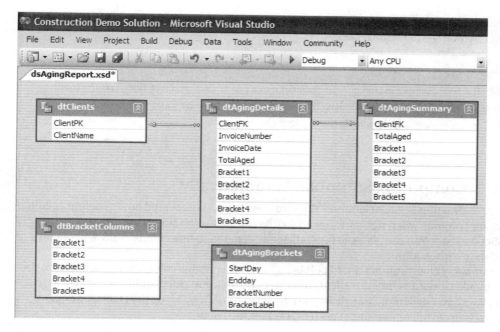

Figure 7-4. *Establishing an ADO.NET relation using typed DataSets*

Listing 7-8 demonstrates a brief but functional example of this, where you take a row from the dtClients table and retrieve all of the related child rows from dtAgingDetails. You don't need to perform a lookup or a FIND or a filter—all you need to do is call the GetdtAgingDetailsRows() method and then process the array of rows that the method returns.

Listing 7-8. *Using Functions from Relations*

```
dsAgingReport odsAgingReport = new dsAgingReport();
// Create an array of DataRows that will store the child rows
DataRow[] aRows;
decimal nAmount = 0;
// Loop through the client rows
foreach (dsAgingReport.dtClientsRow oClientRow in odsAgingReport.dtClients.Rows)
{
    // The strongly-typed client (parent) row has a method (from the typed DataSet)
    // to automatically retrieve the child rows from dtAgingDetails
    aRows = oClientRow.GetdtAgingDetailsRows();
    // You can cast each individual row from the return array as a strongly-typed row
    foreach (dsAgingReport.dtAgingDetailsRow oDetailRow in aRows) {
        nAmount = oDetailRow.Bracket1 + oDetailRow.Bracket2 +
                        oDetailRow.Bracket3 + oDetailRow.Bracket4 +
                        oDetailRow.Bracket5;
    }
}
```

You can also use `DataRelation` objects to automatically compute subtotals from related tables, as you'll see in the next part.

■**Note**   The final example in Listing 7-10 does not make use of data relations. However, you could just as easily have done so. We're showing this part to demonstrate how you'd write code for ADO.NET `DataRelation` objects, should you choose to use them.

Step 9: Computing Subtotals Automatically

In "Step 2: Creating Default Column Values for New Rows," we covered how to define default values for columns when new rows are added, by setting the `DefaultValue` property in the DataSet designer. You can also use the DataSet designer to define column values based on calculation expressions.

Your aging client summary table (`dtAgingSummary`) contains columns that summarize the aging bracket amounts for each client. You can perform those calculations one of two ways. Figures 7-5 and 7-6 demonstrate how you can accomplish it by using the DataSet designer. The goal is to calculate the sum of each bracket for the client.

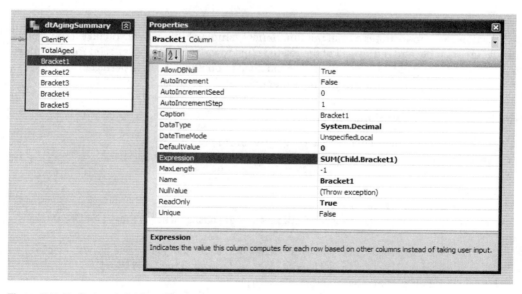

Figure 7-5. *Defining calculated expressions based on a related child table*

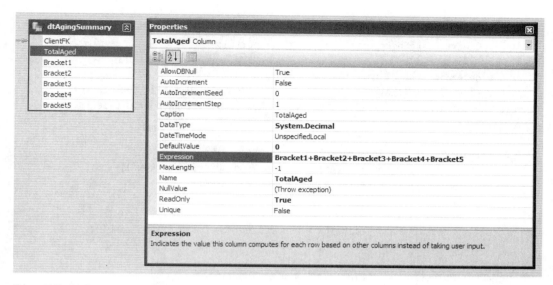

Figure 7-6. *Defining calculated expressions based on specific columns in the same table*

Because you've established a data relation between the client summary parent table (dtAgingSummary) and the aging detail child table (dtAgingDetails), you can utilize the child object and define the expression as Sum(Child.Bracket1). This means that ADO.NET will automatically calculate Bracket1 for each client based on the sum of invoices (from dtAgingDetails) in Bracket1 for that client. (And then you'll repeat the process for brackets 2 through 5.)

Finally, you'll define the calculated expression for the column TotalAged as the sum of brackets 1 through 5.

■**Note** You can only specify parent and child syntax in ADO.NET column expressions if you have previously established ADO.NET DataRelations.

Step 10: Computing Subtotals Manually

The second way to compute subtotals is manually, by using the DataTable method Compute(), demonstrated in Listing 7-9. In the example, you loop through each client row in the dtClients table (which you populated back in Listing 7-7) and use the Compute() method in the dtAgingDetails DataTable.

Listing 7-9. *Subtotals*

```
dsAgingReport odsAgingReport = new dsAgingReport();

// Now determine the client summary subtotals
// For each client (that you populated in dtClients), summarize the brackets
foreach (dsAgingReport.dtClientsRow oClientRow in odsAgingReport.dtClients.Rows)
{

    dsAgingReport.dtAgingSummaryRow oClientSummaryRow =
            odsAgingReport.dtAgingSummary.NewdtAgingSummaryRow();
    oClientSummaryRow.ClientFK = oClientRow.ClientPK;

    string cExpression;
    string cCondition = "ClientFK = " + oClientRow.ClientPK.ToString();
    for (int nCtr = 1; nCtr <= 5; nCtr++)
    {
        cExpression = "SUM(Bracket" + nCtr.ToString() + ")";

        //  Remember that Compute returns an object - you must cast it
        oClientSummaryRow["Bracket" + nCtr.ToString()] =
                (decimal)odsAgingReport.dtAgingDetails.Compute(
                                            cExpression, cCondition);

    }

    oClientSummaryRow.TotalAged =
            oClientSummaryRow.Bracket1 +  oClientSummaryRow.Bracket2 +
            oClientSummaryRow.Bracket3 +  oClientSummaryRow.Bracket4 +
            oClientSummaryRow.Bracket5;

    odsAgingReport.dtAgingSummary.AdddtAgingSummaryRow(oClientSummaryRow);
}
```

You pass two parameters to the Compute method: the calculation (SUM(Bracket1)), and the expression that corresponds to the scope (for ClientFK = the current client value). Note that Compute() returns an object, and, since you may be computing against different data types, you must cast the return value, in this case a decimal.

■**Note** The ADO.NET method Compute returns an object: you must cast the return value to the appropriate data type.

Note that for brevity's sake, you create a loop for the five brackets and define an expression for each bracket calculation.

■**Note** The final result in Listing 7-10 computes the subtotals manually, and does not utilize relations. You could have just as easily used the methodology from Step 9 to compute the subtotals automatically, using DataRelations.

Putting It All Together

Listing 7-10 contains the complete source code for building a relational result set of aging invoice data. This represents an entire function you could implement in the business layer, in the absence of the stored procedure you wrote back in Chapter 3 for the aging receivables report.

This code requires a reference to `ConstructionDemo.Datasets`.

Listing 7-10. *Complete Source Code to Process a Set of Raw Invoice Data*

```
using ConstructionDemo.Datasets;

// Start new function

// Create instance of flat invoice DataSet
dsInvoices odsInvoices = new dsInvoices();

// Manually add invoice data
// (otherwise might have come from a simple query from the database)

odsInvoices.dtInvoices.AdddtInvoicesRow(
        111, "Client 111", new DateTime(2005, 11, 15), "ABC-11", 250.55M);
odsInvoices.dtInvoices.AdddtInvoicesRow(
        111, "Client 111", new DateTime(2005, 11, 17), "ABC-12", 1251.00M);
odsInvoices.dtInvoices.AdddtInvoicesRow(
        111, "Client 111", new DateTime(2006,  2,   7), "XYU-15", 787.00M);

odsInvoices.dtInvoices.AdddtInvoicesRow(
        222, "Client 222", new DateTime(2005, 10, 15), "RWW-86", 694.94M);
odsInvoices.dtInvoices.AdddtInvoicesRow(
        222, "Client 222", new DateTime(2005, 9, 7), "URE-91", 4943.05M);
odsInvoices.dtInvoices.AdddtInvoicesRow(
        222, "Client 222", new DateTime(2005, 8, 17), "JSW-51", 1023.85M);

odsInvoices.dtInvoices.AdddtInvoicesRow(
        333, "Client 333", new DateTime(2006, 2, 5), "SRS-01", 192.01M);
odsInvoices.dtInvoices.AdddtInvoicesRow(
        333, "Client 333", new DateTime(2005, 12, 5), "SJA-01", 1034.84M);
```

```
odsInvoices.dtInvoices.AdddtInvoicesRow(
        333, "Client 333", new DateTime(2005, 8, 17), "LWW-84", 9802.14M);

// Create an instance of the Aging Report DataSet
dsAgingReport odsAgingReport = new dsAgingReport();

// Fill in the aging brackets manually (as if you'd pulled them from the database)
odsAgingReport.dtAgingBrackets.AdddtAgingBracketsRow(
        1, 30, 1, "< 30 days");
odsAgingReport.dtAgingBrackets.AdddtAgingBracketsRow(
        31, 60, 2, "31-60 days");
odsAgingReport.dtAgingBrackets.AdddtAgingBracketsRow(
        61, 90, 3, "61-90 days");
odsAgingReport.dtAgingBrackets.AdddtAgingBracketsRow(
        91, 120, 4, "91-120 days");
odsAgingReport.dtAgingBrackets.AdddtAgingBracketsRow(
        121, 999999, 5, "> 120 days");

// Set the "as-of" date
DateTime dAsOfDate = new DateTime(2006, 3, 1);

int nBracket;
int nDaysAged;
TimeSpan ts;
string cDateExpr;

// Loop through each row in the set of flat invoices
foreach (dsInvoices.dtInvoicesRow oInvRow in odsInvoices.dtInvoices.Rows)
{
    ts = dAsOfDate.Subtract(oInvRow.InvoiceDate);
    nDaysAged = ts.Days;
    if (nDaysAged > 0)
    {   // If it's aged, process it
        dsAgingReport.dtAgingDetailsRow oNewRow =
                odsAgingReport.dtAgingDetails.NewdtAgingDetailsRow();

        oNewRow.ClientFK = oInvRow.ClientPK;
        oNewRow.InvoiceDate = oInvRow.InvoiceDate;
        oNewRow.InvoiceNumber = oInvRow.InvoiceNumber;

        // Need to grab the aging bracket associated with the
        // number of days the invoice has aged
        cDateExpr = "StartDay <= " + nDaysAged.ToString() +
                " AND EndDay >= " + nDaysAged.ToString();

        DataRow[] dr = odsAgingReport.dtAgingBrackets.Select(cDateExpr);
```

```
        // You should only get one row back, so look for the first row
        nBracket = ((dsAgingReport.dtAgingBracketsRow)dr[0]).BracketNumber;

        // You can either reference the corresponding bracket in the result set
        // by a variable name, or you can use a switch/case statement below
        string cColumn = "Bracket" + nBracket.ToString().Trim();
        oNewRow[cColumn] = oInvRow.InvoiceAmount;
        oNewRow.TotalAged = oInvRow.InvoiceAmount;

        //     Or, you can evaluate each bracket manually
        //     switch (nBracket)
        //     {
        //         case 1:
        //             oNewRow.Bracket1 = oInvRow.InvoiceAmount;
        //             break;
        //         etc   (repeat for each bracket)

        odsAgingReport.dtAgingDetails.Rows.Add(oNewRow);
    }
}


// Create a unique list of clients from the entire table of invoices
// and then merge them right into the typed DataSet
// (The ADO.NET equivalent of a SQL SELECT DISTINCT)

odsAgingReport.dtClients.Merge(
    odsInvoices.dtInvoices.DefaultView.ToTable(
                true, "ClientPK", "ClientName"));


// Now determine the client summary subtotals
// For each client (that you populated in dtClients), summarize the brackets
foreach (dsAgingReport.dtClientsRow oClientRow in odsAgingReport.dtClients.Rows)
{

    dsAgingReport.dtAgingSummaryRow oClientSummaryRow =
odsAgingReport.dtAgingSummary.NewdtAgingSummaryRow();
    oClientSummaryRow.ClientFK = oClientRow.ClientPK;

    string cExpression;
    string cCondition = "ClientFK = " + oClientRow.ClientPK.ToString();
    for (int nCtr = 1; nCtr <= 5; nCtr++)
    {
        cExpression = "SUM(Bracket" + nCtr.ToString() + ")";
```

```
        //  Remember that Compute returns an object - you must cast it
        oClientSummaryRow["Bracket" + nCtr.ToString()] =
                (decimal)odsAgingReport.dtAgingDetails.Compute(
                                            cExpression, cCondition);
    }

    oClientSummaryRow.TotalAged =
            oClientSummaryRow.Bracket1 +  oClientSummaryRow.Bracket2 +
            oClientSummaryRow.Bracket3 +  oClientSummaryRow.Bracket4 +
            oClientSummaryRow.Bracket5;

    odsAgingReport.dtAgingSummary.AdddtAgingSummaryRow(oClientSummaryRow);
}


string[] Brackets = new string[5];

for (int nRowCtr = 0; nRowCtr < 5; nRowCtr++)
    Brackets[nRowCtr] = odsAgingReport.dtAgingBrackets[nRowCtr].BracketLabel;

odsAgingReport.dtBracketColumns.AdddtBracketColumnsRow(
        Brackets[0], Brackets[1], Brackets[2], Brackets[3], Brackets[4]);
```

You can examine the results of the typed DataSet by using the new debugging visualizers in Visual Studio 2005. To do this, set a breakpoint on a line of code after the processing is finished, and then run the code with debugging turned on. When you hit the breakpoint, place the mouse pointer over the object you wish to examine (in this case, odsAgingReport). Visual Studio 2005 will display the tooltip (see Figure 7-7). If the object name in the tooltip is followed by a magnifying glass, that indicates that Visual Studio 2005 contains a debugging visualizer for the object type.

Figure 7-7. *The magnifying glass indicates that a debugging visualizer exists.*

If you click the magnifying glass shown in Figure 7-8, Visual Studio 2005 will display a simple grid with the contents of odsAgingReport. Debugging visualizers in Visual Studio 2005 are a major improvement over the debugging features in Visual Studio .NET 2003.

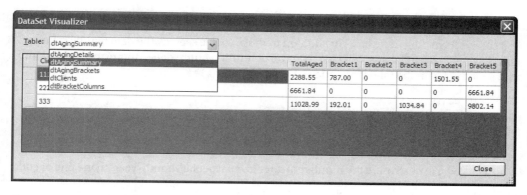

Figure 7-8. *The debugging DataSet Visualizer*

■**Note** Another great new feature in Visual Studio 2005 is the ability to browse DataSets in the debugger.

Some Miscellaneous ADO.NET Tips

In this chapter, we've shown you many different techniques for processing data using ADO.NET. In this final section, you'll learn about some miscellaneous areas where you can use ADO.NET for other data-related tasks. While many of these are outside the scope of your specific application, they are also commonly asked ADO.NET questions.

Reading/Writing NULL Values

Dealing with NULL values can be an annoying but necessary task—we're sure if Mark Twain were alive today, he'd have something pithy to say about NULLs. Fortunately, when using typed DataSets, ADO.NET provides methods for each strongly-typed column object. For example, if you have a row object and a column called HoursWorked, you can set the column or check for NULL values with the following code:

```
// Setting a column to NULL
oRow.SetHoursWorkedNull();
// Check for null value
if(oRow.IsHoursWorkedNull()==true)
```

For each strongly-typed column, the typed DataSet class contains two methods for setting a column value to NULL (Set<ColumnName>Null()) and determining whether a column value is null (Is<ColumnName>Null()).

More Date Handling

You can perform other date tasks in addition to those you've seen by the date handling functions covered back in Listing 7-3. First, you can determine future dates (tomorrow, next month, next year, etc.) with the following code:

```
// Determine future dates
DateTime dNextDay = dtInvoiceDate.AddDays(1);
DateTime dNextMonth = dtInvoiceDate.AddMonths(1);
DateTime dNextYear = dtInvoiceDate.AddYears(1);
```

Also, you can determine the number of days in a particular month/year in one line of code:

```
// Determine # of days in October 2002
int nDaysInMonth = DateTime.DaysInMonth(2002, 10);
```

Finding out if a year is a leap year is just as easy:

```
if(DateTime.IsLeapYear(2006)==true)
```

Sometimes you need to determine the current date/time (down to the second), and other times you just need the current date (and the time expressed as midnight):

```
// Get the current date/time, down to the second
DateTime dNow = DateTime.Now;


// Gets today (time will be midnight)
DateTime dToday = DateTime.Today;
```

Finally, there may be times where you need to determine whether a string represents a valid date. One way is to convert the string to a DateTime variable, and wrap the code inside a try...catch block:

```
// Determine whether a string represents a valid date
public bool IsValidDate(string cText)
{
    bool lIsGoodDate = true;
    // Convert in a try/catch
    try
    {
        DateTime dt = Convert.ToDateTime(cText);
    }
    catch (Exception)
    {
        lIsGoodDate = false;
    }
    return lIsGoodDate;
}
```

Choices, Choices: When to Use RowFilter, When to Use Select()?

ADO.NET provides you with two different ways to filter on data—either by setting the RowFilter property of a data view, or by using the DataTable Select() method. Some ask the question: which is better?

The answer (of course) is, it depends on what you're doing. Use a DataView and a RowFilter when you want to bind the results of a filter. The DataView implements IEnumerable, ICollection, and IList, making it ideal for data binding. You cannot bind a collection of DataRow objects that DataTable.Select() returns.

On the other hand, if you need to scan through the rows of a filter to perform calculations or other processing, you'll want to call the Select() method, which returns an array of DataRow objects. You can do something with a collection of DataRow objects that you cannot do with a DataView: cast each of the rows as one of the strongly-typed objects from a typed DataSet:

```
dsInvoices odsInvoices = new dsInvoices();
// Run some process to populate orders

// Now perform a select and filter
DataRow[] aFilteredRows =
        odsOrder.dtOrderHdr.Select("InvoiceAmount > 1000");

// You can cast the collection of rows
// as the strongly-typed rows from your typed DS

foreach (dsInvoices.dtInvoicesRow oRow in aRows) {
    cInvoiceNumber = oRow.InvoiceNumber;
    // Perform other processing
}
```

Occasionally, you'll encounter a situation where you have to copy a DataView back to a DataTable. You may need to save a DataView to XML, or you may need to bind the results of a DataView to a .NET library or product that does not recognize DataViews (such as Crystal Reports). In Listing 7-7, we showed the new ToTable() method, which allows you to copy a DataView back to a new DataTable, which you can then bind to controls that cannot work with a DataView.

Summary

You've completed the database requirements, learned about stored procedures, tackled the architecture, and even saw data handling in situations where you can't process all the data in the back end. Now it's time to turn your attention to the actual presentation aspect of the text—the creation and delivery of the reports themselves.

PART 4

Report Writers

At the outset of this text, we stated that the report writer was only one portion of a reporting solution. It is certainly a critical portion, but only a portion. The fact that we've spent nine chapters on key components of a reporting solution before we covered the report writer is proof positive of this. It is now time to build the report templates themselves. Chapters 8 and 9 will demonstrate how to use Crystal Reports to construct your reports. For those using other report writers such as ActiveReports and SQL Reporting Services, Chapters 10 and 11 will demonstrate how to handle many of the construction application's reporting requirements using those report writers.

Basic/Intermediate Report Design with Crystal Reports

Crystal Reports by Business Objects is, in our opinion, the best general-purpose reporting tool on the market. We're sure this view is shared by many Crystal Reports users, as Crystal owns roughly half the market share, and the next closest competitor owns roughly 25%. Ironically, Crystal also confuses some individuals, in part because Crystal appeals both to application developers as well as corporate power users.

This book (and specifically the next two chapters) targets application developers and the challenges they face in constructing reports. As you've seen in prior chapters, the overall methodology of this text focuses on constructing result sets outside of the report and **pushing** them into the Crystal report. This methodology reflects the objective of using the report as an extension of the overall user interface.

By contrast, many corporate power users **pull** data from external data sources (SQL Server, Oracle, Access, etc.) into Crystal Reports. In these situations, the data source resides on the same domain (or is easily accessible). Pulling data utilizes many Crystal database access features that are beyond the scope of this book. We are showing you how to use what is known as the **push** model, as opposed to the **pull** model. The data format is common XML. (The section "The Crystal Reports Push Model" later in this chapter illustrates the push model.)

This chapter and Chapter 11 will demonstrate how to construct the physical RPT files that reflect the reporting requirements of the application. We'll take a step-by-step approach to building the reports.

So, where to start? Most Crystal tutorials begin with a basic report to demonstrate Crystal Reports functionality. You'll start with a basic report as well: one that will address one of your reporting requirements.

You defined one of the reporting requirements as a common header and footer for all reports. Crystal Reports provides the ability to built separate reports for the header and footer, and then incorporate them into your reports (as a subreport) as needed. Crystal Reports also allows you to incorporate subreports in such a way that subsequent changes to subreports can be automatically reflected in the parent reports, without the need to manually refresh the subreports. We'll cover this later.

This start will allow you to get your feet wet in building your first report, and also addresses the requirement of building a standard header/footer for reports.

Versions of Crystal Reports

The existence of different versions of Crystal Reports (version 9, version 10, version 11, and the versions that come with Visual Studio .NET 2003 and Visual Studio 2005) often prompt questions in user group meetings, online forums, etc.

The examples in this book are built with the version of Crystal Reports that comes with Visual Studio 2005, which is essentially Crystal Reports 10. This alone should bring a smile to those who struggled with the version of Crystal that came with Visual Studio .NET 2003, which was a subset of Crystal 8.5. In our opinion, the single biggest enhancement to the embedded version of CR .NET from VS 2003 to VS 2005 is the ability to preview reports inside the designer. This fact alone was enough for us to use the embedded CR .NET designer in VS 2005, as opposed to the stand-alone version of Crystal Reports.

Those who follow Crystal Reports know that Business Objects has released Crystal Reports 11. Because the primary focus of this book is based on the technology available with the release of Visual Studio 2005 (and SQL Server 2005), Chapters 8 and 9 do not cover any new capabilities in Crystal Reports 11. Throughout the book, we will refer to this specific version as **Crystal Reports .NET**.

■**Note**   The report examples in this book were built with the version of Crystal Reports that comes with Visual Studio 2005. This is essentially Crystal Reports version 10. While the next two chapters may briefly refer to new functionality in Crystal Reports version 11, the examples are exclusively based on Crystal Reports using Visual Studio 2005. Throughout the book, we will refer to this specific version as Crystal Reports .NET.

The Crystal Reports Push Model

Here we will show you how to utilize what is commonly known as the **push model** for working with Crystal Reports. Figure 8-1 shows an overview of the push model.

The key steps of the push model are as follows:

1. At the heart of the push model are the typed DataSet/schema definitions. They will represent the DataSource for the report. We covered the creation of typed DataSets in Chapter 6. You are storing them in the `ConstructionDemo.Datasets` project.

2. Build the report using the Crystal Reports designer. This chapter and the next will cover the capabilities of the designer. When you build each report, you will specify one of the DataSets in `ConstructionDemo.Datasets` as the design-time DataSource for the report. Each Crystal Reports file contains a `Database` object that stores the information on the DataTables from the DataSource.

3. For your application, you'll save your reports in a separate project called `ConstructionDemo.CrystalReports`. Each report will be stored as a strongly-typed object. The project will contain a reference to `ConstructionDemo.Datasets`.

4. At runtime, any time you need to generate a specific report, you will populate an instance of the typed DataSet associated with that report. (Chapter 6 showed a full example of populating the result set for the aging receivables report.) You will then

create an instance of the report and "push" that DataSet into the report object. Chapter 12 will present a reusable library for the task of pushing runtime DataSets into the `Database` object of an instantiated report object.

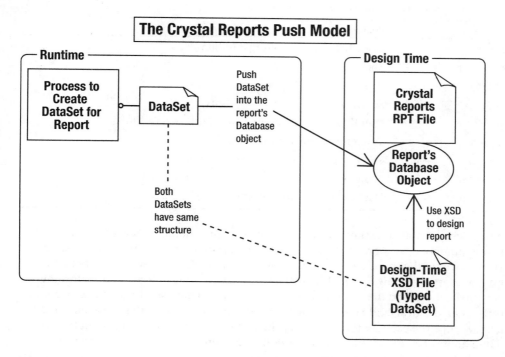

Figure 8-1. *A diagram depicting the Crystal Reports Push Model*

Note In using the Crystal Reports Push Model, you use XML Schemas/typed DataSets to communicate with the Crystal Reports `Database` object. The report contains no information on the back-end database, nor any database login information. You generate the report by pushing XML/DataSet data with the same structure you supplied at design time.

Building a Reusable Header and Footer Subreport

All the way back in Figure 1-1 (in Chapter 1), we presented a draft version of the timesheet report. In the style guide, we covered the requirements for, among other things, a common report header and footer. Your initial foray into Crystal Reports will be to construct a reusable report header and report footer component.

You'll start by identifying the data requirements for a common header and footer report. Table 8-1 lists the data that you'll push into a header and footer. As you can see, these elements are the common report annotations, such as title, footnote, data source, etc.

Table 8-1. *Structure for Common Header and Footer*

ColumnName	Description
HdrCompany	Name of the company/organization
HdrReportTitle	Main report title
HdrSubTitle1	Report subtitle (if necessary)
HdrSubTitle2	Second report subtitle (if necessary)
UserID	User ID of the user running the report
FtrRunBy	Text for user who ran the report
FtrVersion	Text for version of software used to run report
FtrFootNotes	Footnotes
FtrDataSource	Data source used for the report

A brief story, to illustrate the value of data source as an annotation: Years ago, one of us, Kevin, was summoned to work on a vacation day. An important internal user ran the same report twice within the span of a few minutes, and received different results/numbers. To make a long story short, the user had created a test database—the first run was against the production database, and the second run was against a test database. The databases were similar but not identical (and Kevin had no knowledge that the test database existed). Had Kevin known that the two report runs were against different databases, it likely would have saved him hours of investigating (not to mention a vacation day!). So because of that, we always include the data source as a report annotation.

Note that you're using one common structure for both the header and footer. While our examples will have data showing either in a header or footer (but never both), an organization may change their style guide and switch the location of data. Therefore, it makes more sense to maintain one common report information table from which the header and footer can draw.

This structure will be one DataTable within several tables in a result set—but the header/footer will only use this one. We'll revisit this once you fully incorporate reports into the application.

Creating the Generic Report Header and Defining the Data Source

Let's start by creating the header and defining the default design-time data source. As we stated earlier, Visual Studio 2005 includes a version of Crystal Reports that is essentially the same as Crystal Reports version 10. This allows you to create and modify reports as part of a Visual Studio project.

From Solution Explorer, right-click and choose Add New Item. In the Add New Item dialog (see Figure 8-2), select Crystal Report as the template and enter **rptHeader.RPT** for the name of the report.

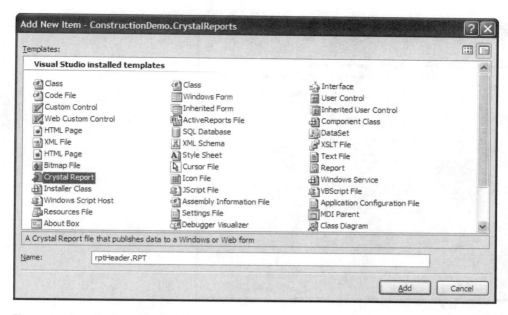

Figure 8-2. *Creating a new report*

After you click Add in Figure 8-2, Crystal Reports will display the Create a New Crystal Report Document screen. Select the option for a blank report, and Crystal Reports .NET will take you to a blank report page. Note that a new pull-down menu appears, called Crystal Reports. This pull-down menu contains options for the major report tasks we'll cover, which are listed in Table 8-2.

Table 8-2. *Major Options in the Crystal Reports .NET Pull-Down Menu*

Option	Description
Insert	Insert different elements into the report, such as special fields, text objects, groups, sections, subreports, lines, boxes, pictures, etc.
Database	Set the report's design-time data source.
Report	Access general report entities, such as the section expert, selection formula, and general report options.
Design	Define page and printer setups, and default designer settings/options.
Preview Report	Preview the current report.
Field Explorer	Access Field Explorer, which allows you to drag/drop report elements and also access report formulas and other report fields.

These options are also available by right-clicking in the main report area.

Now you need to specify the design-time data source that we described in Table 8-1. If you click the Crystal Reports menu and select Database ➤ Database Expert, you will see the Database Expert as shown in Figure 8-3.

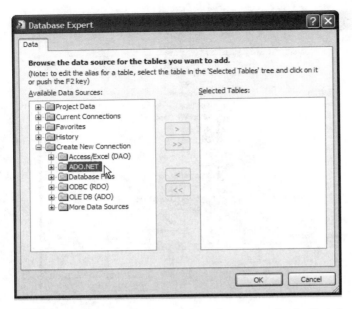

Figure 8-3. *Specifying the design-time data source in the Database Expert*

On the left-side menu, expand the Create New Connection item, select ADO.NET, and choose the option to create a new connection. Crystal Reports .NET will then prompt you for a location of the XML Schema that you'll specify and select as a design-time data source (see Figures 8-4 and 8-5).

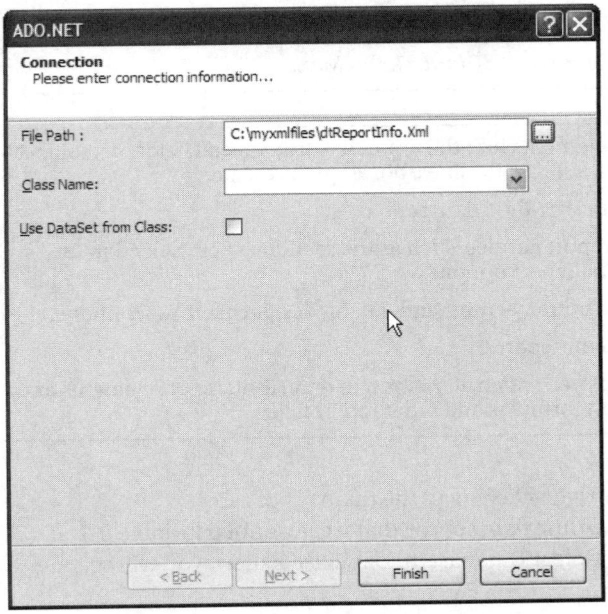

Figure 8-4. *Selecting a design-time data source*

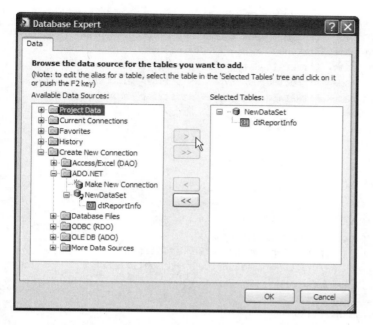

Figure 8-5. *Selecting the tables from the selected data source*

For design-time testing, create a simple XML file in your C:\MyXmlFiles folder called dtReportInfo.xml (see Listing 8-1). It is a one-table XML file with test entries for the columns listed in Table 8-1. It's important to note that the application will programmatically specify the actual data used at runtime for each report (which we'll cover later in the book in Chapter 12). The objective here is to give the RPT a strongly-typed design-time structure that you can use for designing the report and binding the report data elements.

Listing 8-1. *Simple XML File for Design-Time Testing of Report Header/Footer Templates*

```xml
<?xml version="1.0" standalone="yes"?>
<NewDataSet>
  <xs:schema id="NewDataSet" xmlns="" xmlns:xs="http://www.w3.org/2001/XMLSchema"
      xmlns:msdata="urn:schemas-microsoft-com:xml-msdata">
    <xs:element name="NewDataSet" msdata:IsDataSet="true"
        msdata:MainDataTable="dtReportInfo" msdata:UseCurrentLocale="true">
      <xs:complexType>
      <xs:choice minOccurs="0" maxOccurs="unbounded">
        <xs:element name="dtReportInfo">
          <xs:complexType>
            <xs:sequence>
              <xs:element name="HdrCompany" type="xs:string" minOccurs="0" />
              <xs:element name="HdrReportTitle" type="xs:string" minOccurs="0" />
              <xs:element name="HdrSubTitle1" type="xs:string" minOccurs="0" />
```

```
            <xs:element name="HdrSubTitle2" type="xs:string" minOccurs="0" />
            <xs:element name="UserID" type="xs:string" minOccurs="0" />
            <xs:element name="FtrRunBy" type="xs:string" minOccurs="0" />
            <xs:element name="FtrVersion" type="xs:string" minOccurs="0" />
            <xs:element name="FtrFootNotes" type="xs:string" minOccurs="0" />
            <xs:element name="FtrDataSource" type="xs:string" minOccurs="0" />
          </xs:sequence>
        </xs:complexType>
      </xs:element>
    </xs:choice>
  </xs:complexType>
 </xs:element>
</xs:schema>
<dtReportInfo>
  <HdrCompany>Acme Construction Company</HdrCompany>
  <HdrReportTitle>Time Sheet Report with Rates</HdrReportTitle>
  <HdrSubTitle1>Time Period: 11/07/2005 to 11/08/2005</HdrSubTitle1>
  <HdrSubTitle2 />
  <UserID>User 001</UserID>
  <FtrRunBy>Run by John Smith</FtrRunBy>
  <FtrVersion>Version 1.01</FtrVersion>
  <FtrFootNotes>Test of TimeSheet Report, showing labor and overhead rates
    An asterisk indicates subcontractors</FtrFootNotes>
  <FtrDataSource>Source: Test Construction Database</FtrDataSource>
</dtReportInfo>
</NewDataSet>
```

■**Note** In Chapter 12, we'll cover steps to programmatically incorporate this report information table (dtReportInfo) into the application.

Once you have selected the design-time data source(s) for the report by clicking the right-facing arrow, you can drag and drop columns using Field Explorer (see Figure 8-6). Note that Field Explorer contains all available data columns under the Database Fields item. You can also insert special fields (such as page count, print date, etc.).

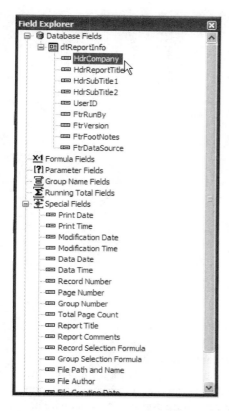

Figure 8-6. *Dragging and dropping data onto the report using Field Explorer*

■**Tip** To include a data column on a report, drag it from Field Explorer onto the area of the report where the data should appear. Once you've dragged data onto the report, you can right-click the data column to use the Crystal Reports formatting options.

Editing Options

Crystal Reports contains different capabilities for editing reports. Some of these capabilities can help you to cleanly implement some of the requirements of the reporting style guide.

First, you can define the default font for all fields and text objects that you place on the report. This allows you to easily adhere to font requirements. To set default fonts, select the Design menu option from the Crystal Reports menu, then choose Default Settings. Crystal Reports .NET will display the dialog shown in Figure 8-7. Note that the Options dialog is divided into sections for different categories, including Fonts.

Figure 8-7. *Report Options dialog (different tabs for different categories)*

By default, when you select an item in the report body and move with any arrow keys, Crystal Reports .NET will move it accordingly by .083 of an inch (the default grid size). If you have situations where you need to move a label or text control or other report object by a smaller margin, you can change the default grid size (see Figure 8-8). The minimum grid size is .01 of an inch.

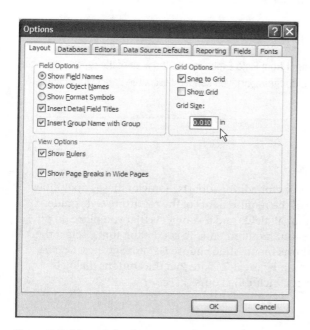

Figure 8-8. *More default settings (changing grid size for moving report objects)*

You can set the margins for a report by choosing the Page Setup option under the Crystal Reports ➤ Design menu option (see Figure 8-9). Under the same Design menu option, you can also use the Printer Setup option to set the orientation (portrait or landscape) for a report.

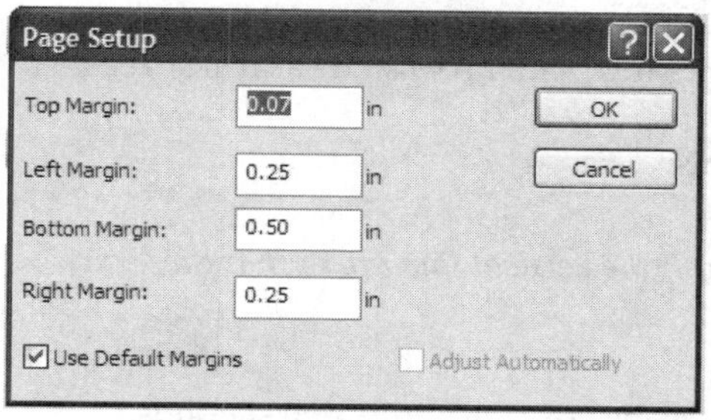

Figure 8-9. *Setting page margins (under Design ➤ Page Setup)*

Finally, some text or field objects may need to stretch vertically. You can turn word wrap on for any report object by right-clicking the object and selecting Format Object. The dialog in Figure 8-10 will appear, and you can select the Can Grow option to allow word wrap.

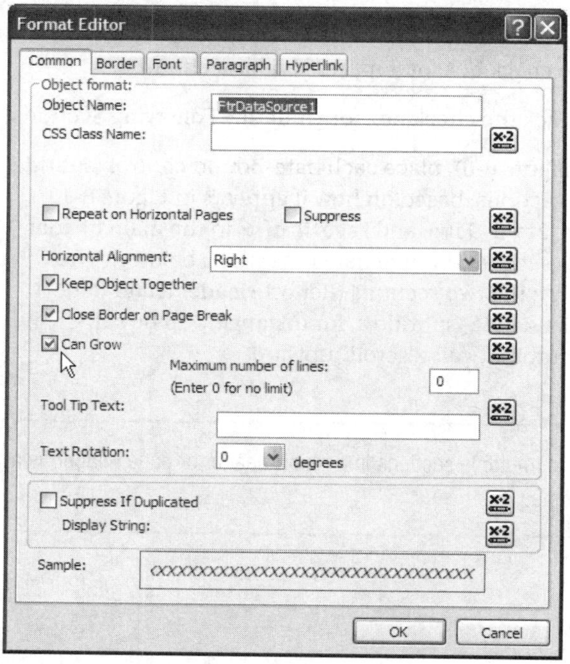

Figure 8-10. *Allowing word wrap*

Using Report Sections to Build the Report Header

The report heading data requirements in Table 8-1 contain columns for a report title and two report subtitles, and the style guide calls for a horizontal line immediately under the report heading text. This immediately raises an issue: some reports will have two subtitles, but other less-complicated reports may only have one (or even none). To preserve vertical space, you want the horizontal bar under the last piece of header text, with no wasted vertical space if any subtitles are blank.

In a nutshell, what you'd like to tell Crystal is this:

If the subtitle is blank, suppress the text and scroll the vertical line up, so that there are no blank lines.

Crystal provides the functionality for you to do so, by creating **additional sections**. Normally, you would place the report title and two report subtitles in the main report header section. To implement the functionality you need, you can do the following:

1. Open the Crystal Reports Section Expert (see Figure 8-11) by selecting the Crystal Reports ➤ Report ➤ Section Expert menu option.

2. Insert multiple sections underneath the main report header section (by clicking the Insert button). This will create subsections under the Report Header section (Report Header a, Report Header b, etc.).

3. For each inserted section, check the check box for Suppress blank section.

4. For the section Report Header a, check the check box for Underlay Following Sections.

5. Using Field Explorer (refer back to Figure 8-6), place each data-bound control (subtitle 1, subtitle 2) in the appropriate subsections, based on how it appears in Figure 8-12. Note that you're placing Print Date, Print Time, and Page N of M in the main header section (Report Header a), and each set of additional data in sections below it. The underlay option will essentially merge the two sections (Report Header a and Report Header b). Also, any section with blank data (subtitle 2, for instance) will be suppressed, and subsequent data will automatically "scroll" upward.

■**Note** Inserting sections with a report band (e.g., multiple sections in a report header or page header) is a great and powerful way to deal with conditional data.

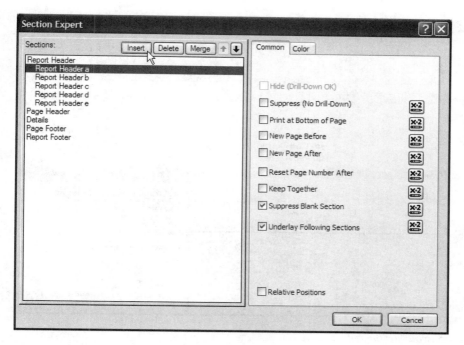

Figure 8-11. *Crystal Reports Section Expert*

As we stated previously, place each data-bound control from the Crystal Reports Field Explorer onto specific sections of the report body, as shown in Figure 8-12. The complete list of data fields you should drag onto the report are as follows:

- Print Date and Print Time (from the Special Fields section)
- Page N of M (from the Special Fields section)
- HdrCompany (from the dtReportInfo section)
- HdrReportTitle (from the dtReportInfo section)
- HdrSubTitle1 (from the dtReportInfo section)
- HdrSubTitle2 (from the dtReportInfo section)

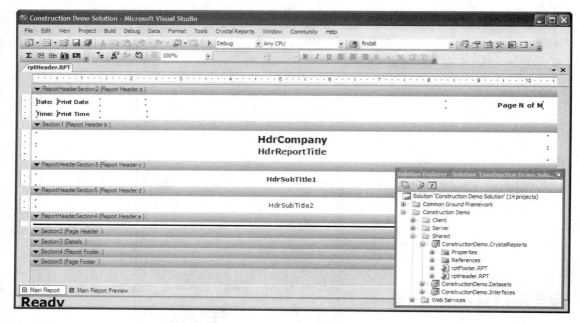

Figure 8-12. *The designer layout for the report header*

After you design the report header, you can preview it (see Figure 8-13) by selecting the Preview Report option under the Crystal Reports menu pad option.

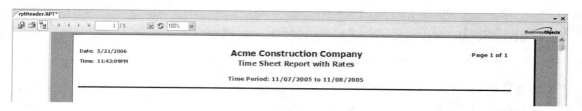

Figure 8-13. *Previewing the report*

Building the Footer Page

You can build a report footer page in the same manner that you created the report heading page. Repeat the general steps from the preceding section, and design the footer report (call it rptFooter.RPT) as shown in Figure 8-14. Remember to create a section underneath the main report heading section, and then drag the following columns from Field Explorer to the report body:

- FtrRunBy
- FtrVersion
- FtrDataSource
- FtrFootNotes

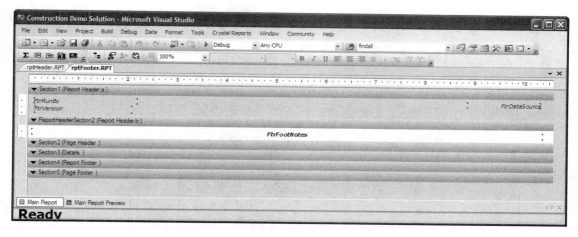

Figure 8-14. *Footer page*

Also, note that the style guide calls for the entire report footer to contain a light-gray background shading. You can define a background color for the entire section area by using the Color tab in the Section Expert (see Figure 8-15).

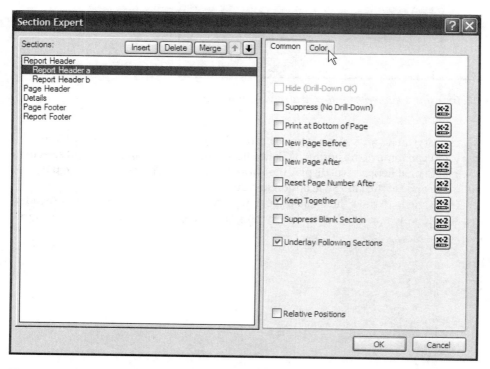

Figure 8-15. *Section expert for footer page (note background color)*

Using the Report Header and Footer in a New Report

Now that you've built a reusable header and footer, let's use them. In the next chapter, you'll create your actual reports and use the header/footer, but for now, you'll just create a simple test report. Create a new report called TestOfHeaderFooter.RPT, right-click the main report, and choose Insert ➤ Subreport to insert a new subreport. Crystal Reports .NET will display a dialog like the one in Figure 8-16. You can select the desired subreport, and then place it into the appropriate area of the main report. You'll want to insert rptHeader.RPT into the page header area and rptFooter.RPT into the page footer area.

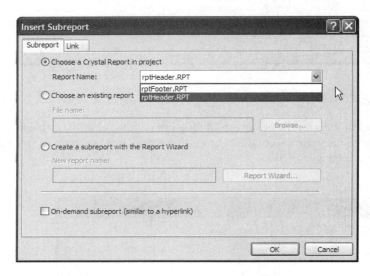

Figure 8-16. *Inserting a subreport into a new report, into the header*

By default, Crystal Reports places a border around any subreport that you insert into a main report. You can remove the border by right-clicking the inserted subreport and selecting Format Object. Crystal Reports will display the Format Editor (see Figure 8-17). Go to the second tab (Border) and set the Line Style option to None.

Figures 8-18 and 8-19 show the final designer and preview for a test report with the header and footer. Now all you have to do is fill in everything else (which you'll do in detail in the next chapter).

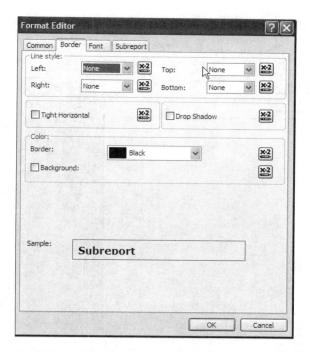

Figure 8-17. *Formatting the subreport (removing borders)*

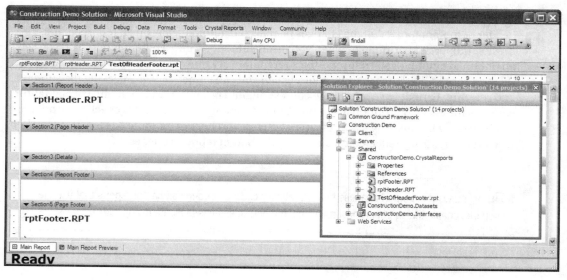

Figure 8-18. *Inserting the footer looks like this.*

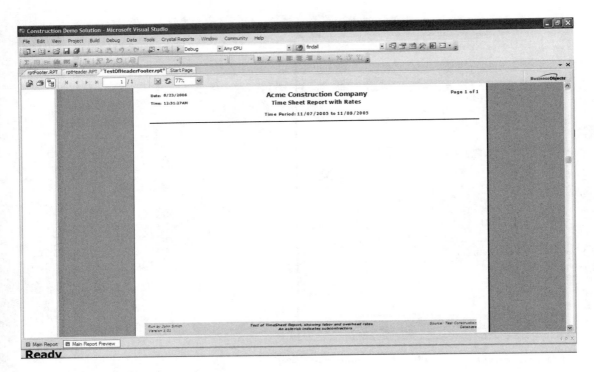

Figure 8-19. *End result*

You may be asking the following questions—"What happens if I have to change the header or footer report? Will the changes be reflected automatically on all reports that use these subreports?" Fortunately, when you insert subreports into a parent report, you can set an option to automatically reimport the subreport every time. Figure 8-20 shows the Crystal Reports Format Editor for the subreport, which you can launch by right-clicking the subreport and selecting Format Object from the context menu. The Subreport tab on the Format Editor contains the check box option Re-import When Opening. By default, this check box option is disabled—but by checking it, any changes to the report header (or footer, as the case may be) will be automatically reflected the next time the parent report is opened.

■Tip If you want subreport changes to automatically cascade through all parent reports that use the subreports, enable the subreport option Re-Import When Opening (see Figure 8-20).

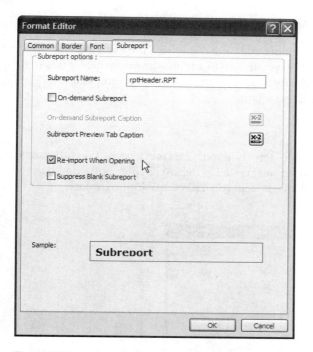

Figure 8-20. *Setting a subreport to automatically reimport*

"Houston, We Have a Problem"

As much as you'd like to move on with the actual reports, there's a small problem that you won't have discovered until you incorporate the header and footer subreports. The problem is the calculation of the current page number and total pages (Page X of Y).

Figure 8-6 showed the Crystal Reports Field Explorer, which includes special fields like Print Date, Page Number, and Total Page Count. You dragged these fields onto the header subreport (as shown previously in Figure 8-12). When you created the test report TestOfHeaderFooter.RPT and previewed it (refer back to Figure 8-19), you saw the (correct) calculation of "Page 1 of 1" in the upper-right corner.

Unfortunately (and you'll be spared the frustration of troubleshooting this), when you insert the header subreport on reports with more than one page, the upper-right corner will repeatedly display "Page 1 of 1" on every page.

Why? Because the page number and page count are being derived/scoped from the subreport, as opposed to the main report. While the main report is calling the header subreport for each page heading, the subreport is truly only printing for a single page at a time, thus repeating "Page 1 of 1". To address this, the main report must "pass" the current page number and total page count to the header subreport. We will address this now.

Implementing a Base Report Template

As stated, you now need to pass the page number and page count from the main (parent) report as parameters to the header reports. So you'll need to address the mechanics of this step.

What would be great is if you could encapsulate this into a base report template, and apply it when you create your regular business reports.

The End Result

The goal at the end of this section is to have three reports in your ConstructionDemo.CrystalReports project: the header and footer subreports that you created in the last chapter, and a new base template report (rptBase.RPT). Figure 8-21 shows what you'll have in Solution Explorer.

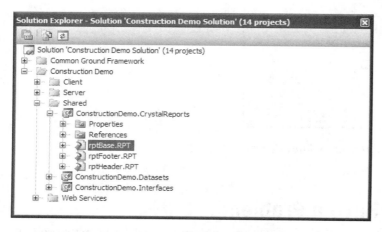

Figure 8-21. *The ConstructionDemo.CrystalReports project, with a new base report*

Integrating the Header Subreport and a New Base Report Template

There are two sets of steps you need to perform. First, you need to modify your header subreport to receive the current page number and page count as parameters from the main report, and also to display these parameters as a Page X of Y string in the upper-right corner of the header report. Second, you need to create a base main report (that all future reports will use as a template) that uses the header (and footer) subreports, and passes the page number and page count as parameters to the header report every time the page header is generated.

■**Note** You place the header subreport onto the Page Heading section of the main base report to generate the contents of the header subreport for each new page. Therefore, your subreport link must pass the current Page Number and Total Page Count from the main report to the subreport.

Step 1: Modifying the Header Subreport to Receive Parameters

We'll take you through a step-by-step approach here. First, open the `rptHeader.RPT` report from Solution Explorer. This will launch Crystal Reports within .NET, with the header report loaded. Next, load Crystal Reports Field Explorer (by clicking the main Crystal Reports menu pull-down button and selecting Field Explorer). In Field Explorer, select the Parameter Fields list option, and then right-click to create a new parameter (see Figure 8-22).

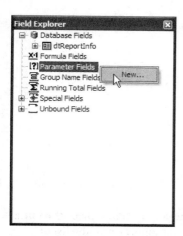

Figure 8-22. *Adding new parameters to rptHeader.RPT*

When you want to add a new report parameter, Crystal Reports .NET prompts you for the name of the parameter (`PageNumber`) and the value type (`Number`), as shown in Figure 8-23. Note that Crystal Reports .NET also prompts for prompting text. This text is what Crystal Reports .NET will display if someone runs the report without a parameter. Since your reporting process will always feed this value from the main (parent) report, you really don't need to worry about this text, so just use the name of the parameter as the prompting text.

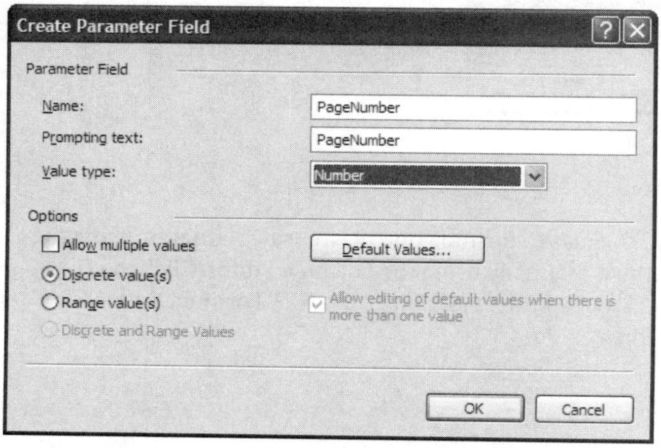

Figure 8-23. *Adding the first of two parameters: PageNumber*

After adding the first parameter for PageNumber, repeat the process shown in Figures 8-22 and 8-23 to create the second parameter for TotalPageCount (see Figure 8-24).

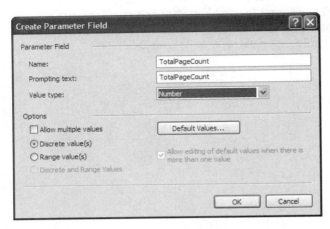

Figure 8-24. *Adding the second of two parameters: TotalPageCount*

You've added the two parameters to the header report. Now you need to replace the initial Page N of M special field that you initially inserted into the header report (from the list of available Crystal Reports .NET special fields) with your own custom formula that uses the new parameters PageNumber and TotalPageCount.

Figure 8-22 showed the Crystal Reports .NET Field Explorer with the list of available parameters, formulas, etc. In the same way you right-clicked the Parameter Fields list option to create a new parameter, you can right-click the Formula Fields list to create a new formula (see Figure 8-25), which you'll call PageXofY. Create the formula and then drag it onto the report, in the upper-right corner where you previously placed Page N of M.

Figure 8-25. *Adding a formula*

Crystal Reports .NET allows you to create a formula one of two ways: either by using the Formula Expert or by typing the formula manually using the Formula Editor. Click the Use Editor button as shown in Figure 8-25 to load the Crystal Reports .NET Formula Editor (see Figure 8-26).

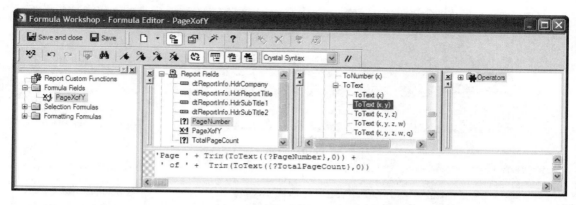

Figure 8-26. *Using the Formula Editor to add a formula for a formatted string*

The goal for your PageXofY formula is to build a string that reads Page X of Y, where X is the PageNumber parameter and Y is the TotalPageCount parameter. You can drag the parameter fields (PageNumber and TotalPageCount) from the Report Fields list onto the editing pane at the bottom—note that Crystal Reports .NET annotates parameters with a question mark (?) prefix. In the formula, you use two Crystal Reports .NET functions, ToText() and Trim(). You use the ToText() function to convert numeric parameters to text/strings (the first argument for ToText() is the numeric value, and the second is the number of decimals you want—since both of your parameters are integer values, you don't want any decimals). Use the Trim() function to trim any excess spaces.

```
'Page ' + Trim(ToText({?PageNumber},0)) +
   ' of ' + Trim(ToText({?TotalPageCount},0))
```

Note The Crystal Reports .NET Formula Editor contains shortcuts to functions by category. If you want to learn more about the Crystal Reports formula language and available functions, browse through the categories in the Formula Editor.

Finally, as you see in Figure 8-27, drag the PageXofY formula from Field Explorer to the upper-right corner of the report.

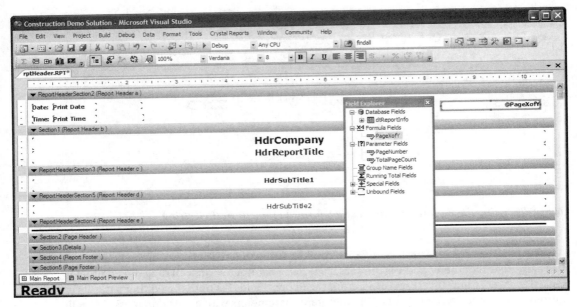

Figure 8-27. *Dragging the PageXofY formula from Field Explorer onto the report body*

Step 2: Creating a Base Template Report

Now that you've modified your rptHeader.RPT header report to accept the parameters, you can create your base template report and utilize rptHeader.RPT (and rptFooter.RPT, which doesn't use any parameters).Your new base template report will serve as the starting point for all new reports you create.

To create your new base template report, do the following:

1. Right-click the ConstructionDemo.CrystalReports project in Solution Explorer.

2. Select Add ➤ New Item from the shortcut menu.

3. Visual Studio .NET will display a dialog box with a list of Visual Studio installed templates. Select Crystal Report from the list of templates, and enter **rptBase.RPT** as the name.

4. This will launch the Crystal Reports .NET designer within Visual Studio 2005. You will see the screen to create a new Crystal Reports document, either as a blank report, or from an existing report. Choose the second option, to create the report as a blank report.

It would be great if you could immediately add your two header/footer subreports, but you have to complete a task before you can do so. Your intention is to pass the current page number and total page count values to the header subreport. Unfortunately, Crystal Reports .NET does not allow you to directly specify the Crystal Reports .NET special fields PageNumber and TotalPageCount when you link the main parent report (rptBase.RPT) with rptHeader.RPT. However, you can create simple formula fields that simply specify the two values, and link the two reports using the simple formula fields. Fortunately, it's just a few steps, and you'll only have to do it once.

As in Figure 8-28, right-click the Formula Fields list option in Field Explorer, and select New.

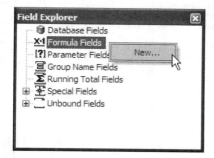

Figure 8-28. *Adding a new formula to the base report template*

Next, as shown in Figure 8-29, you specify the formula name. For clarity's sake, call the formulas the same name as the Crystal Reports .NET special field that the formula represents (in the same way you named the parameter fields for the header subreport). It doesn't matter what order you add them. You can add the formula for TotalPageCount first.

Figure 8-29. *Formula Editor for TotalPageCount formula*

In Figure 8-30, you see the same Formula Editor that you used previously. For the TotalPageCount formula, you want to utilize the Crystal Reports system variable for TotalPageCount. Again, you can type in the name of the variable, or you can drag it from the list of available system functions.

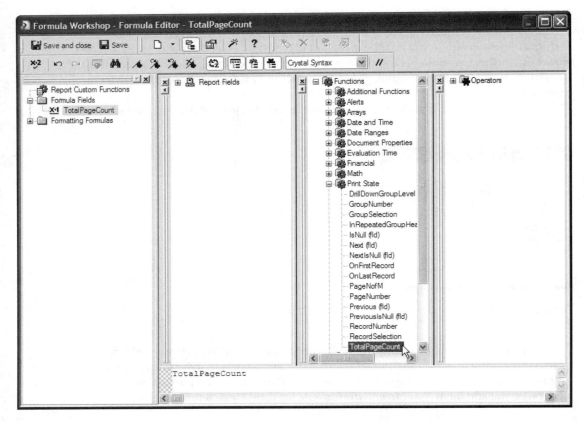

Figure 8-30. *Specifying the print state variable TotalPageCount for the formula expression*

After saving the formula, you can repeat the steps shown in Figures 8-28 through 8-30 to create the formula for PageNumber (see Figure 8-31).

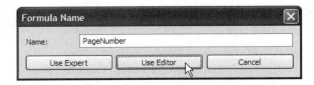

Figure 8-31. *Formula Editor for PageNumber formula*

After creating both formulas, Crystal Reports will display both in Field Explorer (see Figure 8-32).

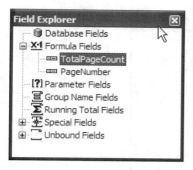

Figure 8-32. *Two new formulas in Field Explorer*

Now that you've created the formulas, you can insert the header subreport and establish the links between formulas and the parameter fields in the subreport. First, right-click the main report body and select Insert ➤ Subreport from the context menu and then click the page header section. Crystal Reports .NET will display the Insert Subreport screen (see Figure 8-33), where you can select rptHeader.RPT.

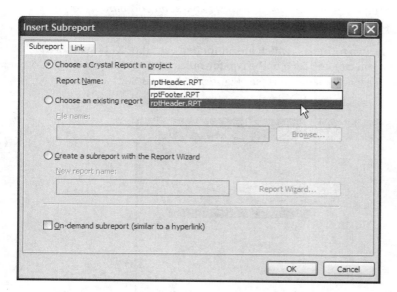

Figure 8-33. *Inserting the rptHeader.RPT header as a subreport*

After you select the subreport, you can establish the links that we've been talking about. The second tab of the Insert Subreport screen in Figure 8-33 allows you to select each of the two formulas (one at a time) and link them to the subreport parameters. Figure 8-34 shows the second tab and the two report formulas on the left.

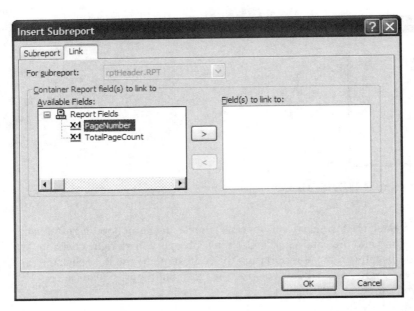

Figure 8-34. *Subreport Link option, to link the two formulas to the subreport parameter fields*

As you select each of the two formulas (which are annotated with the "X+1" symbol in front of the formula name), you can link each of the two formulas to the corresponding parameter fields in the rptHeader.RPT subreport (see Figures 8-35 and 8-36).

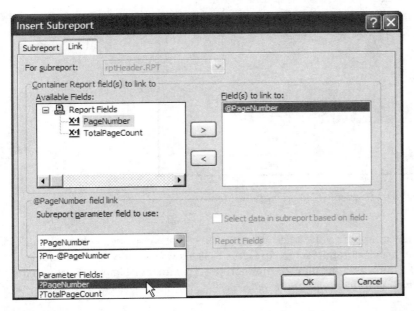

Figure 8-35. *Linking the formula (PageNumber) to the subreport parameter (PageNumber)*

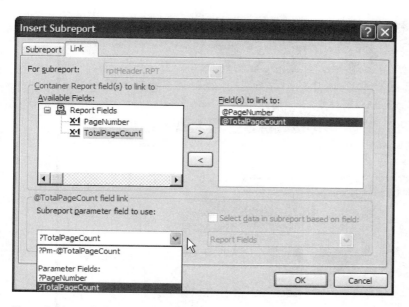

Figure 8-36. *Link the formula (TotalPageCount) to the subreport parameter (TotalPageCount)*

After you click OK in the Insert Subreport dialog, you can physically insert the rptHeader.RPT subreport into the page header of your base template report. You can also repeat the insertion process for the rptFooter.RPT subreport into the page footer of the base template, as shown in Figure 8-37. If you ever need to modify subreport links, you can right-click the subreport and choose the context menu option to change subreport links.

■**Note** It would be convenient to directly pass the Crystal Reports system variables for TotalPageCount and PageNumber to a subreport. However, Crystal Reports .NET only allows you to pass actual report fields (or formula fields) from the parent report to the subreport. So you need to create formulas that simply reference the system variables so that you can pass the formulas to the subreports. While this may seem less than 100% efficient, you only need to solve this puzzle for the base template report.

■**Note** When you insert a subreport, 99 times out of a 100, you'll want to turn ON the option to automatically reimport a subreport when opening the parent report (under the Format Object . . . Subreport options screen). This will ensure that subreport changes are reflected in the parent report.

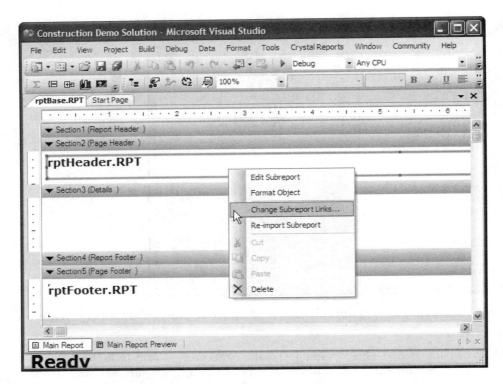

Figure 8-37. *The report header . . . right-click if you need to change the subreport links.*

Using Your New Base Report Template

Now that you've created and saved rptBase.RPT, you can use it as the basis for all future reports that you build. When you create any new reports, Crystal Reports .NET asks if you are building a new report as a blank report, or from an existing report. You can take the third option, which will display an open dialog box where you can select rptBase.RPT.

There's one drawback to this approach. If you create several new reports using rptBase.RPT, and then modify anything in the base template, the changes will not be reflected in reports you previously created from the base template. However, this shouldn't present much of a problem, as the content of your base template report is nothing more than the two subreports. And since you inserted subreports with the option to automatically reimport subreports when opened, any subreport changes will be reflected in new reports that you create from rptBase.RPT. (Any formula changes in the base, however, will not be reflected in newly created reports.)

Summary

This chapter covered some basic Crystal Reports functionality and established a foundation for building reports. While it may initially seem that you didn't accomplish much toward your business reporting requirements, you actually learned many fundamental tasks in report construction and gained some foundation for the actual business reports that we'll cover in the next chapter. We covered the basics of the Crystal Reports Push Model for designing and running reports with XML Schema/typed DataSet data. We talked about different versions of Crystal Reports. We walked you through the steps for building reusable header/footer subreports, how to incorporate them into your actual reports, and how to reimport these subreports back into your main reports when the standard header/footer changes.

Chapter 9 will cover the steps for building the specific reports in the application, as well as constructing powerful charts and report/chart combinations.

CHAPTER 9

■ ■ ■

Advanced Report Design with Crystal Reports

In the previous chapter, you learned the fundamentals of report design and built two reusable report components for common report headings and footers. Now we will turn the focus to the actual business reports for the application. In doing so, you will see how to tackle some of the common challenges in building reports.

This chapter will cover the steps for the following reports:

- Timesheet report

- Gantt chart to show a pictorial history of construction projects

- Customer invoice to demonstrate dynamic images

- Bar chart

- Combined line chart/pie chart/data listing

In doing so, we'll present techniques for the following reporting functionality:

- Creating subtotals

- Keeping a group of data on a page (widow/orphan protection)

- Formatting numeric and Date/DateTime data

- Defining groups

- Linking related tables

- Building subreports and defining subreport links

- Page-break handling

- Underlaying group and detail data to preserve vertical space

- Defining report parameters

- Building and customizing different types of graphs

- Incorporating charting bands with other report bands

- Displaying data stored with RTF (Rich Text Format) codes

- Dynamically displaying data in different colors

This chapter contains five sections, one for each report. For each section, we'll present the end result first, then show the result set, cover the necessary steps to build the report, and then follow up with any additional items.

The other reports indicated in Chapter 1 are part of the download project. We've selected the minimum number of reports that cover all the functionality we're looking to present.

> ■**Note** Some of the examples in this chapter appeared in the January/February 2005 issue of *CoDe Magazine*, in Kevin Goff's article, "The Baker's Dozen: 13 Productivity Tips for Crystal Reports.NET."

Report 1: Implementing the Timesheet Report

The first report is the employee timesheet report with labor dollars. You'll spend the most amount of detail time on this report and follow a step-by-step approach to all the functionality for the report.

The End Result

Figure 9-1 shows a single page of a timesheet report, the end result you're looking to implement. You'll build the report as `RPT_TimeSheet.RPT`, in the `ConstructionDemo.CrystalReports` namespace.

Date: 5/28/2006
Time: 1:21:55AM

Acme Construction Company
Time Sheet Report with Rates

Page 1 of 1

Time Period: 01/01/2006 to 01/30/2006

				Hours			Rate $/Hr			Total
Division	Name	Date	Job #	Reg	OT	Hours	Reg	OT	Overhead	Labor $
Mid-Atlantic	Anderson, Rex	01/02/2006	Job #4	0.50		0.50	25.00		9.35	17.18
			Worker Totals:	0.50		0.50				17.18
	* Boone, Alan	01/03/2006	Job #4	8.00		8.00	22.50		4.89	219.12
			Worker Totals:	8.00		8.00				219.12
	Smith, John	01/09/2006	Job #4	4.00		4.00	22.00		9.55	126.20
			Worker Totals:	4.00		4.00				126.20
Division Totals:				12.50		12.50				362.50
New England	Anderson, Rex	01/02/2006	Job #3	7.00		7.00	25.00		9.35	240.45
		01/03/2006	Job #3	7.25		7.25	25.00		9.35	249.04
			Worker Totals:	14.25		14.25				489.49
	Smith, John	01/02/2006	Job #1	8.00	1.00	9.00	20.00	30.00	9.35	274.15
			Job #2		2.00	2.00	20.00	30.00	9.35	78.70
		01/03/2006	Job #1	8.00	1.00	9.00	20.00	30.00	9.35	274.15
			Worker Totals:	16.00	4.00	20.00				627.00
Division Totals:				30.25	4.00	34.25				1,116.49
Final Totals:				42.75	4.00	46.75				1,478.99

Figure 9-1. *Timesheet report*

The Result Set

Table 9-1 shows the result set definition for the timesheet report, from dsTimeSheets in the ConstructionDemo.Datasets project. Note that the DataSet contains related columns for divisions, employees, and construction jobs. Later in the report, you'll see how to formally define the relations in Crystal Reports. For now, create this DataSet, because you will use it in the next section.

Table 9-1. *Result Set for the Timesheet Report* (dsTimeSheets)

Table	Column	Type
dtDivisions	DivisionFK	Integer
	Description	String
	RegularHours	Decimal
	OtHours	Decimal
	TotHours	Decimal
	TotalLabor	Decimal
dtEmployees	DivisionFK	Integer
	WorkerPK	Integer
	FirstName	String
	LastName	String
	EmployeeFlag	Boolean
	RegularHours	Decimal
	OtHours	Decimal
	TotHours	Decimal
	TotalLabor	Decimal
dtTimeDetails	DivisionFK	Integer
	WorkerFK	Integer
	WorkDate	DateTime
	JobMasterFK	Integer
	RegularHours	Decimal
	OtHours	Decimal
	TotHours	Decimal
	Hourlyrate	Decimal
	Otrate	Decimal
	Overheadrate	Decimal
	TotalLabor	Decimal
dtJobs	JobMasterPK	Integer
	Description	String

The Steps to Build It

First, you'll create a new report by right-clicking `ConstructionDemo.CrystalReports`, selecting Add ➤ New Item, choosing the Crystal Reports template, and calling the new report `RPT_TimeSheet`. When Crystal Reports .NET prompts you for how to create the new report, take the option to create from an existing report, and select your `rptBase.RPT` template from the open dialog box. (If you need a refresher on creating reports, Figure 8-2 back in Chapter 8 covers this.)

Once Crystal Reports .NET loads the report designer with your default template, you can define the data source for your report. Click the VS2005 Crystal Reports menu, then select Database ➤ Database Expert. This will launch the Crystal Reports Database Expert (see Figure 9-2), where you can set the design-time data source (`dsTimeSheets`). Here is where some developers initially get a bit stuck. Your data source resides in another project, so it will not appear in a simple list of available objects. You need to expand the folder option Create New Connection in the Database Expert (again, see Figure 9-2), and then expand the ADO.NET folder underneath and click the option Make New Connection. (If you need a refresher on these steps, check Figures 8-3 through 8-5 back in Chapter 8.)

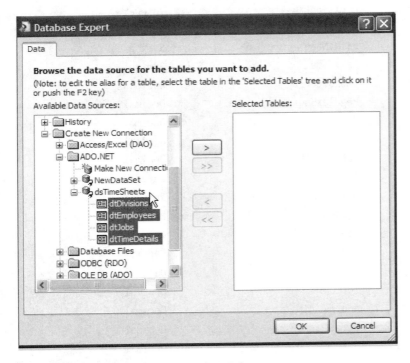

Figure 9-2. *Selecting dsTimeSheets XML Schema*

You will then see an open file dialog box, where you will select the file that contains the schema for the timesheets report (either `dsTimeSheets.XSD` for the empty schema or `dsTimeSheets.XML` if you want the schema with data for design-time report previewing) from the folder where the `ConstructionDemo.Datasets` project resides.

Note If you want to preview a report in design mode, you'll need to select an XML file containing both sample data and the schema. Listing 6-1 (in Chapter 6) showed how to create the XSD Schema from a stored procedure result set, so that you could subsequently use it to create your typed DataSet. You can also create an XML file containing both the result sets **and** the schema by replacing the line `WriteXmlSchema(cXMLFile)` with `WriteXml(cXMLFile,XmlWriteMode.WriteSchema)`. Your project typed DataSet can derive from an XSD Schema, and your reports can use an XML file with data and the schema, **so long as** the underlying schemas are **identical**. If, on the other hand, you don't need to preview, you can simply select the XSD Schema file from the typed DataSet.

Once you select the data source for the report by clicking the right-facing arrow, the Database Expert screen shows a second tab (Links) that allows you to establish links between related columns. As we stated back in the result set discussion of this section, the timesheet DataSet contains relations on the division, employee, and job data. You can use the Links tab to establish these relations (see Figure 9-3) using the Linking Expert inside the Database Expert.

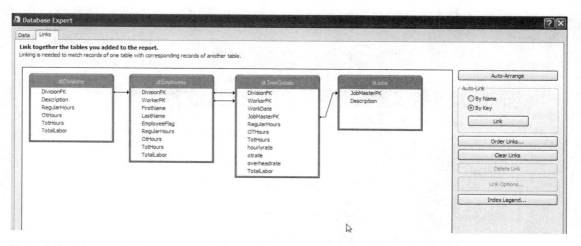

Figure 9-3. *The Linking Expert to establish relations between columns in the DataSet*

You can establish relations/links between columns by clicking one column (the parent column) and dragging the mouse to the related columns (the child columns). Note that given the naming conventions for primary keys and foreign keys (PK and FK suffix), you can't link by name. By default, Crystal Reports establishes a link based on an inner join type—that is, you expect every displayed parent data element to contain at least one corresponding child data element. In the context of your timesheet report, that expectation is valid.

However, you might establish other types of data relationships where not all parent rows will have children rows. An example might be employee notes. Your report might list ten employees, but only three of the ten have notes. In that case, you would need to establish a link based on an outer join type. (If you don't, any employees without employee notes won't show on the report!)

For instances where you need to modify the join type, you can right-click a link (see Figure 9-4).

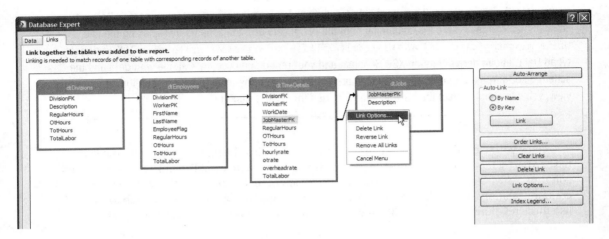

Figure 9-4. *Right-clicking a link to access Link Options*

You can then set the appropriate join type (see Figure 9-5).

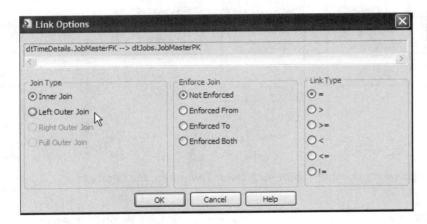

Figure 9-5. *Customizing link options*

■Note If your parent/child relationships between tables can have parent rows without child rows (like the example of notes, where some records will have notes and some will not), make sure to specify Left Outer Join as the join type; otherwise, the childless parent rows will not show.

Next, you can insert the necessary text objects for the report. You can set any necessary alignments by selecting the appropriate text objects and then right-clicking (see Figure 9-6).

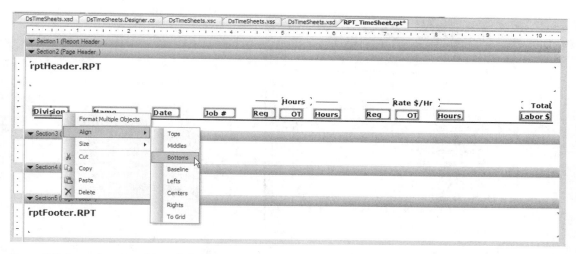

Figure 9-6. *Inserting text objects/labels, and using alignment tools as necessary*

■**Note** Use text objects only for labels that are not likely to change. For example, column headings such as "date" and "Hours" are static. However, you should use data elements instead of labels for any annotations that can and will change.

Your report displays timesheet records by day for each employee and for each division. So you have two groups of data for the report. Using the timesheet DataSet, you will lay out the report to display each division name, then the names of each employee for that division code, and then for each employee the timesheet records for that employee code. To implement this, you must insert a group for both division and employee. You can insert new groups by selecting the Insert pull-down menu from the Crystal Reports main menu. Crystal Reports will display a screen like the one shown in Figures 9-7 and 9-8, where you can select the column identifier for the group.

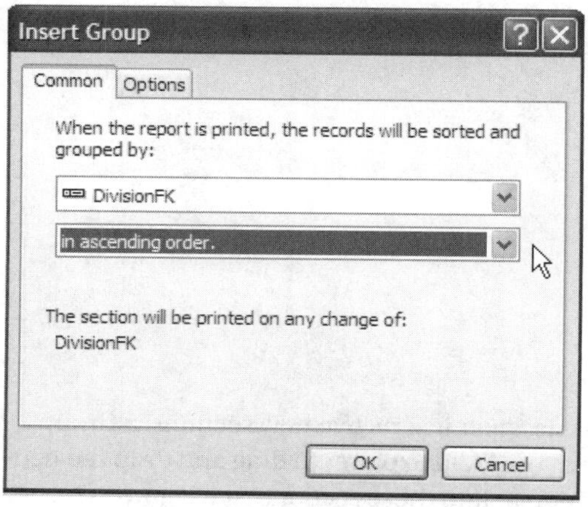

Figure 9-7. *Defining a group*

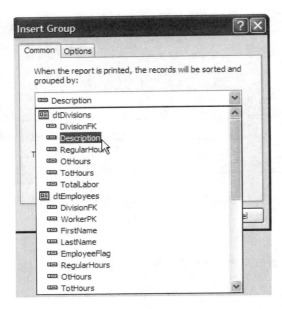

Figure 9-8. *Columns to choose from as the identifier for the group*

The second tab of the Insert Group dialog box allows you to customize the group (see Figure 9-9). For the moment, you will leave these options as is and come back to them a little later when the need surfaces.

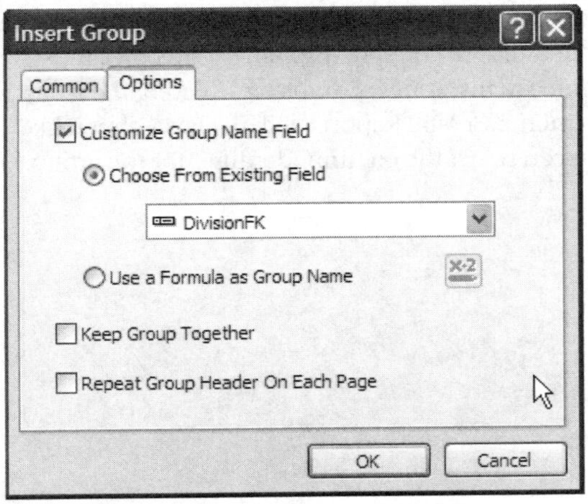

Figure 9-9. *Group options*

After you insert the group, the Crystal Reports designer inserts two new sections: a Group Header section and a Group Footer section. You can use Field Explorer to drag and drop the necessary columns (for example, dtDivisions.Description) into those sections (see Figure 9-10).

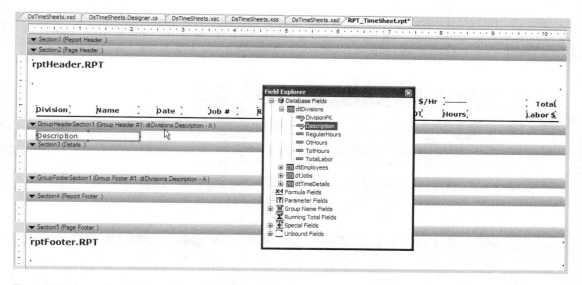

Figure 9-10. *Inserting columns from the Division group as needed*

Now do the same for the employee group using WorkerPK as the column identifier.

Before you insert the employee name into the employee group, stop to consider what you want to display and what columns are available to you. You want to display employee names as a single string (e.g., "John Smith"), instead of two separate columns for first and last name. While you could have created a calculated column in the typed DataSet to concatenate the first and last name, you can also create a formula field in Crystal Reports to display the name in the manner you desire.

As shown in Figure 9-11, load Field Explorer and right-click the Formula Fields item from the list.

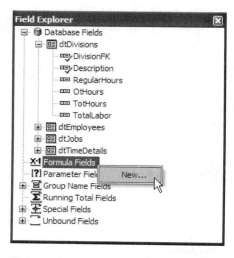

Figure 9-11. *Creating a new formula field*

You will create a new formula called FullName (see Figure 9-12) and click Use Editor to bring up the Formula Editor (see Figure 9-13) to create a calculated field. In the formula, you'll use the TRIM functions to create your formula field.

Figure 9-12. *Giving the new formula a name*

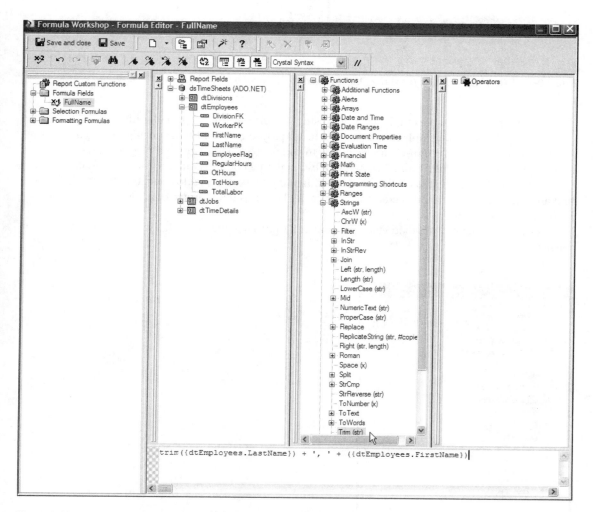

Figure 9-13. *Formula Editor, which provides shortcuts to columns and functions*

Finally, you can drop the formula field directly into the report body (see Figure 9-14).

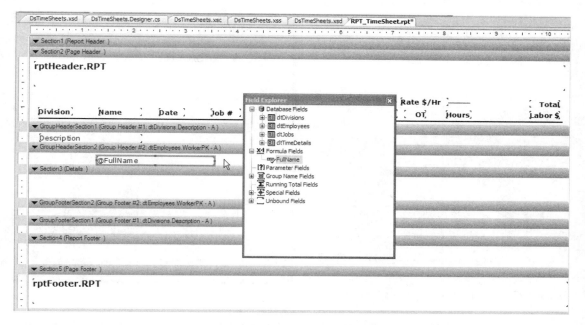

Figure 9-14. *Dropping the FullName formula field into the employee Group Header*

■**Caution** You should limit report formulas to special formatting and display tasks. Don't embed business calculations in formulas. As the report is an extension of the user interface, you shouldn't include business logic in the report any more than you shouldn't include business logic in screens.

Next, you'll drop the numeric and date columns (hours worked, date worked, etc.) onto the report. Crystal Reports gives you many different options for formatting numeric and date data, such as number of decimals and date format mode. Back in Chapter 8, you set default font values for each column and text box object that you create on a report. You can use the same default options screen (by selecting the Crystal Reports menu option, and then selecting Design ➤ Default Settings) to set default values for formatting. Figure 9-15 shows the Format Editor options for numeric data, along with all of the possible format styles. You will set a default format style of -1,123.00. Note that you will not show the currency symbol for each numeric value. For any currency data, you will annotate the column heading to indicate that the column is a currency column.

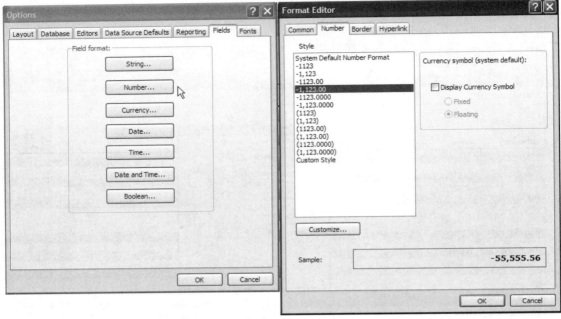

Figure 9-15. *Default format options for numeric data*

Figure 9-16 shows the Format Editor options for date values. By default, you will display dates in MM/DD/YYYY format.

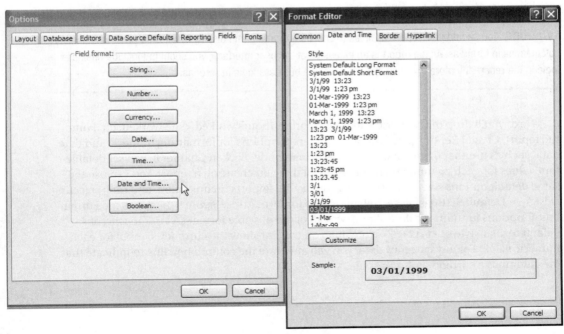

Figure 9-16. *Default format options for date and datetime values*

After you drop all the appropriate data columns onto the report, take a peek at the output using the report preview by clicking the Crystal Reports menu pad option and selecting Preview Report (see Figure 9-17).

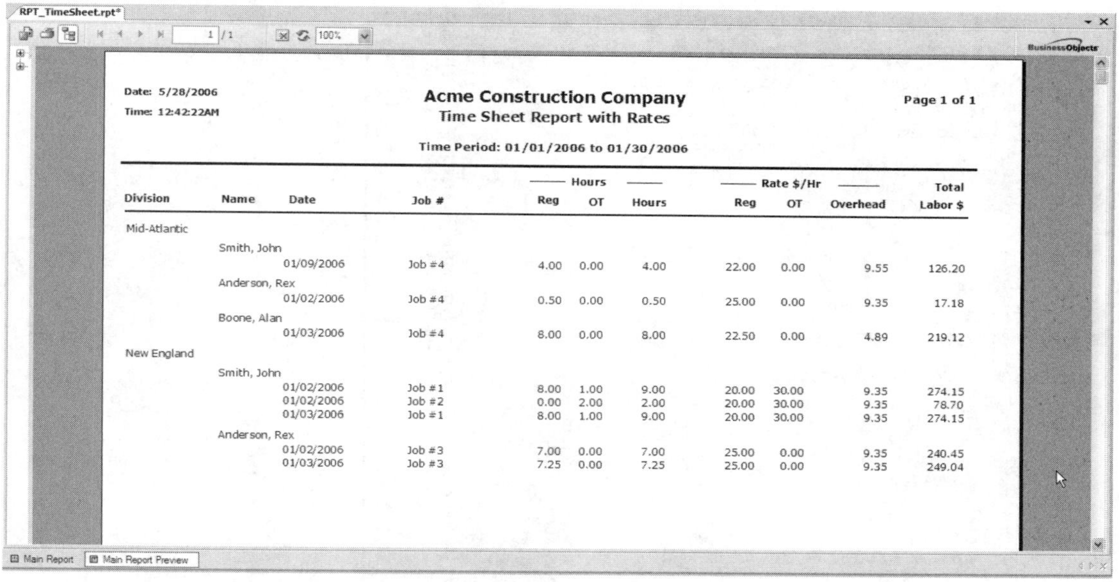
RPT_TimeSheet.rpt*

Date: 5/28/2006
Time: 12:42:22AM

Acme Construction Company
Time Sheet Report with Rates
Time Period: 01/01/2006 to 01/30/2006

Page 1 of 1

Division	Name	Date	Job #	Hours Reg	Hours OT	Hours	Rate $/Hr Reg	Rate $/Hr OT	Overhead	Total Labor $
Mid-Atlantic										
	Smith, John									
		01/09/2006	Job #4	4.00	0.00	4.00	22.00	0.00	9.55	126.20
	Anderson, Rex									
		01/02/2006	Job #4	0.50	0.00	0.50	25.00	0.00	9.35	17.18
	Boone, Alan									
		01/03/2006	Job #4	8.00	0.00	8.00	22.50	0.00	4.89	219.12
New England										
	Smith, John									
		01/02/2006	Job #1	8.00	1.00	9.00	20.00	30.00	9.35	274.15
		01/02/2006	Job #2	0.00	2.00	2.00	20.00	30.00	9.35	78.70
		01/03/2006	Job #1	8.00	1.00	9.00	20.00	30.00	9.35	274.15
	Anderson, Rex									
		01/02/2006	Job #3	7.00	0.00	7.00	25.00	0.00	9.35	240.45
		01/03/2006	Job #3	7.25	0.00	7.25	25.00	0.00	9.35	249.04

Main Report | Main Report Preview

Figure 9-17. *An early preview of the report*

This certainly looks OK; you seem to be on the right track. You still need to implement subtotals for each employee and division; however, there are some other opportunities for improvement:

- First, you have a few instances where a person works on two jobs during a single day. To make it appear more obvious, you'd like to suppress any date value after the first instance.
- Second, you seem to be using a fair amount of vertical space just for one small division—you show a line for a division and a line for the employee, before you show the first line of detail data. Let's look at "sliding up" these values to preserve vertical space.
- Third, all of those zeros make the report look cluttered. You'd like to show blanks if the value is zero.
- Fourth, while you didn't see it in the initial report preview, you want to avoid situations where a page break occurs in the middle of an employee's detail timesheet data. You'll look at protecting an employee group to minimize instances where this would occur.

To address the first issue, Crystal Reports allows you to suppress subsequent duplicate values on a column. If you right-click a column and choose Format Object, Crystal Reports shows the Format Editor. Near the bottom is an option called Suppress If Duplicated (see

Figure 9-18). If you check this option, Crystal Reports will suppress any duplicate instances of a date value within the employee group.

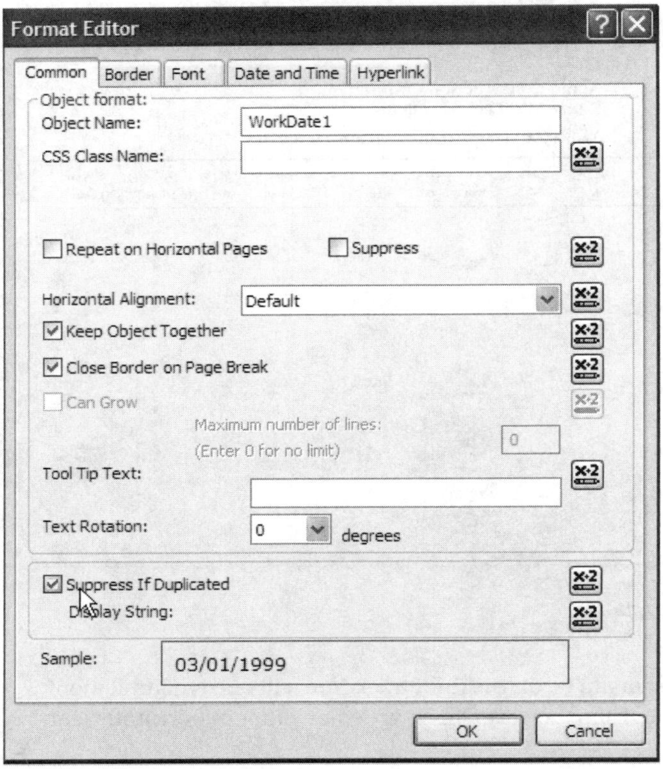

Figure 9-18. *Right-clicking a column, choosing Format Object, and selecting Suppress If Duplicated*

Next, you'll slide up the first line of a timesheet detail record to display on the same line as the employee name, and you'll also slide up the first line of an employee name to display on the same line as the division name. If you'll recall back in Chapter 8, you essentially did the same thing with report heading/footer sections by taking the option to underlay subsequent sections. You can do the same thing here.

As shown in Figure 9-19, you will select the employee Group Header section, load the Section Expert, and check the option to Underlay Following Sections (and then repeat this selection for the division group header). Since the first employee name in a division will appear on the same line as the division name, you'll display the division name in bold to emphasize it.

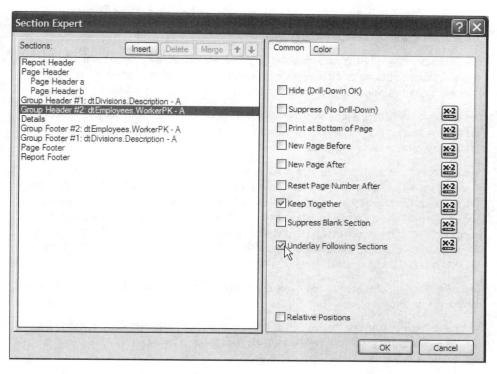

Figure 9-19. *Choosing Underlay Following Sections to merge (slide up) sections*

THE CRYSTAL REPORTS SECTION EXPERT

The Crystal Reports Section Expert is a powerful tool that allows you to manage and customize the different areas (sections) of a report. Here is a list of common tasks where the Section Expert helps you:

- You can insert multiple subsections into a Primary section (Page Header, Page Footer, etc.). You inserted multiple subsections into the report header section in `rptHeader.RPT`, so that you could work with the different vertical pieces of the section. These subsections will follow the behavior of their parent section and allow you to manage and customize these subsections individually and independently of each other.

- You can suppress blank sections. This helps you to cleanly format information that will span a variable number of vertical lines. If you need to display an address that might be three or four or five lines, and don't want to show any white space in between, you can insert a subsection for each line that might be blank (Address Line 2, Address Line 3, etc.), and check the option to Suppress Blank Section. This will eliminate blank spaces.

- You can underlay following sections so that the following section will print in the same vertical space as the current section/subsection.

Continues

- You can color/shade an individual section/subsection.

- You can conditionally suppress a section based on formula. You can store a Boolean column in your result set that indicates whether a section should be printed at runtime, and then write a simple formula that reads the Boolean column and returns a value of true to suppress or false to not suppress.

- You can conditionally force a page break before/after a section prints, based on a formula. Once again, the formula can read from a Boolean column (or some other condition) and return a true or false value to indicate whether a forced page break should occur.

- You can protect a section against being split across two pages by checking the option Keep Together. One example is a Terms and Conditions section of a report. Based on the content of the overall report, the Terms and Conditions section might start at the bottom of one page and continue onto the next page. Since most clients would want this to appear on the same page, checking the Keep Together option will prevent the section from being split. This is basic "widow/orphan" protection for a section. If you need more expansive window/orphan protection for an entire group, check out the same option in the Crystal Reports Group Expert.

- In the Detail band section, you can define multiple columns to print either across and then down, or down and then across.

Just like any other feature or technology, it's best to investigate and experiment with these and other options in the Section Expert to see how they can help you manage your report content.

As for suppressing zero values: since you want this to be a standard formatting rule, you'll go back to the default options for numeric values, click Customize, and then check the option for Suppress if Zero (see Figure 9-20).

Now if you preview the report again (as shown in Figure 9-21), you see that the output looks cleaner and more professional than the initial preview.

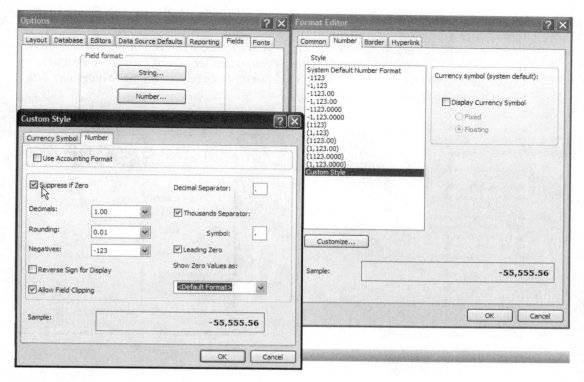

Figure 9-20. *Suppressing if zero*

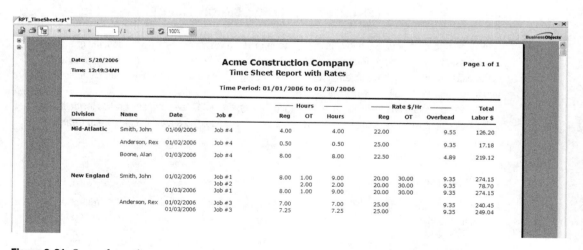

Figure 9-21. *Second preview*

While you didn't have any instances of a page break in the middle of a set of employee records, you can instruct Crystal Reports to keep a group together by loading the Group Expert, selecting the group, and clicking Options (see Figure 9-22). The Group Options dialog box includes a check box option named Keep Group Together. When you check this option, Crystal Reports will force a page break **before** any employee record where the timesheet data would have been split across multiple pages.

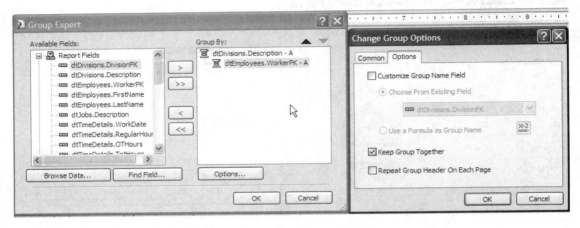

Figure 9-22. *Group option to minimize widow-orphan effect*

THE CRYSTAL REPORTS GROUP EXPERT

Just like the Crystal Reports Section Expert, the Group Expert gives you control over a specific group. A group is essentially a wrapper around a detail band, based on a specific collection (grouping) of data. In your timesheet report, you have an employee group that organizes details by employee and a department group that organizes details by employee group.

The group contains multiple sections: the Group Header, the Detail level and any groups inside it, and the Group Footer. If you need to manage all the sections of the group, you should use the Group Expert, as opposed to the Section Expert.

The Group Expert allows you to do the following:

- You can define the specific data column(s) that define a group.

- You can define the sort order of the group (ascending, descending, or simply by the order of the source data).

- You can repeat the group header on subsequent pages, if a group spans more than one page.

- You can protect an entire group from being split across multiple pages by selecting the option to keep the group together. Just like widow/orphan protection in the Section Expert, you can make sure that a group that would otherwise span multiple pages will begin on a new page.

- Finally, you can specify a Crystal Reports formula as the expression/definition for a group. However, developers should be discouraged from using this option: it may implicitly introduce business logic into the report, and the goal is to treat the report as an extension of the user interface, not a repository for business logic.

    Once again, a little experimenting can go a long way toward learning what the Group Expert can do for you.

Now you can insert subtotals into your employee and division groups. Your division and employee DataTables contain values for subtotals. However, your timesheet DataSet doesn't contain any values for final totals. You can create final totals in your report by right-clicking the column in the detail band you want to aggregate and selecting the option to insert a summary total (see Figure 9-23). This will actually create a new calculated column in the report footer.

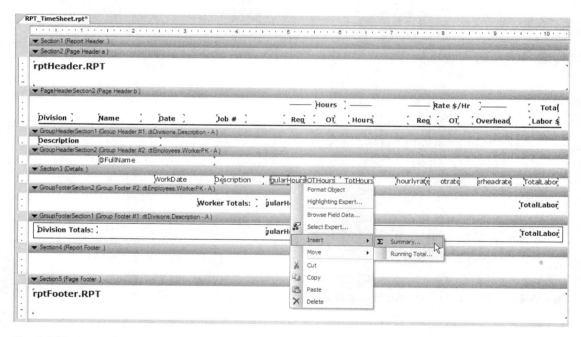

Figure 9-23. *Creating summary totals*

Note Do not create a summary total based on a subtotal in a group column. Always create summary totals based on the column in the detail line. If you create summary totals based on a subtotal, very likely you'll get double (or triple, or quadruple, etc.) counting!

Whoops! You missed one detail: you want to show contractors with an asterisk. You can retrieve the formula field called FullName and modify the formula to display an asterisk if the EmployeeFlag is false (see Figure 9-24).

Note The Crystal Reports formula syntax is a high-level language with VB-like syntax. The Formula Editor Workshop (in Figure 9-24) allows you to explore the list of available functions and operators. In many instances, dragging a function or operator will fill in a partial or complete snippet of the specific syntax. Developers should use formulas judiciously, and restrict them to operations related to formatting and display.

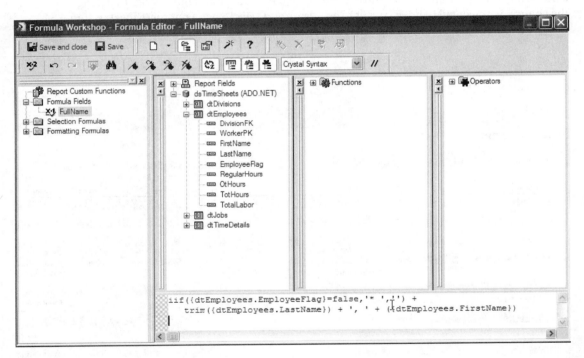

Figure 9-24. *Retrieving the formula field to display contractors with an asterisk*

Tah-dah! You're finished. Figure 9-25 shows the end result.

Acme Construction Company
Time Sheet Report with Rates

Time Period: 01/01/2006 to 01/30/2006

Division	Name	Date	Job #	Hours			Rate $/Hr			Total
				Reg	OT	Hours	Reg	OT	Overhead	Labor $
Mid-Atlantic	Anderson, Rex	01/02/2006	Job #4	0.50		0.50	25.00		9.35	17.18
			Worker Totals:	**0.50**		**0.50**				**17.18**
	* Boone, Alan	01/03/2006	Job #4	8.00		8.00	22.50		4.89	219.12
			Worker Totals:	**8.00**		**8.00**				**219.12**
	Smith, John	01/09/2006	Job #4	4.00		4.00	22.00		9.55	126.20
			Worker Totals:	**4.00**		**4.00**				**126.20**
Division Totals:				**12.50**		**12.50**				**362.50**
New England	Anderson, Rex	01/02/2006	Job #3	7.00		7.00	25.00		9.35	240.45
		01/03/2006	Job #3	7.25		7.25	25.00		9.35	249.04
			Worker Totals:	**14.25**		**14.25**				**489.49**
	Smith, John	01/02/2006	Job #1	8.00	1.00	9.00	20.00	30.00	9.35	274.15
			Job #2		2.00	2.00	20.00	30.00	9.35	78.70
		01/03/2006	Job #1	8.00	1.00	9.00	20.00	30.00	9.35	274.15
			Worker Totals:	**16.00**	**4.00**	**20.00**				**627.00**
Division Totals:				**30.25**	**4.00**	**34.25**				**1,116.49**
Final Totals:				**42.75**	**4.00**	**46.75**				**1,478.99**

Figure 9-25. *The timesheet report*

Final Notes

Of course, there are always additional opportunities for improvement. For example, you could conditionally suppress the employee group footer line if the employee only has one row of data (since the summarized values in the subtotal line should be the same as the one detail line).

Report 2: Implementing the Gantt Chart

Your next report is the project Gantt chart. A Gantt chart is a pictorial chronological representation of data, project schedules, etc. Because of their visual nature (see the example in Figure 9-26 in the next section), they are often easily comprehended by most people. Your Gantt chart will show a timeline of past client construction projects. To increase the value of the report, you'll include an additional detail band to show data for each construction job that the report displays.

The End Result

Figure 9-26 shows the final output for the Gantt chart. You'll build the report as RPT_JobGanttChart.RPT in the ConstructionDemo.CrystalReports namespace. The report contains two bands per page: the Gantt chart on the left and the data recap for the related jobs on the right. Note that the first page displays projects for four clients. Your result set will contain a column for the actual page number—you can set a rule to allow the end user to determine the maximum number of clients to display on one page, and then calculate which clients will show on which page. (We'll cover this further when we talk about the user-interface portion of the reports in Chapter 13.)

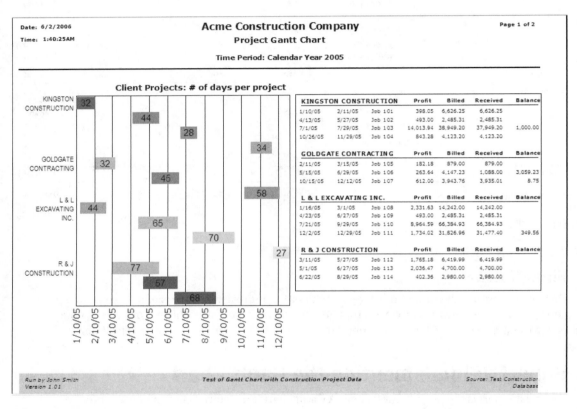

Figure 9-26. *The final result*

The Result Set

Table 9-2 shows the result set for the Gantt chart, from dsJobGanttChart in the ConstructionDemo.DataSets project. dsJobGanttChart contains a parent table for each client and the page to which the client belongs, and a child table that contains the detail data for each client construction job. The page number will drive the main group section for the report.

Table 9-2. *Result Set for the Gantt Chart (dsJobGanttChart)*

Table	Column	Type
dtClients	PageNumber	Integer
	ClientFK	Integer
dtJobs	ClientFK	Integer
	ClientName	String
	StartDate	DateTime
	EndDate	DateTime
	JobNumber	String
	JobDescription	String
	TotalProfit	Decimal
	TotalBilled	Decimal
	TotalReceived	Decimal
	AmountDue	Decimal

The Steps to Build It

Just like you did with the timesheet report, you'll create a new Crystal report in the
ConstructionDemo.CrystalReports namespace and call it RPT_JobGanttChart.RPT. Again,
you'll build the report from an existing report, your base template report. Additionally,
you'll load the Database Expert in Crystal Reports .NET and navigate to either the schema
(dsJobGanttChart.XSD) or the schema with data (dsJobGanttChart.XML), depending on
whether you want to preview the report.

Note For all of the remaining reports, the first set of tasks is the same. Create a new item in the
ConstructionDemo.CrystalReports namespace, specify the item as a Crystal Reports file, provide the
report name, create it from an existing report (your template rptBase.RPT), and then launch the Crystal
Reports Database Expert to select the supporting DataSet structure.

Figure 9-27 shows the linking expert for the two DataTables in the Gantt DataSet definition. You are establishing a link between the client column in the parent table and the client
column in the job detail table.

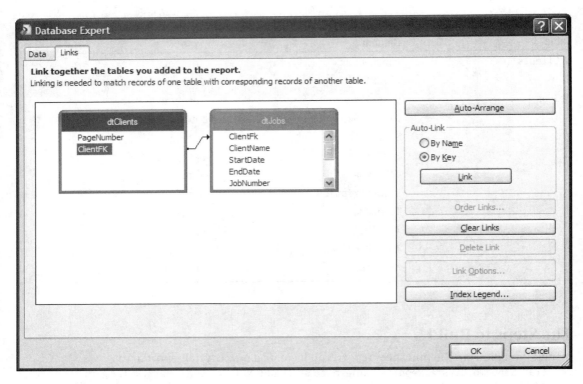

Figure 9-27. *Linking Expert for the Gantt chart*

Next, you need to establish the main group for the report, based on the PageNumber column (see Figure 9-28).

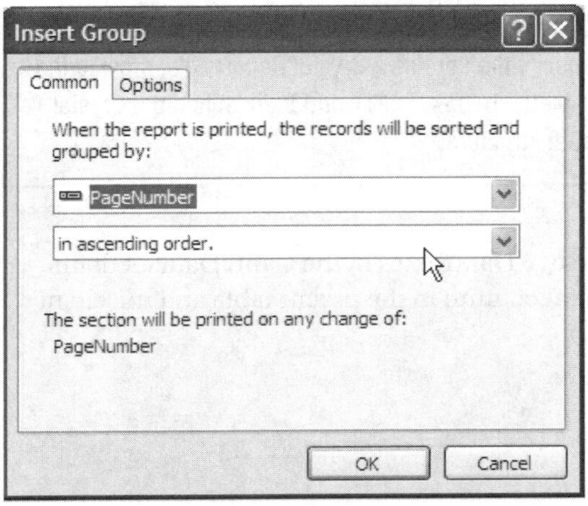

Figure 9-28. *Inserting the main group, based on the PageNumber column*

Inside the Group Header section, you are going to insert two primary items: a chart object (which you'll define as a Gantt chart), and then a subreport to show the supporting data. First, you will insert the new chart. Right-click anywhere in the Group Header section and select Insert ➤ Chart from the shortcut menu. (Alternatively, you can select the main Crystal Reports menu option, and select Insert ➤ Chart.)

Once you tell Crystal to insert a new chart, you'll see the Crystal Reports dialog (see Figure 9-29) that allows you to define a new chart type. Your first step is to define the chart type on the first tab of the Chart Expert. The Chart Expert displays each available chart, along with a description of the chart.

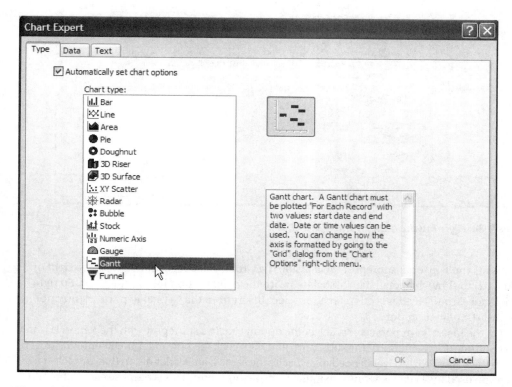

Figure 9-29. *Available chart types*

Next, you need to define the data columns that will drive the chart (see Figure 9-30). Your Gantt chart requires two pieces of information: the column for which you are displaying data (dtJobs.ClientName), and the start-end date of each construction job.

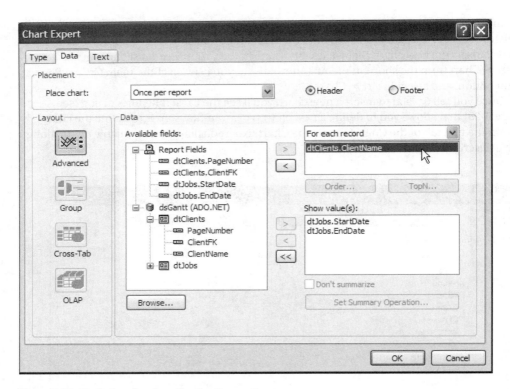

Figure 9-30. *Defining the data for the Gantt chart*

Next, you'll insert a subreport (also inside the Group Header section, and to the right of the chart) to show the detail data associated with the construction jobs in the chart. So right-click in the Group Header section area (or select Insert from the Crystal Reports menu option) and insert a new subreport.

On the Insert Subreport screen, select the option Create a subreport with the Report Wizard, enter **SubJobs** for the name of the subreport, and then click the button for the Report Wizard.

In the Report Wizard, you'll need to respecify the same DataSet definition that you selected when you used the Database Expert to initially create this report. This is because each subreport contains a separate database object. After you specify the same DataSet definition (either the XSD or XML for the job Gantt chart) by clicking the Finish button, you can establish the link between the main page and the subreport that will show all of the construction jobs for the chart page.

The PageNumber column in the main parent table will drive the display of the detail construction job data, as illustrated in the subreport link in Figure 9-31.

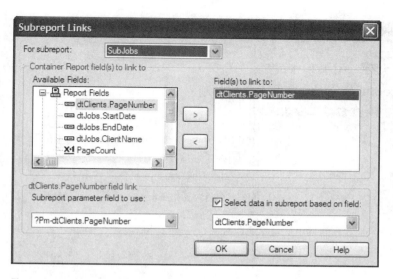

Figure 9-31. *Establishing the links into the subreport that shows the construction job data*

You'll lay out the subreport (SubJobs) as shown in Figure 9-32, using Field Explorer to drag the columns. Since you specified dsJobGanttChart as the data source for the subreport, the columns should appear in Field Explorer for you to select. Note that you have to be careful about horizontal space, as you're showing the Gantt chart and the data listing side by side.

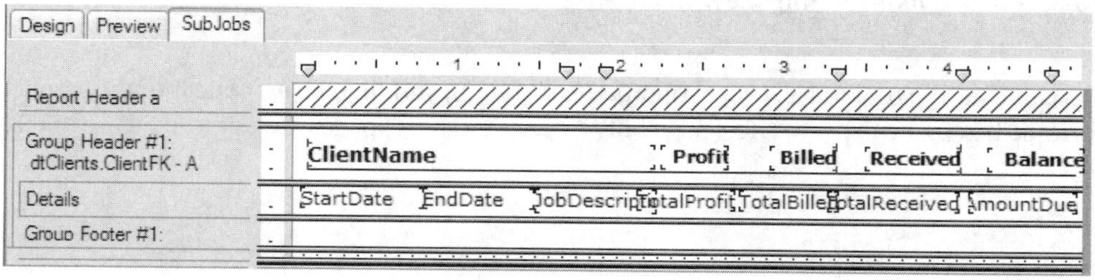

Figure 9-32. *The subreport for the detail construction job data*

Finally, we'll cover an area that often creates confusion with developers using Crystal: how to handle a blank page that may appear at the end of a report. In this instance, you want to tell Crystal not to print a new page if there is no more data to show—specifically if the next key value (PageNumber) is null. The best place to handle this is to load the Section Expert (either by selecting the Crystal Reports menu option, and then Report ➤ Selection Expert, or by right-clicking in the main report area and following the same context menu structure to get to the Section Expert) in the group footer for the PageNumber group (see Figure 9-33).

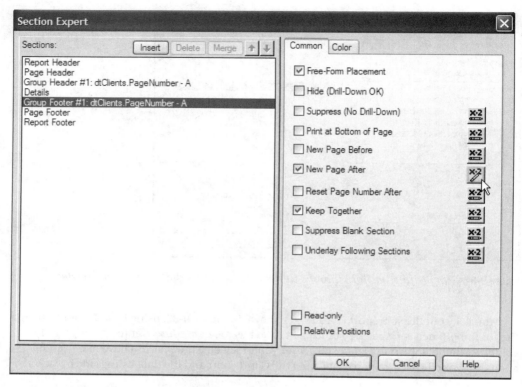

Figure 9-33. *Conditionally setting the next page*

You can click the option New Page After (in Figure 9-33), and then insert code into the associated formula box that will print a new page only if there is a "next" page number (see Figure 9-34).

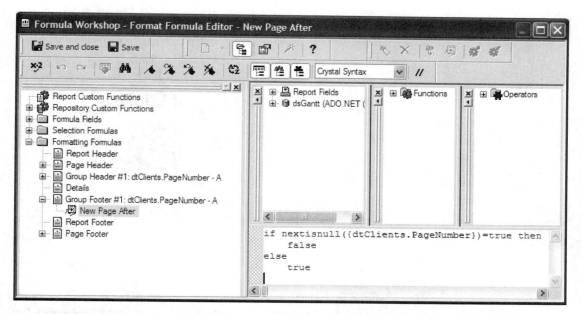

Figure 9-34. *Defining a formula to print the next page only if NextIsNull is false*

Report 3: Implementing Dynamic Images on a Customer Invoice

A common question on Crystal forums is how to generate images dynamically on a report. Your customer invoice contains this requirement. Any time you generate an invoice, whether a single invoice for a single customer or a group of invoices for different customers, you want to display the customer logo on the report.

The End Result

Figure 9-35 shows an example of what you want to accomplish. The customer logo (from a JPG, BMP, or other picture file) appears in the upper-right corner.

Customer Invoice

Customer: **K. GOFF Construction**

Figure 9-35. *Customer invoice*

You'll define a DataColumn in your result set to hold the contents of the image, insert the DataColumn on the report as a BLOB field, and then load the DataColumn at runtime with the appropriate picture file.

The Result Set

You'll need to define a new DataColumn in the DataTable that stores the customer name and other general customer information for the invoice (dtInvoices). You'll call it ClientLogo. The DataType must be base64binary, which you can set in the XML Schema Editor for the typed DataSet. Alternatively, you can define the DataType as a byte array (System.Byte[]) in the standard DataSet Editor.

The Steps to Build It

After you define the binary column in the result set, you must insert the column in the report design area. Note that Crystal Reports will treat the column as a BLOB object, which you can then size and position as needed.

Finally, you need to populate the image at runtime when you populate the rest of the result set contents. Listing 9-1 shows a code sample for creating a binary reader and inserting the picture image into the DataSet.

Listing 9-1. *Code to Load an Image into a Datacolumn, for Use in Crystal Reports*

```
dsInvoices odsInvoices = new dsInvoices();

// Might be read in many different ways
string cPicFileName = "c:\\construction.jpg";
```

```
// Must create a stream and a reader
FileStream fsStream = new FileStream(cPicFileName, FileMode.Open);
BinaryReader br = new BinaryReader(fsStream);

dsInvoices.dtInvoicesRow oRow = odsInvoices.dtInvoices.NewdtInvoiceRow();
oRow.ClientName = "K. GOFF Construction";
oRow.ClientLogo = br.ReadBytes((int)br.BaseStream.Length);
odsInvoices.dtInvoices.Rows.Add(oRow);
```

Report 4: Implementing a Stacked Bar Chart

The fourth report is a stacked bar chart that depicts an organization's costs over the last year and a half. The report displays the cost data by division, broken out by month, and subdivided by cost category. The report also displays total costs for the same time period a year ago. In order to show trends from the previous year, the report uses a single horizontal line to graph the total costs for the prior year. You'll build the report as RPT_CostStackedBarGraph.RPT in the ConstructionDemo.CrystalReports namespace.

The End Result

Figure 9-36 shows the final stacked bar chart.

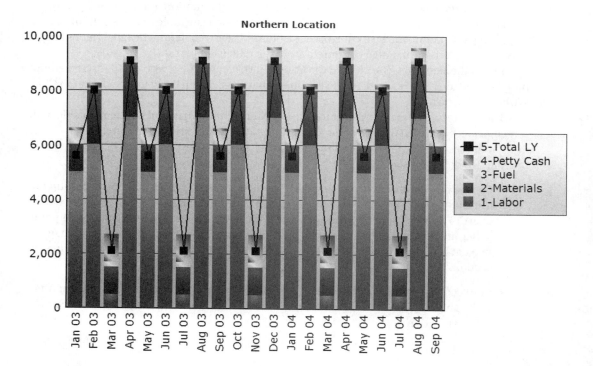

Figure 9-36. *Stacked bar chart*

The Result Set

Table 9-3 shows the result set for the stacked bar chart, from `dsSimpleChart` in the `ConstructionDemo.Datasets` project. As with prior reports, you'll define a parent table that contains the division names and a child table that contains all the data you want to graph. The child table will contain up to five rows for each month's worth of data for a division: one row for each cost data by type (labor, materials, fuel, petty cash, and total amount last year).

Table 9-3. *Result Set for a Bar Chart (dsSimpleChart)*

Table	Column	Type
dtDivisions	DivisionFK	Integer
	Description	String
dtGraph	DivisionFK	Integer
	LegendType (Labor, Materials, etc.)	String
	Label (Jan 03, Feb 03, etc.)	String
	Data	Decimal

The Steps to Build It

Crystal Reports needs data not only for the pictorial representation, but also for legends, x-axis descriptions, etc. Looking back at the result set, the DataTable needs a column (`LegendType`) to define the cost categories, a column (`Label`) to define the labels along the x-axis (for each month), and a column to store the data itself (`Data`).

Just in the same way you created the Gantt chart, create a new report and insert a group based on the `DivisionFK` key. Then insert a new chart, which will bring up the three-tab Chart Wizard dialog box.

The first tab allows you to select the type of chart. Choose Bar, and on the right side of the screen, choose the specific type of bar chart (e.g., side-by-side, stacked bar, etc.).

On the second tab, you will define the data for the graph (see Figure 9-37). You need to provide two definitions:

- For the first definition (On change of), you need to define the group and subgroup for the chart breakdown. (You need a subgroup definition because this is a stacked bar chart.) The main group for the bar chart is the x-axis definition (each month), and the subgroup includes any groupings within each month (the cost categories). So drag the two data columns that represent the month and cost categories into the On change of section.

- The second definition (Show value(s)) represents the actual data that Crystal Reports will chart: drag the data column that contains the actual numeric data into the Show value(s) section.

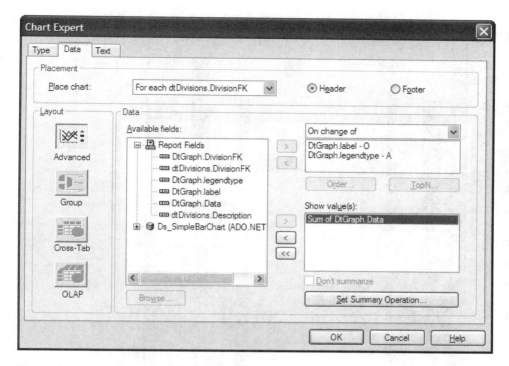

Figure 9-37. *Setting the data for the graph*

At this point, the chart will show a stacked bar for all five legend types (see Figure 9-38). However, you want to display the total costs from last year as a horizontal line, not as a stacked bar. As you can see back in Figure 9-36, this will allow you to easily compare total costs between this year and last year.

In order to do this, you need to preview the report, select the top stacked bar, and right-click (again, see Figure 9-38). Crystal Reports displays the Chart Options submenu: select the Series option, which will display the Series Options dialog shown in Figure 9-39.

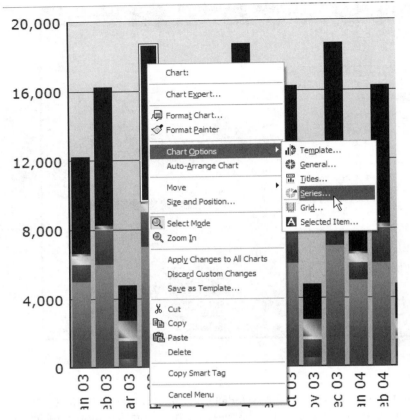

Figure 9-38. *Right-clicking a specific stacked bar to access the Series chart option*

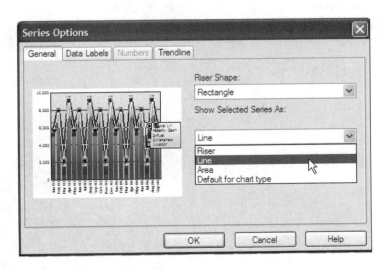

Figure 9-39. *Setting a specific stacked bar as a horizontal line*

This dialog allows you to customize how you display the specific stacked bar that you previously selected. To display the selected stacked bar as a horizontal line instead of the default riser shape, change the Show Selected Series As to Line.

Now that you've defined the data for last year's costs as a line, you can customize the display of the line (color, thickness, etc.) by right-clicking the line on the preview screen and selecting the Selected Item option under the Chart Options menu. You'll then see a dialog that allows you to customize the appearance of the line (as shown in Figure 9-40).

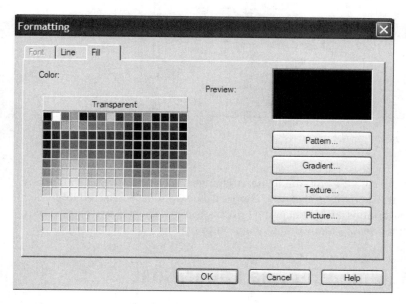

Figure 9-40. *Formatting a specific line item in the graph*

You just need to make a few more adjustments to generate the final finished product. First, you need to define a legend. To show a legend, right-click the graph, choose Chart Options ➤ General, go to the Look tab, and check the check box for Show Legend (see Figure 9-41). Note the options underneath the check box for the placement and appearance of the legend box.

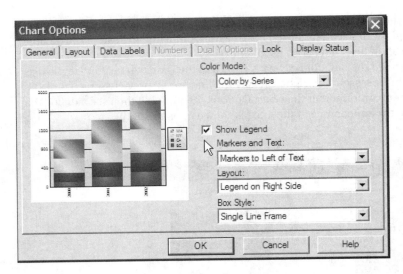

Figure 9-41. *Defining a legend for the graph*

Finally, just as you did with the horizontal line, to change the color/font/gradient for any series, label, etc., select the item, right-click, and choose Chart Options ➤ Selected Item.

You can check these options, and other graph options, by right-clicking a portion of the graph. The context menu provides many different options for customizing chart output.

Report 5: Implementing the Labor/Cost Report/Graph

We've saved the best for last! Your final output is a report with two charts and a detail band on a single page. One of the Holy Grails of business reporting is the ability to cleanly integrate charts and reports using multiple levels of data, and this is an area where Crystal Reports shines. The report also shows how to dynamically display certain pieces of data in a different color based on a specific condition.

The End Result

Figure 9-42 shows a cost profile report that consists of a line chart showing cost trends over time, a pie chart depicting cost by division, and a report band showing additional monthly job labor/cost information. You'll build the report as RPT_CostLaborReportGraph.RPT in the ConstructionDemo.CrystalReports namespace.

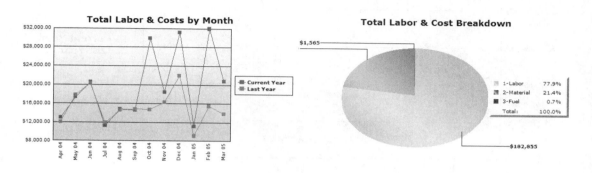

Month Ending	Labor $	Costs $
Apr 04	12,951.23	
May 04	17,338.21	
Jun 04	20,511.56	
Jul 04	11,251.25	
Aug 04	14,797.90	
Sep 04	14,537.15	
Oct 04	14,721.55	15,120.00
Nov 04	17,020.85	1,402.50
Dec 04	21,195.72	9,968.00
Jan 05	9,829.09	1,401.44
Feb 05	14,771.53	17,178.51
Mar 05	13,928.56	6,825.00
Total:	**182,854.60**	**51,895.45**

Figure 9-42. *Preview of the labor/cost report/graph—note the three separate areas.*

The next three figures show each of the three report sections separately (to get a closer look). Figure 9-43 shows the line chart. We will show you how to construct a line chart based on the types of data and the monthly breakdown.

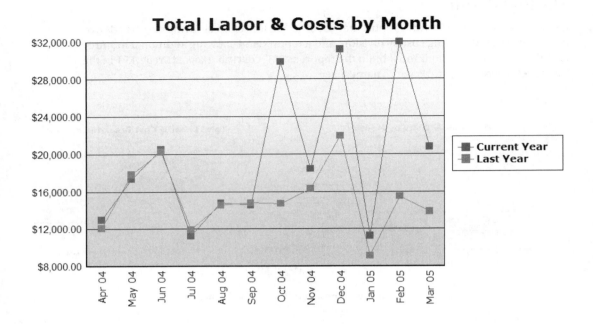

Figure 9-43. *Line chart that breaks out costs by total labor and other costs by month*

Figure 9-44 shows the pie chart. You will see how to construct a pie chart along with a legend, and data annotations for each pie slice.

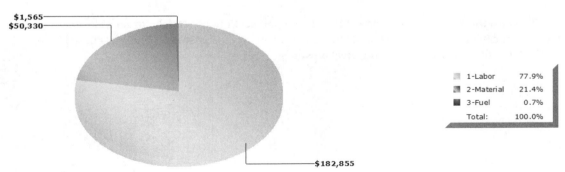

Figure 9-44. *Basic pie chart to break out labor and costs, with a legend and data annotations*

Finally, Figure 9-45 shows the data recap at the bottom of the page. Note that the report displays certain values in red. We'll show how to dynamically display values based on a run-time condition.

Construction Labor/Material Summary

Month Ending	Labor $	Costs $
Apr 04	12,951.23	
May 04	17,338.21	
Jun 04	20,511.56	
Jul 04	11,251.25	
Aug 04	14,797.90	
Sep 04	14,537.15	
Oct 04	14,721.55	15,120.00
Nov 04	17,020.85	1,402.50
Dec 04	21,195.72	9,968.00
Jan 05	9,829.09	1,401.44
Feb 05	14,771.53	17,178.51
Mar 05	13,928.56	6,825.00
Total:	**182,854.60**	**51,895.45**

Figure 9-45. *The data recap as a subreport*

The Result Set

Table 9-4 displays the result set for the entire labor/cost report, from dsCostReportGraph in the ConstructionDemo.Datasets project. The first DataTable contains user-supplied threshold values for displaying the labor/cost recap data in red. The second DataTable will define the group-level data (one page for each division). The third DataTable stores data for the line chart; you will have two rows for each division/month: one for total costs this year, and one for total costs last year. The fourth DataTable stores data for the pie chart (one row per division/cost type, which will represent a single pie slice). Finally, the fifth DataTable contains data for the summarized recap listing at the bottom of the page.

Table 9-4. *Result Set for the Labor/Cost Report/Graph* (dsCostReportGraph)

Table	Column
dtHeader	LaborThreshold
	CostThreshold
dtDivisions	DivisionFK
	Description
dtLineChart	DivisionFK
	MonthEnding
	Legend
	Costs
dtPieChart	DivisionFK
	CostType
	CostAmount

Continues

Table 9-4. *Continued*

Table	Column
dtSummaryData	DivisionFK
	MonthEnding
	LaborAmount
	Costs

The Steps to Build It

For this report, you'll start by displaying the end result of the designer, and then work backwards.

First, create a group by Division, based on the DivisionPK column in dtDivisions.

Second, insert multiple subsections within the Group Header section (using the Section Expert), so that you have Group Headers 1a, 1b, and 1c. You will place subreports in each of these sections.

In the first Group Header (1a), create a subreport called LineChart. In the subreport, set the DataSource to the same XML DataSource as the main report (dsCostReportGraph), and establish a subreport link based on DivisionFK between the dtDivisions and dtLineChart tables. In the second Group Header (1b), create a subreport called PieChart. In the subreport, set the DataSource to the same XML DataSource as the main report (dsCostReportGraph), and establish a subreport link based on DivisionFK between the dtDivisions and dtPieChart tables.

Figure 9-46 shows a group based on the division/location, and separate sections for the LineChart subreport, PieChart subreport, and then the data recap.

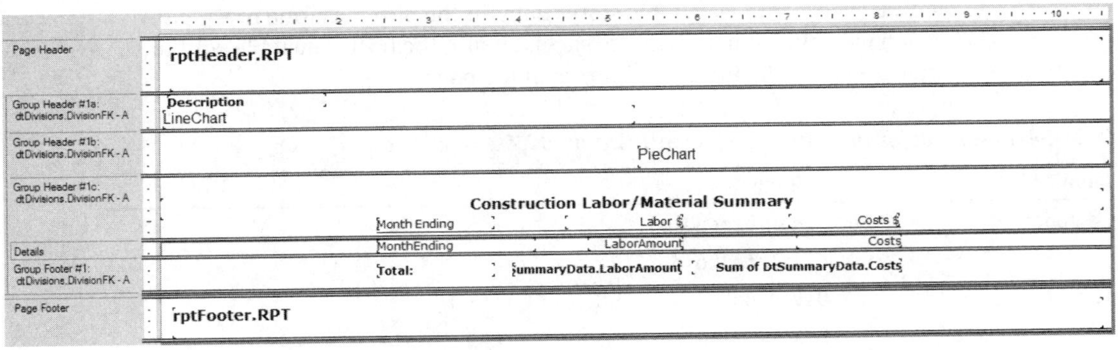

Figure 9-46. *The final designer contents for the report and graph*

As previously seen with subreports, you need to establish links into each subreport—this time, based on the division/location. Figure 9-47 shows the Subreport Links screen where you can link the main report to the LineChart subreport based on the division.

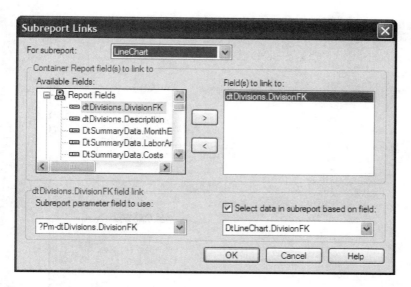

Figure 9-47. *Establishing subreport links for the subreport chart*

Back in the stacked bar chart, you provided information to Crystal Reports on how to use the data for building the chart. The same concept applies for the line chart: you want to generate two lines, one for each legend type within a month, so start off by inserting a line chart into the LineChart subreport. Figure 9-48 shows the Data tab of the Chart Expert, where you graph the sum of costs (Show value(s)) as lines on the change of legend within MonthEnding values (the On change of option). The end result of these options gives you a vertical bar on each change of the MonthEnding column, subdivided by colored stacks on each change of the Legend column within the MonthEnding column.

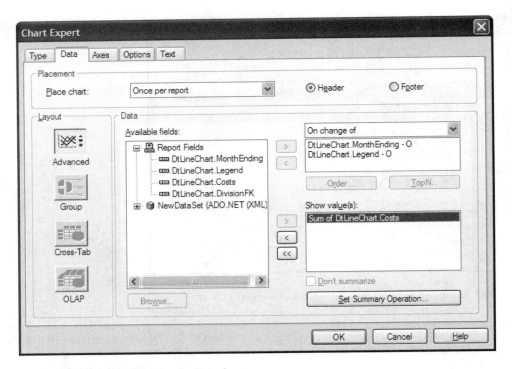

Figure 9-48. *Defining data for the line chart*

Next, you need to insert the pie chart into the `PieChart` subreport and define the data. In Figure 9-49, you instruct Crystal Reports to build a pie chart based on the values in `dtPieChart.CostAmount`, broken out by `dtPieChart.CostType` (the individual pie slices).

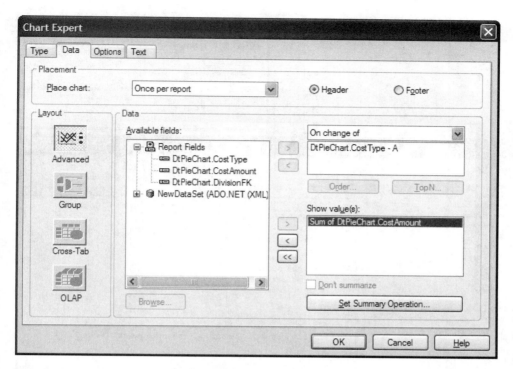

Figure 9-49. *Defining data for the pie chart*

Finally, you need to configure the labor and cost values in the data recap to display in red if they exceed the threshold values stored in the dtHeader table. This is a good example of when you should use formula fields (and also how to use them). Figure 9-50 shows the formula field for the Font Color option for each cost in the data summary recap. Note that the formula returns a value of crRed (a Crystal Reports constant) for any cost value that exceeds the cost threshold, and a value of crBlack (the default) for any values that do not. Note that you do not hard-wire the values for the threshold for the formula: you place the threshold in the DataSet, which the user can define at runtime.

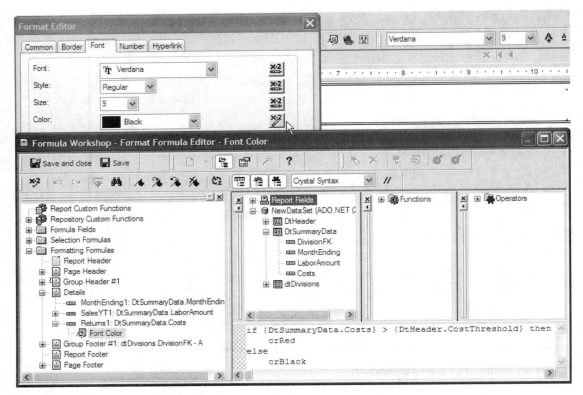

Figure 9-50. *Formula to show data in a different color, based on a value*

Final Note: the Aging Receivables Report

In previous chapters, we covered back-end logic (stored procedures, data access, etc.) for the aging receivables report. In Chapter 12, when we focus on showing you how to integrate your reports with the application, we'll give you a refresher course on the Crystal Reports .NET Designer and cover the necessary steps for building the aging receivables report.

Summary

This concludes our coverage of the Crystal Reports designer. The next two chapters will demonstrate how many of these reporting requirements can be addressed with two other report writers, ActiveReports and SQL Reporting Services. After that, Chapter 12 will demonstrate how you as a developer can programmatically integrate these reports into your application.

■ ■ ■

CHAPTER 10

Using ActiveReports for .NET

In Chapters 8 and 9, you learned about using Crystal Reports for creating basic-to-intermediate reports. This chapter will cover another report writer: ActiveReports for .NET from Data Dynamics. Whereas Crystal Reports is considered more of an end-user reporting tool, ActiveReports is much more a programmer's reporting tool.

While Crystal Reports ships with Visual Studio, there is definitely a good reason to use ActiveReports for .NET. Whereas Crystal Reports is a more self-contained type of report writer, ActiveReports for .NET is more of a set of building blocks for creating reports. These building blocks are all developed in managed code and provide capabilities that will make .NET developers feel right at home. You can create inheritable reports, add custom properties and methods to reports, and build up reports dynamically with VB .NET and C# code.

This chapter will demonstrate using ActiveReports to carry out the tasks you learned how to perform using Crystal Reports in Chapters 8 and 9.

ActiveReports Basics

After installing ActiveReports .NET (version 2.0, available at www.datadynamics.com), you are ready to begin creating reports. The nice thing about ActiveReports for .NET is that its installer places all of its required assemblies into the Global Assembly Cache, integrates its help content into your Visual Studio shell, and adds its components to the Visual Studio IDE. So once you have installed it, you are off to the races. This first section will demonstrate the following tasks:

- Creating a basic report using an XML XSD file

- Binding data to your report

- Creating an application for viewing your report

Creating Your First Reporting Application

When installed, ActiveReports integrates its tools into the Visual Studio IDE. The process of incorporating reports into your Visual Studio is just like it is for all other Visual Studio components. You simply select Add New Item from your Solution Explorer and select ActiveReport from the list of installed items. To begin using ActiveReports, perform the following steps:

1. Create a new C# Windows application, naming it **ARReporting**.

2. After your project has been created, right-click the Solution Explorer window and choose Add New Item.

3. In the Add New Item dialog (see Figure 10-1), select ActiveReports File as the template and specify `rptEmployeeList.rpx` for the name of the report.

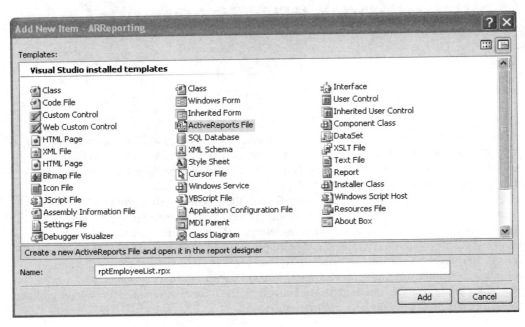

Figure 10-1. *Creating a new ActiveReport item*

Upon creation, your report will be opened in the Visual Studio IDE, as shown in Figure 10-2.

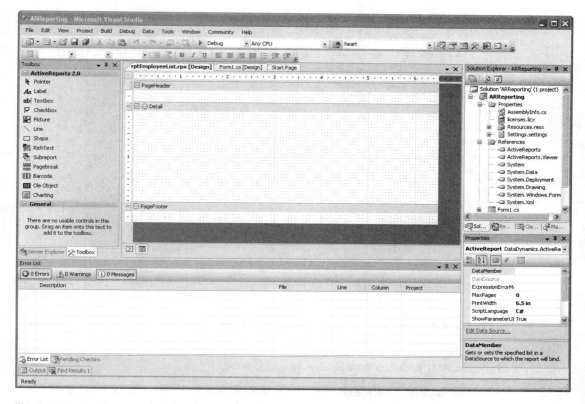

Figure 10-2. *New ActiveReport shown in the Visual Studio IDE*

The ActiveReports designer integrates a number of tools into the Visual Studio IDE. A Report menu bar is added, a Report Explorer is created, and a new toolbox full of ActiveReports controls is included. The **Report menu bar** is where you specify layout characteristics for your report (size, orientation, and styles). The Report menu bar is also used to specify a datasource for your reports. The **toolbox** contains a number of controls that can be added to a report including labels, text boxes, check boxes, pictures, etc. The **Report Explorer** gives you an outline of the bands contained in your report, shows you the data fields retrieved from your datasource, and also allows you to drag and drop data fields onto your report.

Binding to the XML-XSD File

After creating the empty shell of your report, you can begin the process of laying out your report. In a fashion similar to the previous chapters, you will use an XML-XSD file to assist in the creation of your report(s). To incorporate an XML-XSD file into your report, do the following:

1. Select Data Source from the Report menu. Selecting this option opens the Report Data Source dialog (see Figure 10-3).

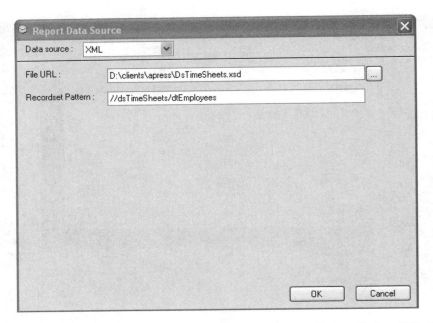

Figure 10-3. *ActiveReports Data Source dialog with XML file specified and XPath syntax*

2. Select XML from the Data Source drop-down list.

3. In the File URL field, specify the path to your XSD file. (If you click the selector button, the dialog opens filters to XML files. Entering ***.xsd** in the File URL field will allow you to select XSD files.) For this example, select the XSD file from Chapter 9.

4. Upon selecting your XSD file, you need to specify the correct XPath notation to retrieve the proper nodes from your XML document. For this example, enter **//dsTimeSheets/ dtEmployees**. This XPath notation tells ActiveReports that fields for this report will be pulled from the dsTimeSheets DataSet and the dtEmployees table.

5. After specifying the XPath notation, you can begin dragging and dropping fields onto your report from the Report Explorer (see Figure 10-4).

Figure 10-4. *ActiveReports Report Explorer with the dtEmployees datatable specified as datasource*

6. Drag the `FirstName`, `LastName`, and `WorkerPK` fields onto your report. When you drag and drop these fields onto your report, ActiveReports will create text box fields for each item.

7. Now you can proceed to doing some simple layout on your report.

Simple ActiveReports Layout

The process of doing layout in ActiveReports is very similar to creating a Windows form or an ASP.NET web page. ActiveReports controls have properties that you can specify in the Visual Studio property sheet. Figure 10-5 shows the property sheet available for an ActiveReports text box.

Figure 10-5. *ActiveReports text box property sheet*

As you can see, the property sheet is used to specify formatting and data-binding information for your report output. You can change information such as colors, fonts, sizes, and data-binding information. In this example, you will change the font information for the controls you just added. You will also add labels to the report header for your controls. Here are the steps you need to take:

1. Select all the controls with your mouse.

2. Expand the Font section of the property sheet.

3. Enter **Tahoma** in the Name field and **14** in the Size field.

4. Resize your controls using the mouse.

5. Select the label control from the ActiveReports toolbox.

6. Select all three controls and change their font to Tahoma and 14pt using the same process as step 3.

7. Change the labels' Text property to **Last Name**, **First Name**, and **Employee #**, respectively.

8. Resize the controls accordingly.

9. You can now also resize the Detail area of the report to a specific size.

10. Select the Detail area.

11. In the Height property, enter a value of **.40**. This will reduce the size of each Detail area to .40 inches.

You report should look like the one in Figure 10-6.

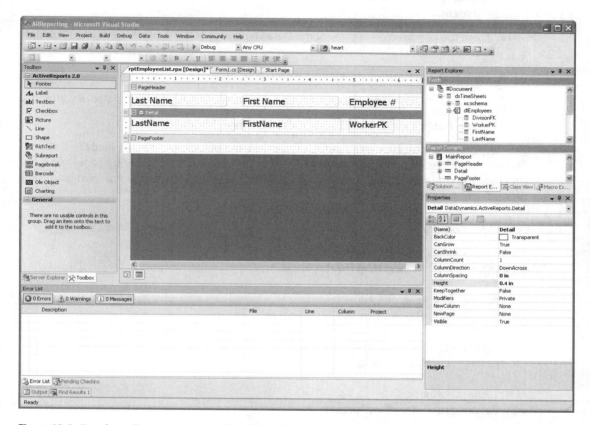

Figure 10-6. *Employee list report in the Visual Studio IDE*

Now that you have the layout for your report completed, you need to create a mechanism for viewing your report. The next section will discuss creating a preview form for running your report.

Creating a Report Viewer

Now that you have created a report, you will want to view the contents of that report. The current version of ActiveReports (2.0) does not have a mechanism for automatically previewing your reports. This means you will need to create your own report viewer. To create a report viewer, carry out the following steps:

1. From the Solution Explorer, select the `Form1.cs` file that was created by default.

2. Rename this file to `frmReportViewer.cs`.

3. Set the `Text` property of your report to **ActiveReports Demo**.

4. You will then need to add an ActiveReports Viewer control to your form. In an existing toolbox or new toolbox, you can add the ActiveReports control by right-clicking in the appropriate toolbox and selecting the Choose Items option from the provided short-cut menu.

5. From the provided dialog, select the Data Dynamics ActiveReports Viewer control from the `ActiveReports` namespace.

6. Now drag and drop a Viewer control onto your form.

7. Set the `Size` and `Anchor` properties to make the viewer correspond to the size of your form.

8. Add a button to your form. Set its `Text` property to **Employee List**.

Now that you have created a report and the skeleton of a viewer, you are ready to load data into your report and view its contents. Listing 10-1 demonstrates creating your DataSet, attaching the contents of that DataSet to your report, and then viewing the report in your viewer form.

Listing 10-1. *Code for Viewing a Simple Employee Listing Using the Report Viewer Control*

```
// Create new instance of timesheet XSD
dsTimeSheets oDs = new dsTimeSheets();

// Load the data from the XML File
oDs.ReadXml("d:\\clients\\apress\\DsTimeSheets.xsd");

// Create instance of the report
rptEmployeeList oRpt = new rptEmployeeList() ;

// Set the datasource
oRpt.DataSource = oDs.dtEmployees;

// Attach the Viewer control
this.viewer1.Document = oRpt.Document;

// Run the report
oRpt.Run();
```

This code creates an instance of your typed DataSet, sets the datasource of the report to the `dtEmployeeList` datatable, attaches the report to the viewer, and runs the report. Figure 10-7 shows the contents of your report running in the viewer form you created in the last step.

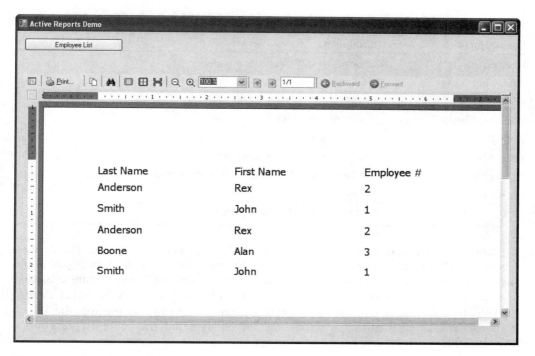

Figure 10-7. *The contents of the employee list report shown in the viewer form*

From this set of steps, you can see that the process of creating a report in ActiveReports is not that difficult. The next section will demonstrate how to create standard report components for your ActiveReports.

Building Header and Footer Subreports

One requirement of this application is the creation of standardized report headers and footers. When you create reports for any application, it is important to have the same look and feel across the reports. This starts with the way the title and report parameters are presented to the consumer of the report. This section will discuss the process of creating reusable header and footer controls for your report.

As specified in Chapter 8, you'll repeat the standard information for your header and footer controls. Table 10-1 lists the data that you'll push into a header and footer. As you can see, these elements are the common report annotations, such as title, footnote, datasource, etc.

Table 10-1. *Structure for Common Header and Footer*

ColumnName	Description
HdrCompany	Name of the company/organization
HdrReportTitle	Main report title
HdrSubTitle1	Report subtitle (if necessary)
HdrSubTitle2	Second report subtitle (if necessary)
UserID	User ID of the user running the report
FtrRunBy	Text for user who ran the report
FtrVersion	Text for version of software used to run report
FtrFootNotes	Footnotes
FtrDataSource	Datasource used for the report

Note that you're using one common structure for both the header and footer. While your examples will have data showing either in a header or footer (but never both), an organization may change its style guide and switch the location of data. Therefore, it makes more sense to maintain one common report information table from which the header and footer can draw.

This structure will be one datatable within several tables in a result set—but the header/footer will only use this one. You'll revisit this once you fully incorporate reports into the application.

Header/Footer Strategy

There are a number of possibilities to creating standardized header and footer controls for an ActiveReport. One possibility is to create a standard report and then cut and paste the controls from that report onto every new report. This has the advantage of your being able to use the ActiveReports designer to create the report using tools you already know how to use. The disadvantage (and a big one at that) is that if you want to make a change to the standard report, you have to cut and paste the contents of that report onto each and every report.

Another possibility is to add standardized controls to a report programmatically. The advantage of this method is that you have 100% control of the look and feel for your controls, and they can be changed on a global basis. The downside is that this is done with code, so it may take quite a while to perfect the look and feel of a report.

Finally, there is a method that has the best of both worlds. This method incorporates the use of standardized subreports for the header and footer for your application. You create your header/footer using the ActiveReports designer and simply merge that report into your new reports using the ActiveReports Subreport control.

Creating the Header

The first step to this process is to create the header report. The process of creating a report header is exactly the same as creating any other report. You will create the new report from the Solution Explorer by selecting Add ➤ New Item, then selecting ActiveReports Item from the Add New Item dialog. Name your report rptHeader.rpx.

After creating your report, attach the XML date source file to your report using the Report Data Source dialog. This example uses the dsReportInfo.xsd file (shown in the following code block). The recordset pattern (XPath) should be specified as **//dsReportInfo/dtReportInfo**. Figure 10-8 demonstrates the proper settings for your report header's datasource.

```xml
<?xml version="1.0" standalone="yes"?>
<dsReportInfo>
  <xs:schema id="dsReportInfo" xmlns=""
xmlns:xs="http://www.w3.org/2001/XMLSchema" xmlns:msdata="urn:schemas-microsoft-
com:xml-msdata">
    <xs:element name="dsReportInfo" msdata:IsDataSet="true"
 msdata:MainDataTable="dtReportInfo" msdata:UseCurrentLocale="true">
      <xs:complexType>
        <xs:choice minOccurs="0" maxOccurs="unbounded">
          <xs:element name="dtReportInfo">
            <xs:complexType>
              <xs:sequence>
                <xs:element name="HdrCompany" type="xs:string" minOccurs="0" />
                <xs:element name="HdrReportTitle" type="xs:string" minOccurs="0" />
                <xs:element name="HdrSubTitle1" type="xs:string" minOccurs="0" />
                <xs:element name="HdrSubTitle2" type="xs:string" minOccurs="0" />
                <xs:element name="UserID" type="xs:string" minOccurs="0" />
                <xs:element name="FtrRunBy" type="xs:string" minOccurs="0" />
                <xs:element name="FtrVersion" type="xs:string" minOccurs="0" />
                <xs:element name="FtrFootNotes" type="xs:string" minOccurs="0" />
                <xs:element name="FtrDataSource" type="xs:string" minOccurs="0" />
              </xs:sequence>
            </xs:complexType>
          </xs:element>
        </xs:choice>
      </xs:complexType>
    </xs:element>
  </xs:schema>
  <dtReportInfo>
    <HdrCompany>Acme Construction Company</HdrCompany>
    <HdrReportTitle>Time Sheet Report with Rates</HdrReportTitle>
    <HdrSubTitle1>Time Period: 11/07/2005 to 11/08/2005</HdrSubTitle1>
    <HdrSubTitle2 />
    <UserID>User 001</UserID>
    <FtrRunBy>Run by John Smith</FtrRunBy>
    <FtrVersion>Version 1.01</FtrVersion>
    <FtrFootNotes>Test of TimeSheet Report, showing labor and overhead rates
An asterisk indicates subcontractors</FtrFootNotes>
    <FtrDataSource>Source: Test Construction Database</FtrDataSource>
  </dtReportInfo>
</dsReportInfo>
```

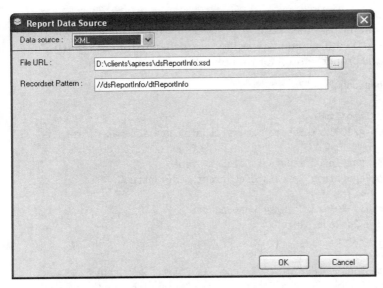

Figure 10-8. *Report header datasource*

Now you can drag and drop your controls from the Report Explorer onto your report. When you drag and drop data elements onto your subreport, add them to the detail section of the report. Subreports are generally run in the detail section of a master report. It is advised that you use the detail section of the report as the target for your header information. After dragging and dropping controls onto your report, you should set the font properties of your controls to **Tahoma 16pt**.

The next step is to add the date and time run to your report. To add the date and time run to your report, do the following:

1. Drag and drop two Label and two Textbox controls from the ActiveReports toolbox onto your report.

2. Change the Name properties of the Label and Textbox controls to **lblDate**, **lblTime**, **txtDate**, and **txtTime**, respectively.

3. Set the font information for the labels to **Tahoma 12pt**, **bold**.

4. Set the font information for the text boxes to **Tahoma 12pt** (nonbold).

5. Change the Text properties for the label controls to **Date** and **Time**, respectively.

6. In the DataField property of the text controls, add code to return the current date: =System.DateTime.Now.

After specifying the DataField properties of your controls, you will want to control the output of these controls. From the code demonstrated earlier, you can see that the information returned from the DateTime.Now function is a full date-time value. In this example, you will want to display the date and time as two discrete elements. This will be done via the OutputFormat property of the Textbox control. The OutputFormat property gives you the ability to apply formatting masks to your data.

There are two methods for applying output formatting masks. The first is to type the mask literal directly into the property sheet. The second is to use the helper that is provided by ActiveReports. To active the helper, select the OutputFormat property in the property sheet and click the ellipsis button. Clicking this button will activate the ActiveReports OutputFormat dialog (see Figure 10-9). From this dialog, select the Date category and select the format that best represents how you want to display your date. Perform the same process for your time field.

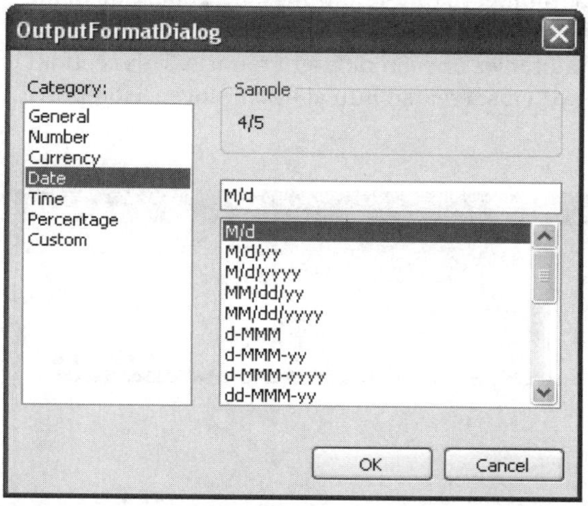

Figure 10-9. *OutputFormat helper dialog*

Now that you have created the layout of your report, it's time to test the report using the viewer form. To test your report, add another button to your viewer form, change its Text property to **Test Header Control**, and add the code in Listing 10-2 to the Click event of the button.

Listing 10-2. *Code to Preview Your Report with a Header Control*

```
// Create new instance of reportinfo XSD
dsReportInfo oDs = new dsReportInfo();

// Load the data from the XML File
oDs.ReadXml("d:\\clients\\apress\\dsReportInfo.xsd");

// Create instance of the report
rptHeader oRpt = new rptHeader();

// Set the datasource
oRpt.DataSource = oDs.dtReportInfo ;
```

```
// Attach the Viewer control
this.viewer1.Document = oRpt.Document;

// Run the report
oRpt.Run();
```

Figure 10-10 shows the output of your header test. Now that you have created and tested your report, you can merge your header document into your report. This is done via a Subreport control. **Subreports** allow you to do a number of different things, the main one being to give developers the ability to have multiple detail bands for a report. These multiple detail bands can derive their data from different datatables or even different reports. This section will discuss incorporating the report header you just created into your employee list report.

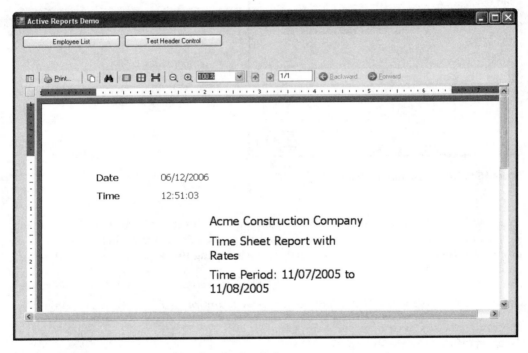

Figure 10-10. *Viewer with the report header loaded*

The steps necessary to adding the header to your employee list report are as follows:

1. Open the rptEmployeeList.rpx report in the ActiveReports designer.

2. Right-click the report design surface. From the context menu provided, select Insert ➤ Report Header/Footer (see Figure 10-11).

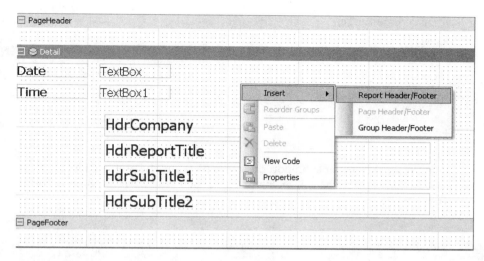

Figure 10-11. *ActiveReports designer adding a report header/footer*

3. From the ActiveReports toolbox, drag and drop a Subreport control from the Active-Reports toolbox and add it to the ReportHeader.

4. Size the subreport to be the same width as the report.

5. Change the name of the Subreport control to **subHeader**.

6. Change the Modifiers property to **public** on the subHeader control. This will expose the subreport for data binding from your viewer code.

7. Add another button to your form for running the report with the header. Change the Text property to **Employee List with Header**.

8. Add the code in Listing 10-3 to the Click event of the button.

Listing 10-3. *Code to Generate a Report with a Report Header*

```
// Create new instance of timesheet XSD
dsTimeSheetsWithReportHeader oDs = new dsTimeSheetsWithReportHeader();

// Load the data from the XML File
oDs.ReadXml("d:\\clients\\apress\\DsTimeSheetsWithReportHeader.xsd");

// Create instance of the report
rptEmployeeList oRpt = new rptEmployeeList();

// Set the datasource
oRpt.DataSource = oDs.dtEmployees;
```

```
// Set the subreport datasource
oRpt.subHeader.Report = new rptHeader();
oRpt.subHeader.Report.DataSource = oDs.dtReportInfo;

// Attach the Viewer control
this.viewer1.Document = oRpt.Document;

// Run the report
oRpt.Run();
```

After you incorporate the header subreport onto your page and the proper code is inserted, you can run the report in the viewer. Figure 10-12 shows the viewer with the report incorporating your new header subreport.

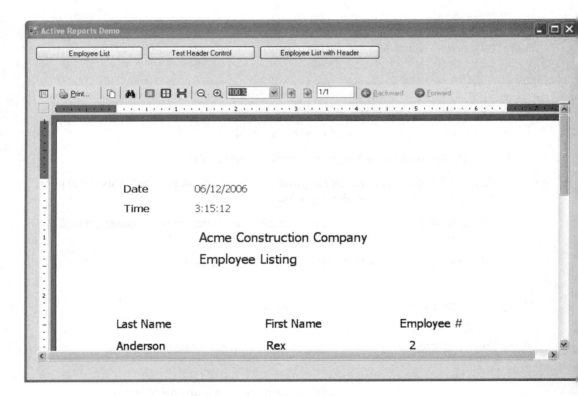

Figure 10-12. *Employee list with header subreport included*

Now that you have successfully created your report header control, you can move on to creating the footer subreport. Creating the report footer follows the same set of steps as for creating the header:

1. Create a new ActiveReport file, and name it rptFooter.rpx.

2. Set the report's datasource to the dsReportInfo.xsd file.

3. Enter **//dsReportInfo/dtReportInfo** to set the XPath for the dsReportInfo datatable.

4. Drag and drop your fields onto your report.

5. Apply any necessary formatting to the subreport.

6. Add a Subreport control to your employee list control.

7. Change the name of the subreport to **subFooter**.

8. Change the subreport's modifiers to **Public**.

9. Add another button to your Viewer control. Change its Text property to **Employee List with Header and Footer**.

10. Add the code in Listing 10-4 to the button's Click event.

Listing 10-4. *Code That Creates an Employee List Report and Shows It in a Preview Form*

```
// Create new instance of timesheet XSD
dsTimeSheetsWithReportHeader oDs = new dsTimeSheetsWithReportHeader();

// Load the data from the XML File
oDs.ReadXml("d:\\clients\\apress\\DsTimeSheetsWithReportHeader.xsd");

// Create instance of the report
rptEmployeeList oRpt = new rptEmployeeList();

// Set the datasource
oRpt.DataSource = oDs.dtEmployees;

// Set the subreport datasource
oRpt.subHeader.Report = new rptHeader();
oRpt.subHeader.Report.DataSource = oDs.dtReportInfo;


// Create the footer and set the subreport datasource
oRpt.subFooter.Report = new rptFooter();
oRpt.subFooter.Report.DataSource = oDs.dtReportInfo;
```

```
// Attach the Viewer control
this.viewer1.Document = oRpt.Document;

// Run the report
oRpt.Run();
```

After adding and running the preceding code, you can view your report. Figure 10-13 shows the report with the header and footer subreports embedded.

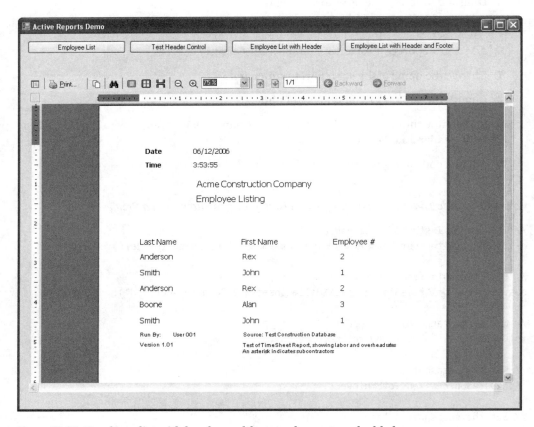

Figure 10-13. *Employee list with header and footer subreports embedded*

The Timesheet Details Report

The reports you have been building so far have been rather simple. This next example will create a more complex timesheet report. The timesheet details report will create a list of timesheets summarizing data by employee. Figure 10-14 shows what the final report will look like.

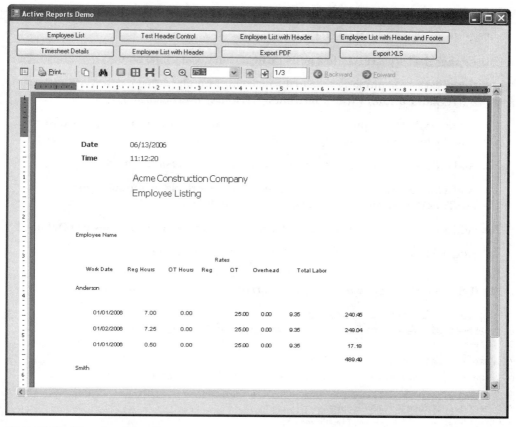

Figure 10-14. *Timesheet details report*

The first step to this process is to create a new report that will display your timesheet data. To create the timesheet details report, perform the following steps:

1. Create a new report from the Solution Explorer.

2. On the Report menu, select Load Layout. This option will present you with a File Open dialog. Search for the rptEmployeeList.rpx file you created earlier.

3. Select this file to import the layout settings from the employee list report.

The next step is to create the subreport that will show the timesheet details for a particular employee. Create a new ActiveReports file via the Solution Explorer, name the file rptEmployeeTimeDetails.rpx, and set the datasource properties to the XSD file as described earlier in this chapter. The only difference this time is that the Recordset Pattern property will be pointed at the dtTimeDetails table (e.g., //dsTimeSheets/dtTimeDetails). Now come the detailed set of steps for creating the timesheet report:

1. Drag and drop the following fields onto the report: WorkDate, RegularHours, OTHours, hourlyrate, otrate, and overheadrate.

2. Format the work date text box's OutputFormat property to show only the date.

3. Format the hour and rate fields to use a numeric format with two decimal points.

4. Add a new text field. Name it `txtTotalLabor`.

5. Change the `OutputFormat` to a numeric field with two decimal points.

6. In the `DataField` property, type in the following formula: **=(RegularHours*hourlyrate) + (OTHours*otrate) + ((RegularHours+OTHours)*overheadrate)**.

7. Set the `RightToLeft` property of the `txtTotalLabor` text box to **true**. This will ensure that the total amounts are right-justified.

8. Add the appropriate header information to your `rptTimesheet` report.

9. Add a Subreport control to your `rptTimeSheet` report. Name the subreport **subTimeDetails** and change its modifiers to **Public**.

10. Add another button to your viewer form. Set its `Text` property to **Timesheet Details**.

11. Add the code in Listing 10-5 to the `Click` event of the button.

Listing 10-5. *Code That Creates a Timesheet Report and Displays It in a Preview Form*

```
// Create new instance of timesheet XSD
dsTimeSheetsWithReportHeader oDs = new dsTimeSheetsWithReportHeader();

// Load the data from the XML File
oDs.ReadXml("d:\\clients\\apress\\DsTimeSheetsWithReportHeader.xsd");

// Create instance of the report
rptTimeSheet oRpt = new rptTimeSheet();

// Set the datasource
oDs.dtEmployees.DefaultView.Sort = "WorkerPK";
oDs.dtTimeDetails.DefaultView.Sort = "WorkerFK";
oRpt.DataSource = oDs;
oRpt.DataMember = "dtEmployees";

// Set the subreport datasource
oRpt.subHeader.Report = new rptHeader();
oRpt.subHeader.Report.DataSource = oDs.dtReportInfo;

// Create the footer and set the subreport datasource
oRpt.subFooter.Report = new rptFooter();
oRpt.subFooter.Report.DataSource = oDs.dtReportInfo;

// Attach the Viewer control
this.viewer1.Document = oRpt.Document;

// Run the report
oRpt.Run();
```

There are a few items that are different with this code. The first is the method of binding the data to the report. In all of the earlier examples, the report's DataSource property was bound directly to the dtEmployees datatable. This code sets the DataSource property to the timesheet's DataSet and sets the DataMember property to the dtEmployees table. This mechanism is the same as binding to the datatable directly with one added benefit. If you need to access the underlying set of data from a report during its run, binding to the datasource will help you do this. Which leads you to your next challenge: filtering the timesheet data by employee.

Running the report with the code shown in Listing 10-5 will simply produce a report with employee data and no timesheet detail. There is one more step. In order to show the timesheet detail, you will need to filter the timesheet detail by employee as the report runs. To add filtering by employee and timesheet, add the code in Listing 10-6 to the Format event of the report's detail band.

Listing 10-6. *Code That Demonstrates Using a Subreport with Filtering for a Master-Child Relation Report*

```
// Create the subreport
rptEmployeeTimeDetails oRpt = new rptEmployeeTimeDetails();

// Grab a handle to the report's underlying data
dsTimeSheetsWithReportHeader ods = (dsTimeSheetsWithReportHeader)this.DataSource;

// Filter the timesheet details
ods.dtTimeDetails.DefaultView.RowFilter = "WorkerFK=" +
this.Fields["WorkerPK"].Value.ToString();

// Bind the report to the filtered details
oRpt.DataSource = ods.dtTimeDetails.DefaultView;

// Bind the report to the Subreport control
this.subTimeDetails.Report = oRpt;
```

This code is used to filter data in a master/detail report like the timesheet details report you are creating. This code has the following behavior: every time the employee record changes (the datasource of the master report), the Format event is called. This code creates an instance of the timesheet details report, creates a reference to the report's underlying data structure, applies a filter to the timesheet details table, and attaches that table's default view to the subreport. Finally, it takes the created report and assigns it to the master report's details subreport.

Creating Subtotals and Totals

This report is almost done. The final step is to add subtotals to each timesheet and a grand total to the bottom of the report. The first task you will accomplish is the creation of the timesheet subtotals. This is a little more complicated because you used a calculated expression to show the total amount of payroll for each work day, and ActiveReports does not allow summarization on calculated fields. Not to worry though, it's pretty simple to add the summarization of a calculated field to a report.

Adding summarization to a calculated field requires you to add an unbound field to your report and then to accumulate the data as the report progresses. When ActiveReports runs a report, its wraps all of the underlying data in a set of field objects that can be accessed as the code runs. You are also able to append new fields to this collection. To add an unbound field to the fields collection, add the following code to the report's `DataInitialize` event:

```
this.Fields.Add("PayrollLineTotal");
```

The next step is to add code to the detail band's `Format` event that will store the calculated data shown in the txtTotalLabor text box. To store the calculated value to the new unbound field, add this code to the `Format` event of the detail band:

```
this.Fields["PayrollLineTotal"].Value = this.txtTotalLabor.Value;
```

Now that you have stored off the calculated payroll values, you can summarize them in the report.

1. Open the `rptEmployeeTimesheetDetails.rpx` report.

2. Add a data grouping to your report.

3. Copy and paste the txtTotalLabor text box and copy it into the footer section of the group you just added.

4. Change the `DataField` property to **PayrollLineTotal**.

5. Change the `SummaryGroup` property to **GroupHeader1**, which is the name of your group band.

6. Change the `SummaryRunning` and `SummaryType` properties to **Group** and **SubTotal**, respectively.

7. Run and test your report. Your report should now show subtotals for each employee's timesheet.

The last step is to add a grand total to your timesheet report. This is a little more involved. The first thing you will need to do is add a public property to the `rptEmployeeTimesheetDetails.rpx` report. The purpose of this property is to expose the subtotal amount to the parent report. Add the following code to the beginning of the `rptEmployeeTimeDetails` class:

```
public double exposedtotal = 0.00;
```

Next you will need to add another line to the `Format` event of the details report. This code will accumulate the details into the exposed total property you just added:

```
this.exposedtotal += (double)this.txtTotalLabor.Value ;
```

The final step is to store the subtotal amounts for each timesheet into a grand total value on your parent report. This is done by adding an unbound field to the master report fields' collection and then accumulating the grand total into that new field. To add your new grand total field, add the following code to the `DataInitialize` event of the parent report:

```
this.Fields.Add("TimesheetGrandTotal");
this.Fields["TimesheetGrandTotal"].Value = 0.00;
```

The next step is to accumulate the exposed total value from the subreport. The best way to do this is to add code to the AfterPrint event of the report's detail band. This event is fired after each detail band has been created (including subreports). Your accumulation code will look like this:

```
this.Fields["TimesheetGrandTotal"].Value
  = (double)this.Fields["TimesheetGrandTotal"].Value + oRpt.exposedtotal;
```

Finally, you can add a new text control to your parent report to display this value. Simply add a text control to the ReportFooter section of your report. Set its DataField property to **TimeSheetGrandTotal**.

Now that you have created some reports, let's take a look at some other things that it's important to know how to do, such as printing and exporting reports to different formats.

Printing

One of the most important tasks in any reporting environment is the act of printing the report. ActiveReports provides a number of mechanisms for printing reports. The simplest mechanism is to print the report from the Viewer control by clicking the Print button. You are also able to print reports programmatically. Printing an ActiveReport with code is as simple as adding one line of code to your report creation process. To print the employee list programmatically, do the following:

1. Add a new button control to your viewer form. Change its Text property to **Print Employee List**.

2. Add the code in Listing 10-7 to the button's Click event.

Listing 10-7. *Code That Demonstrates Printing a Report*

```
// Create new instance of timesheet XSD
dsTimeSheetsWithReportHeader oDs = new dsTimeSheetsWithReportHeader();

// Load the data from the XML File
oDs.ReadXml("d:\\clients\\apress\\DsTimeSheetsWithReportHeader.xsd");

// Create instance of the report
rptEmployeeList oRpt = new rptEmployeeList();

// Set the datasource
oRpt.DataSource = oDs.dtEmployees;

// Set the subreport datasource
oRpt.subHeader.Report = new rptHeader();
oRpt.subHeader.Report.DataSource = oDs.dtReportInfo;

oRpt.Run();
oRpt.Document.Print();
```

The ActiveReports class has a method called Print() that will present you with a printer selection dialog, allowing you to choose the destination for your report output. The print method also has a number of overloads that will suppress the printer selection dialog and the printing progress windows.

Exporting

Another important task when building reporting applications is the ability to export reports to different formats. ActiveReports has capabilities for exporting reports in the following formats:

- PDF

- Microsoft Excel

- Rich Text Format

- HTML

- Text

- TIFF

ActiveReports performs exporting using specialized classes for exporting to the various export types. Each export type has a specialized class that handles its export process. The following steps demonstrate how to export your data to two different formats:

1. Add a reference to the appropriate ActiveReports class library. Figure 10-15 shows the Add Reference dialog with export libraries included with ActiveReports selected.

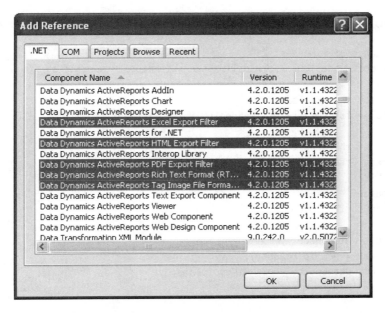

Figure 10-15. *Add Reference dialog with ActiveReports export libraries selected*

2. For this example, you'll add the PDFExport and ExcelExport classes. Add using statements for each class to the top of the viewer form:

```
using DataDynamics.ActiveReports.Export.Pdf;
using DataDynamics.ActiveReports.Export.Xls ;
```

3. Add two buttons to your viewer form. Set their Text properties to **Export PDF** and **Export XLS**, respectively.

4. Copy the code from the printing exercise (see the earlier section "Printing") into each button's Click event.

5. In each button, swap out the Print() method call with the following code:

```
oRpt.Run();
PdfExport oPDF = new PdfExport();
oPDF.Export(oRpt.Document, "d:\\clients\\apress\\pdfexport.pdf");

oRpt.Run();
XlsExport oXLS = new XlsExport();
oXLS.Export(oRpt.Document, "d:\\clients\\apress\\pdfexport.xls");
```

The code just shown runs your report in memory, creates an instance of an export library, and exports the contents of that report to the file specified in the Export() method. Figures 10-16 and 10-17 show the contents of both the PDF and XLS exports.

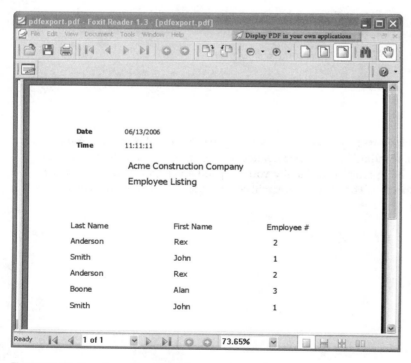

Figure 10-16. *Employee list report in PDF format*

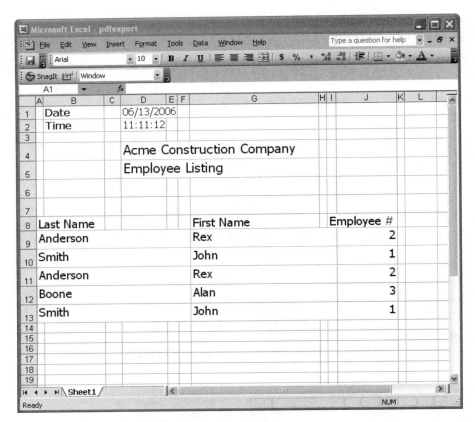

Figure 10-17. *Employee list report in Microsoft Excel format*

Summary

As you can see, ActiveReports has a rich set of tools for creating complex reports. You can achieve a high level of standardization using headers and footers. You can create complex master/child reports using subreports. Finally, you can print and export your reports to a number of different formats. The next chapter will cover the same set of features using Microsoft's Reporting Services.

CHAPTER 11

Using Microsoft SQL Server Reporting Services

In Chapters 8 through 10, you learned how to use Crystal Reports and ActiveReports for creating basic-to-intermediate reports. This chapter will cover another report writer: Microsoft SQL Server Reporting Services (SSRS). Where Crystal Reports and ActiveReports are more developer-oriented report writers, SQL Server Reporting Services is oriented much more toward the data analyst. This chapter will demonstrate using SSRS to create reports from XML data.

What Is SQL Server Reporting Services?

SSRS consists of two parts, the Report Manager and the Report Creator, described here:

- **Report Manager**: The Report Manager is a web application that is used to secure, maintain, manage, schedule, and run your reporting service projects.

- **Report Creator**: When SSRS is installed, it installs a set of tools for creating reports. These tools are installed in a Visual Studio shell. Creating reporting projects will be a very familiar experience to .NET developers, as they are created and managed using the same development shell used to create applications.

SSRS Basics

Creating SSRS projects is done via the Visual Studio shell. This section describes the process for creating and configuring your first SSRS project.

Creating a Report Project

The first step to using SSRS is to create a Report Server Project. Report Server Projects manage the creation of two types of items: data sources and reports. Data sources provide parameters for connecting to databases and other types of data sources. Reports contain the rules for sending queries to data sources and the information for formatting that data and presenting it to end users. To create a new Report Server Project, perform the following steps:

1. Open Visual Studio 2005 (if you do not have Visual Studio 2005, SSRS will install a version for you).

2. Select File ➤ New ➤ Project ➤ Business Intelligence Projects ➤ Report Server Project.

3. Name your project ApressReporting.

Figure 11-1 shows the Visual Studio New Project dialog with the proper options selected. Once you have created your project, you need to configure it.

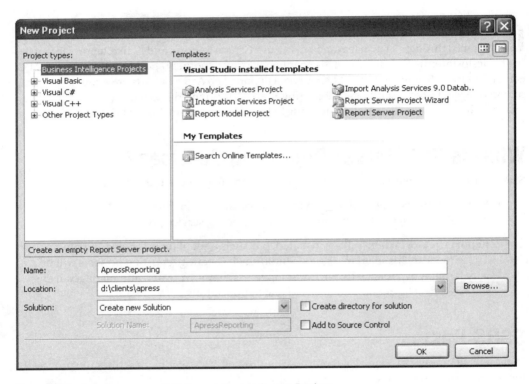

Figure 11-1. *Creating a new SQL Server Report Server Project*

Configuring Your Project

After creating your project, you need to configure a number of parameters that specify how and where your report server application will be deployed. SSRS project parameters are specified using a set of property pages. To configure your project, right-click your project in the Solution Explorer and select Properties. Figure 11-2 shows the property pages for an SSRS project.

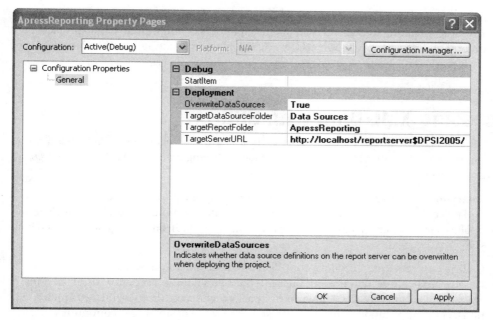

Figure 11-2. *Project Properties page for the SQL Server Reporting Services projects.*

The deployment section of the provided page contains a number of options. These options are defined as follows:

- **OverwriteDataSources**: When you deploy your project, the data sources in that project will be deployed to the reporting server. During development it is wise to make sure this option is set to true.

- **TargetDataSourceFolder**: This option specifies the folder where your data sources will be stored on your reporting server.

- **TargetReportFolder**: This option specifies the folder where your report definitions will be stored on your reporting server.

- **TargetServerURL**: This option specifies the web address of your reporting server. This is where your reporting project will be stored when you deploy it.

Reporting Project Components

Once you have created and configured your project, you can then begin creating your reporting components. You will be creating two major classifications of items: data sources and reports.

- Shared Data Sources: The Shared Data Sources folder contains definitions of your report project's data sources. You can create data sources for OLE DB, ODBC, XML, SQL Server Data, Oracle, and numerous others.

- Reports: The Reports folder is where you will create your reports. This folder is a flat structure, meaning that you cannot create subfolders. If you want to create projects for different folders on your report server, you will need to create a new report project for each one.

Accessing XML Data with SSRS

The original version of SSRS did not support XML as a data source, but SSRS 2005 added support for querying data from XML data sources. When querying data from XML data sources, there are two likely scenarios:

- **Querying static XML data**: There are a number of applications that will prequery XML and place the data into static pages that can then be consumed by applications. These applications may or may not dynamically create their XML data. It is just presented in a static XML format.

- **Calling web services**: A modern approach is to access data via web services. Web services are applications that present their interface and data as a set of XML transactions. These applications are also known as Simple Object Access Protocol (SOAP) applications. SOAP applications subscribe to a standard set of protocols for communicating between heterogeneous applications.

Accessing Data from a Static XML Data Source

This first example demonstrates the mechanisms used to access data from static XML data sources. The basic process for accessing data from a static XML data source is to

- Create a data source pointing at the URL of your XML data source.

- Create a new report.

- Create a report dataset.

- Specify the query syntax for your XML.

- Drag and drop field queried onto your report.

The following example uses data from a file called ReportData.XML. For the examples to work, copy this file to into the root directory of your local web server (typically c:\inetpub\wwwroot). The structure of the XML contained in this file is shown in Listing 11-1.

Listing 11-1. *XML Representing a Customer List*

```
<?xml version="1.0" encoding="utf-8" ?>
<Customers>
  <Customer LastName="Paddock" FirstName="Jessica">
    <Notes>
```

```
      <Note NoteText="Test Note Text 1"/>
      <Note NoteText="Test Note Text 2"/>
    </Notes>
  </Customer>
  <Customer LastName="Anderson" FirstName="Krysta"/>
  <Customer LastName="Paddock" FirstName="Isaiah"/>
  <Customer LastName="Paddock" FirstName="Jessia"/>
</Customers>
```

The first step is to create your data source. The following steps show you how to create an XML data source based on a static XML file:

1. If you already created your project, continue to step 4; otherwise start at step 2.

2. Create your first reporting services project.

3. Name your project ApressReporting.

4. Create your data source by right-clicking the Shared Data Sources folder and selecting Add New Data Source.

5. This will open the Shared Data Source dialog, as shown in Figure 11-3.

6. Specify XML as the type and the following URL as the connection string: http:// localhost/ReportData.XML.

7. Name your data source **StaticDataSource**.

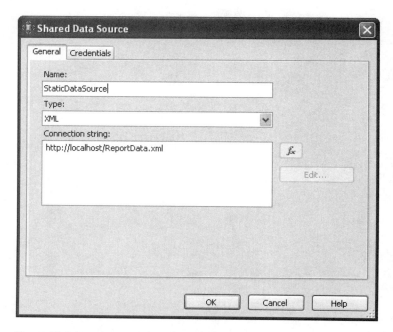

Figure 11-3. *Properties defined for XML data sources*

Creating Your First Report

Now that you have created a data source, you will need to create a report that will consume data from your data source. To create your report:

1. Right-click the Reports folder.

2. Select Add ➤ New Item.

3. From the Add New Item dialog, select Report.

4. Name your report **CustomerList**.

Examining the Report Designer

After creating a new report, a number of new options and tools will be added to your Visual Studio IDE. These tools include a report designer, a Report Items toolbox, a Report menu bar, and a Datasets toolbox.

The first item to examine is the report designer. The report designer is used to create your reports. The designer has three tabs (see Figure 11-4): Data, Layout, and Preview. The Data tab is used to create datasets that will be used for your report. The Layout tab is used to add display elements to your report. The elements that can be added to a report are accessed via the Report Items toolbox. Finally, there is the Preview tab, which allows you to run and preview your report.

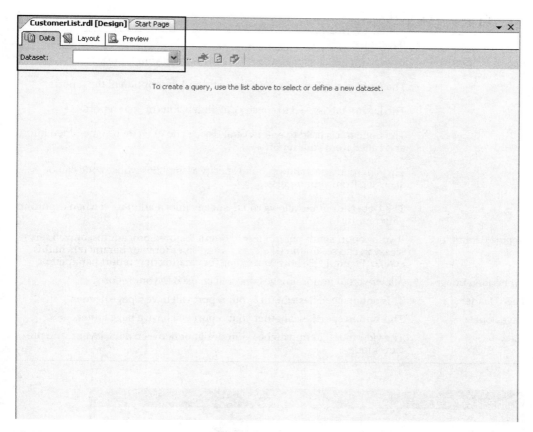

Figure 11-4. *Report designer tabs highlighted in the Visual Studio IDE*

The Report Items toolbox contains the elements that are used to create the layout for your report. These items include labels, text boxes, images, tables, subreports, and graphs.

Next is the Datasets toolbox. This toolbox contains a visual representation of data elements that are available to your report. You can drag and drop elements from the Datasets toolbox onto the layout of your reports.

Finally, there is the Report menu bar. Table 11-1 describes the elements of the Report menu bar.

Table 11-1. *Report Menu Options*

Option	Description
Report Properties	Used to set general and layout characteristics of your report.
	The General tab is used to specify a title and description of the report.
	The Layout tab is used to specify the dimensions of your report.
	The Code tab is used to enter Visual Basic code that can be embedded into and called from your reports.
	The References tab allows you to specify assemblies whose code can be accessed from your reports.
	The Data Output tab allows you to specify information used when exporting your reports to XML.
Report Parameters	If your report sends parameters to queries, stored procedures, or web services, you can set up the UI elements and rules for your parameters in this screen. Figure 11-5 shows the dialog for creating new report parameters.
Embedded Images	Allows you to import images that will be used in your reports.
Page Header	This option specifies whether your report will have a page header.
Page Footer	This option specifies whether your report will have a page footer.
View	The view menu item switches your designer between data, layout, and preview mode.

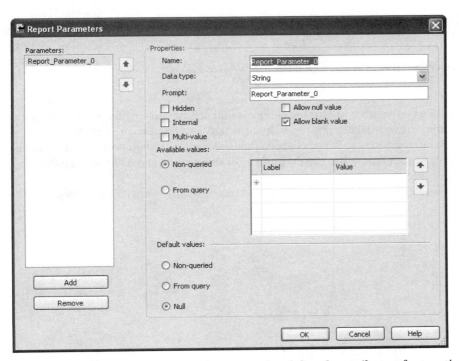

Figure 11-5. *The Report Parameters dialog is used to define the attributes of properties you provide your queries, stored procedures, and web services.*

Creating an SSRS Dataset

Now that you have created your report, you need to create a dataset for your report. This is not an ADO typed DataSet but an SSRS dataset. SSRS datasets are used to send queries to different data sources for display in report layouts. Reports can retrieve data from multiple data sources, meaning that a report can pull data from SQL Server, Oracle, and XML data all in the same layout engine.

As an example, if your report's data source was specified as SQL Server, you would use a dataset to specify a set of T-SQL code to run against the server or a stored procedure to call. Upon specifying these parameters, you can test your query, and its results are presented in a grid viewer screen.

The XML data source has its own proprietary syntax for querying data from static XML and web services. This next section will demonstrate how to query data from an XML data source:

1. Change to the Data tab of your report.

2. From the Dataset drop-down select <New Dataset> (see Figure 11-6). This will open the Dataset dialog.

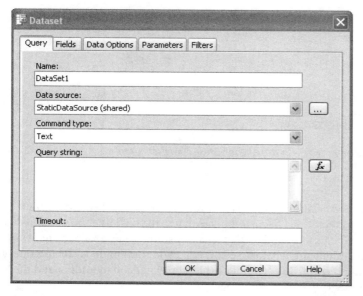

Figure 11-6. *New dataset option called from the SSRS report designer*

3. At this point, you can simply close the dialog. You don't need to enter any parameters because by default the XML data source will flatten your XML document into a list of fields. You can create and view the list of fields extracted from your XML by pressing the refresh button on the Dataset toolbar (see Figure 11-7).

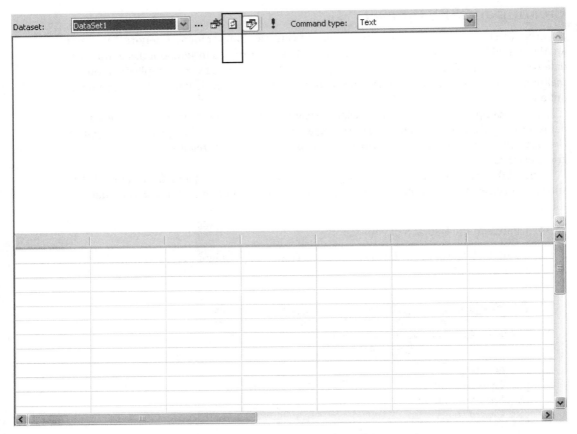

Figure 11-7. *Refresh dataset button on the Data tab of the SSRS report designer*

While it is nice that SSRS flattens your XML structure, this is not always desirable. The goal of this example is to create a list of customers with just the customer information listed. The preceding steps will create a set of data that lists a customer name for each note attached to a customer. This is definitely not what you want. What you want to do is create a query that selects only the customer records. To accomplish this step, you need to understand the XML query syntax used by SSRS.

Basic XML Query Syntax

This section will demonstrate the most basic elements of the XML data source query syntax. When modifying your XML query syntax, you can simply enter the code into the dataset design surface. You can also click the ellipsis (...) button next to your dataset name and a Dataset dialog will come up. Figures 11-8 and 11-9 demonstrate the different places you can put your XML query code.

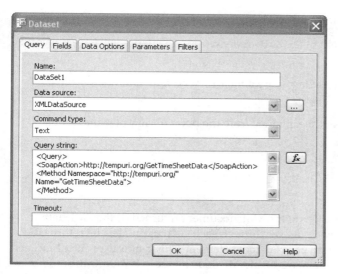

Figure 11-8. *This dialog shows an XML query in the Dataset dialog.*

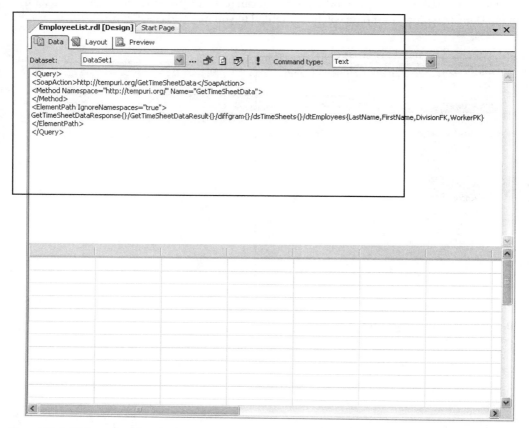

Figure 11-9. *This screen shows an XML query in the Data tab of the report designer.*

This example uses two elements of the XML query syntax:

- `<Query>`: The top-level element of the XML query syntax. All queries will have a `<Query>` element.

- `<ElementPath>`: The element used to query data from your XML data source. It uses a strange notation resembling XPath.

The syntax of `<ElementPath>` is best explained from the point of view of some sample queries:

```
<Query>
  <ElementPath>Customers/Customer{@LastName,@FirstName}</ElementPath>
</Query>
```

This query traverses down the nodes of the XML document returned by the XML data source. It starts with the `Customers` node, moves through each `Customer` node, and returns the `LastName` and `FirstName` attributes from each `Customer` element. This syntax uses curly brackets (`{ }`) to specify specific attributes or elements of an XML node to query. If your XML does not use attributes and is element centric, you need to remove the @ signs from the fields specified for retrieval.

Once you have entered your XML query, you can test it by pressing the exclamation icon on the Dataset toolbar. Your data will be presented to you in a grid (see Figure 11-10).

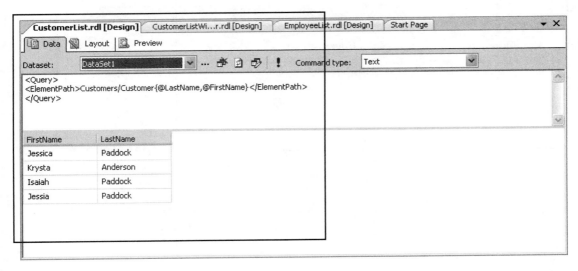

Figure 11-10. *Customer List query result*

You can also specify an element-centric type of query. The following XML query returns just the LastName element of each Customer node. The XML for this example is found in Listing 11-2.

```
<Query>
  <ElementPath>Customers/Customer{LastName}</ElementPath>
</Query>
```

Listing 11-2. *Element-Centic Customer XML*

```
<Customers>
  <Customer>
    <LastName>Paddock</LastName>
    <FirstName>Rod</FirstName>
  </Customer>
  <Customer>
    <LastName>Anderson</LastName>
    <FirstName>Krysta</FirstName>
  </Customer>
  <Customer>
    <LastName>Paddock</LastName>
    <FirstName>Isaiah</FirstName>
  </Customer>
  <Customer>
    <LastName>Paddock</LastName>
    <FirstName>Jessica</FirstName>
  </Customer>
</Customers>
```

Presenting Your Data

Now that you have created your data source, you can add the presentation elements of your report. In this example, you will add the display elements to your report for your customer list. You will then deploy your project to your report server.

Adding presentation elements to your report is done via the Layout tab. Switch to this tab, then select the Report Items toolbox from the Visual Studio IDE. This example will present your data in a simple list. To add your fields to your report, do the following:

1. Select the Table object from the Report Items toolbox and drag one onto your report.

2. Switch to the Datasets tab in the toolbox and drag the LastName and FirstName elements onto your Table object's Detail area. Make sure you are using the ElementPath that contains the FirstName and LastName fields. Figure 11-11 shows the LastName and FirstName fields in the Table object's design surface.

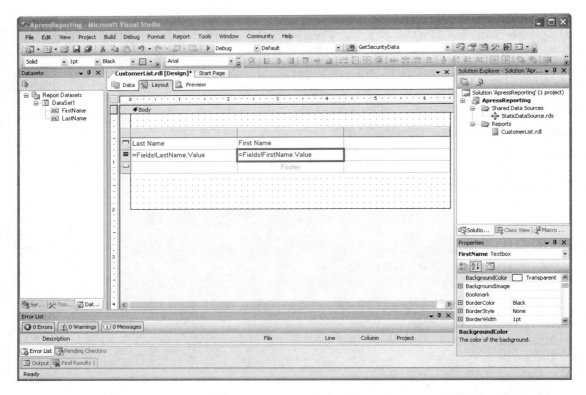

Figure 11-11. *CustomerList report with the LastName and FirstName elements specified in a Table object*

3. If you like, you can set properties of each object via the Properties window (see Figure 11-12).

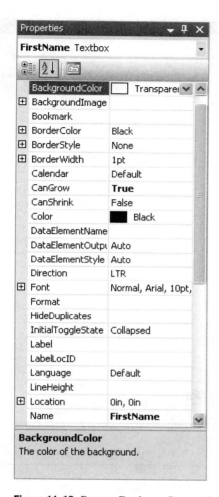

Figure 11-12. *Report Designer Properties sheet*

4. After adding your elements, change to the Preview tab in the report designer. Figure 11-13 shows your report in preview mode.

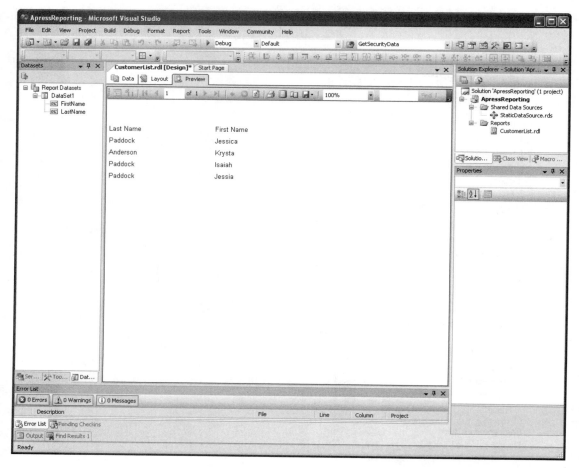

Figure 11-13. *Report designer Preview tab showing the contents of the CustomerList report*

Deploying Your Project

Once you have finished creating your report, you can deploy it. To deploy your project, simply select Build ➤ Deploy <your project name> from the Visual Studio menu. Your project will then be deployed to the server as specified by the TargetServerUrl attribute of your project properties. Now you can go directly into your SSRS Report Manager via Internet Explorer. Simply enter the URL of the web server where you installed your Report Manager. Figure 11-14 shows your CustomerList report running in the Report Manager.

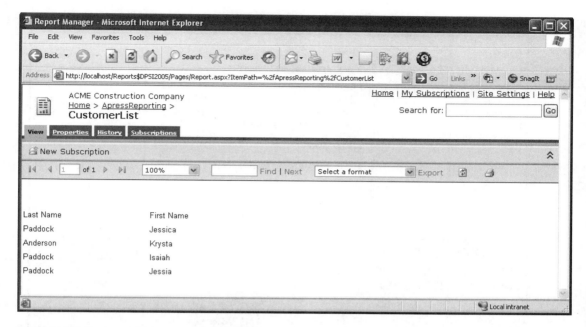

Figure 11-14. *CustomerList report in the SSRS Report Manager*

Accessing Data from Web Services

The next step in XML data access is to query data from a web service. Web services have become a universal mechanism for exchanging data between diverse data sources. Where it was a relatively simple process to query data from a static XML file, web services introduce a new level of complexity. Web services are not just a static link to an XML page; rather they are a set of instructions passed in as XML. These instructions are then processed, and a set of XML is returned to the client.

Creating the Test Web Service

For this example and all subsequent examples, you will retrieve data from a small web service application. This application will provide functions for returning dataset data to the client application.

Creating a web service in Visual Studio 2005 is a simple process. To create your web service, do the following steps:

1. Select File ➤ New Project from within Visual Studio.

2. From your preferred language section (C# or Visual Basic), select ASP.NET Web Service Application. Name your web service ApressWebService (see Figure 11-15).

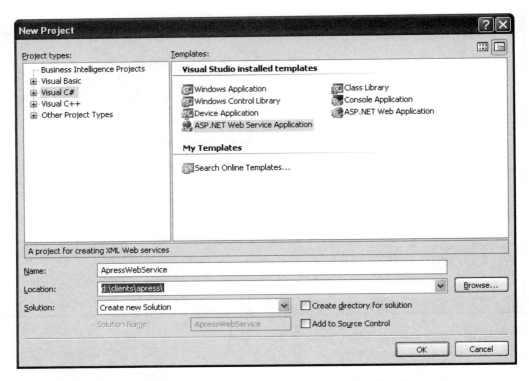

Figure 11-15. *New Project dialog used to create a new web service application*

3. Visual Studio will then create your web service skeleton application. By default, a file called Service1.asmx will be created. Right-click this file in the Solution Explorer and change its name to EmployeeServices.asmx.

4. You will also need to rename the class file that was created to EmployeeServices. Visual Studio will not rename this class automatically.

5. The next step is to add the XSD file that is used to represent your employee timesheet data. To do this, right-click the Solution Explorer and select Add ➤ Existing Item. Locate the dsTimeSheets.XSD file and add it to your project.

6. The next step is to insert your custom code. You need to add the code found in Listing 11-3. This will add two web methods: GetTimeSheetData() and GetTimeSheetDataWithParameter().

7. The first function, GetTimeSheetData(), returns all the timesheet data (dtEmployees, dtTimeSheets, etc.). The second function, GetTimeSheetDataWithParameter(), accepts an integer parameter and returns a DataTable with employees that match your parameter.

8. Next you need to configure your project to run in IIS. To do this, right-click your project in the Solution Explorer and open the Properties dialog. Select the Web tab in this dialog.

9. The first thing to configure is the Specific Page property. Change this value to `EmployeeServices.asmx`.

10. Next you need to configure the web service to run under IIS. To do this, you need to change the Servers option to Use IIS Web server. Specify the location of the IIS installation where you want your web service deployed. Click the Create Virtual Directory button if you haven't already created your web service directory. Figure 11-16 shows you how your project properties should look.

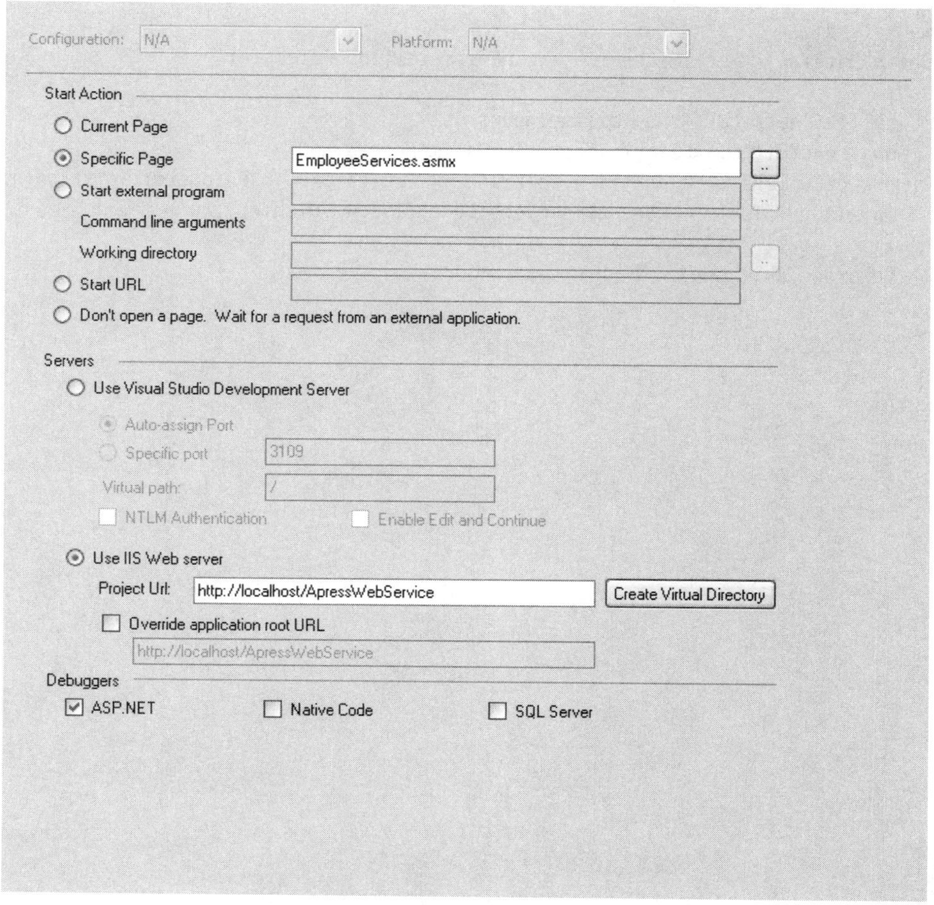

Figure 11-16. *Web properties dialog for web service application*

11. After adding the code, you can test your web service by pressing F5.

Figure 11-17 shows the results of your web service call.

Listing 11-3. *Web Method Code for Returning Datasets to SSRS*

```
[WebMethod]
public dsTimeSheets  GetTimeSheetData()
{
    dsTimeSheets ods = new dsTimeSheets();
    ods.ReadXml("D:\\Clients\\apress\\DsTimeSheets.XSD");
    return ods ;

}
[WebMethod]
public DataTable GetTimeSheetDataWithParameter(int Parameter)
{
    dsTimeSheets ods = new dsTimeSheets();
    ods.ReadXml("D:\\Clients\\apress\\DsTimeSheets.XSD");
    ods.dtEmployees.DefaultView.RowFilter = "workerpk=" + Parameter.ToString();
    DataTable oTable = ods.dtEmployees.DefaultView.ToTable();

    return oTable;
}
```

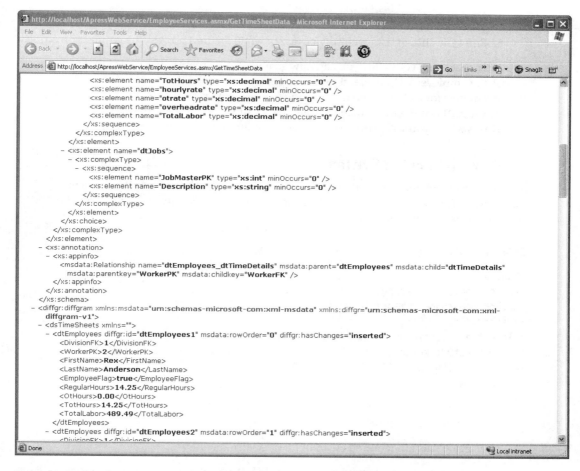

```
            <xs:element name="TotHours" type="xs:decimal" minOccurs="0" />
            <xs:element name="hourlyrate" type="xs:decimal" minOccurs="0" />
            <xs:element name="otrate" type="xs:decimal" minOccurs="0" />
            <xs:element name="overheadrate" type="xs:decimal" minOccurs="0" />
            <xs:element name="TotalLabor" type="xs:decimal" minOccurs="0" />
          </xs:sequence>
        </xs:complexType>
      </xs:element>
      <xs:element name="dtJobs">
      - <xs:complexType>
        - <xs:sequence>
            <xs:element name="JobMasterPK" type="xs:int" minOccurs="0" />
            <xs:element name="Description" type="xs:string" minOccurs="0" />
          </xs:sequence>
        </xs:complexType>
      </xs:element>
    </xs:choice>
  </xs:complexType>
</xs:element>
- <xs:annotation>
  - <xs:appinfo>
      <msdata:Relationship name="dtEmployees_dtTimeDetails" msdata:parent="dtEmployees" msdata:child="dtTimeDetails"
        msdata:parentkey="WorkerPK" msdata:childkey="WorkerFK" />
    </xs:appinfo>
  </xs:annotation>
</xs:schema>
- <diffgr:diffgram xmlns:msdata="urn:schemas-microsoft-com:xml-msdata" xmlns:diffgr="urn:schemas-microsoft-com:xml-
  diffgram-v1">
  - <dsTimeSheets xmlns="">
    - <dtEmployees diffgr:id="dtEmployees1" msdata:rowOrder="0" diffgr:hasChanges="inserted">
        <DivisionFK>1</DivisionFK>
        <WorkerPK>2</WorkerPK>
        <FirstName>Rex</FirstName>
        <LastName>Anderson</LastName>
        <EmployeeFlag>true</EmployeeFlag>
        <RegularHours>14.25</RegularHours>
        <OtHours>0.00</OtHours>
        <TotHours>14.25</TotHours>
        <TotalLabor>489.49</TotalLabor>
      </dtEmployees>
    - <dtEmployees diffgr:id="dtEmployees2" msdata:rowOrder="1" diffgr:hasChanges="inserted">
        <DivisionFK>1</DivisionFK>
```

Figure 11-17. *Results returned from the GetTimeSheetData() function*

Creating the Data Source

Creating the data source for an XML web service is the same as creating an XML data source
for a static XML file. You simply specify the URL for your web service. In this example, you will
specify the ASMX file that was created for your web service application. To create your web
service data source, do the following:

1. Right-click Shared Data Sources in the Solution Explorer.

2. Select Add New Data Source.

3. Name your source **WebServiceDataSource**.

4. Specify XML as type.

5. Enter the URL of your web service (as shown in Figure 11-16) as the connection string.

After specifying your URL, you can now go ahead and create a new report that will show your list of employees. Upon creating your report, you will need to create a dataset that specifies parameters for calling a web method. When you create your dataset object, make sure you specify the XMLDataSource (created earlier) data source as your data source.

This is where you will learn more syntax for calling a web method from SSRS.

Basic Web Service Syntax

The simplest mechanism for calling web services is to call web methods that have no parameters. The syntax in Listing 11-4 shows how to call a web service that returns the XML representation of your timesheet's dataset.

Listing 11-4. *XML Syntax for Querying Timesheet Dataset*

```
<Query>
<SoapAction>http://tempuri.org/GetTimeSheetData</SoapAction>
<Method Namespace="http://tempuri.org/" Name="GetTimeSheetData">
</Method>
<ElementPath IgnoreNamespaces="true">
GetTimeSheetDataResponse{}/GetTimeSheetDataResult{}/diffgram{}/dsTimeSheets{}
/dtEmployees{LastName,FirstName,WorkerPK}
</ElementPath>
</Query>
```

The various elements here are

- `<Query>`: This is a required element for all XML data queries.

- `<SoapAction>`: This element specifies the SOAP web method call that this service will be making. For this example, you will be calling the `GetTimeSheetData` method.

- `<Method>`: This element specifies what web method you want to call. This is done by specifying the method name in the `Name` attribute. Once again, you will be calling the `GetTimeSheetData` function, so enter that value as your property. It may look like the `<SoapAction>` and `<Method>` elements are the same. They are not. The `<Method>` element has extra subelements that facilitate calling web methods with parameters. You will learn about these subelements later in this chapter.

- `<ElementPath>`: Finally the element path is specified. This is the pseudo XPath syntax that is used by the XML query engine to determine what XML data to return as your data source. With a web method, it gets a little more involved. There are a number of unique issues with querying XML data via a web service.

Understanding SOAP Request and Response Packets

When constructing your <ElementPath> elements you need to first understand the concept of SOAP response and result elements. SOAP web service calls wrap their return data in an XML structure known as a SOAP packet. The SOAP packet has two elements that wrap your returned data. These elements are the response and result elements. They are returned in the XML stream with name of your web method prepended to the names Response and Result.

In the preceding example, your web method is named GetTimeSheetData. You will end up with two elements in your resulting XML called GetTimeSheetDataResponse and GetTimeSheetDataResult. The easiest mechanism for determining the names of these two elements is to run your web service from Visual Studio and examine the SOAP information provided by Visual Studio. Figure 11-18 shows the SOAP information returned for your web service call.

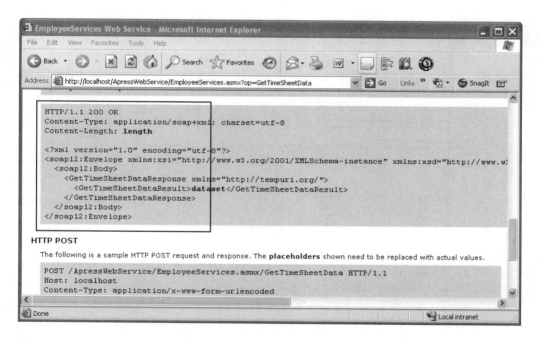

Figure 11-18. *This screen highlights the request and response structures returned from your web service SOAP call.*

Once you have determined the names of the response and result elements, you can enter the element path for your data. As you saw previously, the following syntax represents the <ElementPath> you will use to query your dataset data:

```
<ElementPath IgnoreNamespaces="true">
GetTimeSheetDataResponse{}/GetTimeSheetDataResult{}/diffgram{}/dsTimeSheets{}
/dtEmployees{LastName,FirstName,WorkerPK}
</ElementPath>
```

This syntax tells SSRS query your XML data in the following order:

1. Ignore all namespace elements (this will be a regular XML navigation without namespace notation).

2. Begin at the `GetTimeSheetDataResponse{}` element.

3. Navigate inside the `diffgram{}` element (where your dataset is contained).

4. Navigate inside the `dsTimesheets{}` element (your dataset).

5. Return the `LastName`, `FirstName`, and `WorkerPK` elements from your `dtEmployee{}` data.

Figure 11-19 shows the results of this query in the Visual Studio IDE.

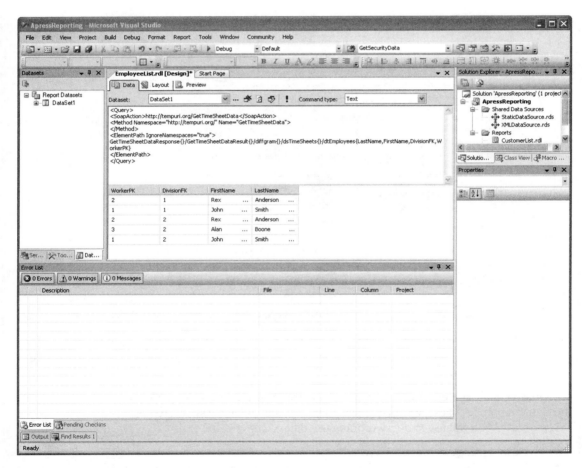

Figure 11-19. *Results of querying a dataset from SSRS*

Parameter Query Syntax

A more real-world example is to query data from web methods that accept parameters. Querying web services that use parameters requires you to add two new elements to the <Method> element of your XML query. These elements are <Parameters> and <Parameter>. The <Parameters> element tells SSRS that (n) number of parameters will be passed to your web method. The <Parameters> element contains <Parameter> elements that define the name and data type of parameters that will be passed to your web method. <Parameter> elements have an optional element called <DefaultValue>, which allows you to specify a default value for your parameter. Listing 11-5 contains an example.

Listing 11-5. *Query Syntax for a Web Service Call with Parameter*

```
<Query>
<SoapAction>http://tempuri.org/GetTimeSheetDataWithParameter</SoapAction>
<Method Namespace="http://tempuri.org/" Name="GetTimeSheetDataDataWithParameter">
<Parameters>
<Parameter Name="nParam" Type="Integer">
<DefaultValue>1</DefaultValue>
</Parameter>
</Parameters>
</Method>
<ElementPath IgnoreNamespaces="true">
GetTimeSheetDataWithParameterResponse{}/GetTimeSheetDataWithParameterResult{}
/DataTable{}/diffgram{}/DocumentElement{}/dtEmployees{LastName,FirstName,DivisionFK,
WorkerPK}
</ElementPath>
</Query>
```

This query will hand in a DefaultValue of 1 to the nParam parameter as specified by the GetTimeSheetDataWithParameter web method. If you want to present an interface for entering this parameter, you can do this by adding a parameter definition to your dataset. To add parameters to your dataset, do the following steps:

1. Open the DataSet dialog from the Data tab of the report designer (click the ellipsis next to the dataset name).

2. Select the Parameters tab.

3. Enter the name of your parameter (nParam) in the Name column.

4. Enter the value of your parameter (1) in the Value column.

5. Figure 11-20 shows the dataset properties screen with the definition for your parameter.

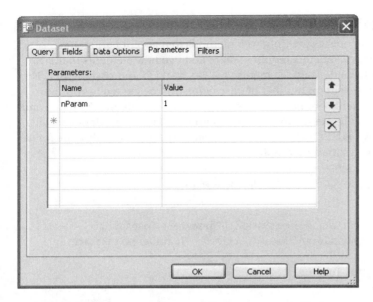

Figure 11-20. *Dataset parameters with parameter specified*

When you run your query in the Data tab, SSRS will present you with a Query Parameters entry screen (see Figure 11-21).

Figure 11-21. *Report Data tab with dialog for entering parameter value*

You can now enter the value of your parameter in a dynamic manner. When an end user runs your report, you want to present a more intuitive interface. This is done via the Report Parameters screen (see Figure 11-22). To define your report parameters, do the following:

1. Open the Layout tab of the report designer.

2. Select Report ➤ Report Parameters from the Visual Studio menu.

3. Click the Add button.

4. Specify `EmployeePK` as the name of your report parameter.

5. Specify **Integer** as the data type.

6. Specify **Employee Number** as the prompt.

7. The dialog should now look like the one in Figure 11-22.

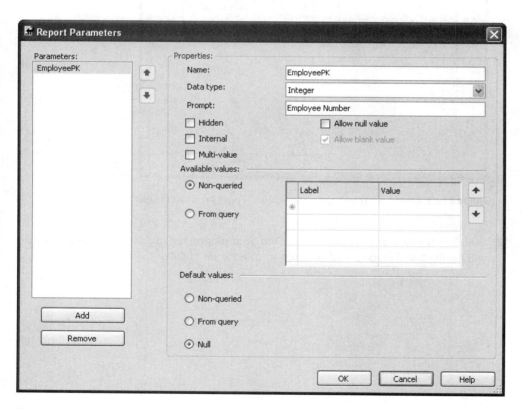

Figure 11-22. *This screen shows the Report Parameters dialog with employee information specified.*

8. Press OK.

9. Change to the Data tab and open your dataset for editing.

10. Switch to the Parameters tab.

11. Select your parameter, which is now displayed in the Value column of the Parameters list (see Figure 11-23).

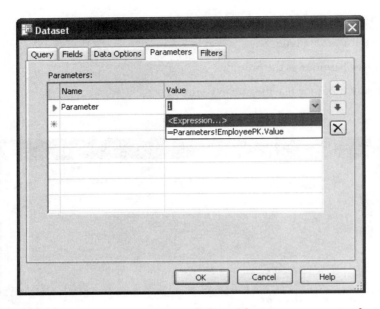

Figure 11-23. *Dataset Parameters dialog with report parameter selected*

12. Switch to the Report Designer Preview tab. Your parameter and the values you entered will be displayed at the top of your report (see Figure 11-24).

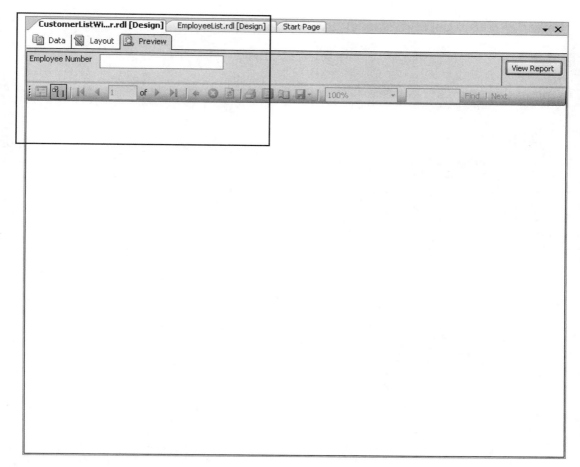

Figure 11-24. *Report running with report parameter information specified.*

Summary

The focus for this chapter is a little different from the other report writer chapters. In this chapter, you learned some very important information for creating and configuring your SSRS projects. The majority of the time was spent explaining the slightly complex process of accessing XML data from SSRS.

Recommended Reading

Peter Blackburn and William R. Vaughn. *Hitchhiker's Guide to SQL Server Reporting Services.* Boston, MA: Addison-Wesley Professional, 2004.

Rodney Landrum and Walter J. Voytek II. Pro SQL Server 2005 Reporting Services. Berkeley, CA: Apress, 2005.

■■■

CHAPTER 12

Integrating the Reporting Tool with the Application

In Chapters 8 and 9, we showed you how to work with the Crystal Reports designer to build the report files. Now we'll focus on integrating the report into the application and generating the report—either to the screen, the printer, or to an export file format such as a Portable Document Format (PDF), Microsoft Word, or Microsoft Excel. To accomplish these tasks, we'll explore the Crystal Reports Object Model. Crystal Reports .NET contains a rich set of properties and methods for developers to implement reporting functionality in a .NET application. This chapter will show how to use the object model to your advantage. The chapter will also present a set of reusable functions for automating Crystal Reports in .NET applications.

Begin with the End in Mind: Your Final Result

The main objective of this chapter is to build a reusable library for managing common Crystal Reports activities. These activities include previewing, printing, and exporting reports, as well as implementing the push model that we covered back in Chapter 8. When you generate reports at runtime, you want to use your library for all of these tasks and not have to duplicate code from the Crystal Reports .NET programming namespaces. In the end, you should be able to create an instance of a specific report, load the corresponding DataSet for the report, and pass both objects to your reusable library for any common reporting task: the library will do the rest.

Figure 12-1 introduces another new project to the Construction Demo solution, CGS.CrystalReportsTools. This is another project in Kevin Goff's **Common Ground Framework for Visual Studio 2005**.

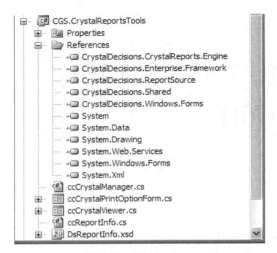

Figure 12-1. *Your newest project, CGS.CrystalReportsTools*

The project is a class library: it contains references to the necessary Crystal Reports .NET managed assemblies and comprises the following:

- A report manager class (ccCrystalManager) that handles most of the functionality

- A Windows Form for setting print options (ccCrystalPrintOptionForm)

- A Windows Form for previewing reports (ccCrystalViewer)

- A class (ccReportInfo.cs) to set the common report header/footer properties (footnote, title, subtitle, etc.)

This project compiles to a separate DLL, CGS.CrystalReportsTools.DLL. Any projects in your demo that need to utilize Crystal Reports functionality will only need to set a .NET reference to this DLL: you won't need to set references to the Crystal Reports assemblies, as your reusable library here will handle all of that!

At the end of the chapter, in Listing 12-9, we'll present a code sample that demonstrates all of the capabilities of this library.

■**Note** CGS.CrystalReportsTools is a .NET class library project that uses the Crystal Reports .NET namespaces and .NET references. They must be added to the project.

Using the Crystal Reports .NET Object Model

Crystal Reports contains a rich and powerful object model—it would require an entire book or books to cover every single property, event, and method, and how to use them effectively. This chapter will focus on those aspects of the Crystal Reports programming model that you as a developer will need to generate your reports.

At the highest level, we'll start with the primary Crystal Reports .NET namespaces (see Table 12-1). You need to add these namespaces as .NET references to any module.

Table 12-1. *The Main Crystal Reports Namespaces for Your Application*

Namespace
CrystalDecisions.CrystalReports.Engine
CrystalDecisions.CrystalReports.ReportSource
CrystalDecisions.Shared
CrystalDecisions.Windows.Forms

In this chapter, we'll examine four of the primary Crystal Reports objects, and we'll present code samples for working with each one:

- The primary ReportDocument object

- The PrintOptions object

- The Export objects

- The ReportPreview object

The ReportDocument Object Model

One of the best ways to explore an object model (any object model) is to interactively utilize the available development tools. In Figure 12-2, we are instantiating the report timesheet object and utilizing IntelliSense to discover the report's properties, events, and methods. Keep in mind that IntelliSense only displays a maximum of roughly 20 items at once: the screen shot has been "doctored and pasted" to show all available items in four adjacent columns.

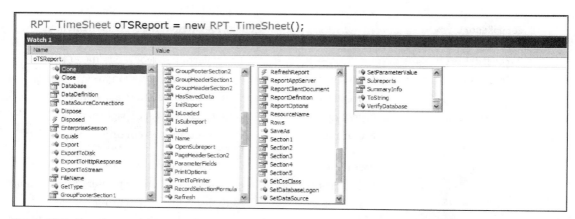

Figure 12-2. *Creating an instance of a report and viewing the object model with IntelliSense*

■Note This is an old adage, but always worth repeating: the best way to learn a rich object model is to explore and experiment with it, often by examining the objects at runtime with the debugger.

Table 12-2 lists the major properties that IntelliSense displayed in Figure 12-1 for the ReportDocument object. Note that many objects are nested and contain multiple levels of sub-objects. You can expand any of the objects to view additional information on the report object (see Figure 12-3).

Table 12-2. *The Main ReportDocument Object Model Properties*

Object	Subobjects	Description
Database	Links	The relational links between tables
	Tables	The collection of design-time table data sources
DataDefinition	FormulaFields	The collection of report formulas
	GroupNameFields	The collection of report group names
	Groups	The collection of report groups
	ParameterFields	The collection of report parameter fields
	RunningTotalFields	The collection of any running total/subtotal fields
	SummaryFields	The collection of any summary fields
DataSourceConnections	DatabaseName	The name of the database to connect to
	IntegratedSecurity	Whether integrated security is being used on the database
	Password	The password to access the database
	ServerName	The name of server (containing the database) to connect to
	UserID	The user ID to access the database
IsSubReport		Flag for whether the report is a main report or a subreport
ParameterFields		The collection of report parameter fields
PrintOptions	ApplyMargins	Applies custom print margins
	CustomPaperSource	Gets or sets a custom paper source
	PageMargins	Gets the current set of page margins
	PaperOrientation	Gets or sets the current printer paper orientation
	PaperSource	Gets or sets the current printer paper source
	PrinterDuplex	Gets or sets the current printer duplex option
	PrinterName	Gets or sets the current printer name

Object	Subobjects	Description
ReportDefinition	Areas	Main collection of report areas
	ReportObjects	Main collection of report objects
	Sections	Main collection of report sections (which also contains report objects)
Subreports		A collection of subreports within the main parent report

oAgingReport.Database.Tables[0].

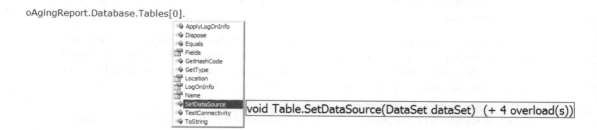

Figure 12-3. *Using IntelliSense to drill down further on report objects*

Finally, Table 12-3 shows the available methods at the main ReportDocument object level.

Table 12-3. *The ReportDocument Object Model Methods*

Method	Description
Export()	Exports a report based on export options
Load()	Loads a report manually
OpenSubReport()	Opens a particular subreport
PrintToPrinter()	Prints a report based on printer options
SetDatabaseLogon()	Set database login information (user ID, password, server, database)

Now that we've listed out the main properties and methods, we'll show you how to utilize them in your application. Your reporting application makes heavy use of tasks such as pushing runtime data to reports, printing, exporting, and previewing reports, so your goal is to build code using the Crystal Reports Object Model to accomplish those tasks.

Using the Database and Subreport Objects to Implement the Push Model

Your overall reporting methodology utilizes the ADO.NET DataSet Push Model, where (as the name implies) you push runtime data into the report. To do so, you need to utilize the ReportDocument's Database object mentioned previously (in Table 12-2). In addition, you need to use the ReportDocument's Subreports object to push data into any report that contains subreports.

Borrowing from the theme that a picture is worth a thousand words, a meaningful code sample can often put in plain words a process (so long as the code sample isn't a thousand lines). Listing 12-1 demonstrates the basics of the push model by doing the following:

1. Set up a method called SetData() that will receive an instance of a report object and an instance of the DataSet you wish to push into the report object.

2. Iterate through the Tables collection object of the report's Database object (oReport.Database.Tables), one Table object at a time.

3. Take the design-time table name of the Table object (oTable.Name.ToString) and set its runtime DataSource to the corresponding table in the DataSet object with the same table name (oTable.SetDataSource()).

Because the code in Listing 12-1 sets the DataSource based on table name, there is no need to worry about table order (a common question from those who are new to Crystal Reports). The only requirement is that the table names at runtime must match the table names that you used at design time (a realistic requirement).

Listing 12-1. *Implementing the Push Model by Setting the Report's Runtime Data Source*

```
private void SetData(DataSet DsReportData, ReportDocument oReport)
{
    // Receives a DataSet and report object.
    // (could be the main object, or a subreport object)

    // Loops through the report object's tables collection,
    // matches up the table name with the corresponding table name in the DataSet,
    // and sets the DataSource accordingly.

    // This function eliminates the need for a developer
    // to know the specific table order in the report.

    foreach (Table oTable in oReport.Database.Tables)
        oTable.SetDataSource( DsReportData.Tables[ oTable.Name.ToString() ]);
}
```

There's one more item we need to address with the push model. Several of your reports contained subreports; therefore, you need to set the runtime DataSource for all table objects in each subreport. This is a segue to our next point, using the report object's Subreports collection.

Once again, a small code listing (see Listing 12-2) should help to demonstrate how you can implement the Push Model with subreports, by doing the following:

1. Call the method SetData() (in Listing 12-1) for the main report object.

2. Iterate through the Subreports collection object of the main report object, one subreport object at a time.

3. Call SetData() for each subreport object.

The beauty here is that Crystal Reports treats each subreport as an actual report object (because it is!): this allows you to call SetData() for all subreports in the main report. Even though each individual subreport may only contain a subset of the data from the final DataSet, the code in your SetData() function (in Listing 12-1) simply iterates through the tables collection of the specified subreport.

Listing 12-2. *Implementing the Push Model for Both the Main Report and Any Subreports*

```
private ReportDocument SetReportData(DataSet DsReportData, ReportDocument oReport)
{
  // Called when a report is generated.
  // Calls SetData for the main report object.
  // Also calls SetData for any subreport objects.

  this.SetData(DsReportData,oReport);

  foreach(ReportDocument oSubReport in oReport.Subreports)
    this.SetData(DsReportData,oSubReport);

  return oReport;
}
```

■**Note** The Crystal Reports .NET managed code assemblies that accompany Visual Studio 2005 cannot read the ADO.NET DataView object. If you try to use the Crystal method SetDataSource() with a DataView, you will receive a blank report. Fortunately, the Visual Studio 2005 method DataView.ToTable() allows developers to easily create a DataTable from a DataView.

Accessing Report Objects on the Fly

In Chapters 8 and 9, you learned how to define specific report content to display (or not display) based on report formulas. Many report object–formatting options contain design-time formulas to define those formatting attributes based on some condition (e.g., a data column rule, etc.). However, some report objects, such as the line and box shapes, do not contain design-time formulas. In a few instances, you may need to conditionally suppress a line or box shape (or if not that, perhaps you may need to conditionally format some other object where a formula does not exist).

Once again, the Crystal Reports object model allows you to programmatically access and modify report objects at runtime. Listing 12-3 shows some miscellaneous examples where you can drill down to the desired section, access specific report objects, and modify formatting attributes. The first section of the listing accesses the specific report objects by name. The second section of the listing demonstrates how to format specific objects in a group if they are of a specific type.

Listing 12-3. *Two Different Ways to Access Report Objects at Runtime*

```
RPT_Invoice oReport = new RPT_Invoice();

// You want to conditionally set a line and a box to invisible.
// The Crystal designer does not provide a formula to conditionally
// suppress a line/box, but you can set the Suppress property at runtime.

// You can do this one of two ways:

// You access the object directly, if you know the property names.

Section oSection = oReport.ReportDefinition.Areas[1].Sections[0];
oSection.ReportObjects["lPageHeaderLine"].ObjectFormat.EnableSuppress = true;
oSection.ReportObjects["lPageHeaderBox"].ObjectFormat.EnableSuppress = true;


// Or, you can iterate through the objects in the section, and
// look for any report objects of type LineObject or BoxObject.

Section oSection = oReport.ReportDefinition.Areas[1].Sections[0];

foreach (ReportObject oObject in oSection.ReportObjects)
  if (oObject is LineObject || oObject is BoxObject)
    oObject.ObjectFormat.EnableSuppress = true;
```

■**Note** A common question is whether a developer can modify the text of a Crystal Reports label at runtime. Report content with conditional labels should be implemented either as formula fields or as database-driven (or business object-driven) data column fields.

Printing with the Print Object

Once you have pushed the necessary runtime data into the report and optionally set any runtime report attributes, you can generate the output. While many introductory texts begin by showing how to build a report preview window (which we'll obviously cover in this chapter), we'll start by covering print capabilities. In many situations, developers need to build processes to either print (or export) directly from the push of a button (or batch job), without the need for a preview window. Therefore, you need direct access to the Crystal Reports Object Model print capabilities.

As you saw back in Table 12-1, the ReportDocument object contains a method called PrintToPrinter() that allows you to print a report object directly to the current default printer. `PrintToPrinter()` receives four parameters: an integer for the number of copies, a Boolean for whether to collate, and two integer options for a page range.

```
RPT_Invoice oReport = new RPT_Invoice();

// Set Page Ranges to zero if you intend to print all pages.
oReport.PrintToPrinter(this.nCopies,this.lCollate,this.nStartPage,this.nEndPage);
```

Table 12-1 also identified a `PrintOptions` object. You can use `PrintOptions` to customize the printed output to something different than what was specified at design time.

```
RPT_Invoice oReport = new RPT_Invoice();

// First, setting a different printer name.
oReport.PrintOptions.PrinterName = this.cPrinterName;

// Second, you can set the PaperSize (see IntelliSense for all possible values).
oReport.PrintOptions.PaperSize = CrystalDecisions.Shared.PaperSize.Paper10x14;

// Third, you can set the paper source (see IntelliSense for all possible values).
oReport.PrintOptions.PaperSource = CrystalDecisions.Shared.PaperSource.Envelope;
oReport.PrintOptions.CustomPaperSource =
  CrystalDecisions.Shared.PaperSource.Envelope;

// Fourth, setting the orientation.
// (if it differs from the default design orientation)
oReport.PrintOptions.PaperOrientation =
  CrystalDecisions.Shared.PaperOrientation.Landscape;

// Finally, Print!
oReport.PrintToPrinter(this.nCopies,this.lCollate,this.nStartPage,this.nEndPage);
```

Exporting Reports

Saving report output to a format that can be viewed by others has become a common function in reporting applications. In many situations, applications will export reports to a Portable Document Format file for a variety of reasons. Perhaps users outside the application domain need to review certain reports, so application users might export reports to PDF and then e-mail the PDF. In other situations, a company may direct all their output to a PDF or other format for batch mail-room printing.

Finally, in this situation, you want to save every printed report to a PDF, so that you can view the output later should any questions arise about the output at the time it was printed (as opposed to printing a duplicate copy and keeping it on file). Figure 12-4 shows an example of report output to PDF.

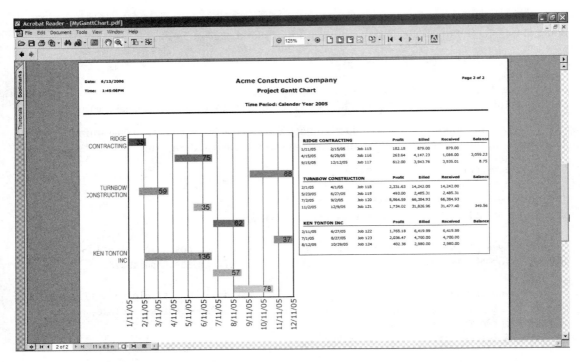

Figure 12-4. *Example of Crystal Reports output to PDF, using the Adobe Acrobat PDF Reader*

Crystal Reports .NET contains a number of functions for exporting report output to a PDF, as well as other file formats such as Microsoft Word and Microsoft Excel. Table 12-4 lists the export objects that Crystal Reports provides in the `CrystalDecisions.Shared` namespace.

Table 12-4. *Export Objects in CrystalDecisions.Shared Namespace*

Object	Available Objects
ExportOptions	ExportDestinationOptions
	ExportDestinationType
	ExportFormatOptions
	ExportFormatType
DiskFileDestinationOptions	DiskFileName
PdfRtfWordFormatOptions	FirstPageNumber
	LastPageNumber
	UsePageRange

Figure 12-5 shows the IntelliSense display of the export formats that the `ExportFormatType` object provides. While you'll focus on PDF output, you can see that Crystal Reports can export to Excel, HTML, Rich Text Format, and Word.

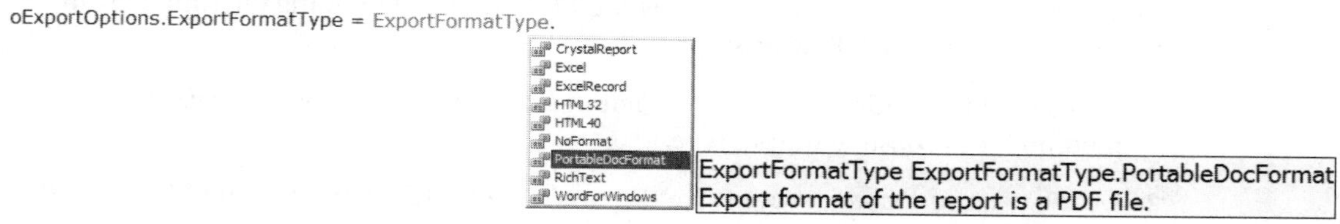

```
oExportOptions.ExportFormatType = ExportFormatType.
```

Figure 12-5. *Using the ExportFormatType object to discover the available file format types*

So now you'll take a crack at writing a function to export a report to a PDF format. Listing 12-4 contains a basic function to export a report object to PDF format. You'll provide the report object and output file name as parameters, and the code will perform the following:

1. Create object instances of the ExportOptions, DiskFileDestinationOptions, and PdfRtfWordFormatOptions objects.

2. Set the DiskFileName property to the name of the file that you supplied as a parameter.

3. Set the ExportFormatType property to PDF.

4. Call the Export() method of the main report object, passing the ExportOptions object as a parameter.

Listing 12-4. *A Basic Function to Export a Report to a PDF Format*

```
private void ExportReport(ReportDocument oReport, string cFile)
{
  // Assume that the class is using the CrystalDecisions.Shared namespace.

  ExportOptions oExport = new ExportOptions();
  DiskFileDestinationOptions oDiskFile = new DiskFileDestinationOptions();
  PdfRtfWordFormatOptions oFormat =  new PdfRtfWordFormatOptions();

  oExport.ExportDestinationType = ExportDestinationType.DiskFile;
  oExport.ExportFormatType = ExportFormatType.PortableDocFormat;

  oDiskFile.DiskFileName = cFile;
  oExport.ExportDestinationOptions = oDiskFile;
  oExport.ExportFormatOptions = oFormat;

  oReport.Export(oExport);
}
```

The code in Listing 12-4 will handle basic exporting functionality. However, you may find that you need to handle other situations. First, you may need to export to different formats. Second, there may be times where you need to export a page range. So your goal is to write a function to expand the functionality from Listing 12-4, while maintaining the simplicity of Listing 12-4. You'll take the following steps:

1. Create a simple enumeration with different export types that you can pass into your method for the desired output type.

2. Define two overloads for your ExportReport() method from the previous listing: in the first overload, you will simply pass the report object, output type, and file name, and in the second overload you will pass all the parameters from the first overload, as well as a start and end page range.

3. Use the FirstPageNumber, LastPageNumber, and UsePageRange properties of the PdfRtfWordFormatOptions object (if you pass a page range as a parameter).

4. Set ExportOptions.ExportFormatType based on the value of the enumeration.

5. Call the Export() method of the main report object, passing the ExportOptions object as a parameter.

Listing 12-5 shows a more robust version of your ExportReport() method.

Listing 12-5. *Exporting Reports*

```
public enum ExportTypes
{
  PDF = 1,
  MSWord = 2,
  MSExcel = 3
}

// ExportReport - two overloads, one for a page range, one without.
this.ExportReport(oReport, "MyOutput.PDF", ExportTypes.PDF);
this.ExportReport(oReport, "MyOutput.PDF", ExportTypes.PDF,2,3);

// ExportReport - First overload (simple one).
public void ExportReport(ReportDocument oReport,string cFile,
            ExportTypes oExportTypes)
{
  // ExportReport - Call second overload with no page range (will export all pages).
  this.ExportReport(oReport, cFile,oExportTypes,0,0);
}

// ExportReport - Second overload (with page range).
public void ExportReport(ReportDocument oReport, string cFile, ExportTypes
                    oExportTypes, int nFirstPage, int nLastPage)
{
  ExportOptions oExportOptions = new ExportOptions();
  PdfRtfWordFormatOptions oFormatOptions =
    ExportOptions.CreatePdfRtfWordFormatOptions();
```

```
DiskFileDestinationOptions oDestinationOptions =
  ExportOptions.CreateDiskFileDestinationOptions();

// Page range, if specified.
if (nFirstPage > 0 && nLastPage > 0)
{
  oFormatOptions.FirstPageNumber = nFirstPage;
  oFormatOptions.LastPageNumber = nLastPage;
  oFormatOptions.UsePageRange = true;
}

switch (oExportTypes)
{
  case ExportTypes.PDF:
    oExportOptions.ExportFormatType = ExportFormatType.PortableDocFormat;
    break;
  case ExportTypes.MSWord:
    oExportOptions.ExportFormatType = ExportFormatType.WordForWindows;
    break;
  case ExportTypes.MSExcel:
    oExportOptions.ExportFormatType = ExportFormatType.Excel;
    break;
}

oExportOptions.ExportFormatOptions = oFormatOptions;
oDestinationOptions.DiskFileName = cFileName;
oExportOptions.ExportDestinationOptions = oDestinationOptions;
oExportOptions.ExportDestinationType = ExportDestinationType.DiskFile;

oReport.Export(oExportOptions);
}
```

Previewing Reports

Now it's time for some eye candy! Figure 12-6 shows an example of the Report Preview toolbar in action. Crystal Reports provides a rich preview window with an attractive toolbar containing built-in options that allow the end user to do the following:

- Export the report to different formats.

- Print the report.

- Navigate to the first/last/next/previous report page, as well as navigate to a specific page number.

- Search for a particular piece of text within the report.

- Zoom in/out of the report.

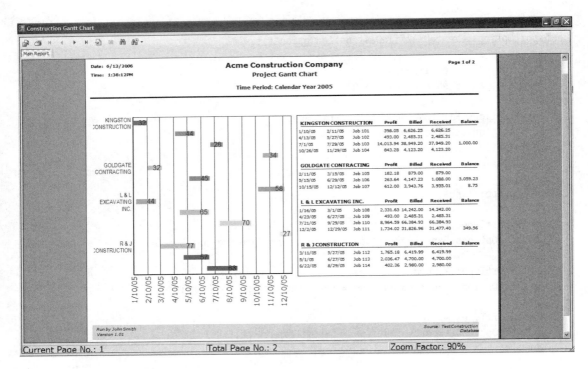

Figure 12-6. *Showing the preview window*

The first step towards creating a report preview window is to drop an instance of the Crystal Reports Preview control on a Windows Form. Figure 12-7 shows a Visual Studio 2005 development environment with Crystal Reports installed: you can select the Crystal Reports tab category in the toolbox and drop an instance of the Crystal Reports Viewer control on a form.

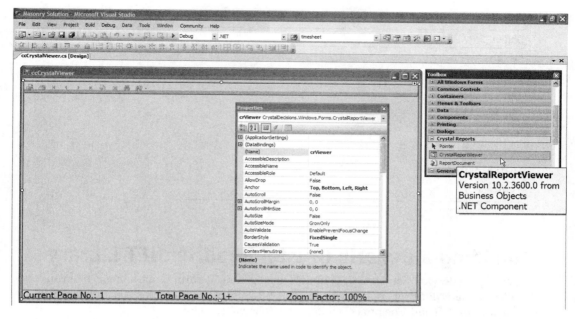

Figure 12-7. *Creating a form with the Crystal Reports Preview control*

The Crystal Reports Preview control contains many properties that you can set to customize the report display at runtime. Table 12-5 shows the properties that you can set for the Crystal Reports Preview control.

Table 12-5. *CrystalDecisions.Windows.Forms.CrystalReportViewer*

Object
EnableToolTips
EnableDrillDown
ReportSource
Zoom
ShowCloseButton
ShowExportButton
ShowGoToPageButton
ShowGroupTreeButton
ShowPageNavigationButtons
ShowPrintButton
ShowRefreshButton
ShowTextSearchButton
ShowZoomButton
ExportReport

Continues

Table 12-5. *Continued*

Object
ShowNthPage
ShowFirstPage
ShowLastPage
ShowNextPage
ShowPreviousPage
ShowGroupTree
SearchForText
PrintReport

Building a Generic Crystal Reports .NET Library

One of your development goals is to build a set of generic reporting components that you can utilize in many different applications. Figure 12-8 shows a Visual Studio 2005 project that you'll use towards that end. The project contains the following pieces:

- A nonvisual report manager class (ccCrystalManager) that contains code to automate the tasks we covered in the previous section:

    - Pushing DataSet information into a report

    - Previewing reports

    - Printing reports (with or without custom print options)

    - Exporting reports

- A generic form to prompt for print options (ccCrystalPrintOptionForm)

- A generic report preview form that you can use to display reports to the screen (ccCrystalViewer)

- A class (ccReportInfo.cs) to set the common report header/footer properties (footnote, title, subtitle, etc.)

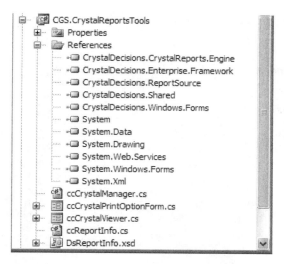

Figure 12-8. *A project of reporting components*

The Generic Report Manager: ccCrystalManager

Table 12-6 shows the public methods in ccCrystalManager that you can use for common report-ing functionality. Table 12-7 shows the available properties, primarily for printing options.

Table 12-6. *Public Methods for ccCrystalManager*

Method	Description
PushReportData()	Passes a report object and DataSet, fills the report, and returns the report object
SetReportInfo()	Sets the report header/footer information
PreviewReport()	Passes a report object and title, and displays the report
PrintReport()	Passes a report object and print options, and prints the report
ExportReport()	Passes a report object, export options, and file name, and exports the report

Table 12-7. *Public Properties for ccCrystalManager*

Name	Description
cPrinterName	Printer name to use
nCopies	Number of copies to print
lAllPages	Prints all pages
lPageRange	Prints a page range
nStartPage	If printing a page range, the starting page number
nEndPage	If printing a page range, the ending page number
lCollate	Whether to collate

Listing 12-6 contains the complete listing for ccCrystalManager. This is the main anchor class for your reporting functionality.

Listing 12-6. *Complete Listing for ccCrystalManager*

```csharp
using System;
using CrystalDecisions.CrystalReports.Engine;
using CrystalDecisions.Shared;
using System.Data;
using System.Windows.Forms;
using System.Collections;
using CrystalDecisions.Windows.Forms;


namespace CGS.CrystalReportsTools
{

    public class ccCrystalManager
    {


        public enum ExportTypes
        {
            PDF = 1,
            MSWord = 2,
            MSExcel = 3
        }


        // Properties utilized by the generic print routine.


        private string _cPrinterName;
        public string cPrinterName
        {
            get {return _cPrinterName ;}
            set {_cPrinterName = value;}
        }


        private int  _nCopies;
        public int nCopies
        {
            get {return _nCopies ;}
            set {_nCopies = value;}
        }
```

```csharp
    private bool  _lAllPages;
    public bool lAllPages
    {
        get {return _lAllPages ;}
        set {_lAllPages = value;}
    }

    private bool  _lPageRange;
    public bool lPageRange
    {
        get {return _lPageRange ;}
        set {_lPageRange = value;}
     }


    private int  _nStartPage;
    public int nStartPage
    {
        get {return _nStartPage ;}
        set {_nStartPage = value;}
     }

    private int  _nEndPage;
    public int nEndPage
    {
        get {return _nEndPage ;}
        set {_nEndPage = value;}
     }

    private bool  _lCollate;
    public bool lCollate
    {
        get {return _lCollate ;}
        set {_lCollate = value;}
    }


public ccCrystalManager()
    {
        this.nCopies = 1;
        this.nStartPage = 0;
        this.nEndPage = 0;
```

```
                    this.cPrinterName = "";
                    this.lAllPages = true;
                    this.lPageRange = false;
                    this.lCollate = true;
        }



        public ReportDocument PushReportData(DataSet DsReportData,
                                                ReportDocument oReport)
        {
        // Called when a report is generated.
        // Calls SetData for the main report object.
        // Also calls SetData for any subreport objects.


                this.SetData(DsReportData,oReport);
                foreach(ReportDocument oSubReport in oReport.Subreports)
                    this.SetData(DsReportData,oSubReport);

                return oReport;

        }

        private void SetData(DataSet DsReportData, ReportDocument oReport)
        {
          // Receives a DataSet and a report object.
          // Could be the main object, could be a subreport object.

          // Loops through the report object's tables collection,
          // matches up the table name with the corresponding table name
          // in the DataSet, and sets the DataSource accordingly.

          // This function eliminates the need for a developer
          // to know the specific table order in the report.

                foreach (Table oTable in oReport.Database.Tables)
                    oTable.SetDataSource(
                      DsReportData.Tables[oTable.Name.ToString()]);
        }

        public void SetReportInfo(ReportDocument oReport, ccReportInfo oReportInfo)
        {
```

```
        // This is a typed DataSet that's also part of the library.
        DsReportInfo odsReportInfo = new DsReportInfo();
        DsReportInfo.dtReportInfoRow oHeaderFooterRow =
          odsReportInfo.dtReportInfo.NewdtReportInfoRow();

        oHeaderFooterRow.FtrDataSource = oReportInfo.FtrDataSource;
        oHeaderFooterRow.FtrFootNotes = oReportInfo.FtrFootNotes;
        oHeaderFooterRow.FtrRunBy = oReportInfo.FtrRunBy;
        oHeaderFooterRow.FtrVersion = oReportInfo.FtrVersion;
        oHeaderFooterRow.HdrCompany = oReportInfo.HdrCompany;
        oHeaderFooterRow.HdrReportTitle = oReportInfo.HdrReportTitle;
        oHeaderFooterRow.HdrSubTitle1 = oReportInfo.HdrSubTitle1;
        oHeaderFooterRow.HdrSubTitle2 = oReportInfo.HdrSubTitle2;
        oHeaderFooterRow.UserID = oReportInfo.UserID;
        odsReportInfo.dtReportInfo.AdddtReportInfoRow(oHeaderFooterRow);

        this.PushReportData(odsReportInfo, oReport);
    }

    public ccCrystalViewer PreviewReport(ReportDocument oReport,
                                         string cTitle,
                                         DataSet DsReportData)
    {
        // Overload of PreviewReport, if you want to push the data
        // and then run the report in one method.
        this.PushReportData(DsReportData, oReport);

        return this.PreviewReport(oReport, cTitle);
    }


    public ccCrystalViewer PreviewReport(ReportDocument oReport,
                                         string cTitle)
    {
        ccCrystalViewer oViewer = new ccCrystalViewer();
        oViewer.crViewer.ReportSource = oReport;
        oViewer.crViewer.Zoom(100);
        oViewer.Text = cTitle;
        oViewer.ShowDialog();

        return oViewer;
    }
```

```
public void PrintReport(ReportDocument oReport)
{
      oReport.PrintOptions.PrinterName = this.cPrinterName;
      oReport.PrintToPrinter(this.nCopies, this.lCollate,
                             this.nStartPage, this.nEndPage);
}


public void ExportReport(ReportDocument oReport,string cFileName,
                         ExportTypes oExportTypes)
{
    this.ExportReport(oReport, cFileName,oExportTypes,0,0);
}


public void ExportReport(ReportDocument oReport, string cFileName,
          ExportTypes oExportTypes, int nFirstPage, int nLastPage)
{
      ExportOptions oExportOptions = new ExportOptions();
      PdfRtfWordFormatOptions oFormatOptions =
                      ExportOptions.CreatePdfRtfWordFormatOptions();
      DiskFileDestinationOptions oDestinationOptions =
                      ExportOptions.CreateDiskFileDestinationOptions();

    if (nFirstPage > 0 && nLastPage > 0)
    {
        oFormatOptions.FirstPageNumber = nFirstPage;
        oFormatOptions.LastPageNumber = nLastPage;
        oFormatOptions.UsePageRange = true;
    }

    switch (oExportTypes)
    {
        case ExportTypes.PDF:
            oExportOptions.ExportFormatType =
                            ExportFormatType.PortableDocFormat;
            break;
        case ExportTypes.MSWord:
            oExportOptions.ExportFormatType =
                            ExportFormatType.WordForWindows;
            break;
        case ExportTypes.MSExcel:
            oExportOptions.ExportFormatType =
                            ExportFormatType.Excel;
            break;
    }
```

```
            oExportOptions.ExportFormatOptions = oFormatOptions;
            oDestinationOptions.DiskFileName = cFileName;
            oExportOptions.ExportDestinationOptions = oDestinationOptions;
            oExportOptions.ExportDestinationType =
               ExportDestinationType.DiskFile;

            oReport.Export(oExportOptions);
         }

      }
}
```

Report Header/Footer Data Objects: ccReportInfo

Table 12-8 shows the properties that you can set for any report header/footer. In code, you'll create an instance of ccReportInfo, populate the properties in Table 12-8, and then pass the object instance to ccCrystalManager (see Listing 12-7), using the method SetReportInfo() in ccCrystalManager. In other words, ccReportInfo is nothing more than a container for the properties listed in the table. The DsReportInfo DataSet also contains these columns in a DataTable called dtReportInfo.

Table 12-8. *Public Methods for ccReportInfo*

Property	Description
FtrDataSource	The annotation for the report data source (shown in the footer)
FtrFootNotes	The user-supplied footnotes (shown in the footer)
FtrRunBy	The name of the user who ran the report (shown in the footer)
FtrVersion	The version of the software used to generate the report (shown in the footer)
HdrCompany	The name of the company (shown in the header)
HdrReportTitle	The main name of the report (shown in the header)
HdrSubTitle1	The subtitle of the report (shown in the header)
HdrSubTitle2	The second subtitle of the report (shown in the header)
UserID	The user ID of the user who ran the report

The Generic Print Options Form: ccCrystalPrintOptionForm

Figure 12-9 shows your print options form, ccCrystalPrintOptionForm.

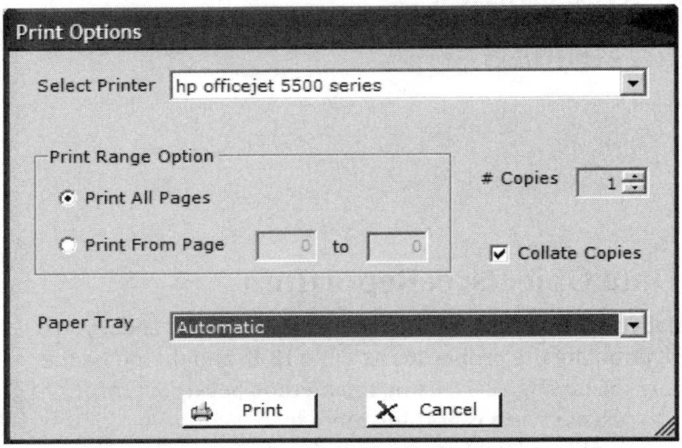

Figure 12-9. *A generic print form*

Getting a List of Installed Printers and Showing the Default

In Figure 12-9, we show the list of available printers and default the list to the current default printer. You can do this as follows:

1. Use the System.Drawing.Printing namespace.

2. Determine the current printer name—create a new PrintDocument object and access the PrinterSettings.PrinterName of the object.

3. Iterate through the PrinterSettings.InstalledPrinters object and populate the printer pull-down list.

Listing 12-7. *Method to Populate the List of Available Printers*

```
private void PopulatePrinterList()
{
  PrintDocument prtdoc = new PrintDocument();
  // Get the current default printer, you'll make that the default in the drop-down.
   // Note: this requires using the System.Drawing.Printing namespace.
  string strDefaultPrinter = prtdoc.PrinterSettings.PrinterName;

  int nCtr = 0;
  // Get list of installed printers.
  foreach(String cPrinter in PrinterSettings.InstalledPrinters)
  {
```

```
this.cboPrinterList.Items.Add(cPrinter); // add the printer to the combobox

if(cPrinter==strDefaultPrinter)
  this.cboPrinterList.SelectedIndex = nCtr;

nCtr++;
  }
}
```

The Generic Report Preview Form: ccCrystalViewer

Figure 12-10 shows your standard report viewer form, ccCrystalViewer. You'll use this form to preview every report. The viewer is simply a Windows form with an instance of the Crystal Reports .NET Viewer control called crViewer. Make sure this control is set with public access.

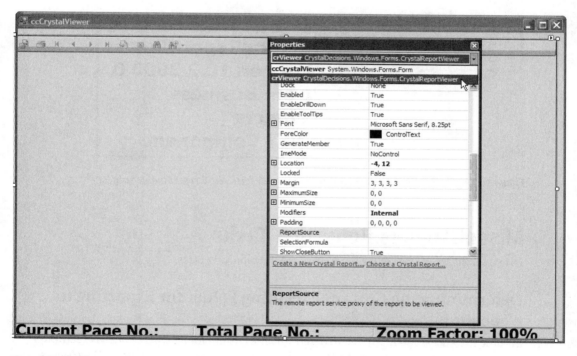

Figure 12-10. *The ccCrystalViewer, a Windows Form with the Crystal viewer object*

To create this report, you can create a new Windows form in the CGS.CrystalReports namespace. In the Visual Studio 2005 Forms designer, load the Windows Forms toolbox and navigate to the Crystal Reports tab (see Figure 12-11), which contains a reference to the CrystalReportsViewer object. Drag the control onto the form and size it to match the dimensions of the form.

When you drop an instance of the CrystalReportsViewer object onto the form, you can set additional properties in the property sheet for the control, such as the Anchor property (to Top, Bottom, Left, Right, so that the control will stretch when the form is maximized).

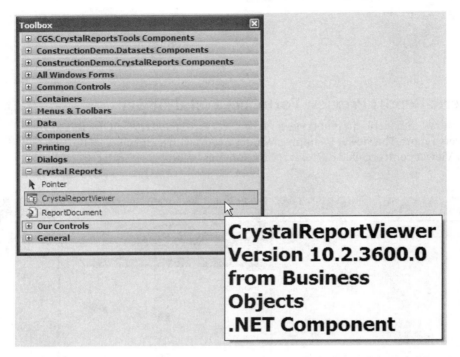

Figure 12-11. *The ccCrystalViewer, a Windows Form with the Crystal viewer object*

Miscellaneous Reporting Tasks

In this section, we'll present some miscellaneous reporting tasks.

Determining the Current Executing Folder for Exporting to a Location

In some instances, you may need to determine the current folder where code is executing—perhaps to determine the root of a folder where you will export report output. Developers sometimes use the following code to determine the current folder:

```
string cFolder = System.IO.Directory.GetCurrentDirectory();
```

Unfortunately, the preceding code will not work if the application has changed the active folder, and is also not fully reliable in a distributed environment. To accurately determine the folder where the current assembly resides, use the following code:

```
AppDomain currentDomain = AppDomain.CurrentDomain;
string cFolder = currentDomain.BaseDirectory.ToString();
```

Loading Untyped Reports

Our text has focused on strongly-typed reports, where you include the report as part of the Visual Studio 2005 application. However, some applications may need to generate a Crystal report that does not reside as part of the application. You can load a report manually with the following code:

```
ReportDocument oReport =
  new CrystalDecisions.CrystalReports.Engine.ReportDocument();
this.oReport.Load("MyExternalReport.RPT");
```

Changing Report Authentication

You have strived to design your reports against a common format (XML/XML Schemas) and to keep database information out of the report. However, some applications, primarily internal (in-house) applications, may run directly off a database server. These applications will often have the reports, database server, and application all under one roof. Developers may design the reports against a test or development server, using database stored procedures as the report's DataSource. Then they will set up a basic interface where internal users will run them off a different server that contains the same stored procedures.

To accomplish this, you need to do the following, as shown in Listing 12-8:

1. Create an instance of the report.

2. Create instances of the Crystal Reports TableLogOnInfo and ConnectionInfo objects.

3. Set the authentication properties in the ConnectionInfo object.

4. Apply the authentication values to each table in the result sets.

Listing 12-8. *Handling Report Authentication*

```
// Create an instance of the report.
ReportDocument oReport =
  new CrystalDecisions.CrystalReports.Engine.ReportDocument();
oReport.Load("MyInternalReport.RPT");

// Set the runtime authentication info.
// (You designed the report to directly work with a stored procedure, which meant
// you authenticated with the database stored proc at design time.)
//
// The report will access a different server at runtime, so it must reauthenticate.

string cServer = "MyServer";
string cDatabase = "MyDatabase";
string cUserID = "kevin";
string cPassword = "kevin7781";
```

```
// Set the connection information, and apply the login information
// for every table/result set from the stored procedure.

TableLogOnInfo logOnInfo = new TableLogOnInfo();
logOnInfo = oReport.Database.Tables[0].LogOnInfo;
ConnectionInfo connectionInfo = new ConnectionInfo ();
connectionInfo = logOnInfo.ConnectionInfo;

connectionInfo.DatabaseName = cDatabase;
connectionInfo.ServerName = cServer;
connectionInfo.Password = cPassword;
connectionInfo.UserID = cUserID;

oReport.Database.Tables[0].ApplyLogOnInfo(logOnInfo);
oReport.Database.Tables[0].LogOnInfo.ConnectionInfo.DatabaseName = cDatabase;
oReport.Database.Tables[0].LogOnInfo.ConnectionInfo.ServerName = cServer;
oReport.Database.Tables[0].LogOnInfo.ConnectionInfo.UserID = cUserID;
oReport.Database.Tables[0].LogOnInfo.ConnectionInfo.Password = cPassword;

// Tricky part: you may need everything before the period character
// of the result set name.
oReport.Database.Tables[0].Location =
  oReport.Database.Tables[0].Location.Substring( ➥
    oReport.Database.Tables[0].Location.LastIndexOf(".") + 1);

myCRViewer.ReportSource = oReport;
```

Utilizing Your Library to Generate a Report

You're approaching the point of the book where things are coming together, and now you can look at generating an actual report from beginning to end. You'll select the aging receivables report. While you haven't (yet) built any kind of interface for users to select a report from a menu option and run it (we'll cover that in Chapter 13), you can combine your back-end efforts (stored procedures, interfaces, back-end data access, and business layer) with your Crystal Reports development.

Building the Aging Receivables Report

If you've already read Chapters 8 and 9 on building reports in Crystal Reports, you'll notice that one report example is conspicuous by its absence: the aging receivables report! Fortunately, we covered most of the fundamental aspects of report construction that are necessary to build your aging receivables report. So you can fast-track creation of the aging receivables report.

The Final Results for the Aging Receivables Report

Figures 12-12 and 12-13 show the end results for the aging receivables report. Figure 12-12 shows the aging receivables report with the option to display individual invoices for each customer (detail option), and Figure 12-13 shows the aging receivables report summarized by customer. You will build one report that supports both options—and just like your other reports, you will use the rptBase.RPT report template.

Date: 9/10/2006 Time: 1:37:32AM			**Test Construction Company** **Aging Receivables Report (Detail)**					Page 1 of 1

Based on Invoices Aged from 3/1/2006

Sorted by Total Aging Amount

Client	Invoice Number	Invoice Date	< 30 Days	31-60 Days	61-90 Days	91-120 Days	> 120 Days	Total
L& L EXCAVATING INC.			1,523.00				30,500.00	32,023.00
	2005-1001	10/18/2005					17,500.00	17,500.00
	2005-0944	08/01/2005					13,000.00	13,000.00
	2006-1391	02/16/2006	1,523.00					1,523.00
KINGSTON CONSTRUCTION			1,032.00	9,624.00	6,500.00		2,000.00	19,156.00
	2006-0133	01/22/2006		8,113.00				8,113.00
	2005-1209	12/18/2005			3,500.00			3,500.00
	2005-2182	12/01/2005			3,000.00			3,000.00
	2005-0778	10/01/2005					2,000.00	2,000.00
	2006-0215	01/23/2006		1,511.00				1,511.00
	2006-3131	02/09/2006	1,032.00					1,032.00
GOLDGATE CONTRACTING						973.00	12,000.00	12,973.00
	2005-1954	05/01/2005					12,000.00	12,000.00
	2005-2393	11/13/2005				973.00		973.00
Grand Total:			**2,555.00**	**9,624.00**	**6,500.00**	**973.00**	**44,500.00**	**64,152.00**

Run by Kevin Goff   *Aging Report Footnotes*   *From Invoice Data*
Version 1.00

Figure 12-12. *Detail aging receivables report*

| Date: 9/10/2006 | | **Test Construction Company** | | | | Page 1 of 1 |
| Time: 1:44:17AM | | **Aging Receivables Report (Summary)** | | | | |

Based on Invoices Aged from 3/1/2006

Sorted by Total Aging Amount

			Aging Range in Days			
Client	< 30 Days	31-60 Days	61-90 Days	91-120 Days	> 120 Days	**Total**
L& L EXCAVATING INC.	1,523.00				30,500.00	32,023.00
KINGSTON CONSTRUCTION	1,032.00	9,624.00	6,500.00		2,000.00	19,156.00
GOLDGATE CONTRACTING				973.00	12,000.00	12,973.00
Grand Total:	**2,555.00**	**9,624.00**	**6,500.00**	**973.00**	**44,500.00**	**64,152.00**

Run by Kevin Goff   *Aging Report Footnotes*   *From Invoice Data*
Version 1.00

Figure 12-13. *Summary aging receivables report*

The Steps to Build It

You'll take a rapid (but complete) step-by-step approach to building the aging receivables report, as shown in the Crystal Reports .NET designer in Figure 12-14. This assumes that you're already familiar with general navigation in Crystal Reports .NET, and you know how to load the Crystal expert functions (Database Expert, Group Expert, Section Expert, etc.). If you need a refresher, check through the examples in Chapters 8 and 9.

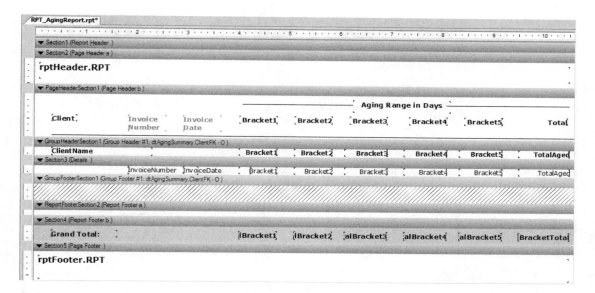

Figure 12-14. *The Crystal Reports .NET designer for the aging receivables report*

1. Add a new item in the ConstructionDemo.CrystalReports project, as a Crystal Report file. Call the new report RPT_AgingReport.RPT.

2. When you are prompted with the screen to create a new Crystal report document, select the third option, From an Existing Report, and click OK. Then navigate to locate the file rptBase.RPT and select it.

3. In the Crystal Reports .NET designer, load the Database Expert, and navigate to the XSD Schema for the aging receivables report (dsAgingReport.XSD). However, instead of selecting every DataTable in the schema, select every one except for dtAgingBrackets. (The reason you don't need this is because of code you wrote in Chapter 7 to produce a nonnormalized table, dtBracketColumns, for the aging column headers.)

4. In the Linking Expert, set links from dtAgingSummary to dtClients, and from dtAgingSummary to dtAgingDetails, as shown in Figure 12-15. Because dtAgingDetails may not contain any data (if the summary option is taken), set the Join Type to a Left Outer Join for the link into dtAgingDetails (see Figure 12-16).

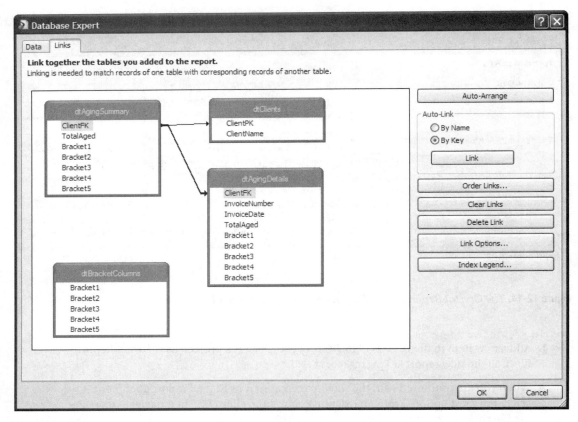

Figure 12-15. *Linking Expert for the aging receivables report*

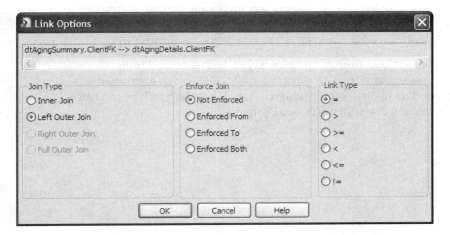

Figure 12-16. *The link options for the aging receivables report; note the Outer Join against* dtAgingDetails.

5. Your aging receivables report will either group invoices by client or summarize by client. Either way, you need to create a group definition based on the client. Using the Group Expert, create a group based on dtAgingSummary.ClientFK. In the Group Expert options, change the sort order for the group to the option "in original order". This will force Crystal Reports to display the customers in the natural order of the source data.

6. You need a flag to determine whether the user is running the report at the detail level or a summary level. As you see in the two screenshots for the report (Figures 12-12 and 12-13 earlier), some labels do not appear in the summary option. You could add a Boolean column to the schema, but you have another option: you can add a Boolean parameter field to the report, and simply pass the corresponding true/false value to the parameter when you launch the report. You created parameter fields for the header and footer reports, so you've already gone through the mechanics of doing so. To create a parameter field, do the following:

   a. Load the Crystal Reports .NET Field Explorer.

   b. In the Parameter Fields option of Field Explorer, right-click, and select New.

   c. In the Create Parameter Field window, give the new parameter a name of ShowDetails. Select Boolean as the value type. Later, you'll use the value of this parameter field to determine whether certain report elements should be displayed.

   d. Finally, when you create an instance of the report, you can set the value of the parameter with the following line of code: oReport.SetParameterValue("ShowDetails", false);.

7. Next, you need to create the page headings. In the Section Expert, insert a new section underneath the Page Header section (so that Page Header a contains the subreport for rptHeader.RPT and Page Header b is blank).

8. In the Page Header b section, add the field objects from Field Explorer for the aging bracket column headers (dtBracketColumns.Bracket1 through dtBracketColumns.Bracket5). Then add the text objects for the remaining columns ("Client", "Invoice Number", etc.)

9. As we stated earlier, certain report objects should only appear if the report is run for details. You need to create a Crystal Reports formula to conditionally suppress the Invoice Number and Invoice Date report headings if the value of your parameter field ShowDetails is false. For both text objects, right-click to load the Format Object/Format Editor screen, and check the Suppress check box on the Common tab. Beside the Suppress check box, click the formula button, and enter the following formula:

```
if {?ShowDetails} = true then
     false
else
     true
```

10. Drag the column dtClients.ClientName from Field Explorer into the Group Header section. Also drag the aging bracket columns from dtAgingSummary (Bracket1 through Bracket5, along with TotalAged) from Field Explorer into the Group Header section, as shown in Figure 12-14.

11. Drag the following columns from Field Explorer into the Detail Section (all from the dtAgingDetails table): InvoiceNumber, InvoiceDate, Bracket1 though Bracket5, and TotalAged.

12. You want to suppress the entire detail section if you're generating the report for the summary option. So load the Section Expert, and for the detail section, check the option to Suppress Blank Section.

13. To create some blank white space between customers (when the detail option is run), expand the vertical space in the Group Footer section. Load the Section Expert, and in the Group Footer section, check the Suppress (No Drill-Down) check box and include the same formula that you used in step 9 (to suppress this section only if the detail option is false).

14. Finally, you need to create the summary totals for the aging brackets. Your first thought might be to create and insert summary total fields from the detail-level aging brackets (from dtAgingDetails). Unfortunately, the aging details table will be empty if the report is generated for the summary option, so you can't use data from dtAgingDetails to create totals. You **also can't** create summary totals from the client summary/subtotal line, because any summary totals from a group-level definition will be incorrect (they'll be double counted for each detail line). So what you need is some type of calculation that summarizes the customer totals on the break of every customer.

Fortunately, Crystal Reports allows you to create a running total field that summarizes based on the change/break of a group. One at a time, right-click each of the bracket columns in the Group Header section, and then select Insert ➤ Running Total from the context menu. This will take you to the Create Running Total Field screen. Check the option to Evaluate on change of group to summarize the bracket every time the group changes as shown in Figure 12-17. Click OK, and insert the new running total into the report footer section (it is found in the Running Total Fields section of Field Explorer).

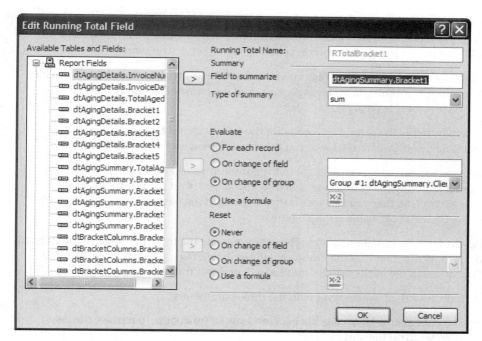

Figure 12-17. *Creating a running total on the change of a group definition*

Running the Aging Receivables Report

This leads to Listing 12-9, which demonstrates execution of the aging receivables report from beginning to end, in a test form. We'll cover the specifics of the client piece in the next chapter: but for now, here are the steps you can take to run your report:

1. On the client side, create a Windows application project called `ConstructionDemo.Client.WinForms`. Add two command buttons to the page, called `btnRemotingTest` and `btnWebServiceTest`. Add a .NET system DLL reference to `CrystalDecisions.CrystalReports.Engine.DLL`. Also add references to the following application DLLs that you've created:

   a. `CGS.CrystalReportsTools.DLL`

   b. `CGS.RemoteAccess.DLL`

   c. `ConstructionDemo.Client.WebReferences`

   d. `ConstructionDemo.CrystalReports`

   e. `ConstructionDemo.DataSets`

   f. `ConstructionDemo.Interfaces`

2. In the Windows form, create an instance of your communication factory class (ClientRemoteAccess) that we covered in Chapter 4. Recall that this class returns an object reference to either a remoting proxy or a web service reference.

3. Set the factory objects tInterface and cServiceName to a typed reference to the aging receivables report interface (IAgingReport) and the name of the aging receivables report class (bzAgingReport).

4. Manually define the three parameters for the aging receivables report (the locations, details flag, and as-of date), since you don't (yet) have a user interface form.

5. Call the method GetAccessObject() in the communication factory. This will return either a remoting proxy object or a web service object. Cast the return object to IAgingReport, so that you can access the methods of the back-end object that implements IAgingReport using strong typing.

6. Call the back-end method GetAgingReport(), passing the three parameters you defined in step 3. Remember that the interface defines that GetAgingReport() will return an XML string. In the back end, this method will perform the following:

   a. Calls your data-access layer with the three parameters.

   b. The data-access layer calls the back-end stored procedure to retrieve the result sets, based on the parameters.

   c. Returns the results back to the client tier, as an XML string.

7. Next, you need to create an instance of the strongly-typed DataSet that you previously used to design the aging receivables report (dsAgingReport).

8. Your goal is to read the contents of the XML string from step 5 into the instance of the aging receivables report DataSet in step 6. To do so, you'll create a StringReader object from the XML string, and then read the StringReader object into the DataSet.

9. Create an instance of the aging receivables report and your Crystal Reports report manager, and then push the DataSet into the report object using the report manager's PushReportData() method.

10. Create an instance of the ccReportInfo object to set the report header/footer information, and then call SetReportInfo.

11. Call the report object's SetParameterValue() method to set the report ShowDetails parameter to either true or false.

12. Call the report manager's methods ExportReport(), PreviewReport(), and PrintReport() to test the different report output processes.

Listing 12-9. *A Walkthrough of Where You Are*

```csharp
using System;
using System.Collections.Generic;
using System.ComponentModel;
using System.Data;
using System.Drawing;
using System.Text;
using System.Windows.Forms;
using System.IO;
using CGS.RemoteAccess;
using ConstructionDemo.Interfaces;
using ConstructionDemo.Client.WebReferences;
using ConstructionDemo.Datasets;
using ConstructionDemo.CrystalReports;
using CGS.CrystalReportsTools;


namespace ConstructionDemo.Client.Winforms
{
    public partial class Form1 : Form
    {
        public Form1()
        {
            InitializeComponent();
        }

        private void Form1_Load(object sender, EventArgs e)
        {
        }


        private void btnWebServiceTest_Click(object sender, EventArgs e)
        {
            this.TestAgingReport
                (ClientRemoteAccess.ConnectionTypeOptions.WebServices);
        }

        private void btnRemotingTest_Click(object sender, EventArgs e)
        {
            this.TestAgingReport
                (ClientRemoteAccess.ConnectionTypeOptions.TcpRemoting);
        }
```

```
private void TestAgingReport
        (ClientRemoteAccess.ConnectionTypeOptions oConnType)
{
    // Return result set for aging receivables report into typed DataSet.
    dsAgingReport dsAgingReport = this.GetAgingReportResult(oConnType);

    // Generate the report, using the typed DataSet.
    this.GenerateAgingReport(dsAgingReport);
}


private dsAgingReport GetAgingReportResult
        (ClientRemoteAccess.ConnectionTypeOptions oConnType)
{
    // Create an instance of your Remote Access Factory class.
    ClientRemoteAccess oRemoteAccess = new ClientRemoteAccess();

    // You need to set five properties for the factory.

    // 1) A type reference to the interface
    oRemoteAccess.tInterface =
                    typeof(ConstructionDemo.Interfaces.IAgingReport<>);

    // 2) The base name of the back-end object
    oRemoteAccess.cServiceName = "AgingReport";

    // 3) Connection type (remoting or web services)
    oRemoteAccess.nConnectionType = oConnType;

    // 4) Back-end server address (could be a URL or TCP server address)
    oRemoteAccess.cTcpServer = "tcp://localhost";
    oRemoteAccess.nTCPPort = 8228;

    oRemoteAccess.cWebServiceURL =
            "http://localhost/ConstructionDemo.WebServices/";

    // 5) If you're using the web, create instance of local web proxy
    //    (subclassed reference)

    if (oRemoteAccess.UsingWebServices() == true)
        oRemoteAccess.wService = new wAgingReportRef();


    // Now that you've set properties for the factory,
    // get an object reference to the back-end object.
    object oReturnObject = oRemoteAccess.GetAccessObject();
```

```
        // Create instance of typed DataSet.
        dsAgingReport dsAgingReport = new dsAgingReport();

        // Set some parameters for the aging receivables report.
        DateTime dAsOfDate = new DateTime(2006, 3, 1);
        bool lUseDetails = false;
        string cClientList = "";
        int nDBKey = 1;

        // If you're using web services, create instance of Interface object
        // (as an XML string),
        // Call back-end method GetAgingReport, and convert the XML string
        // back to your typed DataSet.
        if (oRemoteAccess.UsingWebServices() == true)
        {

            IAgingReport<string> oAgingReport;
            oAgingReport = (IAgingReport<string>)oReturnObject;
            string cXMLResults = oAgingReport.GetAgingReport
                        (dAsOfDate, lUseDetails, cClientList, nDBKey);
            dsAgingReport.ReadXml(new StringReader(cXMLResults),
                        XmlReadMode.InferSchema);
        }
        else
        {
            // If you're using remoting, create instance of Interface object
            // (as your typed DataSet),
            // call back-end method GetAgingReport, which returns result
            // directly into your typed DataSet.
            IAgingReport<dsAgingReport> oAgingReport;
            oAgingReport = (IAgingReport<dsAgingReport>)oReturnObject;
            dsAgingReport = oAgingReport.GetAgingReport
                        (dAsOfDate, lUseDetails, cClientList, nDBKey);
        }

        // At this point, dsAgingReport has been populated!
        // You can use it for your report.

        return dsAgingReport;


    }
```

```
private void GenerateAgingReport(dsAgingReport odsAgingReport)
{

    // Create an instance of the aging receivables report.
    RPT_AgingReport oCrystalAgingReport = new RPT_AgingReport();

    // Create an instance of the Crystal Manager.
    ccCrystalManager oCrystal = new ccCrystalManager();

    // Create an instance of the header/footer object.
    ccReportInfo oReportInfo = new ccReportInfo();
    oReportInfo.FtrDataSource = "From Invoice Data";
    oReportInfo.FtrFootNotes = "Aging Report Footnotes";
    oReportInfo.FtrRunBy = "Run by Kevin Goff";
    oReportInfo.FtrVersion = "Version 1.00";
    oReportInfo.HdrCompany = "Test Construction Company";
    oReportInfo.HdrReportTitle = "Aging Receivables Report (Summary)";
    oReportInfo.HdrSubTitle1 = "Based on Invoices Aged from 3/1/2006";
    oReportInfo.HdrSubTitle2 = "Sorted by Total Aging Amount";
    oReportInfo.UserID = "KSG001";

    oCrystal.SetReportInfo(oCrystalAgingReport, oReportInfo);

    // Push the result set into the report.
    oCrystal.PushReportData(odsAgingReport, oCrystalAgingReport);

    // Set the report ShowDetails Parameter.
    oCrystalAgingReport.SetParameterValue("ShowDetails", false);


    // Show the different capabilities for output...First, do a preview.
    oCrystal.PreviewReport(oCrystalAgingReport, "Preview");

    // Second, show a report export.
    oCrystal.ExportReport(oCrystalAgingReport, "c:\\myexport.pdf",
                          ccCrystalManager.ExportTypes.PDF);


    // Finally, do a print using the printer options dialog.
    ccCrystalPrintOptionForm oPrintOptionsForm =
                        new ccCrystalPrintOptionForm();
    oPrintOptionsForm.ShowDialog();
    if (oPrintOptionsForm.DialogResult == DialogResult.OK)
    {
        oCrystal.lCollate =
            oPrintOptionsForm.chkCollateCopies.Checked;
        oCrystal.nCopies =
```

```
            Convert.ToInt32(oPrintOptionsForm.spnNumPrintedCopies.Value);
        oCrystal.lAllPages =
                oPrintOptionsForm.optPrintAll.Checked;
        oCrystal.lPageRange =
                oPrintOptionsForm.optPrintRange.Checked;
        oCrystal.cPrinterName =
                oPrintOptionsForm.cboPrinterList.Text.ToString();

        if (oPrintOptionsForm.optPrintRange.Checked == true)
        {
            oCrystal.nStartPage =
                Convert.ToInt32(oPrintOptionsForm.txtPrintStartPage.Text);
            oCrystal.nEndPage =
                Convert.ToInt32(oPrintOptionsForm.txtPrintEndPage.Text);
        }
        oCrystal.PrintReport(oCrystalAgingReport);
    }

    }

    }
}
```

Some final notes on the report and on the code in Listing 12-9:

1. Again, this is a test form to demonstrate report generation. In Chapter 13, you'll break out this functionality and implement some user interface modules.

2. Instead of implementing summary report totals for the aging brackets, you could have created a one-row DataTable in the result set to store the results. The reporting methodology in this book definitely creates data-driven subtotals at group levels, but does not create a one-row result set for grand totals.

3. You can use the CGS.CrystalReportsTools library in the middle-tier as well as the presentation layer. You could generate a report in the middle tier and export it to a PDF.

Summary

So, it's time for a check point. What do you need to do that will make your application complete?

- Creating a set of interface forms so that users can make selections for each report

- Allowing the user to save selections for later use

- Allowing the user to view previously exported reports

- Building a testing environment for developers to interactively generate result sets for testing reports

- Generating custom Office output

Recommended Reading

Brian Bischof. *Crystal Reports .NET Programming*. Bischof Systems, 2004.

David McAmis. *Professional Crystal Reports for Visual Studio .NET, Second Edition*. Hoboken, NJ: Wrox, 2004.

The Business Objects Developer Zone. www.businessobjects.com/products/dev_zone/.

Crystal Reports Support Newsgroup, Microsoft.Public.VB.Crystal (on the public news server, News.Microsoft.Com).

■ ■ ■

PART 5

Building the Client Piece

You've reached the final phase of the application, where you construct the user interface modules to interact with all of the back end and support library code that you've built. In previous chapters, you built simple test Windows Forms to launch the modules that you constructed. Now it's time to build the actual client forms. We'll break this into two parts. In Chapter 13, we will cover the basics of Windows Forms and how to build screens for login/authentication and how to launch your reports. In Chapter 14, we'll show you how to build a reusable library for users to generate PowerPoint output from your application.

■ ■ ■

Constructing the User Interface

In this chapter, we'll cover four major pieces:

- We'll show you how to build a set of reusable Windows Forms classes and reusable Windows Forms dialogs. Along the way, we'll cover many different areas and topics dealing with creating controls, visual inheritance, the Windows Forms designer, and subclassing.

- We'll show you how to construct a reusable login/authentication system that allows the user to sign on and set the database/connection to be used. Whereas in prior chapters you had to assign communication settings manually (which server to use, whether to use remoting or web services), this chapter will show how to read these settings out of an XML file, so that the user can select the desired connection at startup.

- We'll walk you through creating basic forms to set report options prior to launching reports.

- We'll show you how to view previously run reports, exactly as they were generated.

■**Note** Just like other chapters in this book, this chapter uses Kevin Goff's **Common Ground Framework for Visual Studio 2005**. One of the goals of the Common Ground Framework is to provide a set of starter, or "productivity," classes for building .NET applications.

Building Reusable Winforms Classes

In this first section, you'll establish some base Windows Forms classes that you can use throughout your client piece. In the same manner that you established a common appearance for report content, you want to establish common appearance and behavior for your base Windows Forms controls. Subclassing .NET Windows Forms controls can be confusing and even frustrating, especially for developers who have used other development products. Fortunately, you can take a guided tour through the process.

In following the motto of beginning with the end in mind, here are some of the things you'll build by the end of this section.

First, you want to build a standard base class Windows Form, from which all of your forms will derive. You want all forms to contain a status label at the bottom of the form to show a message when a process is running (otherwise, the label will be invisible). Figure 13-1 shows the base class form that you'll build, cgsForm, in the CGS.Winforms.Controls namespace. It contains a label, docked to the bottom of the form so that it will stretch to display across the width of the form and always at the bottom. The base form contains two methods so that you can set a message and hide the label.

Figure 13-1. *A base form class (cgsForm) with a status message at the bottom*

Second, you want to build a set of reusable Windows Forms controls (e.g., CheckBox, TextBox, Button, etc.) based on the native Winforms controls. Figure 13-2 shows the end result: controls that you will subclass in the Windows Forms Toolbox that you can subsequently use on any form.

Third, you want to build different classifications of system forms. The first type is a response dialog (otherwise known as a modal form). As the name implies, it is a form that requires a response from a user—generally, either to continue with a process or to cancel. Figure 13-3 shows the form cgsFrmResponse, from the CGS.Winforms.Forms project. The form cgsFrmResponse derives from cgsForm, to inherit the status message functionality. The form also contains two command buttons from your Windows control library that you'll see in the first set of code listings in this chapter.

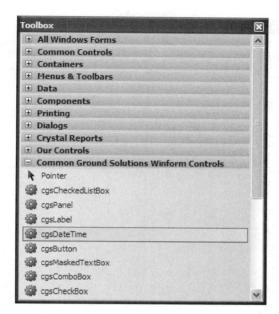

Figure 13-2. *Your base Winforms controls in the VS 2005 Windows Forms Toolbox*

Figure 13-3. *A base response form class* (cgsFrmResponse), *derived from* cgsForm

In this section, you'll be adding two new development projects (as class libraries) to your framework (in Figure 13-4). CGS.Winforms.Controls will contain your subclassed Winforms controls as well as your base Winform class that we showed back in Figure 13-1 (cgsForm). CGS.Winforms.Forms will contain different classifications of system forms (for now, you'll just concentrate on one, your base response form, cgsFrmResponse, in Figure 13-3).

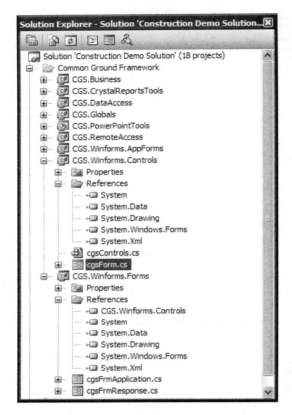

Figure 13-4. *Framework with the CGS.Winforms.Controls and CGS.Winforms.Forms projects*

■**Note** As we stated earlier in the book, .NET does not directly support multiple inheritance. So a single class cannot directly inherit from multiple classes. However, keep in mind that when you create forms that derive from either cgsFrmReponse or cgsFrmApplication, you still pick up the inheritance from whatever those two classes derive from (in this case, cgsForm).

Let's take a look at the steps for each of these.

Creating Winform Classes

Your first step will be to create the form we described back in Figure 13-1. So create a new class library project called CGS.Winforms.Controls. Once Visual Studio loads the project, you need to add .NET references to two .NET components, System.Windows.Forms and System.Drawing (see Figure 13-5). These components are necessary for you to create your Winform classes.

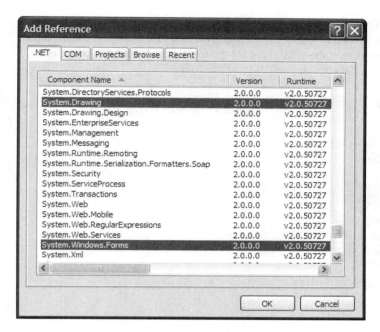

Figure 13-5. *Adding .NET references to a class that subclasses Winforms controls*

After adding the .NET references in Figure 13-5, you can create your new form. Right-click in Solution Explorer on the project to add a new Windows Form, and call the new form cgsForm. Visual Studio will build a default Windows Form in the Visual Studio designer.

By default, you want every form in your application to be centered. The base Windows Form class contains a property called StartPosition that you can set in the property sheet. So right-click the form to retrieve the property sheet, and set the StartPosition property to CenterScreen.

Next, you want to add a status label to the bottom of the form, so that you can display messages when a process is running. So load the Windows Forms Toolbox (by clicking the View pull-down menu and selecting Toolbox), navigate to the Common Controls tab in the Toolbox, and drag an instance of the Label control into the bottom of the form. Now you need to set up the label:

1. Using the property sheet, set the name of the label to lblStatus.

2. Set the label's background color to black, the foreground color to white, and the font to Trubuchet 9.75 (10) point.

3. So that the label will always display at the bottom of the form and will stretch to the width of the form, set the Dock property to Bottom.

4. Finally, so that you'll only see the label when you trigger a function (which we'll cover shortly), set the Visible property for lblStatus to false.

When finished, the form should look exactly like the one back in Figure 13-1.

Finally, you need to add two methods to control the display of the status label lblStatus: one to make the label visible and set its caption, and a second to set the label back to invisible. Listing 13-1 contains the complete code-behind file for the form, which contains two methods, SetMessageOn() and SetMessageOff().

Listing 13-1. *Code for cgsForm*

```
using System;
using System.Collections.Generic;
using System.ComponentModel;
using System.Data;
using System.Drawing;
using System.Text;
using System.Windows.Forms;

namespace CGS.Winforms.Controls
{
    public partial class cgsForm : Form
    {
        public cgsForm()
        {
            InitializeComponent();
        }

        private void cgsForm_Load(object sender, EventArgs e)
        {
        }


        public virtual void SetMessageOn(string cMessage)
        {
            this.lblStatus.Text = cMessage;
            this.lblStatus.Visible = true;
            this.Update();
        }

        public virtual void SetMessageOff()
        {
            this.lblStatus.Visible = false;
            this.lblStatus.Text = "";
        }


    }
}
```

Subclassing the Windows Forms Controls

Also within the CGS.Winforms.Controls project, you'll add a class that subclasses the most common Windows Forms controls that you'll use for the application.

Unlike the Windows Form that you created with ease in the last step, you cannot subclass the Windows Forms controls visually: you must write some code. Fortunately, the code is minimal, and gives you some exposure to the .NET Framework.

You'll focus on the following controls: the Label, MaskedTextBox, ComboBox, DateTimePicker, Panel, CheckedListbox, Button, CheckBox, UserControl, and DataGridView. The purpose of subclassing controls is the same as any other form of subclassing: to define common base appearance/behavior throughout your application. So start by creating a new item in the CGS.Winforms.Controls project, as a class file called cgsControls.cs.

A common example of subclassing Winforms controls appears in Listing 13-2. The code creates a subclass of the Label system class. In the class, you define a default font, Verdana 8 point. Anytime you use this class on a form, the default font will come from this definition.

Listing 13-2. *A Common (but Incorrect) Code Listing for Subclassing the Label Control*

```
using System;
using System.Collections.Generic;
using System.Text;
using System.Windows.Forms;
using System.Drawing;

namespace CGS.Winforms.Controls
{
    public class cgsLabel : Label
    {
        public cgsLabel()
        {
            this.Font = new Font("Verdana", 8);
        }
    }
}
```

Some textbooks use code almost identical to Listing 13-2. Unfortunately, it doesn't quite work. Why? Because of the way the Visual Studio Windows Forms designer works. What happens is as follows:

1. You create some instances of cgsLabel and drop them on a form, and then you change other properties (text, position, etc.) using the property sheet.

2. Consequently, the Windows Forms designer generates code for the form, including code for the value of the font property.

3. Now suppose you later decide that your default font should be Arial 8 instead of Verdana 8. You retrieve the code in Listing 13-2 and change the font to Arial 8, and rebuild the application.

4. Unfortunately, when you load any forms that use cgsLabel, the font is still Verdana 8, because the Windows Forms designer generated code at the time you first created instances of the label class on the form. Your only recourse at this point is to reset the font property for each control using the property sheet.

Of course, this would make subclassing of Winforms controls very inefficient. However, there is a solution. Essentially, you need to use the base constructor and override the Font property, as shown in Listing 13-3.

Listing 13-3. *Correct Way to Subclass a Label Control*

```
using System;
using System.Collections.Generic;
using System.Text;
using System.Windows.Forms;
using System.Drawing;


namespace CGS.Winforms.Controls
{
    public class cgsLabel : Label
    {
        override public Font Font
        {
            get { return base.Font; }
            set { base.Font = value; }
        }

        public cgsLabel()
        {
            base.Font = new Font("Verdana", 8);
        }
    }
}
```

■**Note** You cannot subclass Windows Forms controls visually in Visual Studio 2005. This comes as a surprise to developers who use tools that allow for visual subclassing. However, most developers spend such a small percentage of time subclassing controls, that this isn't much of an issue. In addition, the process of writing the type of code in Listings 13-3 and 13-4 increases exposure to the development language and the .NET Framework.

Now that you've established the mechanics for subclassing, let's take a look at subclassing the rest of the main Windows Forms controls. Table 13-1 shows the main controls that you'll subclass, along with the specific default attributes you want to set.

Table 13-1. *Winforms Controls That You'll Subclass*

Control	Description
CheckedListBox	Sets a default font and sets the check boxes as 3D
Panel	Sets the Border Style and Anchor properties
Label	Sets a default font
DateTimePicker	Sets a default font, width, and date format
Button	Sets a default font and background color
MaskTextBox	Sets a default font, and sets behavior for entering/leaving a text entry control
ComboBox	Sets a default font
CheckBox	Sets a default font

Listing 13-4 shows the complete listing for cgsControls in the CGS.Winforms.Controls namespace. Some important things to note:

- The cgsPanel class sets the Anchor property to all four corners, to stretch consistently with the parent form.

- The cgsButton class sets the background color to white. All of your forms will have some form of a blue/gray background.

- The cgsMaskedTextBox class will set the background color to yellow when the user enters a specific text box (using the Enter event), and back to white when the user leaves the text box (using the Leave event). The class will also treat the Enter key like the Tab key, for users who are accustomed to hitting the Enter key to navigate across fields during data entry (using the KeyDown event).

- The end of the code in Listing 13-4 also contains class definitions for cgsContainer and cgsGrid. These are very basic subclasses of the UserControl and DataGridView controls. You are adding these in now, for when you need them later in the "Creating a Record Selection Screen" section.

Listing 13-4. *Total Listing for Subclassed Controls*

```
using System;
using System.Collections.Generic;
using System.Text;
using System.Windows.Forms;
using System.Drawing;

namespace CGS.Winforms.Controls
{
    public class cgsCheckedListBox : CheckedListBox
    {
        public cgsCheckedListBox()
        {
            this.Font = new Font("Verdana", 8);
```

```
        this.ThreeDCheckBoxes = true;
    }
}

public class cgsPanel : Panel
{
    public cgsPanel()
    {
        this.BorderStyle = System.Windows.Forms.BorderStyle.Fixed3D;

        this.Anchor = ((System.Windows.Forms.AnchorStyles)((((
            System.Windows.Forms.AnchorStyles.Top
            | System.Windows.Forms.AnchorStyles.Bottom)
            | System.Windows.Forms.AnchorStyles.Left)
            | System.Windows.Forms.AnchorStyles.Right)));
    }
}

public class cgsLabel : Label
{
    override public Font Font
    {
        get { return base.Font; }
        set { base.Font = value; }
    }

    public cgsLabel()
    {
        base.Font = new Font("Verdana", 8);
    }
}

public class cgsDateTime : DateTimePicker
{
    override public Font Font
    {
        get { return base.Font; }
        set { base.Font = value; }
    }

    public cgsDateTime()
    {
        base.Font = new Font("Verdana", 8);
        this.Format = DateTimePickerFormat.Short;
        this.Width = 92;
    }
```

```csharp
}

public class cgsButton : Button
{
    override public Font Font
    {
        get { return base.Font; }
        set { base.Font = value; }
    }

    public cgsButton()
    {
        base.Font = new Font("Verdana", 8);
        base.BackColor = Color.White;
    }
}

public class cgsMaskedTextBox : MaskedTextBox
{
    public override Font Font
    {
        get { return base.Font; }
        set { base.Font = value; }
    }

    public cgsMaskedTextBox()
    {
        base.Font = new Font("Verdana", 8);

        this.Enter += new EventHandler(OnEnter);
        this.Leave += new EventHandler(OnLeave);
        this.KeyDown += new KeyEventHandler(OnKeyDown);
    }

    public void OnKeyDown(object sender, System.Windows.Forms.KeyEventArgs e)
    {
        if (e.KeyCode == Keys.Enter)
            SendKeys.Send("{TAB}");
    }

    public void OnEnter(object sender, EventArgs e)
    {
        this.SelectAll();
        if (this.ReadOnly == false)
            this.BackColor = Color.Yellow;
    }
```

```csharp
    public void OnLeave(object sender, EventArgs e)
    {
        if (this.ReadOnly == false)
            this.BackColor = Color.White;
    }
}

public class cgsComboBox : ComboBox
{
    override public Font Font
    {
        get { return base.Font; }
        set { base.Font = value; }
    }

    public cgsComboBox()
    {
        base.Font = new Font("Verdana", 8);
        this.DropDownStyle = ComboBoxStyle.DropDownList;
    }
}

public class cgsCheckBox : CheckBox
{
    override public Font Font
    {
        get { return base.Font; }
        set { base.Font = value; }
    }

    public cgsCheckBox()
    {
        // This call is required by the Windows.Forms Forms designer.
        base.Font = new Font("Verdana", 8);
        this.Width = 88;

        // TODO: Add any initialization after the InitForm call
    }
}

public class cgsContainer : UserControl
{
    public cgsContainer()
    {
        this.BackColor = Color.FromArgb(192, 192, 255);
    }
```

```
    }

    public class cgsGrid : DataGridView
    {
        public cgsGrid()
        {
        }
    }
}
```

■Note When subclassing any Windows Forms controls in a class project, you must add .NET references to System.Windows.Forms. And since your code utilizes the Font object, you must also add a .NET reference to System.Drawing.

You can now build your CGS.Winforms.Controls library, which will create a DLL called CGS.Winforms.Controls.DLL, in the BIN\DEBUG folder of the project location.

Your final step is to make these controls available anytime you want to drop instances of labels, buttons, etc., on a form. In the next section, when you build your base response dialog form, you'll use some of these controls, instead of the standard Windows Forms controls (since you subclassed them to add appearance and functionality). To use them, you need to add them to the Visual Studio Toolbox. In the next section, at the point where you want to add your controls, we'll cover these steps.

Creating an Inherited Windows Form

Your last step is to create the reusable base response form class that we showed back in Figure 13-3 (cgsFrmResponse). You'll use this form as the basis of every form where the user can either continue to the next step or cancel and go back. (In the next section, you'll use this response dialog to create your first actual application form, a login form.)

You'll create cgsFrmResponse in a separate project, CGS.Winforms.Forms. The reason you're creating this form in a separate project is to avoid situations where the Windows Forms designer would otherwise have to display a class that inherits from another class in the same project. While Visual Studio generally supports this (or at least doesn't prevent you from doing so), it can lead to abnormal behavior with the designer, including designer errors that result in either closing or reopening Visual Studio, rebuilding the project, and so on. While it means creating another project, our methodology is to avoid visual inheritance within the same project.

Building the cgsFrmResponse Form

So create a new project as a class library project called CGS.Winforms.Forms. Inside the project, right-click to add a new Windows Form. In the Add New Item screen (see Figure 13-6), select Inherited Form.

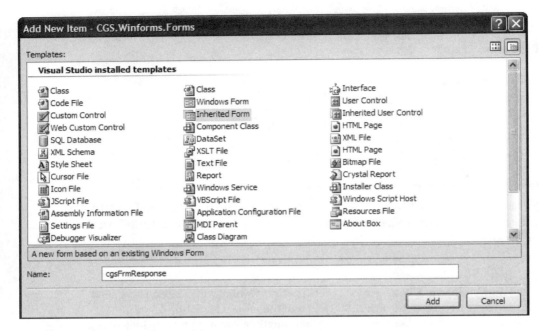

Figure 13-6. *Creating an inherited form*

Next, you need to define the form from which cgsFrmResponse will inherit: the cgsForm base class form from CGS.Winforms.Controls. When you create an inherited form, Visual Studio will prompt for the class from which to inherit (see Figure 13-7). Select the Browse button to navigate to the CGS.Winforms.Controls.DLL file in the BIN\DEBUG folder of the project for CGS.Winforms.Controls.

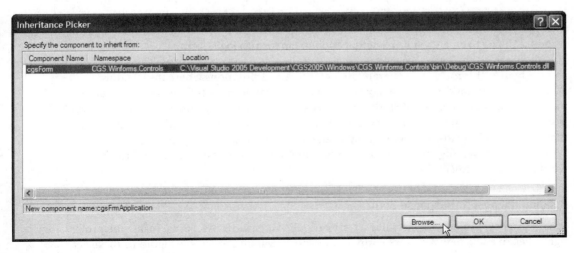

Figure 13-7. *Selecting the class from which to inherit*

After you locate and select cgsForm, you can select OK (in Figure 13-7). That will create the new form cgsFormResponse in your project. If you look at the code-behind file for the form, you'll see that the form indeed inherits from cgsForm:

```
public partial class cgsFrmResponse : CGS.Winforms.Controls.cgsForm
```

Because you're inheriting from your base form, the methods for turning on/off the status label back in Listing 13-1 are exposed (see Figure 13-8).

this.SetMessageOn(

| void cgsForm.SetMessageOn (**string cMessage**) |

Figure 13-8. *Using IntelliSense to demonstrate the inherited methods*

Building a Base Application Form, cgsFrmApplication

Before moving on, you want to create a second base form for your application. Unlike the response dialog you just created (cgsFrmResponse), this second base form will be used for all of your standard report options forms.

You'll call this one cgsFrmApplication. At design time, the only difference is that you'll give the form a different background color, to distinguish it from the response dialog. At run-time, you'll call the form with the standard Show form method, which allows multiple forms to be available. (By contrast, you'll call response dialog forms with the ShowDialog method, which makes the form modal, and therefore the user cannot activate any other form.)

So create the inherited form cgsFrmApplication in the CGS.WinForms.Forms project by repeating the steps in the previous heading that you used to create cgsFrmResponse. Feel free to use any background color you wish, so long as it's something different from the background color for the response dialog. By creating the form as an inherited form from cgsForm, the SetMessageOn method that we showed back in Figure 13-8 will be exposed.

You'll use this application form when you create your aging report options screen later in this chapter in the section "Creating a Report Options Screen."

Adding Your Subclassed Controls to the Toolbox

Your next step is to add command buttons to the bottom of the form, for Continue and Cancel. While it's not absolutely necessary to add your subclassed controls to the Toolbox—you could simply drop instances of the base Winforms controls onto your form and programmatically change where they inherit from—it is easier to add your controls as a new category tab to the Toolbox and then use them.

To do so, load the Windows Forms Toolbox from the View menu item, and then right-click to add a new tab to the Toolbox (see Figure 13-9).

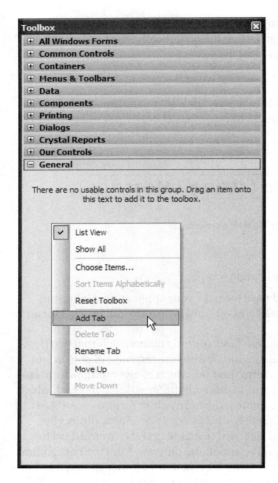

Figure 13-9. *Adding a tab to the Windows Forms ToolBox*

Next, specify a name for the new controls (see Figure 13-10). The name can be any name you choose.

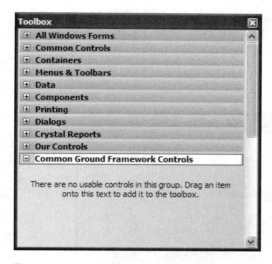

Figure 13-10. *Specifying a tab name*

The next step is to add items to the tab category. So right-click again and select Choose Items (see Figure 13-11).

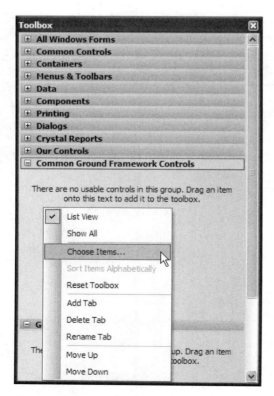

Figure 13-11. *Right-click to choose items.*

This loads the Choose Toolbox Items dialog (see Figure 13-12). Click the Browse button and navigate to the BIN\DEBUG location for the CGS.Winforms.Controls.DLL file. Once you select the file, the screen in Figure 13-12 will automatically select all of the classes from the DLL, so that you can click OK.

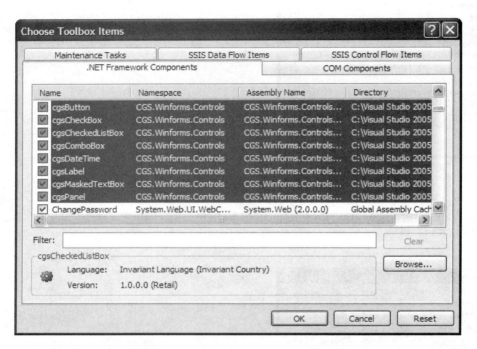

Figure 13-12. *Selecting controls for the Toolbox*

And voila! Your Toolbox tab contains all of the controls (see Figure 13-13). You can now drop them into the form as needed.

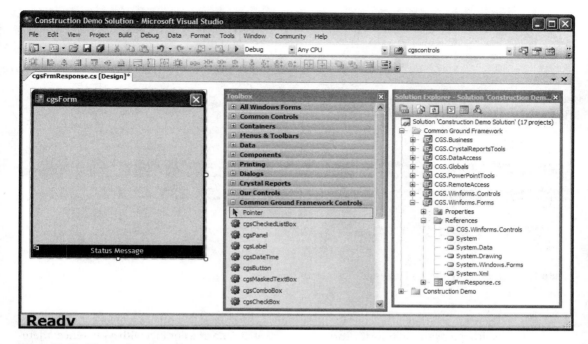

Figure 13-13. *The updated Toolbox*

At this point, you can add command buttons to your response dialog, to make it appear like Figure 13-3. So drag two Button controls from the Toolbox onto the form area, and call the buttons btnContinue and btnCancel. Set the Modifier property for both buttons to Public. Use whatever captions and icons you wish. To achieve the general appearance of both buttons, set the TextAlign property to MiddleRight and the ImageAlign property to MiddleLeft.

Some Commentary on the Visual Studio Forms Designer

Visual Studio 2005 is an outstanding development product, and .NET is a powerful development platform. However, no development product is perfect. Having used Visual Studio heavily for years, there are a few quirks and issues—in this context, with the Visual Studio Forms and UI designer.

Earlier you saw that part of your class methodology is to avoid visual inheritance within the same project. There can be other instances where you load a Winform from Solution Explorer and see a message like the ones in Figures 13-14 and 13-15.

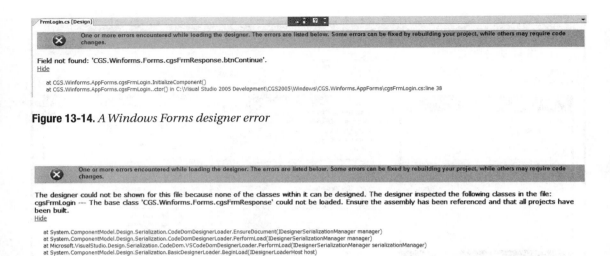

Figure 13-14. *A Windows Forms designer error*

Figure 13-15. *Another Windows Forms designer error*

There are a variety of reasons for these types of messages. Essentially, it means the Windows Forms designer cannot draw the form. It may be as simple as a conflict with a reference; therefore, rebuilding the reference may help. Sometimes you may need to close the project, exit, and then relaunch Visual Studio, and then open the project again. In other instances, your project dependencies may not be correct, and may need to be reviewed. Check the section "Setting Project Dependencies" in Appendix C for more information on project dependencies.

As a practice, I avoid keeping forms open when I am modifying classes that the form uses. Sometimes this means closing a form, just to avoid a strange designer error when I modify and rebuild the class.

So the Visual Studio 2005 Forms designer is not perfect. Many use it for months without experiencing even the slightest hiccup, while others run into these quirks more regularly.

Building an Authentication Screen

Now that you've gone through the mechanics of creating form and control classes, you can focus on building some application components. Where to start? Well, what better place than the first form users will normally see—the login form?

A login form might seem like a rather mundane application form to build. However, in this situation, the login form serves a dual purpose, as you can see by looking at the finished product (shown in Figures 13-16 and 13-17). Your login screen prompts not only for the user ID and password, but also for the connection you plan to use. At the beginning of the book, we stated a requirement that the client piece needed to connect to the back end via web services or remoting, and also that the client piece might need to connect to one of multiple databases. The pull-down menu for Connection to Location prompts the user for the connection and lists the available connections. This section will show how you populate that pull-down menu.

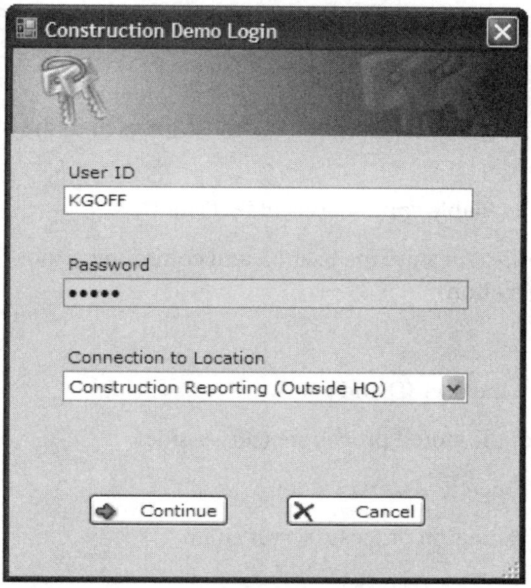

Figure 13-16. *Your login form in action*

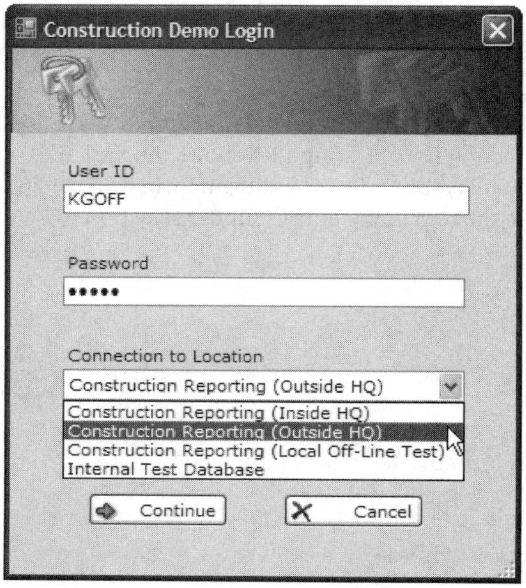

Figure 13-17. *Your login form, with the list of available connections*

Building the Layers, Redux

Because you've been through the mechanics of much of what we're going to cover, you'll take a fast-track approach to building the entire infrastructure for the login form. In previous chapters, you broke up all of the components: now we'll cover them in one section, for each of the physical layers to which they belong:

1. The XML connection file that stores all available connections (client side)

2. A class containing a set of global properties (to store the user ID and communication properties in memory in the client application)

3. The actual base login form (client side)

4. A back-end stored procedure to validate the user ID and password (server side)

5. A typed DataSet that stores the results of the stored procedure (server side)

6. The data access class to call the stored procedure (server side)

7. The back-end interface for the user ID validation process (server side)

8. The business object (server side)

9. The web service (server side, as well as client-side reference and proxy)

10. The client-side code to call out to the back end (client side)

List of Available Connections in XML File

The drop-down menu in Figures 13-16 and 13-17 lists the available connections. You will read these out of an XML file that must reside in the same folder as the actual executable. We'll cover that location a little later (specifically, in Listing 13-7). Listing 13-5 shows the XML file, and Table 13-2 provides a description for each XML column. The client login form will display the descriptions only—and the software will use the remaining entries for the selection to drive how back-end processes are called.

Listing 13-5. *Connect.XML*

```
<Connect>

    <ConnectionInfo>
        <Description>Construction Reporting (Inside HQ)</Description>
        <DBKey>3</DBKey>
        <ConnectionType>2</ConnectionType>
        <ServerAddress>tcp://localhost</ServerAddress>
        <PortNumber>8228</PortNumber>
    </ConnectionInfo>

    <ConnectionInfo>
        <Description>Construction Reporting (Outside HQ)</Description>
        <DBKey>1</DBKey>
```

```
    <ConnectionType>1</ConnectionType>
    <ServerAddress>http://localhost/ConstructionDemo.WebServices/
                        </ServerAddress>
    <PortNumber>0</PortNumber>
</ConnectionInfo>

<ConnectionInfo>
    <Description>Construction Reporting (Local Off-Line Test)</Description>
    <DBKey>1</DBKey>
    <ConnectionType>2</ConnectionType>
    <ServerAddress>tcp://localhost</ServerAddress>
    <PortNumber>8228</PortNumber>
</ConnectionInfo>

<ConnectionInfo>
    <Description>Internal Test Database</Description>
    <DBKey>2</DBKey>
    <ConnectionType>2</ConnectionType>
    <ServerAddress>tcp://localhost</ServerAddress>
    <PortNumber>8228</PortNumber>
</ConnectionInfo>

</Connect>
```

Table 13-2. *List of Columns in Connect.XML*

XML Column	Description
Description	The description for the connection
DBKey	The database key—which is resolved against the database key from Chapter 5
ConnectionType	The connection type (1 = web services, 2 = TCP remoting)
ServerAddress	The main address (either a web service URL or TCP server address)
PortNumber	For TCP remoting, the TCP port number

A Class of Globals

When the user's full name and connection settings are determined at sign-on, you want to hold these and other values in memory to easily access them at different points of the application. For instance, you'll want to know the user's name for any custom messages, and you'll want to know the connection option that user chose. Listing 13-6 shows cgsGlobals.cs, which resides in the CGS.Globals standard class library project.

Other projects that need to reference this information can simply set a reference to CGS.Globals to access these values. Note that the properties in this class are set to static, thus being retained anytime the class is instantiated.

Listing 13-6. *cgsGlobals.cs*

```
using System;

namespace CGS.Globals
{
    public class cgsGlobals
    {
        private static bool _lAppRunning;
        public bool lAppRunning
        {
            get { return _lAppRunning; }
            set { _lAppRunning = value; }
        }

        private static string _cUserID;
        public string cUserID
        {
            get { return _cUserID; }
            set { _cUserID = value; }
        }

        private static int _nUserPK;
        public int nUserPK
        {
            get { return _nUserPK; }
            set { _nUserPK = value; }
        }

        private static string _cUserPassword;
        public string cUserPassword
        {
            get { return _cUserPassword; }
            set { _cUserPassword = value; }
        }

        private static string _cUserName;
        public string cUserName
        {
            get { return _cUserName; }
            set { _cUserName = value; }
        }

        private static string _cCurrentConnection;
        public string cCurrentConnection
        {
```

```
            get { return _cCurrentConnection; }
            set { _cCurrentConnection = value; }
        }

        private static int _nDataBaseKey;
        public int nDataBaseKey
        {
            get { return _nDataBaseKey; }
            set { _nDataBaseKey = value; }
        }

        public cgsGlobals()
        {
            //
            // TODO: Add constructor logic here
            //
            this.cUserID = "";
            this.cUserPassword = "";

            // Default, for internal systems with one database
            this.nDataBaseKey = 1;
        }
    }
}
```

Creating the Base Login Form

Your login form will inherit from the cgsFrmResponse form that you created in the previous section. You will create this form in a new project within the Common Ground Framework solution—you'll call the project CGS.Winforms.AppForms, as the login form represents one of several base application forms in the Framework.

So create a new class library project called CGS.Winforms.AppForms. Very important—add a reference to your remote access factory class, CGS.RemoteAccess, as this login form will set specific connection properties, based on the connection the user selects. Inside the project, add a new inherited form called cgsFrmLogin. When Visual Studio prompts for the inherited form (which we covered back in Figure 13-7), select cgsFrmResponse from the CGS.Winforms.Forms DLL.

In the Windows Forms designer, add Label, MaskedTextBox, and ComboBox controls from the Toolbox (using your Common Ground Framework controls) to the login form area, so that the form resembles the one in Figure 13-18. (The logo at the top with the keychain icon is for aesthetics only—feel free to replace it with your own image.) Call the three entry/pull-down controls txtUserID, txtPassword, and cboConnections. Make sure to set all three controls to Public.

Figure 13-18. *Your base login form, cgsFrmLogin*

Now let's look at the code to support this form. Listing 13-7 contains the complete code for the cgsFrmLogin class. Of particular importance are the following:

- The PopulateConnections() method reads the Connect.XML file and populates the cboConnections pull-down menu.

- When clicked, the button btnContinue calls the UserLogin() form method, which does three things:

  - Sets the status message on to indicate that a login attempt is occurring.

  - Sets the global properties mentioned in cgsGlobals, based on the connection that the user selected.

  - Calls the ValidateUserID() form method. This is a virtual stub method that you'll override when you subclass this form and add your custom logic.

Note that you won't actually run this base form. You'll eventually create your own form in the main Windows application, ConstructionDemo.Client.Winforms.

Listing 13-7. *Code-Behind in cgsFrmLogin Base Form*

```
using System;
using System.Collections.Generic;
using System.ComponentModel;
using System.Data;
```

```csharp
using System.Drawing;
using System.Text;
using System.Windows.Forms;
using CGS.Globals;
using CGS.RemoteAccess;

namespace CGS.Winforms.AppForms
{
    public partial class cgsFrmLogin : CGS.Winforms.Forms.cgsFrmResponse
    {
        DataSet DsAvailableConnections;

        // Set at startup when user logs in and selects the connection profile
        private DataRow _Dr;
        public DataRow Dr
        {
            get { return _Dr; }
            set { _Dr = value; }
        }

        cgsGlobals oGlobals;
        private bool lLoaded = false;

        public cgsFrmLogin()
        {
            InitializeComponent();
        }


        private void cgsFrmLogin_Load(object sender, EventArgs e)
        {
            oGlobals = new cgsGlobals();
            if (oGlobals.lAppRunning == true)
                if (this.lLoaded == false)
                {
                    this.PopulateConnections();
                    this.lLoaded = true;
                }
        }

        protected virtual void PopulateConnections()
        {
            this.DsAvailableConnections = new DataSet();
            if (System.IO.File.Exists(System.IO.Directory.GetCurrentDirectory() +
                            "\\connect.xml"))
            {
```

```
            this.DsAvailableConnections.ReadXml(
                    System.IO.Directory.GetCurrentDirectory() +
                    "\\connect.xml");
            foreach (DataRow Dr in this.DsAvailableConnections.Tables[0].Rows)
                this.cboConnections.Items.Add(Dr["Description"]);

        if (this.cboConnections.Items.Count > 0)
            this.cboConnections.SelectedIndex = 0;
    }
}

private void btnCancel_Click(object sender, EventArgs e)
{
    this.Close();
}

private void btnContinue_Click(object sender, EventArgs e)
{
    this.UserLogin();
}


protected virtual bool ValidateUserID()
{
    return false;
}

protected virtual void UserLogin()
{
    this.SetMessageOn("Connecting for user " +
                oGlobals.cUserID.ToString().Trim() + "...please wait");
    this.SetConnectionInfo();
    if (this.ValidateUserID() == true)
    {
        this.DialogResult = DialogResult.OK;
        this.Close();
    }
    this.SetMessageOff();
}


protected virtual void SetConnectionInfo()
{
    // Set the communcation properties

    ClientRemoteAccess oRemoteAccess = new ClientRemoteAccess();
    this.Dr = this.DsAvailableConnections.Tables[0].Rows
```

```
                                    [this.cboConnections.SelectedIndex];

        oRemoteAccess.nConnectionType =
                (ClientRemoteAccess.ConnectionTypeOptions)
                        Convert.ToInt32(Dr["ConnectionType"]);
        oRemoteAccess.cWebServiceURL = (string)Dr["ServerAddress"];
        oRemoteAccess.cTcpServer = (string)Dr["ServerAddress"];
        oRemoteAccess.nTCPPort = Convert.ToInt32(Dr["PortNumber"]);
        oRemoteAccess.cDescription = (string)Dr["Description"];
        oGlobals.nDataBaseKey = Convert.ToInt32(this.Dr["DbKey"]);
    }


  }
}
```

■**Note** The code in the base login class is an example of framework design that allows for extensibility. The virtual Boolean method `ValidateUserID()` is simply a stub that the developer can override to implement the necessary custom login process.

Stored Procedure to Validate User ID

The login prompt requires two pieces of information from the user: user ID and password. So you need a basic stored procedure that queries the user table to determine whether the user exists. Listing 13-8 shows a stored procedure that reads `UserFile` based on the user ID and password, and also performs an outer join on the `Status` table to determine the user's current status (Active, Suspended, etc.).

Listing 13-8. *Stored Procedure to Validate User ID*

```
CREATE PROCEDURE [dbo].[ValidateUserID]
    (@cUserID nChar(10), @cPassword nchar (10))
 AS
BEGIN
-- Introduces new table, Status    (StatusPK int, Description char(100)

SELECT UserPK, UserName,
      COALESCE(StatusPK,0) AS StatusFK,
      COALESCE(Status.Description,'') AS StatusDescription
    FROM UserFile
    LEFT JOIN Status ON StatusFK = StatusPK
    WHERE UserID = @cUserID AND Password = @cPassword

END
```

The Typed DataSet

In Chapter 6, you built typed DataSets to store results of your queries and for any post-query data processing or data manipulation. Figure 13-19 shows the dsUser typed DataSet for your stored procedure's results. You'll store this DataSet in the same project you used in Chapter 6, namely ConstructionDemo.DataSets.

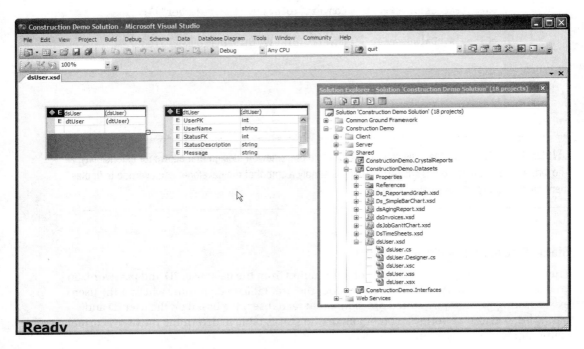

Figure 13-19. *Typed DataSet for dsUser*

The stored procedure that you'll build in the next heading will return the UserPK, UserName, StatusPK, and StatusDescription columns. You'll build a custom message in your business object for any instances where the login should be refused.

Data Access Class

Back in Chapter 5, you built data access classes to interact with your stored procedures, in the project ConstructionDemo.DataAccess. You'll need to add a new class to call your stored procedure from Listing 13-8. So create a new class inside ConstructionDemo.DataAccess, and call it daUser (see Listing 13-9). daUser will inherit from your base data access class cgsDataAccess, which you built in Chapter 5.

Just like the data access classes you built in Chapter 5, daUser will receive parameters (the user ID and password), along with the database key to use. The GetUser() method will create an instance of the typed DataSet dsUser and call the stored procedure using the base data access method ReadIntoTypedDS().

Listing 13-9. *Data Access Class daUser in the ConstructionDemo.DataAccess Project*

```
using System;
using System.Collections.Generic;
using System.Text;
using System.Data;
using System.Data.SqlClient;
using CGS.DataAccess;
using ConstructionDemo.Datasets;


namespace ConstructionDemo.DataAccess
{
    public class daUser : cgsDataAccess
    {
        public dsUser GetUser(string cUserID, string cPassword, int nDBKey)
        {
            List<SqlParameter> oParms = new List<SqlParameter>();

            oParms.Add(new SqlParameter("@cUserID", cUserID));
            oParms.Add(new SqlParameter("@cPassword", cPassword));

            dsUser odsUser = new dsUser();
            odsUser =
              this.ReadIntoTypedDs(odsUser, "[dbo].[ValidateUserID]",
                                   oParms, nDBKey);

            return odsUser;
        }
    }
}
```

The Interface

In Chapter 4, we covered the value of interfaces to maintain strong typing in the client piece. You'll need an interface here for the validation process. Your interface will require a back-end function called GetUser(), that receives a user ID, a password, and a database key, and returns either an XML string or a DataSet.

```
public interface IUser<T>
{
    T GetUser(string cUserID, string cPassword, int nDBKey);
}
```

You can add this interface directly into your ReportInterfaces.cs file in the ConstructionDemo.Interfaces project, or you can create a new interface class in the project. For purposes of simplicity, you'll just add this interface to ReportInterfaces.cs.

Business Object

Next, you need to build your business object, which you'll call bzUser, in the ConstructionDemo. Business project (see Listing 13-10). bzUser will inherit from your base business object (to pick up the necessary inheritance to System.MarshalByRefObject for remoting), and will also implement the IUser interface we just covered.

The GetUser() method will call daUser (see Listing 13-9) to retrieve the user information. GetUser() will also construct a custom message if the user's status is anything other than Active by using the UserStatus enumeration.

Listing 13-10. *Business Object bzUser in the ConstructionDemo.Business Project*

```
using System;
using System.Collections.Generic;
using System.Text;
using ConstructionDemo.Datasets;
using ConstructionDemo.DataAccess;
using CGS.Business;
using ConstructionDemo.Interfaces;

namespace ConstructionDemo.Business
{
    public class bzUser : cgsBaseBusinessObject, IUser< dsUser>
    {

        public enum UserStatus  { Active = 1,
                                  TemporarilyInActive = 2,
                                  Inactive = 3,
                                  Suspended = 4,
                                  Deleted = 5};

        public dsUser GetUser(string cUserID, string cPassword, int nDBKey)
        {
            dsUser odsUser = new dsUser();
            odsUser = new daUser().GetUser(cUserID, cPassword, nDBKey);

            if (odsUser.dtUser.Rows.Count > 0)
            {
                dsUser.dtUserRow oRow = odsUser.dtUser[0];
                if (oRow.StatusFK != (int)UserStatus.Active)
                    oRow.Message = "Cannot login: User Status is currently " +
                                        oRow.StatusDescription.Trim();
```

```
            else
                oRow.Message = String.Empty;
        }
        else
        {
            dsUser.dtUserRow oBlankRow = odsUser.dtUser.NewdtUserRow();
            oBlankRow.Message = "User ID/Password was not found";
            odsUser.dtUser.AdddtUserRow(oBlankRow);
        }

        return odsUser;
    }
  }
}
```

■**Note** If your database application uses a combination of status/type codes and enumerations, consider writing a tool to autogenerate your enumerations from the database. This reduces maintenance and keeps things a little more synchronized.

The Web Service

Moving right along, you now need to build your web service. Again, you can follow the lead of Chapter 4, where you built web services in the ConstructionDemo.WebServices project.

Listing 13-11 shows the web service to validate the user ID: you'll call it wUser, in the same project as the other web services. Just as you did with other web services, wUser will implement IUser, but specifying an XML string for the return value.

Listing 13-11. *The Web Service wUser*

```
using System;
using System.Data;
using System.Web;
using System.Collections;
using System.Web.Services;
using System.Web.Services.Protocols;
using System.ComponentModel;
using ConstructionDemo.Interfaces;
using ConstructionDemo.Business;

namespace ConstructionDemo.WebServices
{
    /// <summary>
```

```
/// Summary description for wUser
/// </summary>
[WebService(Namespace = "http://tempuri.org/")]
[WebServiceBinding(ConformsTo = WsiProfiles.BasicProfile1_1)]
[ToolboxItem(false)]
public class wUser : System.Web.Services.WebService, IUser<string>
{
    [WebMethod]
    public string GetUser(string cUserID, string cPassword, int nDBKey)
    {
        string cXML = new bzUser().GetUser(cUserID, cPassword, nDBKey).GetXml();

        return cXML;
    }
}
}
```

The Client-Side Web Service Reference

You're getting close! On the client side, you need to add a web reference to your web service
wUser.asmx. Chapter 4 covered the steps for adding a web reference, if you need a refresher on
the process.

As also stated in Chapter 4, you want to subclass the web reference proxy to implement your interface (in this case, IUser). So after adding the web reference to wUser in
ConstructionDemo.Client.WebReferences, you'll subclass the web reference (see Listing 13-12)
as wUserRef (also in ConstructionDemo.Client.WebReferences). Remember that there is nothing in the way of code when you subclass your web references—the only objective is for the
web service reference to implement the interface.

Listing 13-12. *Web Service Proxy Reference Subclass*

```
// wUserRef.cs
// Subclasses the web service reference for wUser, to implement IUser
using System;
using System.Collections.Generic;
using System.Text;
using ConstructionDemo.Interfaces;

namespace ConstructionDemo.Client.WebReferences
{
    public class wUserRef : wUser.wUser, IUser<string>
    {
    }
}
```

Finally! The Client Form

You've reached the final point. In your main windows application (ConstructionDemo.Client.Winforms), you can subclass the base login form (cgsFrmLogin) to your own login form, and implement your methods to call the back end. There are a few steps you need to perform to create this, as described in the next sections.

First, the .NET References

Figure 13-20 shows all of the .NET references that you'll ultimately need in your client application. Note that some are from your CGS set of libraries, and others are from your client-side libraries in the ConstructionDemo namespace.

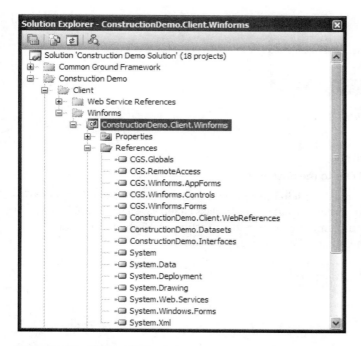

Figure 13-20. *All the .NET references in your Windows application*

Second, Creating the Form

Once again, you'll create an inherited form, your last level of inheritance. So in the ConstructionDemo.Client.Winforms project, create an inherited form called FrmLogin, and inherit from cgsFrmLogin in the CGS.Winforms.AppForms DLL. This will create a new Windows Form in your client project (see Figure 13-21). You can set the form caption to whatever you wish, and you can add any additional information that you might need on the form.

Figure 13-21. *Final login form with your caption*

Third, Writing the Code to Call Out to the Back End

Last, but certainly not least, you need to fill in the code in the client form. Back in Listing 13-7, you saw a stub Boolean method in the base cgsFrmLogin class called ValidateUserID(). You can override that function and implement your own logic. Listing 13-13 shows the code-behind for the FrmLogin form in your local Winform application.

Listing 13-13. *Code-Behind for FrmLogin*

```
using System;
using System.Collections.Generic;
using System.ComponentModel;
using System.Data;
using System.Drawing;
using System.Text;
using System.Windows.Forms;
using CGS.Globals;

namespace ConstructionDemo.Client.Winforms
{
    public partial class FrmLogin : CGS.Winforms.AppForms.cgsFrmLogin
    {
        FrmLoginManager oLoginManager;
        public FrmLogin()
```

```
    {
        InitializeComponent();
    }

    private void FrmLogin_Load(object sender, EventArgs e)
    {
    }

    protected override bool ValidateUserID()
    {
        cgsGlobals oGlobals = new cgsGlobals();
        bool lRetVal = true;
        string cUserID = this.txtUserID.Text.Trim();
        string cPassword = this.txtPassword.Text.Trim();
        oGlobals.cCurrentConnection = this.cboConnections.Text;

        oLoginManager = new  FrmLoginManager();

        string cMessage = oLoginManager.ValidateUserID(cUserID, cPassword);
        if(cMessage.Length > 0) {
            MessageBox.Show(cMessage,oGlobals.cCurrentConnection);
            lRetVal = false;
        }

         return lRetVal;
    }

    private void btnContinue_Click(object sender, EventArgs e)
    {
    }

    private void btnCancel_Click(object sender, EventArgs e)
    {
    }
    }
}
```

■**Note** The base virtual method SetConnectionInfo in cgsFrmLogin automatically sets the connection properties such as cTcpServer, cWebServiceUrl, etc., in the ClientRemoteAccess class, when the user makes a connection selection. You can use this capability as is. However, if you need to tap into it to add additional logic, declare an override method as protected override void SetConnectionInfo(). Inside the method, call the base behavior with the line base.SetConnectionInfo(), and then add your own custom logic.

You probably noticed something interesting in Listing 13-13, particularly in the override for ValidateUserID(). You don't have much code, just a call out to another function in an object called FrmLoginManager? What gives? Read on . . .

The Form's Right-Hand Man, a Form Manager

Your form's methodology in the client piece will implement two classes for each form: the form itself (which ultimately inherits from some base Windows Form), and a form manager class. You'll minimize any lengthy code in the form itself and delegate that responsibility to the corresponding form manager. At the top of Listing 13-13, you see a line of code that declares an object reference to the form manager, and then further down you see two lines that create an instance of the manager and then call the form manager.

```
FrmLoginManager oLoginManager;

oLoginManager = new  FrmLoginManager();
string cMessage = oLoginManager.ValidateUserID(cUserID, cPassword);
```

The code for the login manager (FrmLoginManager.cs) appears in Listing 13-14. Note that the form manager takes care of all the actual calling out to the back end, through the communications factory classes that we covered in prior chapters.

Listing 13-14. *Login Manager*

```
using System;
using System.Collections.Generic;
using System.Text;
using ConstructionDemo.Interfaces;
using ConstructionDemo.Datasets;
using CGS.RemoteAccess;
using ConstructionDemo.Client.WebReferences;
using CGS.Globals;
using System.IO;
using System.Data;

namespace ConstructionDemo.Client.Winforms
{
    class FrmLoginManager
    {
        private dsUser GetUser(string cUserID, string cPassword)
        {
            cgsGlobals oGlobals = new cgsGlobals();
            ClientRemoteAccess oRemoteAccess = new ClientRemoteAccess();
            oRemoteAccess.tInterface = typeof(ConstructionDemo.Interfaces.IUser<>);
```

```
            oRemoteAccess.cServiceName = "User";

            if (oRemoteAccess.UsingWebServices() == true)
                oRemoteAccess.wService = new wUserRef();

            object oReturnObject = oRemoteAccess.GetAccessObject();
            dsUser odsUser = new dsUser();

            if (oRemoteAccess.UsingWebServices() == true)
            {
                IUser<string> oUser;
                oUser = (IUser<string>)oReturnObject;
                string cXMLResults =
                  oUser.GetUser(cUserID, cPassword, oGlobals.nDataBaseKey);
                odsUser.ReadXml(new StringReader(cXMLResults),
                            XmlReadMode.InferSchema);
            }
            else
            {
                IUser<dsUser> oUser;
                oUser = (IUser<dsUser>)oReturnObject;
                odsUser = oUser.GetUser(cUserID, cPassword, oGlobals.nDataBaseKey);
            }

            return odsUser;
        }

        public string ValidateUserID(string cUserID, string cPassword)
        {
            string cMessage = "";
            dsUser odsUser = this.GetUser(cUserID, cPassword);

            if (odsUser.dtUser.Count == 0)
                cMessage = "User not found";
            else
                cMessage = odsUser.dtUser[0].Message;

            return cMessage;
        }
    }
}
```

Creating a Report Options Screen

Your next step is to build a screen for users to run a report. Since we've focused on the aging receivables report, you'll build the options screen for the user to run the aging receivables report. Figures 13-22 and 13-23 show the end result: an options screen that prompts for the report parameters (aging date, details option, and list of clients), and the report preview screen when the user runs the report. Some of the options are ones that you'll want to use across other areas, so you'll build some reusable tools for selecting items from a list and entering a footnote. This section will walk through the steps to create these visual components.

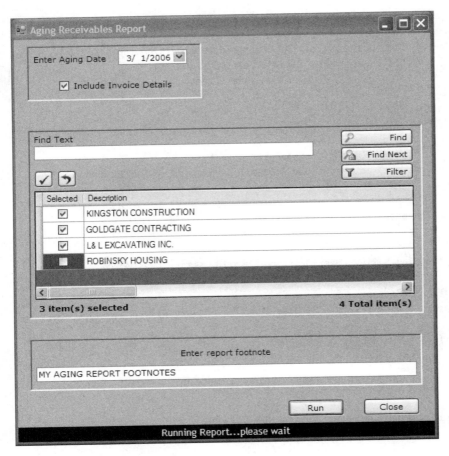

Figure 13-22. *End result of an options screen*

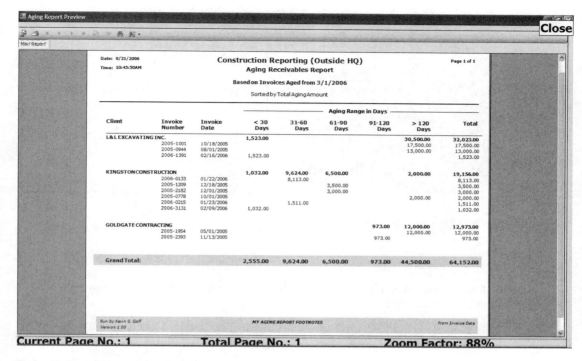

Figure 13-23. *Preview of the aging receivables report*

Creating a Reusable Record Selection Screen

Figure 13-22 contains a component that displays the list of available clients and allows the user to select the desired clients for the report. The component also allows the end user to search for a specific entry and filter the list based on the same entry—capabilities that will be valuable for long lists of clients.

You could certainly build specific functionality for this situation (selecting clients); however, in other areas of the application, you will want to utilize this same functionality to select workers, construction jobs, invoices, etc. So instead you can build a reusable record selection screen that handles different types of lists and provides the functionality described previously.

Up to this point, you've built two types of controls: single Windows Forms controls, and Windows Forms classes. But in this situation, you want to build a set or collection of controls into one composite control, and drop that composite control on a form. In .NET, this is called a UserControl—though some developers refer to this as a **container** (since it contains multiple controls).

So you'll create a generic record-selection UserControl called ctrRecordSelect in the CGS.Winforms.Containers namespace (see Figure 13-24).

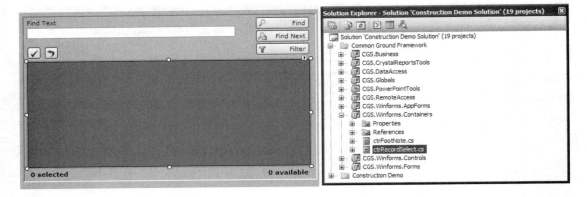

Figure 13-24. *A reusable selection screen*

To create this, do the following:

1. Create a new class library project in the Common Ground Framework solution called CGS.Winforms.Containers.

2. In the project, add .NET references to CGS.Winforms.Controls.DLL, as well as the .NET system libraries System.Windows.Forms.DLL and System.Drawing.DLL.

3. In the new project, add a new item, as an inherited user control, and call it ctrRecordSelect. You want to inherit from your base container class (cgsContainer, in your CGS.Winforms.Controls library back in Listing 13-4). Note that in the inheritance picker screen that we covered back in Figure 13-7, you may need to browse to navigate to the DLL.

4. In the new UserControl, drop instances of TextBox, Label, Grid, and Button controls as show in Figure 13-24. Make sure to drop instances of these controls from your Common Ground Framework Winforms controls tab in the Windows Forms Toolbox. Name the controls as follows:

   - *For the single textbox,* txtSearch: This will be the text for the user to perform a find, find next, or filter operation.

   - *For the three command buttons in the upper right,* btnFind, btnFindNext, *and* btnFilter: These work with the text search to perform finds and filters on the list.

   - *For the grid,* grdSelect: This will contain the list of items that you want to display.

   - *For the two command buttons above the grid and on the left-hand side,* chkSelectAll *and* chkUnselectAll: These two buttons provide a fast means to check/uncheck all items in the list for selection.

   - *For the two labels at the bottom,* lblSelected *and* lblTotalItems: These display the counts of selected and available items.

5. In the code-behind for the UserControl, add the code in Listing 13-15. The main aspects of the code are as follows:

- Public properties for the grid's DataSource (dtSource), the DataSource column name that stores the selection flag (SelectColumn), the DataSource column name that contains the description for each row to display in the grid (DescriptionColumn), and the DataSource column name that stores the unique PK identifier for each row (PKColumn). Since you'll want to use this container class for many different types of data, you need to set these properties for the method code in the container.

- A public property (PKList) that contains a comma-separated list of all PK values that the user has selected in the grid. You can ultimately read this property and pass it as a parameter that the stored procedures will use to query against those specific values. The code always keeps PKList in synch with the checked selections in the grid every time the user selects/unselects an entry.

- Code in the Enter event to set the DataSource of the grid, and to establish the columns in the grid for the selection check box and the description.

- The method MarkAll(), called from the check/uncheck command buttons, to set the selected column for each row to either true or false.

- The method SetCount(), which shows the total number of items in the list, and the number of items selected. The method performs a DataTable Select() method to determine the number of checked items.

- The method TextSearch(), which reads the text search and loops through the DataSource (either from the top or the current row using the BindingManager position), depending on whether the user is doing a find or a find next.

- The method FilterList(), which uses the RowFilter property of the DataSource to filter the list, based on the search text.

Listing 13-15. *Code for ctrRecordSelect.CS*

```
using System;
using System.Collections.Generic;
using System.ComponentModel;
using System.Data;
using System.Drawing;
using System.Text;
using System.Windows.Forms;

namespace CGS.Winforms.Containers
{
    public partial class ctrRecordSelect : CGS.Winforms.Controls.cgsContainer
    {
        private bool lFilterOn = false;
```

```csharp
private DataTable _dtSource;
public DataTable dtSource
{
    get { return _dtSource; }
    set { _dtSource = value; }
}

private string _SelectColumn ;
public string SelectColumn
{
    get { return _SelectColumn; }
    set { _SelectColumn = value; }
}

private string _DescriptionColumn ;
public string DescriptionColumn
{
    get { return _DescriptionColumn; }
    set { _DescriptionColumn = value; }
}

private string _PKColumn;
public string PKColumn
{
    get { return _PKColumn; }
    set { _PKColumn = value; }
}

private string _PKList;
public string PKList
{
    get { return _PKList; }
    set { _PKList = value; }
}

public ctrRecordSelect()
{
    InitializeComponent();
}

private void ctrRecordSelect_Load(object sender, EventArgs e)
{
}
```

```
private void CheckFilterChanged(object sender, DataColumnChangeEventArgs e)
{
    this.SetCount();
}


private void ctrRecordSelect_Enter(object sender, EventArgs e)
{
    this.dtSource.DefaultView.AllowNew = false;

    this.grdSelect.DataSource = this.dtSource.DefaultView;
    this.grdSelect.CellContentClick += new
        DataGridViewCellEventHandler(grdSelect_CellContentClick);

    foreach (DataColumn dc in this.dtSource.Columns)
    {
        try
        {
            this.grdSelect.Columns.Remove(dc.ColumnName.ToString());
        }
        catch (Exception)
        {
        }
    }

    DataGridViewCheckBoxColumn fld1 = new DataGridViewCheckBoxColumn();
    fld1.DataPropertyName =  this.SelectColumn;
    fld1.HeaderText = "Selected";
    fld1.Width = 55;
    fld1.ReadOnly = false;
    this.grdSelect.Columns.Insert(0, fld1);

    DataGridViewTextBoxColumn fld2 = new DataGridViewTextBoxColumn();
    fld2.DataPropertyName = this.DescriptionColumn;
    fld2.HeaderText = "Description";
    fld2.Width = this.grdSelect.Width - fld1.Width - 11;
    fld2.ReadOnly = true;
    this.grdSelect.Columns.Insert(1, fld2);

    this.SetCount();
}
```

```
void grdSelect_CellContentClick(object sender, DataGridViewCellEventArgs e)
{
    this.grdSelect.CommitEdit(DataGridViewDataErrorContexts.Commit);
    this.SetCount();
}

private void MarkAll(bool lMark)
{
    foreach (DataRow dr in this.dtSource.Rows)
        dr[this.SelectColumn] = lMark;
    this.SetCount();
}

private void chkSelectAll_Click(object sender, EventArgs e)
{
    this.MarkAll(true);
}

private void chkUnselectAll_Click(object sender, EventArgs e)
{
    this.MarkAll(false);
}

private void SetCount()
{
    this.lblTotalItems.Text =
            this.dtSource.DefaultView.Count.ToString().Trim() +
                    " Total item(s)";

    string cFilter = this.SelectColumn + " = true ";

    DataRow[] drSelections =
        this.dtSource.DefaultView.ToTable().Select(cFilter);

    int nCount = drSelections.Length;
    this.lblSelected.Text = nCount.ToString().Trim() + " item(s) selected";

    this.PKList = String.Empty;
    foreach (DataRow dr in drSelections)
        this.PKList += dr[this.PKColumn].ToString().Trim() + ",";

    if (this.PKList != String.Empty)
        this.PKList = this.PKList.Substring(0, this.PKList.Length - 1);
```

```csharp
}


private void btnFilter_Click(object sender, EventArgs e)
{
    this.FilterList();
}


private void TextSearch(bool lStartAtTop)
{
    BindingManagerBase bMgr =
            this.grdSelect.BindingContext
                    [this.grdSelect.DataSource,this.grdSelect.DataMember];

    // Will scan through rows for a hit
    int nStartRow;
    bool lFound = false;

    int nRowCount = bMgr.Count;

    string cSearchText = this.txtSearch.Text.ToString().Trim();
    if (cSearchText.Length > 0)
    {
        int nPos = bMgr.Position;
        if (lStartAtTop == true)
            nStartRow = 0;
        else
            nStartRow = bMgr.Position + 1;

        int nRowCtr;
        for (nRowCtr = nStartRow; nRowCtr < nRowCount; nRowCtr++)
        {
            if (this.dtSource.DefaultView
                            [nRowCtr][this.DescriptionColumn].
                                ToString().IndexOf(cSearchText) > 0)
            {
                bMgr.Position = nRowCtr;
                lFound = true;
                break;
            }
        }

        if (lFound == false)
            MessageBox.Show("End of the result list reached!");
    }
}
```

```
private void FilterList()
{
    if (this.lFilterOn == false)
    {
        this.btnFilter.Text = "Filter Off";
        string cFilter =
                this.DescriptionColumn + " Like '%" +
                        this.txtSearch.Text.ToString().Trim() + "%'";
        this.dtSource.DefaultView.RowFilter = cFilter;
    }
    else
    {
        this.btnFilter.Text = "Filter On";
        this.dtSource.DefaultView.RowFilter = "";
    }

    this.lFilterOn = !this.lFilterOn;
    this.SetCount();
}

private void btnFind_Click(object sender, EventArgs e)
{
    this.TextSearch(true);
}

private void btnFindNext_Click(object sender, EventArgs e)
{
    this.TextSearch(false);
}

private void cgsPanel1_Paint(object sender, PaintEventArgs e)
{
}
    }
}
```

■Note The record selection screen `ctrRecordSelect` is a reusable container that we can utilize anytime we need to allow the user to make multiple selections. We can drop an instance of `ctrRecordSelect` on a form, and set the properties `dtSource`, `DescriptionColumn`, `SelectColumn`, and `PKColumn` for the DataSource containing the selections to display, the string column representing the selection descriptions, the boolean column for whether the user has selected a row, and an integer column for each row's primary key value. Listing 13-16 will show an example of utilizing `ctrRecordSelect`.

Creating a Reusable Footnote Entry Screen

Figure 13-25 shows your second UserControl, ctrFootNote: a small but useful control to prompt users for a report footnote. You can create this control in the same manner you created the previous UserControl (ctrRecordSelect). Call the text box txtFootNote and make sure it is public.

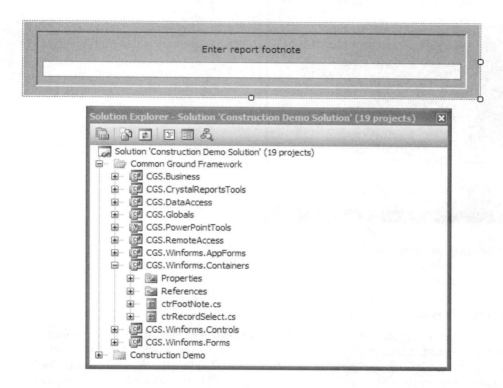

Figure 13-25. *A reusable footnote screen*

Building Your Report Options Screen

Figure 13-26 shows the end result: an aging report form options screen (FrmAgingReport) in the main windows application. You'll drop instances of your two UserControls onto the form, and then add the miscellaneous options.

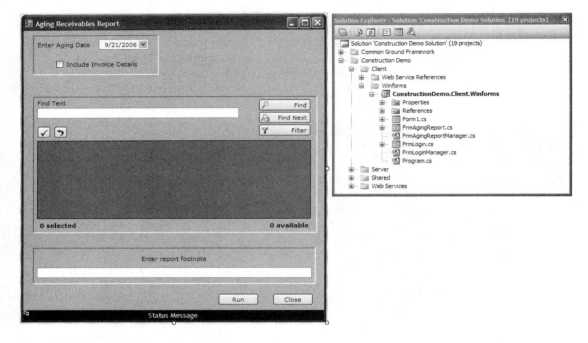

Figure 13-26. *Your aging report options form*

Adding Your User Controls

To create instances of your UserControls (so that you can select clients and enter a footnote), you'll add your base UserControls to the Windows Forms Toolbox. You'll do it the same way you did it for your base Winforms controls, by loading the Windows Forms Toolbox, adding a new tab (which you'll call Common Ground Framework Winform Containers), and then choosing new items. Then you can navigate to the BIN\DEBUG folder that contains CGS.Winforms.Containers.DLL. At the end, you'll see the two UserControls in the Toolbox, as shown in Figure 13-27.

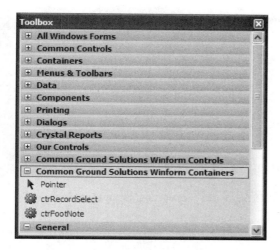

Figure 13-27. *Your new tab in the Toolbox for your containers/UserControls*

You can drag the two UserControls onto your form and call them ctrAgingReportSelect and ctrAgingFootNote.

Adding Additional Options

After you add the two UserControls, you add a DateTime control and a CheckBox control (again, from your library of controls) for the aging date and the check box for including detail invoices. Call them dAgingDate and chkDetails, respectively.

The Code for the Form and the Form Manager

Listings 13-16 and 13-17 show the code for the FrmAgingReport form, as well as the corresponding form manager, FrmAgingReportManager.cs.

Note the following in Listing 13-16:

- We are going to have you do a little bit of cheating for purposes of demonstration—you are hand-coding the list of clients and setting the dtSource property of ctrRecordSelect to that hand-coded list. Normally you would want to retrieve the data from your client's database through a stored procedure and through the mechanisms we've already described in this book.

- The code sets the other properties for ctrRecordSelect so that the container can work with the specific columns of the source table.

- The click event of the run button creates an instance of the report's form manager (shown in Listing 13-17). The form manager contains properties for the list of clients, aging date, and details options, which correspond to the options you send to the back end to return the result set.

Listing 13-16. *Code-Behind for Form FrmAgingReport*

```
using System;
using System.Collections.Generic;
using System.ComponentModel;
using System.Data;
using System.Drawing;
using System.Text;
using System.Windows.Forms;

namespace ConstructionDemo.Client.Winforms
{
    public partial class FrmAgingReport : CGS.Winforms.Forms.cgsFrmApplication
    {
        public FrmAgingReport()
        {
            InitializeComponent();
        }

        private void FrmAgingReport_Load(object sender, EventArgs e)
        {
            DataTable dtClients = new DataTable();

            dtClients.Columns.Add("Selected", typeof(System.Boolean));
            dtClients.Columns.Add("ClientPK", typeof(System.Int32));
            dtClients.Columns.Add("ClientName", typeof(System.String));

            dtClients.Rows.Add(false, 1, "KINGSTON CONSTRUCTION");
            dtClients.Rows.Add(false, 2, "GOLDGATE CONTRACTING");
            dtClients.Rows.Add(false, 3, "L&L EXCAVATING INC.");
            dtClients.Rows.Add(false, 4, "ROBINSKY HOUSING");

            this.ctrAgingReportSelect.dtSource = dtClients;
            this.ctrAgingReportSelect.DescriptionColumn = "ClientName";
            this.ctrAgingReportSelect.SelectColumn = "Selected";
            this.ctrAgingReportSelect.PKColumn = "ClientPK";
        }

        private void ctrRecordSelect1_Load(object sender, EventArgs e)
        {
        }

        private void cgsButton2_Click(object sender, EventArgs e)
        {
        }
```

```csharp
        private void btnRun_Click(object sender, EventArgs e)
        {
            this.SetMessageOn("Running Report...please wait");

            FrmAgingReportManager oAgingClass = new FrmAgingReportManager();

            oAgingClass.cClientList = this.ctrAgingRecordSelect.PKList;
            oAgingClass.cFootNote =
                this.ctrAgingFootNote.txtFootNote.Text.ToString().Trim();
            oAgingClass.dAgingDate =  this.dAgingDate.Value;
            oAgingClass.lDetails = this.chkDetails.Checked;

            oAgingClass.RunAgingReport();

            this.SetMessageOff();
        }
    }
}
```

The code in the aging report form manager (see Listing 13-17) is similar to the code for the login form manager earlier in this chapter. You take your parameters from the aging report form itself and call out to the necessary back-end functions. This ties together code that you've built in previous chapters for retrieving the result set and generating the report.

Listing 13-17. *FrmAgingReportManager.cs*

```csharp
using System;
using System.Collections.Generic;
using System.Text;
using ConstructionDemo.Interfaces;
using ConstructionDemo.Datasets;
using CGS.RemoteAccess;
using ConstructionDemo.Client.WebReferences;
using CGS.Globals;
using System.IO;
using System.Data;
using ConstructionDemo.CrystalReports;
using CGS.CrystalReportsTools;

namespace ConstructionDemo.Client.Winforms
{
    class FrmAgingReportManager
    {
        private string _cClientList ;
        public string cClientList
```

```csharp
{
    get { return _cClientList; }
    set { _cClientList = value; }
}

private DateTime _dAgingDate ;
public DateTime dAgingDate
{
    get { return _dAgingDate; }
    set { _dAgingDate = value; }
}

private bool _lDetails ;
public bool lDetails
{
    get { return _lDetails; }
    set { _lDetails = value; }
}

private string _cFootNote ;
public string cFootNote
{
    get { return _cFootNote; }
    set { _cFootNote = value; }
}

public void RunAgingReport()
{
    dsAgingReport odsAgingReport = this.GetAgingReportResultSet();
    this.PreviewReport(odsAgingReport);
}

private void PreviewReport(dsAgingReport odsAgingReport)
{
    cgsGlobals oGlobals = new cgsGlobals();
    RPT_AgingReport oRPTAgingReport = new RPT_AgingReport();

    // Create an instance of the Crystal Manager
    ccCrystalManager oCrystal = new ccCrystalManager();

    // Create an instance of the header/footer object
    ccReportInfo oReportInfo = new ccReportInfo();
    oReportInfo.FtrDataSource = "From Invoice Data";
    oReportInfo.FtrFootNotes = this.cFootNote;
    oReportInfo.FtrRunBy = "Run by " + oGlobals.cUserName;
```

```
    oReportInfo.FtrVersion = "Version 1.00";
    oReportInfo.HdrCompany = oGlobals.cCurrentConnection;
    oReportInfo.HdrReportTitle = "Aging Receivables Report";
    oReportInfo.HdrSubTitle1 = "Based on Invoices Aged from " +
                dAgingDate.ToShortDateString();
    oReportInfo.HdrSubTitle2 = "Sorted by Total Aging Amount";
    oReportInfo.UserID = oGlobals.cUserID;

    oCrystal.SetReportInfo(oRPTAgingReport, oReportInfo);

    oCrystal.PushReportData(odsAgingReport, oRPTAgingReport);

    // Set the report ShowDetails Parameter
    oRPTAgingReport.SetParameterValue("ShowDetails", lDetails);

    // Show the different capabilities for output...first, do a preview
    oCrystal.PreviewReport(oRPTAgingReport, "Aging Report Preview");
}

private dsAgingReport GetAgingReportResultSet()
{
    cgsGlobals oGlobals = new cgsGlobals();
    ClientRemoteAccess oRemoteAccess = new ClientRemoteAccess();
    oRemoteAccess.tInterface =
                typeof(ConstructionDemo.Interfaces.IAgingReport<>);
    oRemoteAccess.cServiceName = "AgingReport";

    if (oRemoteAccess.UsingWebServices() == true)
        oRemoteAccess.wService = new wAgingReportRef();

    object oReturnObject = oRemoteAccess.GetAccessObject();
    dsAgingReport odsAgingReport = new dsAgingReport();

    if (oRemoteAccess.UsingWebServices() == true)
    {
        IAgingReport<string> oAgingReport;
        oAgingReport = (IAgingReport<string>)oReturnObject;
        string cXMLResults = oAgingReport.GetAgingReport
                (this.dAgingDate, this.lDetails, this.cClientList,
                    oGlobals.nDataBaseKey);
        odsAgingReport.ReadXml(new StringReader(cXMLResults),
                    XmlReadMode.InferSchema);
    }
    else
    {
```

```
                IAgingReport<dsAgingReport> oAgingReport;
                oAgingReport = (IAgingReport<dsAgingReport>)oReturnObject;
                odsAgingReport = oAgingReport.GetAgingReport
                        (this.dAgingDate, this.lDetails, this.cClientList,
                              oGlobals.nDataBaseKey);
            }

            return odsAgingReport;
        }
    }
}
```

Viewing Previously Saved PDF Files

Finally, if you want to view previously saved PDF files (to view what reports looked like at the time you generated them), you can create a Windows Form with an instance of the Adobe Acrobat ActiveX control, and then use the control to load a specific PDF.

To do so, first you need to add an instance of the Adobe Reader to your Toolbox. When you choose the Toolbox items this time (as in Figure 13-28), you will search in the COM Components tab, and select the Adobe Acrobat Reader.

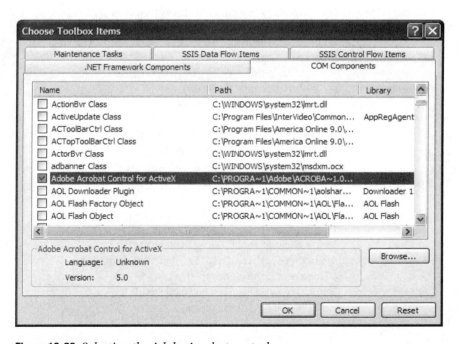

Figure 13-28. *Selecting the Adobe Acrobat control*

This will add the Adobe Acrobat control to the Toolbox, in whichever tab you specified (see Figure 13-29).

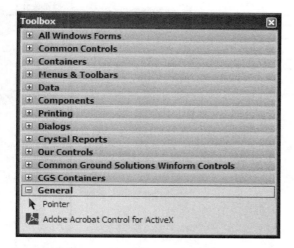

Figure 13-29. *The Adobe Reader control in the Windows Forms Toolbox*

This allows you to drag an instance of the control onto a form and utilize the following code (this assumes the default name of the control is axPdf1):

```
this.axPdf1.LoadFile("c:\\MyAgingReport.PDF");
this.axPdf1.Anchor = AnchorStyles.Left & AnchorStyles.Right &
                                AnchorStyles.Bottom & AnchorStyles.Top;

;
```

That will allow you to view PDF inside a Windows Form (see Figure 13-30).

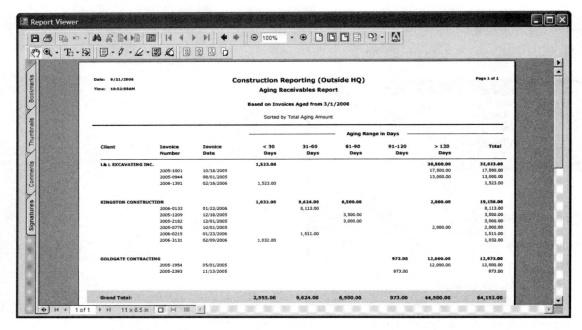

Figure 13-30. *Viewing a previously generated PDF*

Summary

In this chapter, we covered the basics of Winforms and Winforms controls and also established how to integrate your client piece with your back-end functionality. You built a reusable authentication component that you can use for this and other applications, and you also built some reusable components for making report selections. In the next and final chapter, you'll learn to extend the end-user experience by generating Microsoft PowerPoint slideshow output from your application.

■ ■ ■

CHAPTER 14

Building Report Output Using Microsoft PowerPoint

We'll end this text with some eye candy: generating PowerPoint output. Many power users build PowerPoint presentations using data from Excel or other data sources. PowerPoint output should not be confused with general business reporting; each slide should be a synthesized and self-contained unit, and must not reference information on other slides. But presentation slides still serve a valuable purpose in conveying information in a highly summarized and graphical manner.

This chapter shows how to automate Microsoft PowerPoint 2003 from within a Visual Studio 2005 application. The chapter presents a class called `PowerPointTools`, which creates several different types of slides, including slides that integrate tables and charts.

`PowerPointTools` is written in Visual Basic 2005, thus demonstrating the usage of multiple .NET languages in a solution. In this chapter, we'll show how the `PowerPointTools` library helps to automate the following tasks:

- Loading an instance of PowerPoint, and starting a new presentation with a template and title page

- Generating a table of contents (TOC) page with multiple levels of bullet points

- Building and displaying an Excel table with data

- Generating common charts (pie chart, bar chart, line chart), and even displaying a chart and a table on the same slide

- Setting animations and slide transitions

- Defining slide footer information

- Saving the presentation

Introducing PowerPointTools

`PowerPointTools` heavily utilizes the PowerPoint and Excel Object Libraries. However, any external class that utilizes `PowerPointTools` does not need to reference the PowerPoint and

Excel libraries. As such, `PowerPointTools` demonstrates an example of the Façade design pattern. A **Façade design pattern** is a class that provides a simple interface to a larger and more complex class. Some of the characteristics of a Façade pattern are as follows:

- Simplifies access to the larger body of classes (in this case, the PowerPoint and Excel libraries). In a nutshell, the Façade class provides developer-friendly access to the classes you ultimately want to use.

- Potentially makes the interface to the larger body of classes more readable.

- The larger body of classes may contain a larger number of functions that are not necessary for you. The Façade class exposes only those functions you need through an interface that you design.

Creating PowerPointTools: Begin with the End in Mind, Times Two!

Throughout this book, we've often taken the approach of first looking at the end result in some form and then working backwards. This chapter will do the same, times two. Building an Office Automation can be a tricky and difficult task, so we'll start by unveiling the entire project, and then spend the rest of the chapter going over the individual pieces.

An Overview of PowerPointTools

`PowerPointTools` is a DLL, written in Visual Basic 2005. It contains a .NET reference to `System.Drawing.DLL`. It also contains COM references to the Microsoft Excel 11.0 and Microsoft PowerPoint 11.0 Object Libraries, as well as COM references to Microsoft Core Office Library and Visual Basic for Application Extensibility. Visual Studio 2005 automatically adds these references when you add the PowerPoint and Excel Object Libraries.

You may be wondering, "Everything else in this book was C# code . . . why VB all of a sudden?" There are two reasons: one practical, one philosophical, either one conclusive.

First, as Office Automation is historically rooted in VBA (Visual Basic for Applications), VB is better suited for Office Automation and often requires less code as compared to C#. This is more notable when dealing with optional parameters for Office functions, and also comes into play with parameterized properties and late binding. The second reason is more demonstrative: to show that you can use VB 2005 to build a reusable project class and then call it from a C# application.

Figure 14-1 shows the project `CGS.PowerPointTools` as part of the `Common Ground Framework` project folder. The project is a VB 2005 project, built as a class library project. The project has two source code class files, `PowerPointTools.VB` and `PPTBulletList.VB`: we'll cover them shortly.

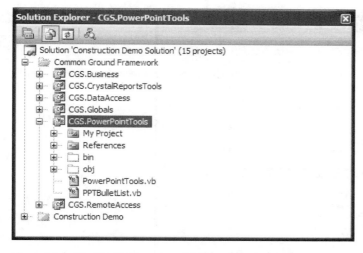

Figure 14-1. *The VB 2005 project CGS.PowerPointTools*

Adding COM References to the PowerPoint and Excel Object Models

Your first order of business in the CGS.PowerPointTools project is to add the COM references we mentioned earlier: the Microsoft Excel 11.0 and Microsoft PowerPoint 11.0 Object Libraries. To do so, navigate to the References folder in Figure 14-1, right-click, and choose Add Reference. From the Add Reference window, click the COM tab and scroll down to the Microsoft Excel and Microsoft PowerPoint Object Libraries to select them (see Figures 14-2 and 14-3).

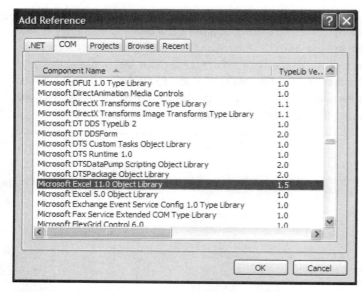

Figure 14-2. *Adding the Microsoft Excel 11.0 Object Library*

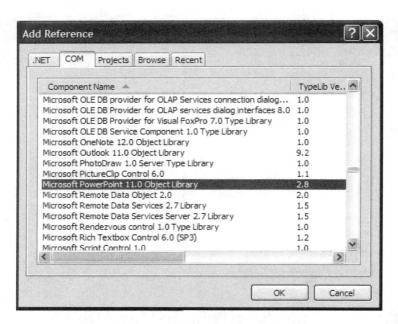

Figure 14-3. *Adding the Microsoft PowerPoint 11.0 Object Library*

After adding the two COM references, add a .NET reference to System.Drawing.DLL. After you do so, the project in Solution Explorer should look like Figure 14-4. Note that even though you only added two COM references, Visual Studio 2005 automatically retrieved references for three other COM objects.

■**Note** Depending on which version(s) of Microsoft Office (production and/or beta) you have installed, you may receive compilation errors when trying to build CGS.PowerPointTools. If this occurs, check the properties for the COM references to Microsoft.Office.Core and Office to ensure that both have the Copy Local property set to FALSE. If either is set to TRUE, set it to FALSE. If you still receive compilation errors on the project, you may need to delete the references to Microsoft.Office.Core and Office, and manually set a COM reference to the Office.DLL file in the Global Assembly Cache.

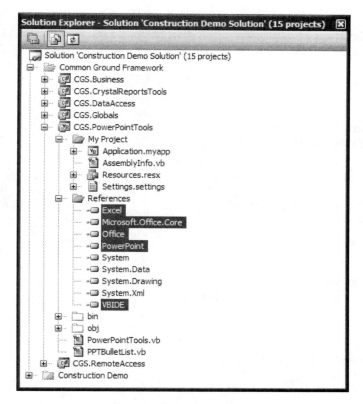

Figure 14-4. *The PowerPointTools project with the COM references*

The Source Code for PowerPointTools

Listing 14-1 contains the complete listing for the main class, PowerPointTools.VB. Throughout this chapter, we will cover the different functions in the class.

Listing 14-1. *Complete Listing for PowerPointTools.VB*

```vb
Imports PowerPoint = Microsoft.Office.Interop.PowerPoint
Imports Excel = Microsoft.Office.Interop.Excel
Imports System.Drawing
Imports System.Collections.Generic


Public Class PowerPointTools

    Private _SlideNumber As Integer
    Public Property SlideNumber() As Integer
        Get
            Return _SlideNumber
```

```vb
        End Get
        Set(ByVal value As Integer)
            _SlideNumber = value
        End Set
    End Property


    Private _oPPTApp As PowerPoint.Application
    Public Property oPPTApp() As PowerPoint.Application
        Get
            Return _oPPTApp
        End Get
        Set(ByVal value As PowerPoint.Application)
            _oPPTApp = value
        End Set
    End Property

    Private _oPPTPres As PowerPoint.Presentation
    Public Property oPPTPres() As PowerPoint.Presentation
        Get
            Return _oPPTPres
        End Get
        Set(ByVal value As PowerPoint.Presentation)
            _oPPTPres = value
        End Set
    End Property

    Private _oExcel As Excel.Application
    Public Property oExcel() As Excel.Application
        Get
            Return _oExcel
        End Get
        Set(ByVal value As Excel.Application)
            _oExcel = value
        End Set
    End Property


    Private _oSheet As Excel.Worksheet
    Public Property oSheet() As Excel.Worksheet
        Get
            Return _oSheet
        End Get
        Set(ByVal value As Excel.Worksheet)
            _oSheet = value
        End Set
    End Property
```

```
Public Sub LaunchPPT()
    ' Creates instances of PPT and Excel

    Me.oPPTApp = New PowerPoint.Application
    Me.oPPTApp.Visible = True

    Me.oExcel = New Excel.Application
    Me.oExcel.Visible = False

    Me.SlideNumber = 0

End Sub

Public Sub AddPicture(ByVal PicFile As String)
    Dim oBitmap As Bitmap
    oBitmap = New Bitmap(PicFile)
    Dim PicWidth As Int32
    Dim PicHeight As Int32

    PicWidth = oBitmap.Width
    PicHeight = oBitmap.Height

    Dim StartTop As Int32 = (540 - PicHeight) / 2
    Dim StartWidth As Int32 = (720 - PicWidth) / 2

    Me.oPPTApp.ActiveWindow.Selection.SlideRange.Shapes.AddPicture _
                    (PicFile, False, True, StartWidth, StartTop)

End Sub

Public Sub DisplayPPT()

    Me.oPPTApp.Visible = True
    Me.oPPTApp.WindowState = _
        PowerPoint.PpWindowState.ppWindowMaximized

    Me.oExcel = Nothing

End Sub



Public Sub SetTemplate(ByVal TemplateFilename As String)

    Me.oPPTPres = Me.oPPTApp.Presentations.Add

    Me.oPPTPres.ApplyTemplate(TemplateFilename)
```

```vbnet
        Me.AddSlide(PowerPoint.PpSlideLayout.ppLayoutTitle)

End Sub



Public Sub AddSlide(ByVal oLayout As PowerPoint.PpSlideLayout)
    ' Increment the active slide number,
    ' add a new slide based on that number/layout,
    ' and go to the slide.

    Me.SlideNumber = Me.SlideNumber + 1
    Me.oPPTApp.ActivePresentation.Slides.Add(Me.SlideNumber, oLayout)
    Me.oPPTApp.ActiveWindow.View.GotoSlide(Me.SlideNumber)

End Sub



Public Sub BuildTitlePage(ByVal MainTitle As String, _
                          ByVal SubTitleTemplate As String)

    Me.AddText("Rectangle 2", MainTitle)
    Me.AddText("Rectangle 3", SubTitleTemplate)

End Sub

Public Sub AddText(ByVal ShapeName As String, ByVal PPTText As String)

    Me.oPPTApp.ActiveWindow.Selection.SlideRange.Shapes(1).Select()
    Me.oPPTApp.ActiveWindow.Selection.TextRange.Text = PPTText

End Sub



Public Sub BuildBulletPage(ByVal MainTitle As String, _
                    ByVal BulletList As List(Of PPTBulletList))

    Me.AddSlide(PowerPoint.PpSlideLayout.ppLayoutText)

    Me.AddText("Rectangle 2", MainTitle)
    ' Note the indentlevel property, from IndentLevel in the DataTable source.

    Me.SelectMainRectangle()

    Dim TextCounter As Int32 = 0
```

```vb
        For Each oBulletItem As PPTBulletList In BulletList
            oPPTApp.ActiveWindow.Selection.TextRange.InsertAfter( _
                            oBulletItem.BulletItem + Chr(13))
            TextCounter = TextCounter + 1
            oPPTApp.ActiveWindow.Selection.TextRange.Paragraphs( _
                    TextCounter, 1).IndentLevel = oBulletItem.BulletItemIndent
        Next

End Sub

Public Sub BuildLineChartPage(ByVal MainTitle As String, _
            ByVal DtLineChartData As DataTable, ByVal xAxisTitle As String, _
            ByVal yAxisTitle As String)

    Me.AddSlide(PowerPoint.PpSlideLayout.ppLayoutChart)
    Me.AddText("Rectangle 2", MainTitle)
    Me.BuildExcelLineChart(DtLineChartData, xAxisTitle, yAxisTitle)
    Me.SelectMainRectangle()
    Me.oPPTApp.ActiveWindow.View.Paste()


End Sub

Public Sub BuildTablePieChartPage(ByVal MainTitle As String, _
            ByVal DtTableEntries As DataTable, ByVal DtHeadings As DataTable, _
            ByVal ChartTitle As String, ByVal DtPieChartData As DataTable)

    ' Add the slide, based on the Text/PieChart layout.
    Me.AddSlide(PowerPoint.PpSlideLayout.ppLayoutTextAndChart)
    Me.AddText("Rectangle 2", MainTitle)

    ' Build the table, paste it into the slide.
    Me.SelectMainRectangle()
    Me.BuildExcelTable(DtTableEntries, DtHeadings)
    Me.oPPTApp.ActiveWindow.View.Paste()

    ' Build the table for the pie chart, generate the chart, and paste the chart
    Me.BuildExcelPieChart(DtPieChartData, ChartTitle)

    Me.oPPTApp.ActiveWindow.Selection.SlideRange.Shapes(3).Select()
    Me.oPPTApp.ActiveWindow.View.Paste()

End Sub

Public Sub SavePresentation(ByVal PPTName As String)

    Me.oPPTApp.ActivePresentation.SaveAs(PPTName)
```

```vbnet
End Sub

Public Sub SetSlideTransitions()

    ' Basic demonstration of looping through the slideshow collection.
    ' Use this as a guide to change settings at the slide level.

    For Each oSlide As PowerPoint.Slide In Me.oPPTApp.ActivePresentation.Slides
        oSlide.SlideShowTransition.EntryEffect = _
                PowerPoint.PpEntryEffect.ppEffectBlindsVertical
    Next

End Sub


Public Sub BuildFooter(ByVal FooterText As String)
    ' Possible enhancement could be making the slide number and date optional

    With Me.oPPTApp.ActivePresentation.SlideMaster.HeadersFooters
        .DateAndTime.Visible = True
        .DateAndTime.Format = _
                PowerPoint.PpDateTimeFormat.ppDateTimeMMddyyhhmmAMPM
        .DateAndTime.Text = ""
        .DateAndTime.UseFormat = True

        .Footer.Text = FooterText
        .SlideNumber.Visible = True
        .DisplayOnTitleSlide = False
    End With

End Sub

Public Sub BuildExcelPieChart(ByRef DtTableEntries As DataTable, _
                ByRef ChartTitle As String)

    Dim TableCellRange As String
    TableCellRange = Me.BuildExcelTable(DtTableEntries)

    Me.oExcel.Charts.Add()

    Me.oExcel.ActiveChart.ApplyCustomType(Excel.XlChartType.xl3DPieExploded)

    'Me.oExcel.ActiveChart.ChartType = Excel.XlChartType.xl3DPie
    Me.oExcel.ActiveChart.SetSourceData(Me.oSheet.Range(TableCellRange), _
                Excel.XlRowCol.xlColumns)

    Me.oExcel.ActiveChart.Location(Excel.XlChartLocation.xlLocationAsObject, _
                "Sheet1")
```

```
    Me.oExcel.ActiveChart.HasTitle = True
    Me.oExcel.ActiveChart.ChartTitle.Characters.Text = ChartTitle
    Me.oExcel.ActiveChart.HasLegend = False

    Me.oExcel.ActiveChart.SeriesCollection(1).HasDataLabels = True
    oExcel.ActiveChart.ApplyDataLabels _
            (Excel.XlDataLabelsType.xlDataLabelsShowLabelAndPercent)

    Me.oExcel.ActiveChart.PlotArea.Select()
    Me.oExcel.Selection.Interior.ColorIndex = 0
    Me.oExcel.Selection.Border.LineStyle = 0


    Me.oExcel.ActiveChart.ChartArea.Select()
    Me.oExcel.Selection.Interior.ColorIndex = 0
    Me.oExcel.Selection.Border.LineStyle = 0
    Me.oExcel.ActiveChart.ChartArea.Select()
    Me.oExcel.ActiveChart.ChartArea.Copy()


End Sub



Public Sub BuildBarChartPage(ByVal MainTitle As String, _
            ByVal DtBarChartData As DataTable, ByVal xAxisTitle As String, _
            ByVal yAxisTitle As String, ByVal DtBarChartHeadings As DataTable)

    Me.AddSlide(PowerPoint.PpSlideLayout.ppLayoutChart)
    Me.AddText("Rectangle 2", MainTitle)
    Me.BuildExcelBarChart(DtBarChartData, xAxisTitle, DtBarChartHeadings)
    Me.SelectMainRectangle()
    Me.oPPTApp.ActiveWindow.View.Paste()

End Sub



Public Sub BuildExcelBarChart(ByRef DtTableEntries As DataTable, _
        ByRef ChartTitle As String, ByRef DtHeadings As DataTable)

    Dim TableCellRange As String
    TableCellRange = Me.BuildExcelTable(DtTableEntries, DtHeadings)

    Me.oExcel.Charts.Add()

    Me.oExcel.ActiveChart.ApplyCustomType(Excel.XlChartType.xlColumnStacked)
```

```vbnet
    Me.oExcel.ActiveChart.SetSourceData(Me.oSheet.Range(TableCellRange), _
        Excel.XlRowCol.xlColumns)

    Me.oExcel.ActiveChart.Location(Excel.XlChartLocation.xlLocationAsObject, _
        "Sheet1")
    Me.oExcel.ActiveChart.HasTitle = True
    Me.oExcel.ActiveChart.ChartTitle.Characters.Text = ChartTitle

    Me.oExcel.ActiveChart.Axes(1).Select()
    Me.oExcel.Selection.TickLabels.Alignment = Excel.Constants.xlCenter
    Me.oExcel.Selection.TickLabels.Offset = 40
    Me.oExcel.Selection.TickLabels.Orientation = Excel.XlOrientation.xlUpward

    Me.oExcel.ActiveChart.SeriesCollection(5).Select()
    Me.oExcel.Selection.ChartType = Excel.XlChartType.xlLine

    Me.oExcel.ActiveChart.ChartArea.Select()
    Me.oExcel.Selection.Interior.ColorIndex = 0
    Me.oExcel.Selection.Border.LineStyle = 0

    Me.oExcel.ActiveChart.SeriesCollection(1).Select()
    Me.oExcel.Selection.Interior.ColorIndex = 4

    Me.oExcel.ActiveChart.SeriesCollection(2).Select()
    Me.oExcel.Selection.Interior.ColorIndex = 26

    Me.oExcel.ActiveChart.SeriesCollection(3).Select()
    Me.oExcel.Selection.Interior.ColorIndex = 27

    Me.oExcel.ActiveChart.SeriesCollection(4).Select()
    Me.oExcel.Selection.Interior.ColorIndex = 42

    Me.oExcel.ActiveChart.ChartArea.Select()
    Me.oExcel.ActiveChart.ChartArea.Copy()


End Sub



Public Sub BuildExcelLineChart(ByRef DtTableEntries As DataTable, _
        ByRef xAxisTitle As String, ByRef yAxisTitle As String)


    Dim TableCellRange As String
    TableCellRange = Me.BuildExcelTable(DtTableEntries)

    Me.oExcel.Charts.Add()
```

```
Me.oExcel.ActiveChart.ChartType = Excel.XlChartType.xlLineMarkers

Me.oExcel.ActiveChart.Location(Excel.XlChartLocation.xlLocationAsObject, _
        "Sheet1")


Me.oExcel.ActiveChart.PlotArea.Select()
Me.oExcel.Selection.Interior.ColorIndex = 36   ' light yellow
Me.oExcel.Selection.Border.LineStyle = 0


Me.oExcel.ActiveChart.ChartArea.Select()
Me.oExcel.Selection.Interior.ColorIndex = 0
Me.oExcel.Selection.Border.LineStyle = 0


Me.oExcel.ActiveChart.Axes(1).Select()
Me.oExcel.Selection.TickLabels.Alignment = Excel.Constants.xlCenter
Me.oExcel.Selection.TickLabels.Offset = 40
'       Me.oExcel.Selection.ReadingOrder = Excel.Constants.xlContent
Me.oExcel.Selection.TickLabels.Orientation = Excel.XlOrientation.xlUpward


Me.oExcel.ActiveChart.ChartArea.Select()
Me.oExcel.ActiveChart.ChartArea.Copy()


End Sub



Public Sub BuildTablePage(ByVal MainTitle As String, _
        ByVal DtTableEntries As DataTable, ByVal DtHeadings As DataTable)

    ' Create a new slide for the table page.
    AddSlide(PowerPoint.PpSlideLayout.ppLayoutTable)


    ' Add the title inside the first shape.
    AddText("Rectangle 2", MainTitle)

    ' Select the body shape.
    Me.SelectMainRectangle()
    ' Generate the Excel table from the table entries/headings.
    Me.BuildExcelTable(DtTableEntries, DtHeadings)
```

```
        ' Paste the generated Excel table.
        Me.oPPTApp.ActiveWindow.View.Paste()



End Sub

Public Sub SelectMainRectangle()
    Me.oPPTApp.ActiveWindow.Selection.SlideRange.Shapes("Rectangle 3").Select()
End Sub


' Note that BuildExcelTable has an overload for either 1 or 2 parameters.

Function BuildExcelTable(ByVal DtTableEntries As DataTable) As String
    Dim EmptyTable As DataTable
    EmptyTable = New DataTable()
    Dim ReturnVal As String = BuildExcelTable(DtTableEntries, EmptyTable)
    Return ReturnVal
End Function

Function BuildExcelTable(ByVal DtTableEntries As DataTable, _
            ByVal DtHeadings As DataTable) As String

    ' Add a workbook and reference the first sheet.
    Dim oBook As Excel.Workbook = Me.oExcel.Workbooks.Add()
    Me.oSheet = oBook.Worksheets(1)

    Dim RowCounter As Int32 = 1
    Dim ColumnCounter As Int32 = 0
    Dim LastCell As String = ""
    Dim Cell As String = ""
    Dim Columnletter As String = ""
    Dim NumRows As Int32 = DtTableEntries.Rows.Count + 1

    ' Write out the column headings (if a heading table was provided).
    For Each Dr As DataRow In DtHeadings.Rows
        ' Determine cell.
        Columnletter = Chr(Asc("A") + ColumnCounter)
        'Cell = Columnletter + RowCounter.ToString().Trim()
        Cell = Columnletter + "1"

        ColumnCounter += 1
        Me.WriteExcelCell(Me.oSheet.Range(Cell), Dr(0), True)

        ' Apply the alignment to the column.
        Me.oSheet.Range(Columnletter + "1:" + _
                Columnletter + NumRows.ToString().Trim()).Select()
```

```vb
            If Convert.ToBoolean(Dr(1)) = True Then
                Me.oExcel.Selection.HorizontalAlignment = 4
            Else
                Me.oExcel.Selection.HorizontalAlignment = 2
            End If
            'Me.oExcel.Selection.HorizontalAlignment = Dr(1)
        Next


        For Each Dr As DataRow In DtTableEntries.Rows
            RowCounter += 1
            ColumnCounter = 0
            For Each Dc As DataColumn In DtTableEntries.Columns
                Cell = Chr(Asc("A") + ColumnCounter) + RowCounter.ToString().Trim()
                LastCell = Cell
                ColumnCounter += 1
                Me.WriteExcelCell(Me.oSheet.Range(Cell), Dr(Dc), False)
            Next
        Next

        Me.oSheet.Range("A1:" + LastCell).Select()
        Me.oExcel.Selection.Copy()

        Return ("A1:" + LastCell)

    End Function




    Public Sub WriteExcelCell(ByVal oRange As Excel.Range, _
            ByVal Col As Object, ByVal CellBold As Boolean)

        With oRange
            .Value = Col
            .Font.Name = "Verdana"
            .Font.Size = 12
            .Font.Bold = CellBold
        End With

    End Sub


End Class
```

CGS.PowerPointTools also contains a second class for populating bullet-point items on a PowerPoint slide. Listing 14-2 contains the source code for PPTBulletList.VB, a custom class that we will cover a little later.

Listing 14-2. *Complete Listing for PPTBulletList.VB*

```
Public Class PPTBulletList

    Public Enum IndentLevel
        NoIndent = 1
        Indent1 = 2
        Indent2 = 3
    End Enum


    Private BulletItemValue As String
    Public Property BulletItem() As String
        Get
            Return BulletItemValue
        End Get
        Set(ByVal value As String)
            BulletItemValue = value
        End Set
    End Property


    Private BulletItemIndentValue As Integer
    Public Property BulletItemIndent() As Integer
        Get
            Return BulletItemIndentValue
        End Get
        Set(ByVal value As Integer)
            BulletItemIndentValue = value
        End Set
    End Property


    Public Sub New(ByVal Bullet As String, ByVal Indent As IndentLevel)
        Me.BulletItemValue = Bullet
        Me.BulletItemIndentValue = Indent
    End Sub

End Class
```

Table 14-1 and Table 14-2 list all the public properties and methods of PowerPointTools. PowerPointTools also contains a few support methods for common tasks, and these appear in Table 14-3.

Table 14-1. *PowerPointTools Properties*

Property	Description
oPPTApp	Object reference to the PowerPoint application
oExcel	Object reference to the Excel application
SlideNumber	Current slide number
oSheet	Object reference to the current Excel worksheet

Table 14-2. *Primary PowerPointTools Public Methods*

Method	Description
LaunchPPT()	Creates an instance of PowerPoint and Excel
SetTemplate()	Defines the default template to be used
SetFooter()	Defines the footer of the PPT
BuildTitlePage()	Builds the PPT title page slide
BuildBulletPage()	Builds a slide of bullet points, using a DataTable source
BuildTablePage()	Builds a slide with a table, using a DataTable source
BuidTableChartPage()	Builds a slide with a table and chart, using DataTable sources
BuildChartPage()	Builds a slide with a chart, using a DataTable source
SavePPT()	Saves the generated PPT
DisplayPPT()	Displays the generated PPT
AddPicture()	Adds a picture to be centered on the current slide
BuildFooter()	Builds a footer
SetSlideTransitions()	Sets the transition effect for each slide in the presentation

Table 14-3. *PowerPointTools Support Methods*

Method	Description
AddSlide()	Adds a new slide using a specific slide layout
AddText()	Adds text to the slide, inside a preexisting shape in the layout
BuildExcelTable()	Creates an Excel table from a DataTable source
WriteExcelCell()	Writes out a single value to a cell
SelectMainRectangle()	Selects the Main Rectangle on a slide, for subsequent editing

The remaining figures in this chapter demonstrate the output that you can generate with this project. We'll now cover the steps to build output with PowerPointTools.

Using PowerPointTools

We'll show you how you can use `PowerPointTools` by utilizing the functionality we listed in Tables 14-1 through 14-3. We'll do that by walking you through the creation of a test form as a stand-alone Windows Forms project in C#. The purpose of the test form will be to launch the `PowerPointTools` library and generate a sample set of presentation slides.

Our approach will be to break this into sections. With each section, we'll show the necessary C# calls in the form to `PowerPointTools`, and then we'll talk about the actual VB 2005 code that's running in `PowerPointTools`.

So, create a Windows Forms application using the C# language, and add a .NET reference to `CGS.PowerPointTools.DLL`. Even though the DLL was written in VB 2005, you can still utilize all of the methods in the library.

Creating an Instance of PowerPointTools

Kicking off `PowerPointTools` is easy—as we just stated, add a reference to `CGS.PowerPointTools.DLL` to your test Windows application project.

Next, in the Windows Forms file (assume you're just using the standard `Form1` for the form in the Windows application), create an object reference to the `PowerPointTools` library, just underneath the class declaration for the form:

```
public partial class Form1 : Form
{
    PowerPointTools oPPT;
```

This creates an object reference (`oPPT`) to the library that you can use throughout the form. You'll create separate methods in the form to cover the different slides that you want to create.

Before you call any functionality, you first need to create an instance of `PowerPointTools`. So in your Windows application, you can use the following code:

```
// Create instance of PowerPointTools in your Windows app test form
PowerPointTools oPPT = new PowerPointTools ();
oPPT.LaunchPPT();
```

The code for `LaunchPPT()` in `CGS.PowerPointTools` (see Listing 14-3) creates new instances for PowerPoint 2003 and Excel. Note that the method utilizes the object property references to `oPPTApp` and `oExcel`, which other methods in the class will use.

Listing 14-3. *LaunchPPT in CGS.PowerPointTools*

```
Public Sub LaunchPPT()
  Me.oPPTApp = New PowerPoint.Application
  Me.oPPTApp.Visible = True

  Me.oExcel = New Excel.Application
  Me.oExcel.Visible = False

  Me.SlideNumber = 0
End Sub
```

Now that you have the basic setup, let's do something more interesting with `PowerPointTools`.

Starting a New Presentation with a Template and a Title Page

After creating an instance of PowerPoint, you can create a new presentation and specify the template and a title page, using three public methods from `PowerPointTools`. So in your Windows application test form, add the following three lines:

```
oPPT.SetTemplate("C:\\MyTemplates\\Pixel.pot");
oPPT.BuildTitlePage("Construction Demo",
            "Prepared by Common Ground Solutions");
oPPT.AddPicture("C:\\construction.jpg");
```

First, the `PowerPointTools` code for `SetTemplate()`, shown in Listing 14-4, provides your first exposure to the PowerPoint object model.

Listing 14-4. *SetTemplate in CGS.PowerPointTools*

```
Public Sub SetTemplate (ByVal TemplateFilename As String)

        Me.oPPTPres = Me.oPPTApp.Presentations.Add
        Me.AddSlide(PowerPoint.PpSlideLayout.ppLayoutTitle)
        Me.oPPTPres.ApplyTemplate(TemplateFilename)

End Sub
```

`SetTemplate()` adds a new presentation and stores an object reference to `oPPTPres`. The method also calls one of the `PowerPointTools` support methods, `AddSlide()` (see Listing 14-5).

Listing 14-5. *AddSlide in CGS.PowerPointTools*

```
Public Sub AddSlide(ByVal oLayout As PowerPoint.PpSlideLayout)
    ' Increment the active slide number,
    ' add a new slide based on that number/layout,
    ' and go to the slide.

    Me.SlideNumber = Me.SlideNumber + 1
    oPPTApp.ActivePresentation.Slides.Add(Me.SlideNumber, oLayout)

    oPPTApp.ActiveWindow.View.GotoSlide(Me.SlideNumber)

End Sub
```

When you call `AddSlide()`, you pass one of the PowerPoint predefined layout templates. You can use IntelliSense to view the available slide layouts (see Figure 14-5).

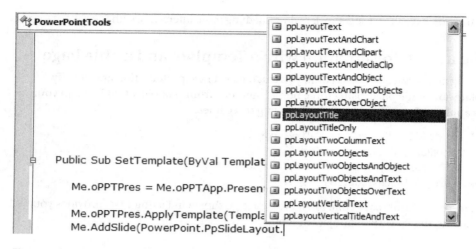

Figure 14-5. *Using IntelliSense to display available slide layouts*

Second, the PowerPointTools code for BuildTitlePage() utilizes another internal method called AddText(), to place text inside predefined shapes for the current slide layout (see Listing 14-6).

Listing 14-6. *BuildTitlePage and AddText Methods in CGS.PowerPointTools*

```
Public Sub BuildTitlePage(ByVal MainTitle As String, ➥
                          ByVal SubTitleTemplate As String)

  Me.AddText("Rectangle 2", MainTitle)
  Me.AddText("Rectangle 3", SubTitleTemplate)

End Sub

Public Sub AddText(ByVal ShapeName As String, ByVal PPTText As String)

    Me.oPPTApp.ActiveWindow.Selection.SlideRange.Shapes(1).Select()
    Me.oPPTApp.ActiveWindow.Selection.TextRange.Text = PPTText

End Sub
```

Finally, PowerPointTools contains the method AddPicture(), which displays an image on the center of the current slide (see Listing 14-7).

Listing 14-7. *AddPicture Method in CGS.PowerPointTools*

```
Public Sub AddPicture(ByVal PicFile As String)

  Dim oBitmap As Bitmap
  oBitmap = New Bitmap(PicFile)
```

```
Dim PicWidth As Int32 = oBitmap.Width
Dim PicHeight As Int32 = oBitmap.Height

Dim StartTop As Int32 = (540 - PicHeight) / 2
Dim StartWidth As Int32 = (720 - PicWidth) / 2

Me.oPPTApp.ActiveWindow.Selection.SlideRange.Shapes.AddPicture(➥
PicFile, False, True, StartWidth, StartTop)

End Sub
```

So far, this leads to the generation of the first title slide, shown in Figure 14-6.

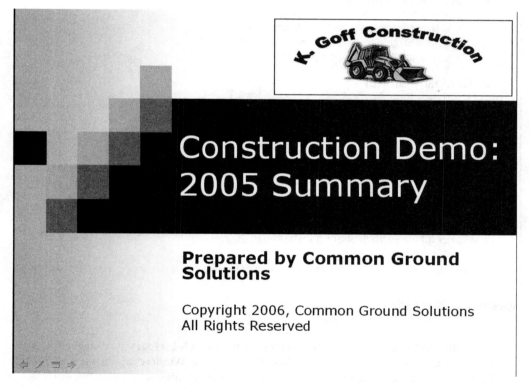

Figure 14-6. *Title slide built with PowerPointTools*

Again, PowerPointTools contains wrapper functions so that a developer doesn't have to access the PowerPoint object model directly. However, there may be times when a developer will need to access the PowerPoint object model directly. If so, the developer will need to add a COM reference to the PowerPoint Object Model Library in the application code.

Creating a Text-Only Slide with a Title and a Set of Bullet Points

The next step is to create a table-of-contents slide, with a title at the top and bullet points in the body of the slide. PowerPointTools must account for a variable-sized list of bullet points, and some of those bullet points may be indented.

PowerPointTools provides a method called BuildBulletPage() for generating individual slides with bullet-point content (see Figure 14-7).

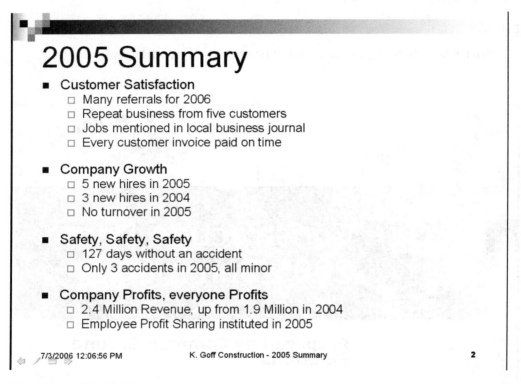

Figure 14-7. *Slide of bullet points*

To use this method, you can create instances of the PowerPointTools custom class PPTBulletList that we covered back in Listing 14-2. So in your Windows application test form, add the following code to create a generic list of PPTBulletList objects that matches the bullet-point items that you wish to create, and pass them to PowerPointTools (see Listing 14-8).

Listing 14-8. *Using PowerPointTools to Create a Slide of Bullet Points*

```
List<PPTBulletList> oBulletList = new List<PPTBulletList>();

// Note the indent level that you set.

oBulletList.Add(new PPTBulletList("Customer Satisfaction",
                        PPTBulletList.IndentLevel.NoIndent));
```

```
oBulletList.Add(new PPTBulletList("Many referrals for 2006",
                                  PPTBulletList.IndentLevel.Indent1));

oBulletList.Add(new PPTBulletList("Repeat business from five customers",
                                  PPTBulletList.IndentLevel.Indent1));

oBulletList.Add(new PPTBulletList("Jobs mentioned in local business journal",
                                  PPTBulletList.IndentLevel.Indent1));

oBulletList.Add(new PPTBulletList("Every customer invoice paid on time",
                                  PPTBulletList.IndentLevel.Indent1));


oBulletList.Add(new PPTBulletList("Company Growth",
                                  PPTBulletList.IndentLevel.NoIndent));

oBulletList.Add(new PPTBulletList("5 new hires in 2005",
                                  PPTBulletList.IndentLevel.Indent1));

oBulletList.Add(new PPTBulletList("3 new hires in 2004",
                                  PPTBulletList.IndentLevel.Indent1));

oBulletList.Add(new PPTBulletList("No turnover in 2005",
                                  PPTBulletList.IndentLevel.Indent1));

// Etc., etc.

oPPT.BuildBulletPage("2005 Summary", oBulletList);
```

The BuildBulletPage() method in PowerPointTools (see Listing 14-9) uses the ppLayoutText slide layout to build a bullet page. The method adds a new slide, sets the slide title, and scans through the generic list. The method examines the Indent column to set the IndentLevel for each bullet point.

Listing 14-9. *BuildBulletPage in CGS.PowerPointTools*

```
Public Sub BuildBulletPage(ByVal MainTitle As String,
            ByVal BulletList As List(Of PPTBulletList))

  Me.AddSlide(PowerPoint.PpSlideLayout.ppLayoutText)

  Me.AddText("Rectangle 2", MainTitle)
  ' Note the indentlevel property

  Me.SelectMainRectangle()

  Dim TextCounter As Int32 = 0
```

```
For Each oBulletItem As PPTBulletList In BulletList
    oPPTApp.ActiveWindow.Selection.TextRange.InsertAfter(
                    oBulletItem.BulletItem + Chr(13))
    TextCounter = TextCounter + 1
    oPPTApp.ActiveWindow.Selection.TextRange.Paragraphs
                (TextCounter, 1).IndentLevel = oBulletItem.BulletItemIndent
Next

End Sub
```

■**Note** There is one aspect of `PowerPointTools` that is essentially experimental, and that is the format of the data you pass to build slides. Some developers prefer to use DataSets, some prefer to use custom collections. `PowerPointTools` demonstrates both. You're encouraged to tweak and customize the `PowerPointTools` interface to suit your particular needs.

Building an Excel Table to Be Used As the Source of a PowerPoint Table

Often, creating/generating a PowerPoint slide also involves creating an Excel table. It may be a temporary table, where the contents are pasted into a PowerPoint table or used to create an Excel Chart Object (also pasted into PowerPoint). The next few sections will cover examples of this. The contents may be all numeric entries or a combination of entries, and they may or may not include column headings and alignment definitions.

PowerPointTools includes a method called `BuildExcelTable()` to generate a temporary Excel table (see Listing 14-10). This method receives two parameters: a DataTable representing the rows/columns (`DtTableEntries`), and a DataTable containing column headings and alignment definitions (`DtHeadings`). `BuildExcelTable` also has an overload for instances where no headings exist: the overload receives the parameter for `DtTableEntries`, and passes an empty table to the method with two parameters. `BuildExcelTable` performs the following:

1. Adds a new workbook to the `oExcel` application object

2. Writes out column heading lines and sets the alignment for each column (using `DtHeadings`)

3. Writes out the actual data (by scanning through `DtTableEntries`)

4. Selects the entire range of cells written out, and copies them to the system clipboard (for subsequent pasting into PowerPoint)

5. Returns a string representing the range of cells ("A1: D10")

Note that all instances of the type of DataTable are referring to the ADO.NET DataTable.

Listing 14-10. *BuildExcelTable in CGS.PowerPointTools: Method to Build a Table from Data*

```
Function BuildExcelTable(ByVal DtTableEntries As DataTable, ➥
  ByVal DtHeadings As DataTable) As String

  ' Add a workbook, and reference the first sheet.
  Dim oBook As Excel.Workbook = Me.oExcel.Workbooks.Add()
  Me.oSheet = oBook.Worksheets(1)

  Dim RowCounter As Int32 = 1
  Dim ColumnCounter As Int32 = 0
  Dim LastCell As String = ""
  Dim Cell As String = ""
  Dim Columnletter As String = ""
  Dim NumRows As Int32 = DtTableEntries.Rows.Count + 1

  ' Write out the column headings (if a heading table was provided).
  For Each Dr As DataRow In DtHeadings.Rows
          ' Determine cell.
          Columnletter = Chr(Asc("A") + ColumnCounter)
          Cell = Columnletter + RowCounter.ToString().Trim()
          ColumnCounter += 1
          Me.WriteExcelCell(Me.oSheet.Range(Cell), Dr(0), True)
          ' Apply the alignment to the column.
          Me.oSheet.Range(Columnletter + "1:" + Columnletter + ➥
              NumRows.ToString().Trim()).Select()
      Me.oExcel.Selection.HorizontalAlignment = Dr(1)
  Next

  For Each Dr As DataRow In DtTableEntries.Rows
    RowCounter += 1
    ColumnCounter = 0
    For Each Dc As DataColumn In DtTableEntries.Columns
        Cell = Chr(Asc("A") + ColumnCounter) + ➥
              RowCounter.ToString().Trim()
        LastCell = Cell
        ColumnCounter += 1
        Me.WriteExcelCell(Me.oSheet.Range(Cell), Dr(Dc), False)
    Next
  Next

  Me.oSheet.Range("A1:" + LastCell).Select()
  Me.oExcel.Selection.Copy()

  Return ("A1:" + LastCell)

End Function
```

```
Public Sub WriteExcelCell(ByVal oRange As Excel.Range, ➡
  ByVal Col As Object, ByVal CellBold As Boolean)

  With oRange
      .Value = Col
      .Font.Name = "Verdana"
      .Font.Size = 12
      .Font.Bold = CellBold
  End With
End Sub
```

Note that Listing 14-10 also contains a method called WriteExcelCell(). As the name implies, this method writes out a value for a particular cell. Calling methods use it when iterating through row/column objects. The next section will present some code to utilize this capability.

■Note The method WriteExcelCell represents a very basic but important tenet in building libraries—always isolate repeated tasks into a single block of code.

Creating a Slide That Displays an Excel Table

Now that you have a class to build a table, you can provide some data to populate it. Listing 14-11 shows an example of calling PowerPointTools with data to build a table that will result in your third slide (see Figure 14-8).

Listing 14-11. *Code in Your Test Form to Call PowerPointTools to Build a Slide with a Table*

```
// Code to generate a page with a title and a table.

DataTable DtJobTable = new DataTable();

DtJobTable.Columns.Add("Job Number", typeof(String));
DtJobTable.Columns.Add("Client", typeof(String));
DtJobTable.Columns.Add("Completed", typeof(String));
DtJobTable.Columns.Add("TotLabor", typeof(Decimal));
DtJobTable.Columns.Add("TotMaterial", typeof(Int32));
DtJobTable.Columns.Add("TotProfit", typeof(Int32));

DtJobTable.Rows.Add("167 - New Visitor Center", "Smithson Masonry", "Jul 2005",
                    5010, 72116, 19120);
DtJobTable.Rows.Add("212 - Summit Center", "Dave Hamilton", "Sep 2005", 10111,
                    32118, 11120);
DtJobTable.Rows.Add("321 - Manxler Homes", "Smithson Masonry", "Nov 2005", 9227,
                    29012, 10020);
```

```
DtJobTable.Rows.Add("177 - Summit Center", "Dave Hamilton", "Sep 2005", 10111,
                    32118, 11120);
DtJobTable.Rows.Add("109 - K.T. Repairs", "Lexington Construction", "Apr 2005",
                    4119,15023, 7020);

DataTable DtJobHeading = new DataTable();
DtJobHeading.Columns.Add("ColumnName", typeof(String));
DtJobHeading.Columns.Add("Alignment", typeof(Int32));
DtJobHeading.Rows.Add("Job #/Description", 2);
DtJobHeading.Rows.Add("Client", 2);
DtJobHeading.Rows.Add("Completed", 2);
DtJobHeading.Rows.Add("Labor $", 4);
DtJobHeading.Rows.Add("Material $", 4);
DtJobHeading.Rows.Add("Profit $", 4);

oPPT.BuildTablePage("Top Five Construction Jobs for 2005",
    DtJobTable,DtJobHeading);
```

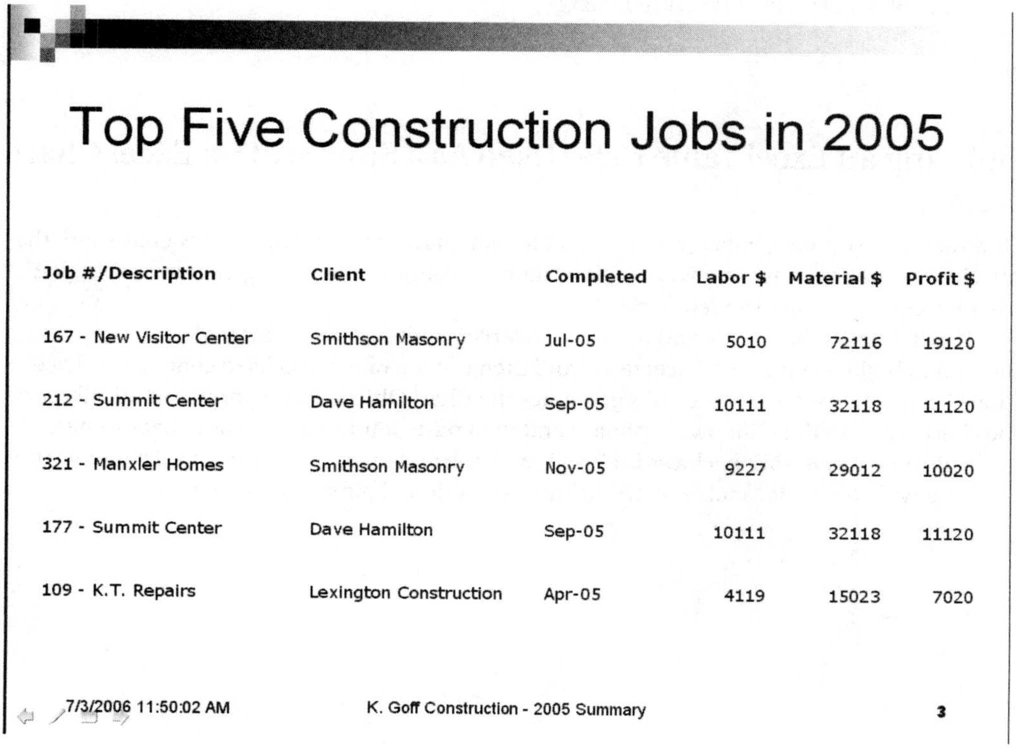

Top Five Construction Jobs in 2005

Job #/Description	Client	Completed	Labor $	Material $	Profit $
167 - New Visitor Center	Smithson Masonry	Jul-05	5010	72116	19120
212 - Summit Center	Dave Hamilton	Sep-05	10111	32118	11120
321 - Manxler Homes	Smithson Masonry	Nov-05	9227	29012	10020
177 - Summit Center	Dave Hamilton	Sep-05	10111	32118	11120
109 - K.T. Repairs	Lexington Construction	Apr-05	4119	15023	7020

7/3/2006 11:50:02 AM   K. Goff Construction - 2005 Summary   3

Figure 14-8. *Slide built from an Excel table*

Listing 14-12 shows the code in `PowerPointTools` for `BuildTablePage` that actually builds the slide.

Listing 14-12. *BuildTablePage in PowerPointTools, to Construct the Table*

```
Public Sub BuildTablePage(ByVal MainTitle As String, ➡
    ByVal DtTableEntries As DataTable, ByVal DtHeadings As DataTable)


    ' Create a new slide for the table page.
    AddSlide(PowerPoint.PpSlideLayout.ppLayoutTable)
    ' Add the title inside the first shape.
    AddText("Rectangle 2", MainTitle)
    ' Select the body shape.
    Me.SelectMainRectangle()

    ' Generate the Excel table from the table entries/headings.
    Me.BuildExcelTable(DtTableEntries, DtHeadings)
    ' Paste the generated Excel table.
    Me.oPPTApp.ActiveWindow.View.Paste()

End Sub
```

Building an Excel Table to Be Used As a Source of an Excel Chart Object

Now that we've covered bullet points and tables, let's have some fun and throw charts into the mix. In the same manner that you provided data to `PowerPointTools` to generate a table, you can do the same thing to generate charts.

If you define a DataTable and pass it to `PowerPointTools`, `PowerPointTools` can use the method to build a temporary Excel table, and then use the range of cells to generate an Excel Chart Object. Once `PowerPointTools` generates the Chart Object, it can programmatically copy the chart image to the Windows clipboard and then paste it into a slide that utilizes a chart.

This time you'll work backwards ("begin with the end in mind"). Figure 14-9 contains the slide you want to create: a table on the left and an exploded pie chart on the right.

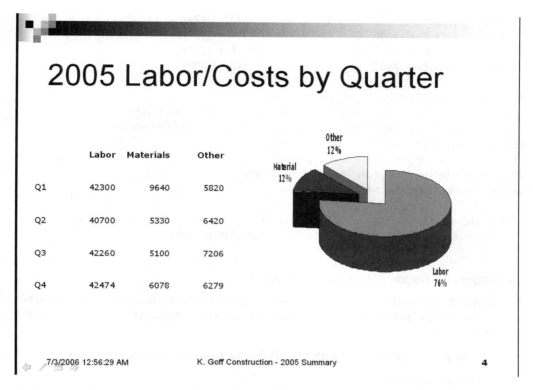

Figure 14-9. *Slide incorporating a pie chart and supporting Excel table data*

Listing 14-13 shows how to call PowerPointTools from your Windows application to generate this output. The following two sections cover the actual PowerPointTools methods to create the chart.

Listing 14-13. *Code in Your Windows Application to Call PowerPointTools to Build a Pie Chart*

```
DataTable DtPieChart = new DataTable();
DtPieChart.Columns.Add("Category", typeof(System.String));
DtPieChart.Columns.Add("Amount", typeof(System.Int32));

DtPieChart.Rows.Add("Labor", 167734);
DtPieChart.Rows.Add("Material", 26148);
DtPieChart.Rows.Add("Other", 13805 + 11920);

DataTable dtLaborCostData = new DataTable();
dtLaborCostData.Columns.Add("Quarter", typeof(System.String));
dtLaborCostData.Columns.Add("Labor", typeof(System.Int32));
dtLaborCostData.Columns.Add("Materials", typeof(System.Int32));
dtLaborCostData.Columns.Add("Other", typeof(System.Int32));
```

```
dtLaborCostData.Rows.Add("'Q1", 42300, 9640, 3400 + 2420);
dtLaborCostData.Rows.Add("'Q2", 40700, 5330, 2860 + 3560);
dtLaborCostData.Rows.Add("'Q3", 42260, 5100, 3666 + 3540);
dtLaborCostData.Rows.Add("'Q4", 42474, 6078, 3879 + 2400);

DataTable DtLaborCostHeading = new DataTable();
DtLaborCostHeading.Columns.Add("ColumnName", typeof(System.String));
DtLaborCostHeading.Columns.Add("RightAlign", typeof(System.Boolean));
DtLaborCostHeading.Rows.Add("Quarter", false);
DtLaborCostHeading.Rows.Add("Labor", true);
DtLaborCostHeading.Rows.Add("Materials", true);
DtLaborCostHeading.Rows.Add("Other", true);

oPPT.BuildTablePieChartPage("2005 Labor/Costs by Quarter", dtLaborCostData,
    DtLaborCostHeading, "Labor/Costs Breakdown",DtPieChart);
```

Customizing the Display of an Excel Chart Object

Listing 14-14 demonstrates how to create an Excel chart, using the method BuildExcelPieChart() in PowerPointTools. Building a pie chart (and for the most part, building any chart) involves the following:

1. Calling BuildExcelTable() with a DataTable containing the data for the chart.

2. Adding a new chart.

3. Using either ActiveChart.ChartType or ApplyCustomType() to define the type of chart. IntelliSense will provide the list of available chart types.

4. Setting the source data for the active chart, using the cell range that BuildExcelTable() returns.

5. Setting other properties relevant to the chart type (legend, X and Y axis, etc.).

6. Setting the ColorIndex and LineStyle of the chart's ChartArea and PlotArea. This is very important to the overall display of the chart.

7. Selecting the entire chart area and copying it to the Windows clipboard.

Listing 14-14. *BuildExcelPieChart in CGS.PowerPointTools, to Construct a Pie Chart*

```
Public Sub BuildExcelPieChart(ByRef DtTableEntries As DataTable, ➥
    ByRef ChartTitle As String)

    Dim TableCellRange As String
    TableCellRange = Me.BuildExcelTable(DtTableEntries)
    Me.oExcel.Charts.Add()
```

```
Me.oExcel.ActiveChart.ApplyCustomType(➡
                Excel.XlChartType.xl3DPieExploded)

Me.oExcel.ActiveChart.SetSourceData(➡
        Me.oSheet.Range(TableCellRange), Excel.XlRowCol.xlColumns)

Me.oExcel.ActiveChart.Location(➡
        Excel.XlChartLocation.xlLocationAsObject, "Sheet1")

Me.oExcel.ActiveChart.HasTitle = True

Me.oExcel.ActiveChart.ChartTitle.Characters.Text = ChartTitle

Me.oExcel.ActiveChart.HasLegend = False

Me.oExcel.ActiveChart.SeriesCollection(1).HasDataLabels = True
oExcel.ActiveChart.ApplyDataLabels(➡
        Excel.XlDataLabelsType.xlDataLabelsShowLabelAndPercent)

Me.oExcel.ActiveChart.PlotArea.Select()
Me.oExcel.Selection.Interior.ColorIndex = 0
Me.oExcel.Selection.Border.LineStyle = 0
Me.oExcel.ActiveChart.ChartArea.Select()
Me.oExcel.ActiveChart.ChartArea.Copy()
```

End Sub

Creating a Slide that Displays Both a Table and a Pie Chart

The code back in Listing 14-14 directly calls the PowerPointTools method
BuildTablePieChartPage() (see Listing 14-15) to build the slide with a table and a chart
(to produce Figure 14-9). BuildTablePieChartPage() does the following:

1. Creates a new slide based on the ppLayoutTextAndChart layout

2. Adds a slide title

3. Calls BuildExcelTable() for the table data, and pastes the results into the table section
   of the slide

4. Calls BuildExcelPieChart() for the chart data, and pastes the results into the chart
   section of the slide

5. Sets other properties relevant to the chart type (legend, X and Y axis, etc.)

Listing 14-15. *BuildTablePieChartPage in CGS.PowerPointTools*

```
Public Sub BuildTablePieChartPage(ByVal MainTitle As String,
    ByVal DtTableEntries As DataTable,
    ByVal DtHeadings As DataTable, ByVal ChartTitle As String,
    ByVal DtPieChartData As DataTable)

    ' Add the slide, based on the text/pie chart layout.
    Me.AddSlide(PowerPoint.PpSlideLayout.ppLayoutTextAndChart)
    Me.AddText("Rectangle 2", MainTitle)
    ' Build the table, paste it into the slide.
    Me.SelectMainRectangle()
    Me.BuildExcelTable(DtTableEntries, DtHeadings)
    Me.oPPTApp.ActiveWindow.View.Paste()
    ' Build the table for the pie chart, generate the chart, and
    ' paste the chart in.
    Me.BuildExcelPieChart(DtPieChartData, ChartTitle)
    Me.oPPTApp.ActiveWindow.Selection.SlideRange.
                                        Shapes(3).Select()
    Me.oPPTApp.ActiveWindow.View.Paste()

End Sub
```

■**Note** The general pattern for charting is consistent. First you build an Excel table containing data for the chart, then you build the chart from the Excel table range of data, and then you paste the chart into PowerPoint.

Creating a Slide That Displays a Line Chart

Now that you've displayed a chart as part of a slide, you'll create a chart that occupies the entire slide. Figure 14-10 shows a line chart that plots monthly labor and costs for 2004 and 2005.

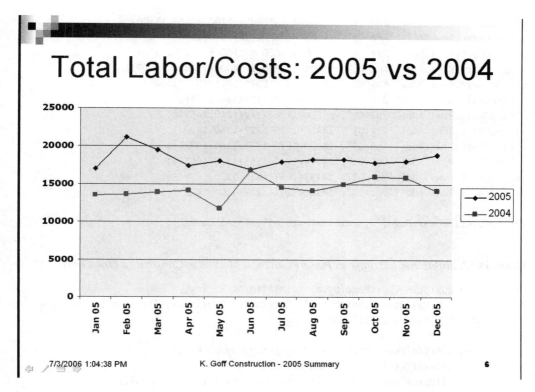

Figure 14-10. *Slide for a basic line chart*

Once again, in your Windows application, you'll create data to drive the table (see Listing 14-16), and then call the method `BuildLineChartPage` in `PowerPointTools` (see Listing 14-17). This method will create a new slide (this time based on the `ppLayoutChart` layout), and will call the method `BuildExcelLineChart` (also in Listing 14-17) to physically construct the line chart. Again, similar to the pie chart example, the code builds a chart image based on a chart type and source data.

Listing 14-16. *Windows Application Code to Call PowerPointTools to Build a Line Chart*

```
DataTable dtLineChart = new DataTable();
// Column names are not important.
// Just need to define the first column as the X-axis,
// and columns 2-N as the groups for the Y-axis.

dtLineChart.Columns.Add("Month", typeof(String));
dtLineChart.Columns.Add("Costs2005", typeof(Decimal));
dtLineChart.Columns.Add("Costs2004", typeof(Decimal));

dtLineChart.Rows.Add(System.DBNull.Value, 2005, 2004);
```

```
dtLineChart.Rows.Add("'Jan 05",    14000 + 1780 + 1100 + 140,13500);
dtLineChart.Rows.Add("'Feb 05", 14100 +4780+1200+1140,13600);
dtLineChart.Rows.Add("'Mar 05", 14200 + 3080 + 1100 + 1140,13900);
dtLineChart.Rows.Add("'Apr 05", 13000 + 1980 + 1300 + 1180, 14200);
dtLineChart.Rows.Add("'May 05", 13800   + 1580+1450+1240, 11800);
dtLineChart.Rows.Add("'Jun 05", 13900+1770+110+1140,16788);
dtLineChart.Rows.Add("'Jul 05", 13960+1710+1111+1240,14591);
dtLineChart.Rows.Add("'Aug 05", 14200+1720+1222+1140,14204);
dtLineChart.Rows.Add("'Sep 05", 14100+1670+1333+1160,15021);
dtLineChart.Rows.Add("'Oct 05", 14075+1120+1555+1170,16015);
dtLineChart.Rows.Add("'Nov 05", 14133+1667+1111+1120, 15943);
dtLineChart.Rows.Add("'Dec 05", 14266+3291+1213+110, 14201);

oPPT.BuildLineChartPage("",  dtLineChart, "","Total Costs");
```

Listing 14-17. *BuildLineChartPage in PowerPointTools Method to Construct a Line Chart*

```
Public Sub BuildLineChartPage(ByVal MainTitle As String, _
        ByVal DtLineChartData As DataTable, ByVal xAxisTitle As String, _
        ByVal yAxisTitle As String)

    Me.AddSlide(PowerPoint.PpSlideLayout.ppLayoutChart)
    Me.AddText("Rectangle 2", MainTitle)
    Me.BuildExcelLineChart(DtLineChartData, xAxisTitle, yAxisTitle)
    Me.SelectMainRectangle()
    Me.oPPTApp.ActiveWindow.View.Paste()

End Sub


Public Sub BuildExcelLineChart(ByRef DtTableEntries As DataTable, _
        ByRef xAxisTitle As String, ByRef yAxisTitle As String)

    Dim TableCellRange As String
    TableCellRange = Me.BuildExcelTable(DtTableEntries)

    Me.oExcel.Charts.Add()
    Me.oExcel.ActiveChart.ChartType = Excel.XlChartType.xlLineMarkers
    Me.oExcel.ActiveChart.Location(Excel.XlChartLocation.xlLocationAsObject, _
        "Sheet1")


    Me.oExcel.ActiveChart.PlotArea.Select()
    Me.oExcel.Selection.Interior.ColorIndex = 36   ' light yellow
    Me.oExcel.Selection.Border.LineStyle = 0
```

```
        Me.oExcel.ActiveChart.ChartArea.Select()
        Me.oExcel.Selection.Interior.ColorIndex = 0
        Me.oExcel.Selection.Border.LineStyle = 0

        Me.oExcel.ActiveChart.Axes(1).Select()
        Me.oExcel.Selection.TickLabels.Alignment = Excel.Constants.xlCenter
        Me.oExcel.Selection.TickLabels.Offset = 40
        Me.oExcel.Selection.TickLabels.Orientation = Excel.XlOrientation.xlUpward

        Me.oExcel.ActiveChart.ChartArea.Select()
        Me.oExcel.ActiveChart.ChartArea.Copy()


    End Sub
```

Creating a Slide That Displays a Bar Chart

We'll round out our coverage of graphs by showing how to build a slide that contains a bar chart. Back in Chapter 9, you constructed a bar chart that depicted monthly costs by category as a stacked bar chart. You also saw how to display the total costs for the previous year as a line chart that cuts across the graph. Figure 14-11 shows an example of this very graph that you can build as a slide page using `PowerPointTools`.

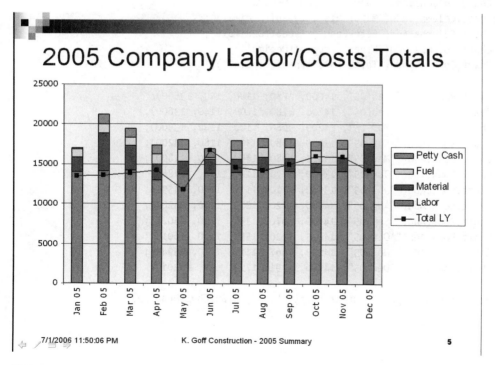

Figure 14-11. *Slide for a bar chart, showing the totals for last year as a line instead of a bar*

Once again, you'll create data to drive the table (see Listing 14-18) and then call the method BuildBarChartPage in PowerPointTools (see Listing 14-19). This method will create a new slide (this time based on the ppLayoutChart layout) and will call the method code BuildExcelBarChart (also in Listing 14-19) to construct the bar chart.

Listing 14-18. *Code in Your Windows Application to Call PowerPointTools to Build a Bar Chart*

```
DataTable DtBarChartHeading = new DataTable();
DtBarChartHeading.Columns.Add("ColumnName", typeof(System.String));
DtBarChartHeading.Columns.Add("RightAlign", typeof(System.Int32));
DtBarChartHeading.Rows.Add("Week Number", false);
DtBarChartHeading.Rows.Add("Labor", true);
DtBarChartHeading.Rows.Add("Materials", true);
DtBarChartHeading.Rows.Add("Fuel", true);
DtBarChartHeading.Rows.Add("Petty Cash", true);
DtBarChartHeading.Rows.Add("Total LY", true);

DataTable dtBarChart = new DataTable();
// Column names are not important.
// Just need to define the first column as the X-axis,
// and columns 2-N as the groups for the Y-axis.

dtBarChart.Columns.Add("WeekNumber",typeof(String));
dtBarChart.Columns.Add("Labor", typeof(Decimal));
dtBarChart.Columns.Add("Materials", typeof(Decimal));
dtBarChart.Columns.Add("PettyCash", typeof(Decimal));
dtBarChart.Columns.Add("Other", typeof(Decimal));
dtBarChart.Columns.Add("Total LY", typeof(Decimal));

dtBarChart.Rows.Add("'Jan 05", 14000, 1780, 1100, 140, 13500);
dtBarChart.Rows.Add("'Feb 05", 14100, 4780, 1200, 1140, 13600);
dtBarChart.Rows.Add("'Mar 05", 14200, 3080, 1100, 1140, 13900);
dtBarChart.Rows.Add("'Apr 05", 13000, 1980, 1300, 1180, 14200);
dtBarChart.Rows.Add("'May 05", 13800, 1580, 1450, 1240, 11800);
dtBarChart.Rows.Add("'Jun 05", 13900, 1770, 110, 1140, 16788);
dtBarChart.Rows.Add("'Jul 05", 13960, 1710, 1111, 1240, 14591);
dtBarChart.Rows.Add("'Aug 05", 14200, 1720, 1222, 1140, 14204);
dtBarChart.Rows.Add("'Sep 05", 14100, 1670, 1333, 1160, 15021);
dtBarChart.Rows.Add("'Oct 05", 14075, 1120, 1555, 1170, 16015);
dtBarChart.Rows.Add("'Nov 05", 14133, 1667, 1111, 1120, 15943);
dtBarChart.Rows.Add("'Dec 05", 14266, 3291, 1213, 110, 14201);

oPPT.BuildBarChartPage("", dtBarChart, "", "", DtBarChartHeading);
```

Listing 14-19. *PowerPointTools Methods to Build a Bar Chart Slide*

```
Public Sub BuildBarChartPage(ByVal MainTitle As String, _
            ByVal DtBarChartData As DataTable, ByVal xAxisTitle As String, _
            ByVal yAxisTitle As String, ByVal DtBarChartHeadings As DataTable)

        Me.AddSlide(PowerPoint.PpSlideLayout.ppLayoutChart)
        Me.AddText("Rectangle 2", MainTitle)
        Me.BuildExcelBarChart(DtBarChartData, xAxisTitle, DtBarChartHeadings)
        Me.SelectMainRectangle()
        Me.oPPTApp.ActiveWindow.View.Paste()


    End Sub

Public Sub BuildExcelBarChart(ByRef DtTableEntries As DataTable, _
            ByRef ChartTitle As String, ByRef DtHeadings As DataTable)

        Dim TableCellRange As String
        TableCellRange = Me.BuildExcelTable(DtTableEntries, DtHeadings)

        Me.oExcel.Charts.Add()

        Me.oExcel.ActiveChart.ApplyCustomType(Excel.XlChartType.xlColumnStacked)

        Me.oExcel.ActiveChart.SetSourceData(Me.oSheet.Range(TableCellRange), _
            Excel.XlRowCol.xlColumns)

        Me.oExcel.ActiveChart.Location(Excel.XlChartLocation.xlLocationAsObject, _
            "Sheet1")
        Me.oExcel.ActiveChart.HasTitle = True
        Me.oExcel.ActiveChart.ChartTitle.Characters.Text = ChartTitle

        Me.oExcel.ActiveChart.Axes(1).Select()
        Me.oExcel.Selection.TickLabels.Alignment = Excel.Constants.xlCenter
        Me.oExcel.Selection.TickLabels.Offset = 40
        Me.oExcel.Selection.TickLabels.Orientation = Excel.XlOrientation.xlUpward

        Me.oExcel.ActiveChart.SeriesCollection(5).Select()
        Me.oExcel.Selection.ChartType = Excel.XlChartType.xlLine

        Me.oExcel.ActiveChart.ChartArea.Select()
        Me.oExcel.Selection.Interior.ColorIndex = 0
        Me.oExcel.Selection.Border.LineStyle = 0
```

```
        Me.oExcel.ActiveChart.SeriesCollection(1).Select()
        Me.oExcel.Selection.Interior.ColorIndex = 4

        Me.oExcel.ActiveChart.SeriesCollection(2).Select()
        Me.oExcel.Selection.Interior.ColorIndex = 26

        Me.oExcel.ActiveChart.SeriesCollection(3).Select()
        Me.oExcel.Selection.Interior.ColorIndex = 27

        Me.oExcel.ActiveChart.SeriesCollection(4).Select()
        Me.oExcel.Selection.Interior.ColorIndex = 42

        Me.oExcel.ActiveChart.ChartArea.Select()
        Me.oExcel.ActiveChart.ChartArea.Copy()

    End Sub
```

■**Note** The code in Listing 14-19 produces a bar chart that assumes five data elements (`SeriesCollections`)— four columns for the stacked bars, and a fifth for the horizontal line depicting data for the previous year. An exercise would be to modify the method `BuildExcelBarChart` to handle a variable number of data elements to graph, and also to identify the element to chart using the `Excel.XLChartType.xlLine`.

Setting Animations and Slide Transitions

Of course, no fancy PowerPoint presentation is complete without some type of slide transition. Listing 14-20 shows a method, `SetSlideTransitions`, that sets a slide-by-slide transition of vertical blinds. PowerPoint offers a number of slide transitions and animation schemes— the listing is just one brief example. Figure 14-12 illustrates the value of IntelliSense to view the different available options.

The value of the code in Listing 14-20 isn't so much the specific result as much as it is a basic demonstration of iterating through a collection of PowerPoint objects.

Listing 14-20. *PowerPointTools Method to Set Slide Transitions*

```
Public Sub SetSlideTransitions()
    ' Basic demonstration of looping through the slideshow collection.
    ' Use this as a guide to change settings at the slide level.

    For Each oSlide As PowerPoint.Slide In Me.oPPTApp.ActivePresentation.Slides

        oSlide.SlideShowTransition.EntryEffect = ➡
            PowerPoint.PpEntryEffect.ppEffectBlindsVertical
```

```
    Next

End Sub


  Public Sub SetSlideTransitions()

    ' Basic demonstration of looping through the slideshow collection
    ' use this as a guide to change settings at the slide level

    For Each oSlide As PowerPoint.Slide In Me.oPPTApp.ActivePresentation.Slides
        oSlide.SlideShowTransition.EntryEffect =
    Next

  End Sub
```

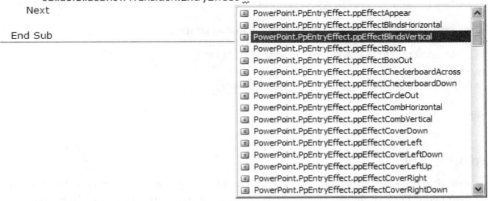

Figure 14-12. *Using IntelliSense to view the available slide transition effects*

Defining Slide Footer Information

PowerPointTools provides a method called BuildFooter() (see Listing 14-21) so that a developer can define footer text for each slide. The method uses the ActivePresentation.SlideMaster.HeaderFooters object hierarchy.

Listing 14-21. *PowerPointTools Method to Set a Common Slide Footer*

```
Public Sub BuildFooter(ByVal FooterText As String)
  ' Possible enhancement could be making the
  ' slide number and date optional.

    With Me.oPPTApp.ActivePresentation.SlideMaster.HeadersFooters
        .DateAndTime.Visible = True
        .DateAndTime.Format = ➥
            PowerPoint.PpDateTimeFormat.ppDateTimeMMddyyhmmAMPM
        .DateAndTime.Text = ""
        .DateAndTime.UseFormat = True
```

```
            .Footer.Text = FooterText
            .SlideNumber.Visible = Microsoft.Office.Core.MsoTriState.msoCTrue
            .DisplayOnTitleSlide = False
        End With

End Sub
```

Saving the Presentation

Finally, `PowerPointTools` provides a simple method to save a presentation:

```
oPPT.SavePresentation("c:\\2005Summary.PPT");
```

The method code for `SavePresentation()` is just as simple:

```
Public Sub SavePresentation(ByVal PPTName As String)

    Me.oPPTApp.ActivePresentation.SaveAs(PPTName)

End Sub
```

Closing Excel

You've seen that the `PowerPointTools` library utilizes Excel to generate tables and charts. After you've saved your PowerPoint presentation, you can release the Excel object with the following code:

```
Me.oExcel.DisplayAlerts = False
Me.oExcel.Quit()
Me.oExcel = Nothing
```

The first line (which uses the `DisplayAlerts` property) prevents Excel from prompting to save the temporary worksheet that you created. The second line terminates Excel, and the third line sets your object reference to nothing.

When in Doubt, Use Office Macros!

If you're not sure how to perform a specific programming task in PowerPoint (or any Microsoft Office product), you can create a macro, perform the task manually, and then review the macro code. In most instances, the code in the VBA macro will show you the way.

This approach was helpful in researching the Excel object model for creating charts from data. For example, to create a bar chart, you manually create some data, start a new macro (as shown in Figure 14-13), build the bar chart manually using the Excel Charting Wizard, stop recording the macro, and then examine the code for the macro (see Figure 14-14).

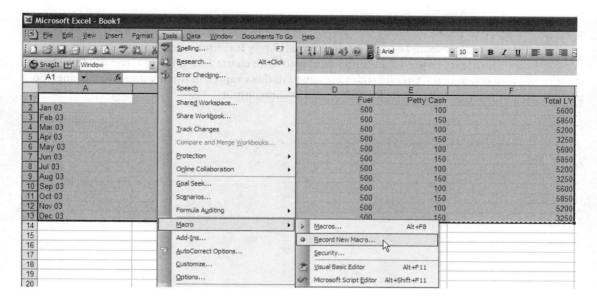

Figure 14-13. *Creating a macro to examine the necessary VBA code to perform a task*

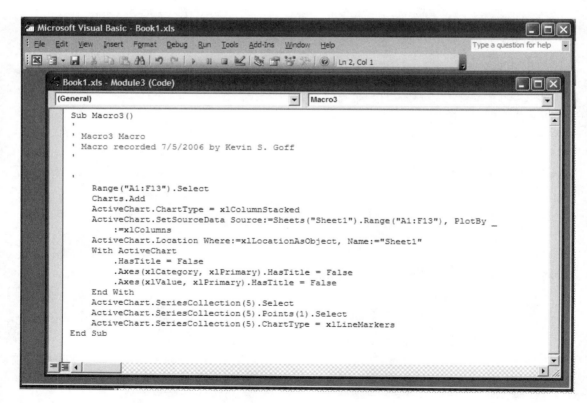

Figure 14-14. *Viewing the resulting macro code*

Summary

This chapter presented a basic but functional library for automating PowerPoint slide generation. The library utilized Excel functionality to drive charts and tables. You can use this library as is to generate the types of slides presented in this chapter, or modify it to adapt to specific needs you may have for high-quality presentation output.

PART 6

■■■

Appendixes

This book contains three appendixes. Appendix A covers the client specs we covered in Chapter 1. Appendix B lists the database contents we covered in Chapters 2 and 3. Appendix C covers the .NET classes for the application that we discuss in the remainder of the book.

Client Specs

When clients request new reports, they will often provide drafts in Excel or Microsoft Word format. In some situations, they may specify some of the report rules. Our job as developers is to review what they provide, ask questions, and look for undocumented rules. Often you'll want to communicate back to the client what you understand their requirements to be: in some instances, the client may think you're doing nothing more than repeating back their needs but in slightly different words, and in other instances the follow-up communication might lead to meaningful discussions.

Appendix A covers all of the samples received from our fictional client. Let's take a look at them.

1. Timesheet Report

Figure A-1 shows a sample of the timesheet report: the client currently builds this semimanually in Excel using macros. They have indicated some rules for the report, such as hiding rates and dollar amounts based on user roles. They have also requested several options, such as running the report for a specific division, worker, or construction job. One of the areas you can provide value is to allow users to select a variable number of works/jobs in a single report run.

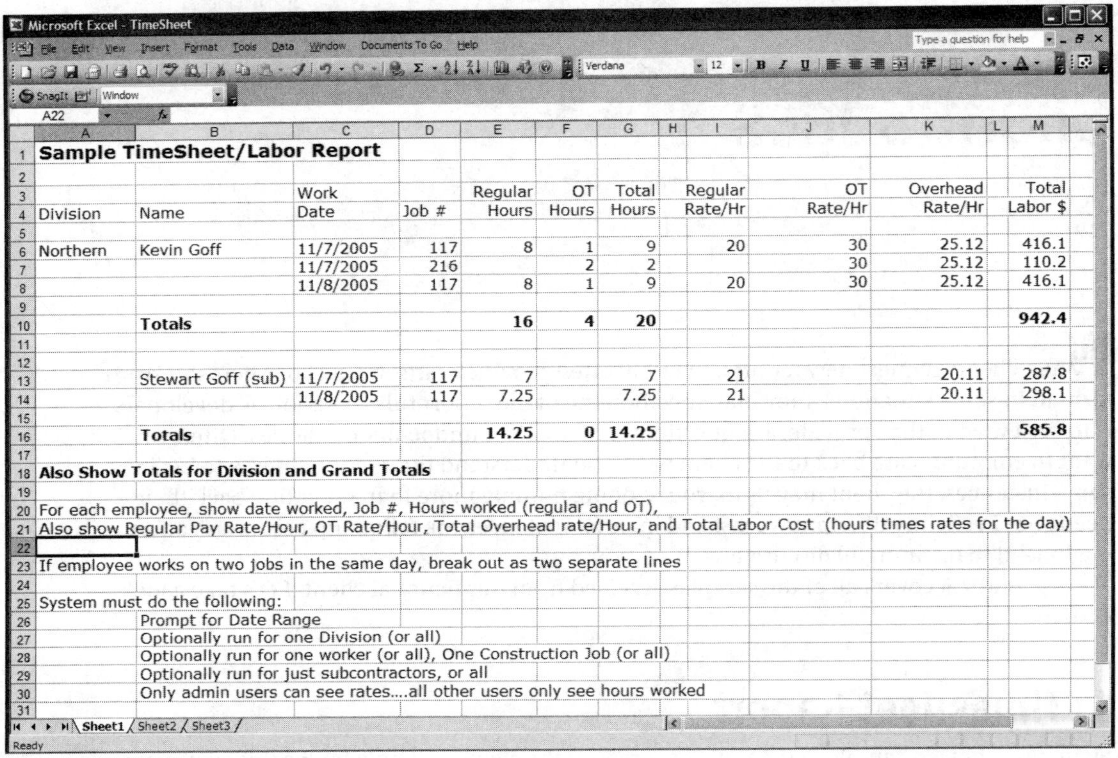

Sample TimeSheet/Labor Report

Division	Name	Work Date	Job #	Regular Hours	OT Hours	Total Hours	Regular Rate/Hr	OT Rate/Hr	Overhead Rate/Hr	Total Labor $
Northern	Kevin Goff	11/7/2005	117	8	1	9	20	30	25.12	416.1
		11/7/2005	216		2	2		30	25.12	110.2
		11/8/2005	117	8	1	9	20	30	25.12	416.1
	Totals			**16**	**4**	**20**				**942.4**
	Stewart Goff (sub)	11/7/2005	117	7		7	21		20.11	287.8
		11/8/2005	117	7.25		7.25	21		20.11	298.1
	Totals			**14.25**	**0**	**14.25**				**585.8**

Also Show Totals for Division and Grand Totals

For each employee, show date worked, Job #, Hours worked (regular and OT),
Also show Regular Pay Rate/Hour, OT Rate/Hour, Total Overhead rate/Hour, and Total Labor Cost (hours times rates for the day)

If employee works on two jobs in the same day, break out as two separate lines

System must do the following:
Prompt for Date Range
Optionally run for one Division (or all)
Optionally run for one worker (or all), One Construction Job (or all)
Optionally run for just subcontractors, or all
Only admin users can see rates....all other users only see hours worked

Figure A-1. *Client sample of a timesheet report*

2. Construction Job Summary/Profit Report

At first glance, the profit summary report in Figure A-2 is a simple report that summarizes labor and material data for each construction job. However, client has requested a few additional options: the ability to sort in descending sequence on any numeric column, and the ability to specify one or more filters.

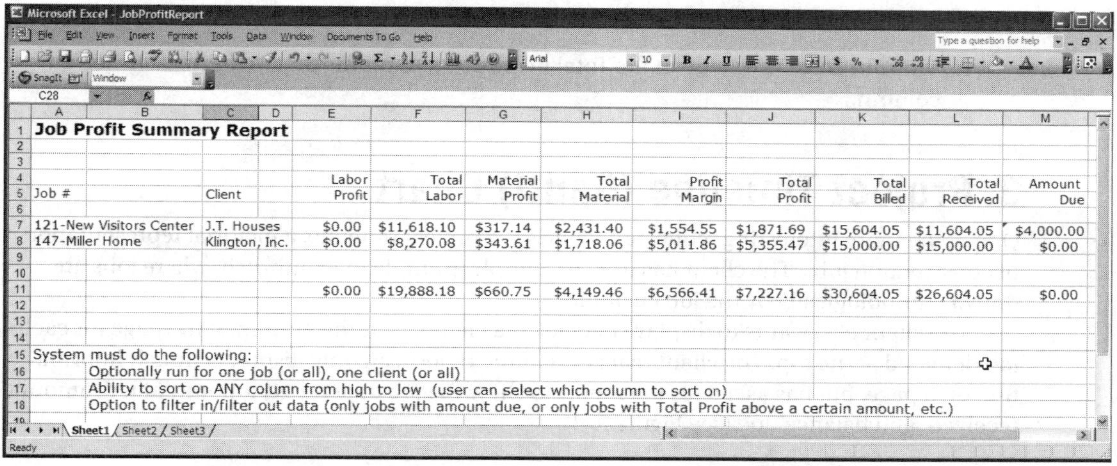

Job Profit Summary Report

Job #	Client	Labor Profit	Total Labor	Material Profit	Total Material	Profit Margin	Total Profit	Total Billed	Total Received	Amount Due
121-New Visitors Center	J.T. Houses	$0.00	$11,618.10	$317.14	$2,431.40	$1,554.55	$1,871.69	$15,604.05	$11,604.05	$4,000.00
147-Miller Home	Klington, Inc.	$0.00	$8,270.08	$343.61	$1,718.06	$5,011.86	$5,355.47	$15,000.00	$15,000.00	$0.00
		$0.00	$19,888.18	$660.75	$4,149.46	$6,566.41	$7,227.16	$30,604.05	$26,604.05	$0.00

System must do the following:
Optionally run for one job (or all), one client (or all)
Ability to sort on ANY column from high to low (user can select which column to sort on)
Option to filter in/filter out data (only jobs with amount due, or only jobs with Total Profit above a certain amount, etc.)

Figure A-2. *Client sample for a job construction summary report*

The client has subsequently provided definitions for the following columns:

1. **Labor Profit**: The client assigns an hourly profit rate for each construction job. The labor profit is the total hours on the job, multiplied by this hourly profit rate. Some jobs do not have a labor profit rate, so the labor profit will be zero. (In lieu of a labor profit rate, the client may prefer to add a lump sum labor profit figure during the invoicing stage.)

2. **Total Labor**: The total hours on the job, multiplied by the appropriate rates (regular hours, overtime hours), plus any labor profit (value from Labor Profit column).

3. **Material Profit**: The client assigns a material markup percentage for each construction job. The material profit is the total material costs for the job, multiplied by this markup percentage. Some jobs do not have a material markup percentage, so the material profit will be zero.

4. **Total Material**: The total materials purchased for the job, plus any material profit (value from Material Profit column).

5. **Profit Margin**: While the client refers to this as a profit margin, it is actually a lump sum labor profit the client assigns at invoice time. On jobs for some customers, the construction company will assign a labor profit rate per hour; on other jobs, the company will leave the labor profit rate per hour as zero, and then assign a lump sum labor profit (which they refer to as the profit margin) as part of the invoice.

6. **Total Profit**: The sum of the values in the Labor Profit, the Material Profit, and the Profit Margin (lump sum profit) columns.

7. **Total Billed**: The sum of the values in the Total Labor, Total Material, and Profit Margin columns.

8. **Total Received**: The total amount of invoices received for each construction job.

9. **Amount Due**: The value in the Total Billed column minus that in the Total Received column.

3. Project Timeline (Gantt) Chart

One of the more interesting requested reports is a project timeline, a pictorial representation of construction jobs. The client has drawn a simple example in Paintbrush, where jobs are drawn chronologically by the job customer.

The client also wants to display specific data elements at the bottom of the page for each job depicted at the top. The client realizes that the report can only display so much information on a page, but has asked for the report to show the job date range, amount billed, amount received, and balance due (see Figure A-3).

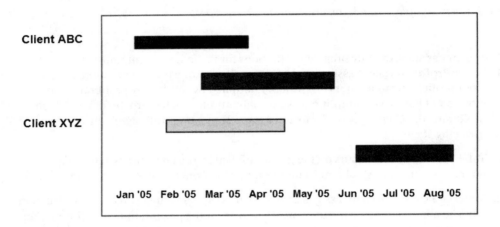

Show timeline for each job

Also show the following for each job:
Client, Date Range, Total Profit, Total Amount Billed, Total Amount Received, and Balance Due

Figure A-3. *Project timeline chart*

4. Client Invoice

The client has been preparing invoices using an inexpensive off-the-shelf program and welcomes the opportunity to design their invoices. Figure A-4 shows the customer invoice. The client has stated that the job customer mailing address must appear three inches from the top of the page and four inches from the left, so that a folded invoice can display the customer address in the envelope window. The client also wants the invoice to display the customer logo at the top of the invoice.

```
                              INVOICE

                         [Show Customer Logo]

 [Invoice #]              [Customer
 [Invoice Date]           Mailing
                          Address]
 ┌──────────────────────────────────────────────────────┐
 │ Jobs:                                                  │
 │     Job Number/Description        Work Dates           │
 ├──────────────────────────────────────────────────────┤
 │ Labor:                                                 │
 │     (Total # of Job Hours)              Total Labor Amt│
 ├──────────────────────────────────────────────────────┤
 │ Materials:                                             │
 │     Material          Purchase Date            Amt     │
 │     Material          Purchase Date            Amt     │
 │                                   Total Material Amt   │
 ├──────────────────────────────────────────────────────┤
 │ Notes:                                                 │
 │     Here are any invoice notes                         │
 ├──────────────────────────────────────────────────────┤
 │ Past Due Invoices:                                     │
 │     Invoice #         Invoice Date        Past Amt Due │
 └──────────────────────────────────────────────────────┘

                                   Total Amount Due

                     Terms (from Invoice File):

   Our company name, address, phone # and company logo at the bottom
```

Figure A-4. *Draft of client invoice*

Note that the Labor section will only show a single line for total hours on the job. However, the Materials and Past Due invoices sections will show one line per material purchase and past due invoice, respectively.

5. Aging Receivables Report

One of the most common accounting reports is an aging receivables report. An aging receivables report displays past due invoices based on the invoice date with respect to the current date (or an as-of date). A standard aging receivables report categorizes these invoices based on the number of days the invoice has aged (i.e., the number of days between the invoice date and the report as-of date): in most cases, the categories are 1–30 days old, 31–60 days old, etc. The primary objectives of an aging report include identifying customers with a large number of overdue invoices, and to also show a company total for outstanding receivables.

Figure A-5 shows the aging receivables report the client wishes to run. For the most part, it is a standard aging receivables report, where the user will specify the report date and whether to show data by invoice or summarize aging results by client. They have also requested basic options to sort by client, by invoice number, or by total amount due.

Aging Receivables Report

- Show invoices unpaid as of a certain date
- Option to show all invoices, or summarize by client
- User should be able to enter a description
- Currently we use standard aging brackets (1-30, 31-60).
  - However, an admin user may need to run and specify different brackets (1-45 days, etc.)
- Sort options: by Client, or by Invoice #, or by Total Amount Due

Detail by Client - Invoice

Client	Invoice #	< 30 days old	31-60 days	61-90 days	91-120 days	> 120 days	Total
ABC	123	100				100	200
	245			100			100
Client Total		**100**	**100**			**100**	**300**
DEF	789				200	200	400
	888			100			100
Client Total				**100**	**200**	**200**	**500**
Final Total		**100**	**200**	**200**	**200**	**100**	**800**

Summarized by Client

Client	< 30 days old	31-60 days	61-90 days	91-120 days	> 120 days	Total
ABC	100	100			100	300
DEF		100	200	200		500
Final Total	**100**	**200**	**200**	**200**	**100**	**800**

Figure A-5. *Aging receivables report, either detail by invoice or summarized by client*

They have also requested the ability (for admin users) to customize the brackets. The client sometimes wants to see the aging receivables report for bracket categories other than 1–30 days, 31–60 days, etc. So the design must account for this requirement.

6. Combination Report/Graph of Labor and Costs

The most challenging (or as we like to call it, "adventurous") report is something the client has offered to pay more for, if you can deliver. They are very conscious of labor and cost trends, and monitor them on a monthly basis. They also want to compare labor and cost amounts versus the same time the prior year.

The client has requested two charts and a listing (Figures A-6, A-7, and A-8) on one page. They want to run this for one location, multiple locations, or all locations. The first chart is a line chart (see Figure A-6) that shows total labor and costs for the past year (and the same time period last year) as a line chart.

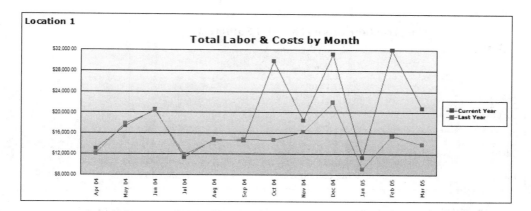

Figure A-6. *First of three outputs on a page, labor and costs by month in a line chart*

The second chart is a pie chart (see Figure A-7) that simply divides total costs by category for the specified report period.

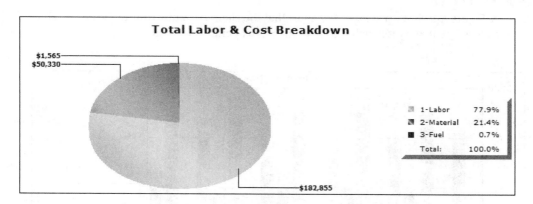

Figure A-7. *Second of three outputs on a page, total labor/costs in a pie chart*

The third and final section of the page is a listing (see Figure A-8) that displays the supporting data for the preceding charts. The client also wants users to be able to specify a display threshold: any months with labor or costs above a runtime specified value displays in red.

Construction Labor/Material Summary

Month Ending	Labor $	Costs $
Apr 04	12,951.23	
May 04	17,338.21	
Jun 04	20,511.56	
Jul 04	11,251.25	
Aug 04	14,797.90	
Sep 04	14,537.15	
Oct 04	14,721.55	15,120.00
Nov 04	17,020.85	1,402.50
Dec 04	21,195.72	9,968.00
Jan 05	9,829.09	1,401.44
Feb 05	14,771.53	17,178.51
Mar 05	13,928.56	6,825.00
Total:	**182,854.60**	**51,895.45**

Figure A-8. *Third of three outputs on a page, simple data listing with thresholds in red*

7. Stacked Bar Chart Showing Labor/Costs by Month

Finally, Figure A-9 shows a stacked bar chart that the client currently runs in Excel. The chart shows costs by category for each month of the report period specified.

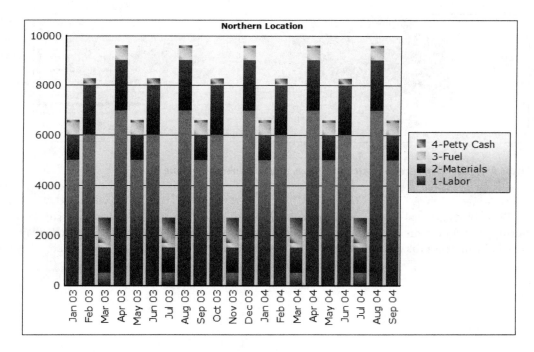

Figure A-9. *Stacked bar chart—client also wants to plot costs from last year as a horizontal line.*

The client has also requested one additional piece of information: the graph should show the total costs from the prior year as a black horizontal line.

8. Construction Job Profile Report

Finally, the client has asked for a report that shows all details on a construction job. Figures A-10 through A-13 show the four parts of a detailed report. The client wants to run this report from a list of jobs: they may select one job or a range of jobs. Figure A-10 shows the heading for the report, which contains general job information, along with summary totals for labor and materials. Typically, the client will run this report after a job has been closed out.

Job Closeout Report			
Job #:	452	Contract Amount:	$34,575.90
Client:	TIMLEY CONSTRUCTION INC.	Labor Costs:	$27,216.12
Description:	BLOCK GARAGE, FRONT PORCH AREA, STANDARD CONCRETE	Material Costs:	$7,101.00
Creation Date:	03/12/2005	Profit/Loss:	$258.77
Close Date:	11/21/2005	Percentage:	0.7%

Figure A-10. *Part 1 of 4—closeout report heading*

Figure A-11 shows the labor breakdown section of the closeout report. It lists employees in name order, along with the total hours worked on each job and the total labor burden (labor rates, as well as overhead rates).

Labor:

Employee Name	Hours	Total Labor
JASON ANDERSON	228.00	$6,449.63
BILL BAILEY	178.00	$6,666.98
JIMMY COCHRAN	8.00	$231.12
CARL FISHER	27.00	$915.03
ANDREW MATTSON	40.00	$1,138.80
PAUL RILEY	56.00	$1,567.88
RICH TRIKOWSKI	164.00	$3,429.83
AARON ZIEGLAR	81.00	$1,891.85
MATT ZIMMERMAN	206.00	$4,925.03

Figure A-11. *Part 2 of 4—closeout report labor summary*

Figure A-12 shows the material purchase breakdown for the closeout report. It lists each purchase and the purchase type, date, and amount.

Materials:

Point Of Sale	Type	Date	Amount
STANDARD 10934	Material	03/30/2005	100.34
STANDARD 044	Material	04/11/2005	77.71
FUEL SURCHARGES	Fuel	04/29/2005	1,400.00
KSM HH 19345	Material	04/30/2005	296.63
KSM PYY 10123	Material	05/12/2005	59.36
STANDARD CONCRETE 34645	Material	06/11/2005	1,418.64
KSM LAKE BUILDING 45687	Material	07/06/2005	125.00
KSM HH 66542	Material	07/07/2005	296.63
STANDARD 055336	Material	07/13/2005	1,545.32
STANDARD 053722	Material	07/18/2005	1,673.25
STANDARD	Material	08/23/2005	108.12

Figure A-12. *Part 3 of 4—closeout report material history*

Finally, Figure A-13 shows the overhead breakdown for the closeout report. This fourth and final section lists each client overhead labor category and the amount applied to the job (the total labor hours on the job multiplied by the overhead rate). The cumulative totals column calculates the overhead **for all closed jobs** in the year of the report. In this example, the job is the only closed job for 2005, so both columns are the same. However, as more jobs are closed, the cumulative total will increase.

Overhead Breakdown:

Category	Amount	2005 Cumulative Total
ACCOUNTANTS FEES	$690.20	$690.20
ADVERTISING	$216.92	$216.92
ESTIMATED TAX/QTRLY235	$1,027.08	$1,027.08
EXTRA: FUEL	$266.22	$266.22
HEALTH INSURANCE	$1,540.62	$1,540.62
LIABILITY INSURANCE	$187.34	$187.34
MISC EQUIPMENT	$216.92	$216.92
MOBIL PHONES	$315.52	$315.52
OFFICE PHONES	$104.61	$104.61
RENT	$494.52	$494.52
SKID LOADER	$581.74	$581.74
TRUCK INSURANCE	$216.92	$216.92
TRUCKS	$2,129.76	$2,129.76
UTILITIES	$47.55	$47.55
W. COMP	$1,027.08	$1,027.08
Please include "Number of Jobs closed for 2005" and the #	**$9,063.00**	**$9,063.00**

Figure A-13. *Part 4 of 4—closeout report overhead/cumulative totals for all closed jobs*

Database Schema

This appendix lists all of the tables and columns in the `Construction Demo` database and also provides a brief explanation of the different categories of data.

Database Schema

Tables B-1 and B-2 list the database tables and database columns for the application.

Table B-1. *List of Database Tables for the Construction and Job-Costing Application*

Table Name	Table Description
Address	A table of addresses
AgingBrackets	A table of configuration aging receivables brackets
Client	One row for each client
ClientAddr	Cross-reference table of addresses for each client
ClientPhone	Cross-reference table of phones for each client
Division	Division master table (Northern, Southern, etc.)
Invoices	One row per invoice
InvoiceJob	Stores link to invoice and associated jobs
JobMaster	Job construction master, one row per job, reference to client
LKAddrType	Address types (business, residence, etc.)
LKInvTerms	Invoice terms (net 30, upon receipt, etc.)
LKMaterialType	Material type categories (regular materials, fuel, etc.)
LKOverHead	Overhead categories (workman's comp, etc.)
LKPhoneType	Business phone, cell, fax
LKRateType	Regular rate, OT rate
Materials	Materials purchased for a job
OverheadRate	Overhead rate, effective date, amount, and whether it applies to contractors
Phone	A table of phone numbers
Receipts	Stores one row per receipt/invoice

Continues

Table B-1. *Continued*

Table Name	Table Description
Reports	A master table of the reports in the application
Status	A table of user status codes (Active, Suspended, etc.)
TimeSheets	One row per worker/work date/job number/LKRateType
UserFile	A table of users who can access the application
Worker	One row for each worker, with a flag to indicate subcontractors
WorkerAddr	Cross-reference table of addresses for each worker
WorkerPhone	Cross-reference table of phones for each worker
WorkerRate	Pay rates for each worker, with an effective date

Table B-2. *Database Columns*

Table Name	Column Name	Column Type	Column Description
Address	AddressPK	Int	Unique identifier
	AddressLine1	Char	First line of address
	AddressLine2	Char	Second line of address
	City	Char	City
	State	Char	State
	ZipCode	Char	ZIP code
	DateCreated	DateTime	Date row was created
	DateModified	DateTime	Date row was last modified
AgingBrackets	StartDay	Int	The first day of the bracket range (e.g., 1)
	EndDay	Int	The last day of the bracket range (e.g., 30)
	BracketNumber	Int	The column order number of the bracket (e.g., 1)
	BracketLabel	Char	A description (e.g., "< 30 days")
Client	ClientPK	Int	Unique identifier
	ClientName	Char	Client name
	ContactName	Char	Main contact name
	Comments	Text	Miscellaneous remarks
	DateCreated	DateTime	Date row was created
	DateModified	DateTime	Date row was last modified
ClientAddr	ClientAddrPK	Int	Unique identifier
	ClientFK	Int	Pointer to PK in Client
	AddressFK	Int	Pointer to PK in Address
	LKAddrTypeFK	Int	Pointer to PK in LKAddrType
	EffectiveDate	DateTime	Date address goes into effect

Table Name	Column Name	Column Type	Column Description
ClientAddr	ExpireDate	DateTime	Date address is no longer in effect
	DateCreated	DateTime	Date row was created
	DateModified	DateTime	Date row was last modified
ClientPhone	ClientAddrPK	Int	Unique identifier
	ClientFK	Int	Pointer to PK in Client
	PhoneFK	Int	Pointer to PK in Phone
	LKPhoneTypeFK	Int	Pointer to PK in LKPhoneType
	EffectiveDate	DateTime	Date address goes into effect
	ExpireDate	DateTime	Date address is no longer in effect
	DateCreated	DateTime	Date row was created
	DateModified	DateTime	Date row was last modified
Division	DivisionPK	Int	Unique identifier
	Description	Char	Description
	DateCreated	DateTime	Date row was created
	DateModified	DateTime	Date row was last modified
Invoices	InvoicePK	Int	Unique identifier
	InvoiceNumber	Char	Invoice number
	ClientFK	Int	Pointer to PK in Clients
	LKInvTermsFK	Int	Pointer to PK in LKInvTerms
	InvoiceDate	DateTime	Invoice date
	LaborNotes	Char	Notes for labor
	MaterialNotes	Char	Notes for materials
	InvoiceNotes	Char	General invoice notes
	InvoiceAmount	Decimal	Invoice amount
	InvoiceClosed	Bit	Boolean for whether invoice is closed
	DateCreated	DateTime	Date row was created
	DateModified	DateTime	Date row was last modified
InvoiceJob	InvoiceJobPK	Int	Unique identifier
	InvoiceFK	Int	Pointer to PK in Invoices
	JobMasterFK	Int	Pointer to PK in JobMaster
	InvoiceAmount	Decimal	Invoice amount (for the specific job)
	DateCreated	DateTime	Date row was created
	DateModified	DateTime	Date row was last modified
JobMaster	JobMasterPK	Int	Unique identifier
	Description	Char	Job description
	DivisionFK	Int	Pointer to PK in Division
	ClientFK	Int	Pointer to PK in Client

Continues

Table B-2. *Continued*

Table Name	Column Name	Column Type	Column Description
JobMaster	MaterialMarkupPct	Decimal	Material markup % on job (profit)
	AdditionalHourlyRate	Decimal	Additional hourly rate (profit)
	AdditionalLabor	Decimal	Additional labor amount
	JobClosed	Bit	Flag for when job is closed
	CreateDate	DateTime	Date job was created
	CloseDate	DateTime	Date job was closed—no more activity
	DateCreated	DateTime	Date row was created
	DateModified	DateTime	Date row was last modified
LKAddrType	LKAddrTypePK	Int	Unique identifier
	Description	Int	Description (business, residence, etc.)
	DateCreated	DateTime	Date row was created
	DateModified	DateTime	Date row was last modified
LKInvTerms	LKInvTermsPK	Int	Unique identifier
	Description	Char	Description (net 30, upon receipt, etc.)
	DateCreated	DateTime	Date row was created
	DateModified	DateTime	Date row was last modified
LKMaterialType	LKMaterialTypePK	Int	Unique identifier
	Description	Char	Description
	DateCreated	DateTime	Date row was created
	DateModified	DateTime	Date row was last modified
LKOverHead	LKOverHeadPK	Int	Unique identifier
	Description	Char	Description
	DateCreated	DateTime	Date row was created
	DateModified	DateTime	Date row was last modified
LKPhoneType	LKPhoneTypePK	Int	Unique identifier
	Description	Int	Description (main phone, cell, fax)
	DateCreated	DateTime	Date row was created
	DateModified	DateTime	Date row was last modified
LKRateType	LKRateTypePK	Int	Unique identifier
	Description	Char	Description
	DateCreated	DateTime	Date row was created
	DateModified	DateTime	Date row was last modified
Materials	MaterialPK	Int	Unique identifier
	JobMasterFK	Int	Pointer to PK in JobMaster
	LKMaterialTypeFK	Int	Pointer to PK in LKMaterialType
	PurchaseAmount	Decimal	Amount of material purchase
	PurchaseDate	DateTime	Date of material purchase

Table Name	Column Name	Column Type	Column Description
Materials	PurchaseNotes	VarChar	Notes for material purchase
	DateCreated	DateTime	Date row was created
	DateModified	DateTime	Date row was last modified
OverHeadRate	OverHeadRatePK	Int	Unique identifier
	LKOverHeadFK	Int	Pointer to PK in LKOverHead
	HourlyRate	Decimal	Rate per hour
	EffectiveDate	DateTime	Date the rate goes into effect
	EmployeeFlag	Bit	Whether this rate is for employees only
	DateCreated	DateTime	Date row was created
	DateModified	DateTime	Date row was last modified
Phone	PhonePK	Int	Unique identifier
	AreaCode	Char	Area code
	MainNumber	Char	Main number
	Extension	Char	Extension
	DateCreated	DateTime	Date row was created
	DateModified	DateTime	Date row was last modified
Receipts	ReceiptPK	Int	Unique identifier
	InvoiceFK	Int	Pointer to PK in Invoices
	JobMasterFK	Int	Pointer to PK in JobMaster
	AmountReceived	Decimal	Amount received
	DateCreated	DateTime	Date row was created
	DateModified	DateTime	Date row was last modified
Reports	ReportPK	Int	Unique identifier
	Name	Char	The name of the report
	Description	Char	A description for the report
Status	StatusPK	Int	Unique identifier
	Description	Char	Description (active, suspended, inactive, etc.)
TimeSheets	TimeSheetPK	Int	Unique identifier
	WorkerFK	Int	Pointer to PK in Worker
	DivisionFK	Int	Pointer to PK in Division
	JobMasterFK	Int	Pointer to PK in JobMaster
	LKRateTypeFK	Int	Pointer to PK in LKRateType
	HoursWorked	Decimal	Actual hours worked
	WorkDate	DateTime	Date worked
	DateCreated	DateTime	Date row was created
	DateModified	DateTime	Date row was last modified
UserFile	UserPK	Int	Unique identifier

Continues

Table B-2. *Continued*

Table Name	Column Name	Column Type	Column Description
UserFile	UserID	Char	User ID (e.g., KGOFF)
	Password	Char	The user's password
	UserName	Char	The full user name (e.g., Kevin S. Goff)
	StatusFK	Int	Pointer to PK in Status
Worker	WorkerPK	Int	Unique identifier
	DivisionFK	Int	Pointer to PK in Division
	FirstName	Char	First name
	LastName	Char	Last name
	EmployeeFlag	Bit	Whether the worker is an employee
	Comments	Text	Miscellaneous remarks
	EmailAddress	Char	The worker's e-mail address
	LastUpdated	DateTime	Date row was last updated
	DateCreated	DateTime	Date row was created
	DateModified	DateTime	Date row was last modified
WorkerAddr	WorkerAddrPK	Int	Unique identifier
	WorkerFK	Int	Pointer to PK in Worker
	AddressFK	Int	Pointer to PK in Address
	LKAddrTypeFK	Int	Pointer to PK in LKAddrType
	EffectiveDate	DateTime	Date address goes into effect
	ExpireDate	DateTime	Date address is no longer in effect
	DateCreated	DateTime	Date row was created
	DateModified	DateTime	Date row was last modified
WorkerPhone	WorkerPhonePK	Int	Unique identifier
	WorkerFK	Int	Pointer to PK in Worker
	PhoneFK	Int	Pointer to PK in Phone
	LKPhoneTypeFK	Int	Pointer to PK in LKPhoneType
	EffectiveDate	DateTime	Date address goes into effect
	ExpireDate	DateTime	Date address is no longer in effect
	DateCreated	DateTime	Date row was created
	DateModified	DateTime	Date row was last modified
WorkerRate	WorkerRatePK	Int	Unique identifier
	LKRateTypeFK	Int	Pointer to LKRateType.LKRateTypePK
	WorkerFK	Int	Pointer to Worker.WorkerFK
	HourlyRate	Decimal	Rate per hour
	EffectiveDate	DateTime	Date the rate goes into effect
	DateCreated	DateTime	Date row was created
	DateModified	DateTime	Date row was last modified

Categories of Data

For your reporting application, there are six categories of data that you will read and process. Let's take a few minutes and review them.

Employees and Rates and Rate Types

Figure B-1 displays some test data for the Worker, Division, WorkerRate, and LKRateType tables. Note that the database can store multiple labor rates for each worker, rates for regular hours and overtime hours, and rates with effective dates. This allows the application to calculate (and retroactively calculate) labor figures for a specific point in time. Chapters 2 and 3 cover the SQL code to retrieve rates based on effective dates.

	WorkerPK	DivisionFK	FirstName	LastName	EmployeeFlag	Comments	EmailAddress
1	1	1	John	Smith	1	NULL	NULL
2	5	2	Kevin	Goff	0	NULL	NULL

	DivisionPK	Description
1	1	New England
2	2	Mid-Atlantic

	WorkerRatePK	WorkerFK	LKRateTypeFK	HourlyRate	EffectiveDate
1	1	1	1	20.00	2006-01-01 00:00:00.000
2	2	1	2	30.00	2006-01-01 00:00:00.000
3	7	1	1	22.00	2006-01-09 00:00:00.000
4	8	1	2	33.00	2006-01-09 00:00:00.000
5	6	5	1	19.00	2006-01-01 00:00:00.000

	LKRateTypePK	Description
1	1	Regular Rate
2	2	OT Rate

Figure B-1. *Worker, Division, WorkerRate, and LKRateType tables*

Overhead Rates

The client stores overhead rates per hour: some rates apply to all workers on construction jobs, while other rates apply only to regular employees (as opposed to subcontractors). Figure B-2 shows some sample overhead rates for the application.

	OverHeadRatePK	LKOverHeadFK	HourlyRate	EffectiveDate	EmployeeFlag
1	1	1	0.70	2006-01-01 00:00:00.000	0
2	9	9	0.11	2006-01-01 00:00:00.000	1
3	17	1	0.85	2006-01-09 00:00:00.000	0
4	18	9	0.16	2006-01-09 00:00:00.000	1

	LKOverHeadPK	Description
1	1	ACCOUNTANTS FEES
2	2	ADVERTISING
3	3	ESTIMATED TAX/QTRLY235
4	4	EXTRA: FUEL
5	5	HEALTH INSURANCE
6	6	LIABILITY INSURANCE
7	7	MISC EQUIPMENT
8	8	MOBIL PHONES
9	9	OFFICE PHONES
10	10	RENT
11	11	SKID LOADER
12	12	TRUCK INSURANCE
13	13	TRUCKS

Figure B-2. *OverHeadRate and LKOverHead tables*

The database supports multiple rates per each overhead category (health insurance, rent, etc.), based on an effective date. This allows the application to calculate (and retroactively calculate) overhead figures for a specific point in time. In the example data in Figure B-2, on January 9, 2006, accountants' fees and office phones increased from $.70 per hour and $.11 per hour to $.85 per hour and $.16 per hour, respectively.

Construction Job Master Data

Figure B-3 shows the JobMaster table. When the construction company enters a new job, the company specifies the division for the job, as well as the client. Note that for each job, the construction company can enter the following:

- MaterialMarkupPct: This is essentially an upcharge on any materials purchased, passed on to the client during the invoice (material profit).

- AdditionalHourlyRate: This is a labor profit rate per hour on all hours worked on the job, passed on to the client during the invoice (labor profit).

- AdditionalLabor: The construction company may choose to specify labor profit as a lump sum figure, as opposed to an hourly profit rate.

- JobClosed: Once a job is closed, users can no longer post labor or material purchases for the job.

	JobMasterPK	DivisionFK	Description	ClientFK	MaterialMarkupPct	AdditionalHourlyRate	AdditionalLabor	JobClosed	CreateDate
1	1	1	Job #1	1	0.07	2.00	0.00	NULL	2005-01-01
2	2	1	Job #2	2	0.05	0.00	0.00	NULL	2005-01-01
3	3	2	Job #3	3	0.08	0.00	0.00	NULL	2005-01-01
4	4	2	Job #4	4	0.05	0.00	1500.00	NULL	2005-01-01

	ClientPk	ClientName	ContactName	Comments
1	1	KINGSTON CONSTRUCTION	STEPHEN EASON	NULL
2	2	GOLDGATE CONTRACTING	IAN RALEIGH	NULL
3	3	L& L EXCAVATING INC.	CHUCK WENDELL	NULL
4	4	ROBINSKY HOUSING	JASON MITCHELL	NULL

Figure B-3. *JobMaster and Client tables*

Timesheet/Labor Data

Figure B-4 shows the TimeSheet table. The database supports the most complex labor scenario possible: a worker who works for multiple jobs in multiple divisions for a single day.

	TimeSheetPK	DivisionFk	WorkerFK	JobMasterFK	LKRateTypeFK	HoursWorked	WorkDate
1	1	1	1	1	1	8.00	2006-01-02 00:00:00.000
2	2	1	1	1	2	1.00	2006-01-02 00:00:00.000
3	3	1	1	2	2	2.00	2006-01-02 00:00:00.000
4	4	1	1	1	1	8.00	2006-01-03 00:00:00.000
5	5	1	1	1	2	1.00	2006-01-03 00:00:00.000
6	6	1	2	3	1	7.00	2006-01-02 00:00:00.000
7	7	1	2	3	1	7.25	2006-01-03 00:00:00.000
8	8	2	3	4	1	8.00	2006-01-02 00:00:00.000
9	9	2	2	4	1	0.50	2006-01-02 00:00:00.000
10	10	2	1	4	1	4.00	2006-01-09 00:00:00.000

Figure B-4. *Timesheet data*

Material Purchases

The construction company may purchase a variety of materials for a job, such as different forms of equipment, supplies, fuel, etc. The database stores both material purchases, as well as the categories of materials for reporting purposes (see Figure B-5).

	MaterialPK	JobMasterFK	LKMaterialTypeFK	PurchaseAmount	PurchaseDate	PurchaseNotes
1	1	1	1	1000.00	2006-01-01 00:00:00.000	NULL
2	2	2	1	2000.00	2006-01-01 00:00:00.000	NULL
3	3	3	1	3000.00	2006-01-01 00:00:00.000	NULL
4	4	4	1	500.00	2006-01-01 00:00:00.000	NULL
5	NULL	4	2	200.00	2006-01-01 00:00:00.000	NULL
6	NULL	4	3	100.00	2006-01-01 00:00:00.000	NULL

	LKMaterialTypePK	Description
1	1	Materials
2	2	Petty Cash
3	3	Fuel

Figure B-5. *Materials and LKMaterialType tables*

■**Note** Some jobs may have labor, but no material purchases, or vice-versa. For any model with multiple parent-child relationships, make sure that all queries and joining functions recognize that parent rows may have child rows in some tables, but not others.

Jobs and Invoices and Invoice Receipts

Figure B-6 shows an example of two different customer invoices for two different construction jobs. In the example, the company invoiced Client 1 twice, for Job 1 and Job 2. The client paid all but $100 for Job 1, and paid for all of Job 2 in two separate payments. The example demonstrates what the application can store in the Invoices, InvoiceJob, and Receipts tables. The following rules apply:

- An invoice is generated for one client (Invoices.ClientFK).

- An invoice can reference multiple construction jobs for the client (InvoiceJob table). While this example only stores one job for each invoice, the application needs to support multiple jobs on an invoice (provided they are all for the same client). In that instance, the Invoices.InvoiceAmount column will store the sum of the InvoiceJob.InvoiceAmount values for the invoice.

- The construction company may receive payment multiple times on an invoice, so the Receipts table may contain more than one payment received row for the invoice.

	InvoicePK	InvoiceNumber	ClientFK	LKInvTermsFK	InvoiceDate	LaborNotes	MaterialNotes	InvoiceNotes	InvoiceAmount	InvoiceClosed
1	1	2005-1871	1	1	2005-12-01 ...	NULL	NULL	NULL	1654.30	1
2	2	2005-0662	1	1	2005-09-01 ...	NULL	NULL	NULL	2178.70	0

	InvoiceJobPK	InvoiceFK	JobMasterFK	InvoiceAmount
1	1	1	1	1654.30
2	2	2	2	2178.70

	ReceiptPK	InvoiceFK	JobMasterFK	AmountReceived	DateReceived
1	1	1	1	1554.30	2005-06-01 ...
2	2	2	2	2000.00	2005-06-01 ...
3	3	2	2	178.70	2005-06-02 ...

	LKInvTermsPK	Description
1	1	Net 30 days

Figure B-6. *Invoices, InvoiceJob, Receipts, and LKInvTerms tables*

Technical Roadmap and Reference

This final appendix provides a reference for the application components we covered throughout the book: the framework components as well as the specific projects for the construction demo. You can find the entire project (source code and database) on Kevin Goff's web site, at www.commongroundsolutions.net\downloads. At the conclusion, we'll also include some final notes on the libraries.

Application Component Reference

This section will list all of the projects in the entire Visual Studio 2005 solution, along with a list of the classes in each solution, and a description for each one.

The Common Ground Framework Library

As stated throughout the book, the reporting application makes heavy use of Kevin Goff's **Common Ground Framework for Visual Studio 2005**. This framework focuses on distributed applications and contains reusable productivity classes for reporting, as well as data access, business objects, remoting, and client-side access.

Class Library Project: CGS.Business

This is the base class library, from which all business objects will inherit. Chapter 4 covers this project in detail.

Class File: cgsBaseBusinessObject.cs

This class inherits from System.MarshalByRefObject, which is required for all classes that use .NET remoting. When creating a class that inherits from cgsBaseBusinessObject, set a reference to CGS.Business, and do the following:

```
using CGS.Business;
public class bzMyBackEndClassForRemoting : cgsBaseBusinessObject
```

Any classes that inherit from cgsBaseBusinessObject will automatically inherit from System.MarshalByRefObject. If you have any base methods or properties that you want to expose to all your business objects, you should place them in this class.

Class Library Project: CGS.CrystalReportsTools

This library contains reusable tools to automate Crystal Reports. Instead of writing code using the Crystal Reports API every time the application generates a report, the developer can utilize this library, which in turn makes function calls to the Crystal API. The library contains a class manager for general Crystal functionality (pushing runtime DataSource items into a report and previewing/printing/exporting reports); form class files for viewing reports and setting printer options; and a class for setting report header/footer information.

Chapter 12 covers this library in detail. In particular, Listing 12-9 in Chapter 12 shows a complete example of using this library.

Class File: ccCrystalManager.cs

This is the primary class file in the project. It contains the methods to generate reports. Tables C-1 and C-2 show the properties and methods in ccCrystalManager.

Table C-1. *Properties in ccCrystalManager*

Name	Description
cPrinterName	String property for the printer name to use
nCopies	Numeric property for number of copies, when printing
lAllPages	Boolean property for whether to print all pages
lPageRange	Boolean property for whether to print a page range
nStartPage	Numeric property for starting page (if printing a page range)
nEndPage	Numeric property for ending page (if printing a page range)
lCollate	Boolean property for whether to collage pages
ExportTypes	Enumeration for supported export types

Table C-2. *Public Methods in ccCrystalManager*

Name	Description
PushReportData()	Method to push a DataSet into a report—automatically handles subreports
SetReportInfo()	Method to set report header/footer information (see Table C-3 for details)
PreviewReport()	Method to launch the report previewer
PrintReport()	Method to print a report
ExportReport()	Method to export a report

Form File: ccCrystalPrintOptionForm.cs

This is a reusable form for the user to set common print options.

Form File: ccCrystalViewer.cs

This is a reusable form to preview Crystal Reports output in a Windows Form.

Class File: ccReportInfo.cs

This is a class that can be used to set common report header/footer annotations. Table C-3 lists the available properties.

Table C-3. *Public Properties in ccReportInfo*

Name	Description
FtrDataSource	Property to show report DataSource
FtrFootNotes	Property to show user footnotes
FtrRunBy	Property to show the user who ran the report
FtrVersion	Property to show the software version
HdrCompany	The name of the company
HdrReportTitle	The name of the report
HdrSubTitle1	The report subtitle
HdrSubTitle2	A second report subtitle
UserID	The user ID of the user running the report

Class Library Project: CGS.DataAccess

This is the base data access library. It contains the functionality to retrieve data from SQL Server.

Class File: cgsDataAccess.cs

This is the base data access class. All application-specific data access will inherit from this class. Table C-4 lists the public method in cgsDataAccess.

Table C-4. *Public Method in cgsDataAccess*

Name	Description
ReadIntoTypedDs()	Method that executes a stored procedure, based on a set of parameters and a custom timeout, and returns the result directly into a typed DataSet

Chapter 5 covers this class in detail. In particular, Listing 5-10 in Chapter 5 demonstrates an example of using this data access class.

Class Library Project: CGS.Globals

This project stores global settings that are used through the application. Chapter 13 shows how the application uses these settings.

Class File: cgsGlobals.cs

This is the single class in the project. It contains static properties, mainly set at startup, for retaining through the application session. Table C-5 lists the available properties.

Table C-5. *Public Properties in cgsGlobals*

Name	Description
cUserID	The user ID of the user signed on
nUserPK	The user PK integer value of the user signed on
cUserName	The name of the user signed on (for messages to show the user's name)
cUserPassword	The password of the user signed on
cCurrentConnection	The name of the current selection (from the local Connect.XML file)
lAppRunning	A Boolean property to indicate that the application is running (This will prevent the Windows Forms designer from trying to draw certain content at design time.)
nDataBaseKey	The database key specified at startup

Class Library Project: CGS.PowerPointTools

This is a Visual Basic project library to help automate the creation of PowerPoint slides and charts. Chapter 14 shows many examples of creating PowerPoint output using this library.

Class File: PowerPointTools.VB

This class file provides the major functionality for the PowerPointTools class. Tables C-6 and C-7 list the available properties and methods.

Table C-6. *Public Properties in PowerPointTools*

Name	Description
SlideNumber	Property that gets/sets the current slide number
oPPTApp	Object reference to PowerPoint application class
oPPTPres	Object reference to PowerPoint presentation class
oExcel	Object reference to Excel application class
oSheet	Object reference to Excel worksheet

Table C-7. *Public Methods in PowerPointTools*

Name	Description
AddPicture()	Adds an image to the current slide
AddSlide()	Creates a new slide
AddText()	Adds text to the current slide
BuildBarChartPage()	Builds a new slide page with a bar chart
BuildBulletPage()	Builds a new slide page with bullet points
BuildExcelTable()	Builds an Excel table for display
BuildFooter()	Sets the footer for the PowerPoint presentation
BuildLineChartPage()	Builds a new slide page with a line chart
BuildTablePage()	Builds a new slide page with an Excel table
BuildTablePieChartPage()	Builds a new slide page with a pie chart and a table
BuildTitlePage()	Sets the main title page
DisplayPPT()	Displays the active PowerPoint presentation
LaunchPPT()	Launches the PowerPointTools library
SavePresentation()	Saves the created presentation
SelectMainRectangle()	Selects the main body rectangle of the current slide page
SetSlideTransitions()	Sets the transition effect between slides
SetTemplate()	Sets the PPT background to use for the presentation
WriteExcelCell()	Writes out a cell or range of cells based on a specific value

Class File: PPTBulletList.VB

This class file contains a custom class for generating slide bullet point lists. Table C-8 lists the available properties.

Table C-8. *Public Properties in PPTBulletList*

Name	Description
BulletItem	Bullet point string
BulletItemIndent	Indent level (using enumeration, as in the next entry)
IndentLevel	Enumeration (NoIndent, Indent1, Indent2)

Class Library Project: CGS.RemoteAccess

This is a reusable class library that provides a communication factory class, to simplify creating web service and remoting calls. Chapter 4 covers this class in detail, as do Chapters 6 and 13.

Class File: ClientRemoteAccess.cs

This class file contains the main remote factory access class. Tables C-9 and C-10 list the available properties and methods.

Table C-9. *Public Properties in ClientRemoteAccess*

Name	Description
ConnectionTypeOptions	Enumeration (WebServices = 1, TcpRemoting)
cServiceName	Base name of the back-end object/web service name being accessed
cTcpServer	TCP server address, for remoting
cWebServiceURL	URL, for web services
nConnectionType	Current connection type (of type ConnectionTypeOptions)
nTCPPort	TCP port, for remoting
tInterface	Type reference to the back-end interface
wService	Object reference to the local web reference proxy, for web services

Table C-10. *Methods in cgsRemoteAccess*

Name	Description
GetAccessObject()	Based on supplied properties, creates an object reference to either a back-end web service or a remoting object
UsingWebServices()	Indicates whether application is actively using web services (Boolean method)

Class Library Project: CGS.Winforms.AppForms

This is a reusable class library containing base application-level forms.

Form File: cgsFrmLogin.cs

This class file contains the reusable login form, as described in Chapter 13.

Class Library Project: CGS.Winforms.Containers

This is a reusable class library containing user controls, covered in Chapter 13.

Class User Control File: ctrFootNote.cs

This user control prompts for a footnote to appear on a report.

Class User Control File: ctrDateRange

This user control prompts for a date range. Although not specifically mentioned in Chapter 13, note that this is a reusable container with two `DateTimePicker` controls that can be used for any report options screen that prompts for a date range.

Class User Control File: ctrPDFViewer

This user control displays a PDF file. Although not specifically mentioned in Chapter 13, note that this is a reusable container that can be dragged and dropped onto any Windows Form to display a PDF file.

Class User Control File: ctrRecordSelect.cs

This user control displays any DataTable and allows the user to make selections. See Chapter 13 for details.

Class Library Project: CGS.Winforms.Controls

This is a reusable class library containing base Winform controls, covered in Chapter 13.

Form File: cgsControls.cs

This class file contains subclassed versions of the most commonly used Winform controls.

Form File: cgsForm.cs

This class file contains the base class form.

Class Library Project: CGS.Winforms.Forms

This is a reusable class library containing base Winform forms, covered in Chapter 13.

Form File: cgsFrmResponse.cs

This is a base form class for response dialogs/modal forms.

Form File: cgsFrmApplication.cs

This is a base form class for application forms.

The Construction Demo Solution

The following projects make up the entire application-level solution for the construction demo.

Class Library Project: ConstructionDemo.Client.WebReferences

Chapter 4 showed how to create a web service that implements an interface. However, when you add the web reference proxy to the client application, Visual Studio drops the interface implementation. You can subclass the proxy to implement the interface—that way, any time you update any web references, you'll retain the interface implementation.

The following is a code excerpt from a subclassed web reference, to implement the back-end interface IAgingReport.

```
using System;
using System.Collections.Generic;
using System.Text;
using ConstructionDemo.Interfaces;


namespace ConstructionDemo.Client.WebReferences
{
    public class wAgingReportRef : wAgingReport.wAgingReport,
                IAgingReport<string>
    {
    }
}
```

Table C-11 lists all of the subclassed web references. The base web references have the same name, but without the Ref suffix.

Table C-11. *Web References*

Web Reference Class	Description
wAgingReportRef	Subclassed web reference for the aging receivables report
wCostLaborReportRef	Subclassed web reference for the combination report/graph of labor and costs
wCostStackedBarGraph	Subclassed web reference for the stacked bar chart showing labor/costs by month
wClientInvoiceRef	Subclassed web reference for the client invoice report
wJobGanttChartRef	Subclassed web reference for the construction job timeline Gantt chart
wTimeSheetsRef	Subclassed web reference for the timesheet/labor report
wJobProfitSummaryRef	Subclassed web reference for the construction job summary/profit report
wJobCloseOutRef	Subclassed web reference for the construction job profile (closeout) report
wUserRef	Subclassed web reference for the user validation function

Class Library Project: ConstructionDemo.Business

Our application contains server-side business objects that interact with the data access layer. The client layer will interact with these business objects via .NET remoting. We cover this in detail in Chapters 4 and 5.

Each class in this project inherits from the cgsBaseBusinessObject class in the CGS.Business project, which inherits from the .NET system class System.MarshalByRefObject. This is required for .NET remoting.

```
using ConstructionDemo.Datasets;
using ConstructionDemo.DataAccess;
using CGS.Business;

public class bzAgingReport : cgsBaseBusinessObject,
                                    IAgingReport<dsAgingReport>
{
    public dsAgingReport GetAgingReport
        (DateTime dAsOfDate, bool lDetails, string cClientList, int nDBKey)
    {
        dsAgingReport odsAgingReport = new dsAgingReport();
        odsAgingReport = new daAgingReport().GetAgingReport
                    (dAsOfDate, lDetails, cClientList, nDBKey);

        return odsAgingReport;
    }
}
```

Table C-12 lists all of the business object classes in the project.

Table C-12. *Business Objects*

Class	Description
bzAgingReport	Business object for the aging receivables report
bzCostLaborReportGraph	Business object for the combination report/graph of labor and costs
bzCostStackedBarGraph	Business object for the stacked bar chart showing labor/costs by month
bzClientInvoice	Business object for the client invoice report
bzJobGanttChart	Business object for the construction job timeline Gantt chart
bzTimeSheets	Business object for the timesheet/labor report
bzJobProfitSummary	Business object for the construction job summary/profit report
bzJobCloseOut	Business object for the construction job profile (closeout) report
bzUser	Business object for the user validation function

Class Library Project: ConstructionDemo.DataAccess

Each class in this project inherits from the data access class cgsDataAccess, in the CGS.DataAccess project, which exposes the base data access methods for retrieving data from SQL Server. Each class in this project contains at least one method that does the following:

- Receives parameters from a business object, along with the database key that represents the actual database to be used

- Creates a List object of SqlParameters

- Creates an instance of the typed DataSet associated with the result set

- Calls the base data access method ReadIntoTypedDs() and passes the following:

  - The object instance of the typed DataSet, which the base method will fill

  - The name of the stored procedure

  - The object list of SqlParameters

  - The database key

- Returns the object instance of the typed DataSet

The following excerpt from the aging report data access class demonstrates the data access methodology:

```
using System.Data.SqlClient;
using CGS.DataAccess;
using ConstructionDemo.Datasets;

public class daAgingReport : cgsDataAccess
{
        public dsAgingReport GetAgingReport(DateTime dAsOfDate, bool lDetails,
                                            string cClientList, int nDBKey)
        {

            List<SqlParameter> oParms = new List<SqlParameter>();

            oParms.Add(new SqlParameter("@cCustomerList", cClientList));
            oParms.Add(new SqlParameter("@dAgingDate", dAsOfDate));
            oParms.Add(new SqlParameter("@lShowDetails", lDetails));

            // We can have a base data access class read the results
            // of a stored procedure DIRECTLY into a typed dataset....
            // no need to do a MERGE
            dsAgingReport odsAgingReport = new dsAgingReport();
            odsAgingReport = this.ReadIntoTypedDs
                (odsAgingReport, "[dbo].[GetAgingReceivables]", oParms,nDBKey);

            return odsAgingReport;
        }
}
```

Table C-13 lists all of the data access classes in the project.

Table C-13. *Data Access Classes*

Class	Description
daAgingReport	Data access class for the aging receivables report
daCostLaborReportGraph	Data access class for the combination report/graph of labor and costs
daCostStackedBarGraph	Data access class for the stacked bar chart showing labor/costs by month

Class	Description
daClientInvoice	Data access class for the client invoice report
daJobGanttChart	Data access class for the construction job timeline Gantt chart
daTimeSheets	Data access class for the timesheet/labor report
daJobProfitSummary	Data access class for the construction job summary/profit report
daJobCloseOut	Data access class for the construction job profile (closeout) report
daUser	Data access class for the user validation function

Windows Application Project: ConstructionDemo.RemotingServer

This project contains a reference to all the back-end business objects in ConstructionDemo.
Business. It launches a test remoting server that registers all back-end objects as
WellKnownServiceType objects on a specific TCP port, so that client-side modules can
activate them. See the .NET remoting discussion in Chapter 4 for details.

Form Class File: frmRemotingServer.cs

This form serves as a test listener for the remoting server. In a true production environment,
the remoting server would be an actual Windows service.

Class Library Project: ConstructionDemo.CrystalReports

The example application uses Crystal Reports for the actual report files. Chapters 8, 9, and
12 cover many techniques for using Crystal Reports. The application stores the reports in a
stand-alone DLL—any modules using the reports just needs to set a reference to this DLL.
Table C-14 lists the report files in the application.

Table C-14. *Crystal Report RPT Files*

Class	Description
RPT_AgingReport	File for the aging receivables report
RPT_CostLaborReportGraph	File for the combination report/graph of labor and costs
RPT_CostStackedBarGraph	File for the stacked bar chart showing labor/costs by month
RPT_ClientInvoice.rpt	File for the client invoice report
RPT_JobGanttChart.rpt	File for the construction job timeline Gantt chart
RPT_TimeSheet	File for the timesheet/labor report
RPT_JobProfitSummaryReport	File for the construction job summary/profit report
RPT_JobCloseOut	File for the construction job profile (closeout) report
RPTFooter	File for the reusable footer subreport
RPTHeader	File for the reusable header subreport
RPTBase	File for the reusable report template

Class Library Project: ConstructionDemo.Datasets

The example application uses strongly typed DataSets to store the result sets. Chapters 6 and 7 cover the use of typed DataSets. Table C-15 lists the primary typed DataSets in the application.

Table C-15. *Typed DataSets*

Class	Description
dsAgingReport	Typed DataSet for the aging report result set
dsCostLaborReportGraph	Typed DataSet for the combination report/graph of labor and costs
dsCostStackedBarGraph	Typed DataSet for the stacked bar chart showing labor/costs by month
dsClientInvoice	Typed DataSet for the client invoice report
dsJobGanttChart	Typed DataSet for the construction job timeline Gantt chart
dsTimeSheets	Typed DataSet for the timesheet/labor report
dsJobProfitSummary	Typed DataSet for the construction job summary/profit report
dsJobCloseOut	Typed DataSet for the construction job profile (closeout) report
dsUser	Typed DataSet for the user validation results.

Class Library Project: ConstructionDemo.Interfaces

As we covered in Chapter 4, the application uses interfaces to support strongly typed references on the client side to the server-side components.

Class File: ReportInterfaces.cs

This class file contains all of the interfaces for the application. Each interface contains a signature for the method that the business object or web service will use. Table C-16 lists all of the interfaces in this class file.

Table C-16. *Interfaces for the Application*

Interface	Description
IAgingReport	Interface for the aging receivables report
ICostLaborReportGraph	Interface for the combination report/graph of labor and costs
ICostStackedBarGraph	Interface for the stacked bar chart showing labor/costs by month
IClientInvoice	Interface for the client invoice report
IJobGanttChart	Interface for the construction job timeline Gantt chart
ITimeSheets	Interface for the timesheet/labor report
IJobProfitSummary	Interface for the construction job summary/profit report
IJobCloseOut	Interface for the construction job profile (closeout) report
IUser	Interface for the user validation result set

Class Library Project: ConstructionDemo.WebServices

This project contains all the server-side web services. The project contains .NET references to the CGS.Business library, as well as the ConstructionDemo.Business, ConstructionDemo.Datasets, and ConstructionDemo.Interfaces libraries. Chapter 4 covers these web services in detail.

Each web service implements the same interface as its corresponding business object. The web service receives specific parameters, as well as an integer for the necessary database key to use. The web service calls the corresponding business object and returns an XML representation of a result set. The following is an excerpt from wAgingReport:

```
using ConstructionDemo.Interfaces;
using ConstructionDemo.Business;

public class wAgingReport : System.Web.Services.WebService,  IAgingReport<string>
{
    [WebMethod]
    public string GetAgingReport
        (DateTime dAsOfDate, bool lDetails, string cClientList, int nDBKey)
    {
        string cXML = new bzAgingReport().GetAgingReport
                (dAsOfDate, lDetails, cClientList, nDBKey).GetXml();

        return cXML;
    }
}
```

On the client side, you'll subclass the references to these web services: in the subclass, you'll implement the same interface.

Table C-17 lists all of the web services in the project.

Table C-17. *Web Service ASMX files*

Web Service	Description
wAgingReport	Web service for the aging receivables report
wCostLaborReportGraph	Web service for the combination report/graph of labor and costs
wCostStackedBarGraph	Web service for the stacked bar chart showing labor/costs by month
wClientInvoice	Web service for the client invoice report
wJobGanttChart	Web service for the construction job timeline Gantt chart
wTimeSheets	Web service for the timesheet/labor report
wJobProfitSummary	Web service for the construction job summary/profit report
wJobCloseOut	Web service for the construction job profile (closeout) report
wUser	Web service for the user validation function

Main Windows Application: ConstructionDemo.Client.Winforms

Finally, the Windows application `ConstructionDemo.Client.Winforms` contains a series of report options forms, along with corresponding form managers. Chapter 13 covers a complete example of the aging report options form (`FrmAgingReport`), along with the related form manager (`FrmAgingReportManager`).

Table C-18 lists all of the forms in the application. In addition to the options forms, the application also contains a basic main menu form (`FrmMain`), along with a basic report selection/launcher form (`FrmAgingLauncher`).

Table C-18. *Forms and Form Managers*

Form	Form Manager
FrmMain	FrmMainManager
FrmReportLauncher	FrmReportLauncherManager
FrmAgingReport	FrmAgingReportManager
FrmCostLaborReportGraph	FrmCostLaborReportGraphManager
FrmCostStackedBarGraph	FrmCostStackedBarGraphManager
FrmClientInvoice	FrmClientInvoiceManager
FrmJobGanttChart	FrmJobGanttChartManager
FrmTimeSheets	FrmTimeSheetsManager
FrmJobProfitSummary	FrmJobProfitSummaryManager
FrmJobCloseOut	FrmJobCloseOutManager
FrmLogin	FrmLoginManager

Some Final Notes

Finally, we'll cover some areas that didn't fit into any specific part of this book, but are still worth mentioning.

Setting Project Dependencies

The example application splits components into separate projects and sets references to these projects. You must also define project dependencies. If project X contains references to components B and C, you'll want the compiler to compile B and C before compiling X. Visual Studio 2005 allows you to set project dependencies for each project by right-clicking a project and selecting Project Dependencies from the context menu.

Figure C-1 shows the Project Dependencies screen for the `CGS.Winforms.AppForms` project. We've checked four of the projects that serve as .NET references for the current project. This instructs VS 2005 to compile those projects before compiling the current project.

Figure C-1. *Setting .NET project dependencies*

Note that the second tab of the Project Dependencies screen in Figure C-1 lists the build order for the entire solution. Visual Studio automatically determines the build order of solution, based on the dependencies that you set.

Alternative Approaches

The techniques in this book are being used in production, in one form or another. They work. They may or may not work for specific readers, depending on what types of applications they are building and how they use .NET. There are aspects of the book's framework that could have been done different ways. Some might be better for some situations, some not as effective.

The interface-based approach we present to result sets from either .NET remoting DLLs or web services utilizes a generic interface to handle two essentially disparate data types (XML string and DataSet). This allows you to use the same interface and the same back-end method, although you need some code in the client piece to work with the different return types. You could have utilized some flags on the back end instead, or you could have just used slightly different method names between the web service and the business object.

Having said that, the use of generic interfaces still paves the way for an architecture that can handle either DataSets or custom collections as result sets. It's possible you may only be using .NET remoting, in which case you can simply remove the web service functionality.

The example application also makes heavy use of stored procedures and typed DataSets. Some feel that applications using this model tend to require a number of code changes when the database schema changes. The truth is that schema changes are often likely to require code changes somewhere, regardless of the model being used. Some tackle this by writing utilities to autogenerate source code.

Handling Master Tables

There are a few techniques in the application that we didn't really cover in the book. One is handling lookups in master tables. In Chapter 13, we had you hard-code a list of clients for a client pick list because we hadn't walked through the creation of classes to store items such as client lists, employee lists, etc.

The companion download application contains basic functionality for handling basic master file and pick lists. The functionality consists of the following:

- Basic stored procedures to return data from these master files.

- DataSet definitions for these results.

- A local class that optionally writes these to local XML files when the application closes.

- A method in the application that reloads the XML at subsequent startup, and simply checks the back end to see whether the last modified date of the file back on the server is more recent than the version date on the local end. In doing this, you are retaining user selections by storing a flag with each item to indicate whether the user checked it on or off during a selection process.

Looking at the User Interface

Finally, let's take a look at some miscellaneous aspects of the user interface. These are ones you can "mix and match."

Showing a Status Bar

Just as you can display common annotations on report header and footer areas, you can also display common information on a main system screen. Visual Studio 2005 allows you to add a StatusStrip control to the bottom of any Windows Form, and then add individual StatusLabel controls to the StatusStrip control. Figure C-2 shows an example of a status bar that you can incorporate into your application: a StatusStrip control that contains three StatusLabel controls for the current user, connection, and available disk space.

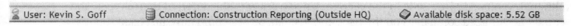

Figure C-2. *A status bar to display system information*

You can create a status bar to the one shown in Figure C-2 by doing the following:

1. In any Windows Form that you've created, load the Windows Forms Toolbox and expand the category for Menus & Toolbars (see Figure C-3).

Figure C-3. *The menu and toolbar controls for Visual Studio 2005*

2. Drag an instance of the StatusStrip control onto your form.

3. Click the StatusStrip control on your form (see Figure C-4) to add items to the status bar. Add three new StatusLabel controls called toolStripStatusLblUser, toolStripStatusLblConnection, and toolStripStatusLblDiskSpace.

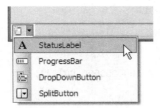

Figure C-4. *Adding controls to the StatusStrip control*

4. Finally, set the text for each of the StatusLabel controls using the code in Listing C-1. You can utilize the global properties that we covered back in Table C-5.

Listing C-1. *A Method to Show Information in a Windows Forms ToolStrip Control*

```
using System;
using System.Collections.Generic;
using System.ComponentModel;
using System.Data;
using System.Drawing;
using System.Text;
using System.Windows.Forms;
using CGS.Globals;
using System.Management;
```

```csharp
private void SetStatus()
{
    cgsGlobals oGlobals = new cgsGlobals();

    // Show the user and connection.
    this.toolStripStatusLblUser.Text =
                        "User: " + oGlobals.cUserName;
    this.toolStripStatusLblConnection.Text =
                        "Connection: " + oGlobals.cCurrentConnection;

    // Now calculate the amount of free disk space.

    // If the local drive is not the C drive, you'd need to determine it.
    ManagementObject disk =
        new ManagementObject("win32_logicaldisk.deviceid='c:'");

    disk.Get();
    long availFree = long.Parse(disk["Freespace"].ToString());
    string cMessage = "";

    // If we have at least 1GB left, show in terms of GB.
    if(availFree > 1000000000)
    {
        decimal nGB =
            System.Math.Round((decimal)(availFree / 1000000000.00),2);
        cMessage = nGB.ToString().Trim() + " GB";
    }
    else
      // Show in terms of MB.
        {
        decimal nMB =
            System.Math.Round((decimal)(availFree / 1000000.00), 2);
        cMessage = nMB.ToString().Trim() + " MB";
        }

    this.toolStripStatusLblDiskSpace.Text =
        "Available disk space: " + cMessage;
}
```

■**Note** You will need to add a .NET reference to the System.Management namespace to use the code in Listing C-1.

Displaying a Menu List of Available Reports

The demo application provides a basic interface for displaying a list of available reports and allowing the user to launch a specific report. Figure C-5 shows a basic report launcher form: a Windows Form that inherits from the base response dialog form (cgsFrmResponse, in the CGS.Windows.Forms project).

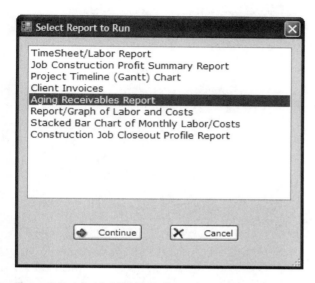

Figure C-5. *A basic Windows Form for a user to select a report*

The form populates a simple ListBox control from the Reports table (see Appendix A for information on the Reports table). The code in the application simply reads the SelectedItem property of the listbox and calls the corresponding report options form using a simple C# switch statement. For an application with a fairly fixed number of reports that are more disparate than similar, an approach like this is usually sufficient.

Some applications contain categories of reports with some level of commonality: in those instances, the system can display the report categories/hierarchy with a visual tool (such as a treeview control). These applications will likely use some level of abstraction to launch the report, based on specific report properties, or an interface, or some other means. For example, a medical software application might produce a high number of forms that fall into a small number of categories. The application might make use of report definitions and attributes to launch the reports using a generic interface or some other means of abstraction.

Also, the Reports database contains a description column to store information on a report. You could modify the screen in Figure C-5 to show the description when the user highlights a specific report. This would be especially helpful in conveying information to end users about specific report content.

Index

You Need the Companion eBook

Your purchase of this book entitles you to buy the companion PDF-version eBook for only $10. Take the weightless companion with you anywhere.

We believe this Apress title will prove so indispensable that you'll want to carry it with you everywhere, which is why we are offering the companion eBook (in PDF format) for $10 to customers who purchase this book now. Convenient and fully searchable, the PDF version of any content-rich, page-heavy Apress book makes a valuable addition to your programming library. You can easily find and copy code—or perform examples by quickly toggling between instructions and the application. Even simultaneously tackling a donut, diet soda, and complex code becomes simplified with hands-free eBooks!

Once you purchase your book, getting the $10 companion eBook is simple:

❶ Visit **www.apress.com/promo/tendollars/**.

❷ Complete a basic registration form to receive a randomly generated question about this title.

❸ Answer the question correctly in 60 seconds, and you will receive a promotional code to redeem for the $10.00 eBook.

2560 Ninth Street • Suite 219 • Berkeley, CA 94710

eBookshop

ASP **Today**

Apressᵉ
THE EXPERT'S VOICE™

Offer valid through 5/20/2007.